BLITZ

Original creation: Cédric BISCAY
Illustrator: Daitaro NISHIHARA
Written by Cédric BISCAY & Harumo SANAZAKI

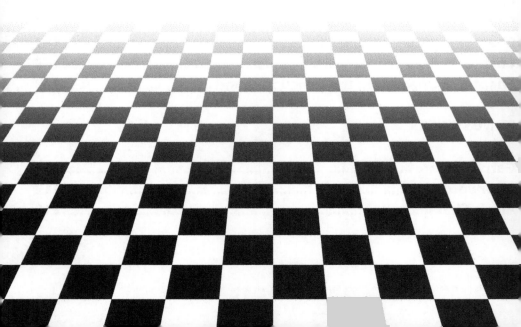

BLiTZ

TABLE OF CONTENTS

BONUS PAGES

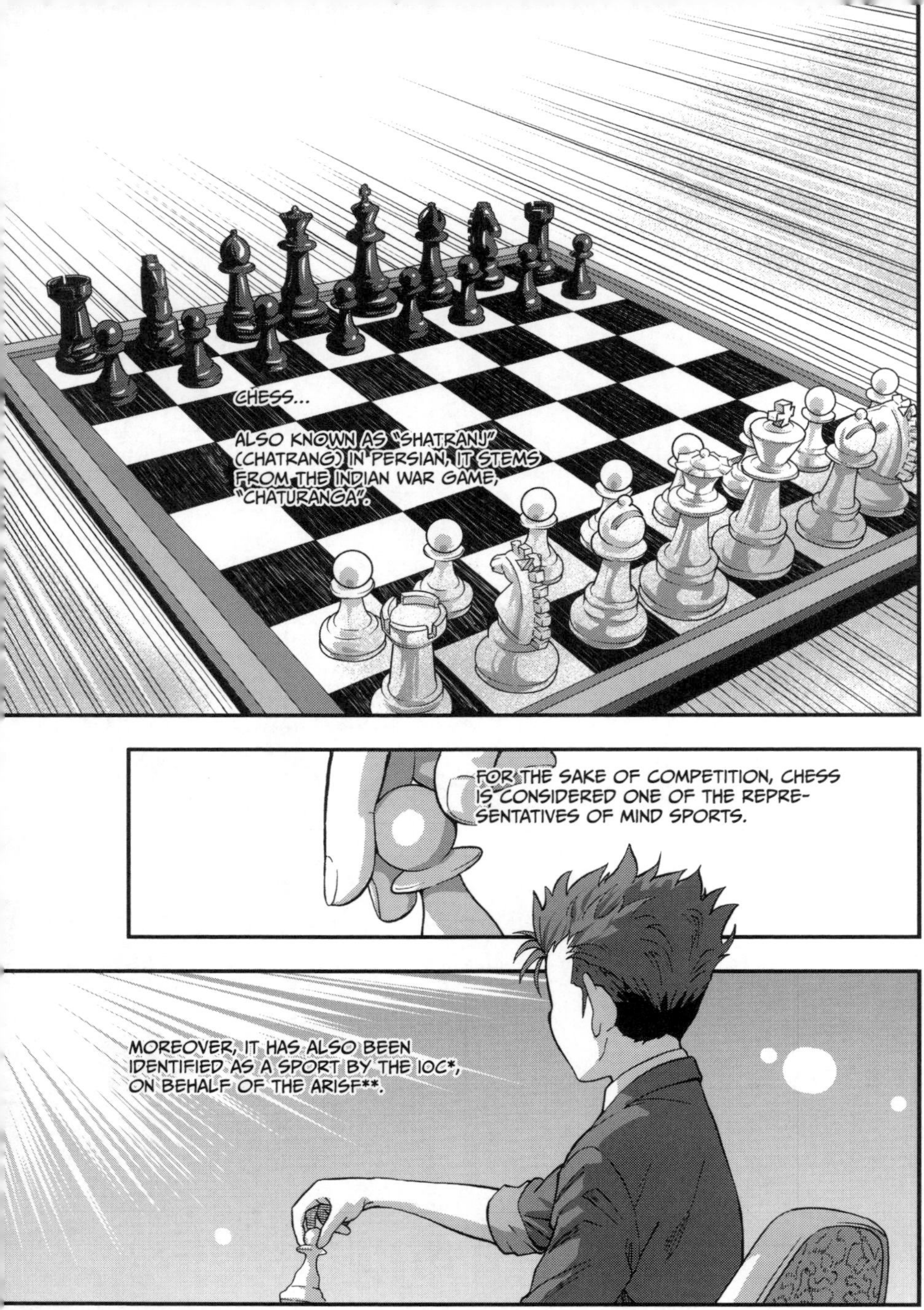
CHESS...
ALSO KNOWN AS "SHATRANJ" (CHATRANG) IN PERSIAN, IT STEMS FROM THE INDIAN WAR GAME, "CHATURANGA".
FOR THE SAKE OF COMPETITION, CHESS IS CONSIDERED ONE OF THE REPRESENTATIVES OF MIND SPORTS.
MOREOVER, IT HAS ALSO BEEN IDENTIFIED AS A SPORT BY THE IOC*, ON BEHALF OF THE ARISF**.

*IOC: INTERNATIONAL OLYMPIC COMMITTEE.

**ARISF: ASSOCIATION OF IOC RECOGNIZED INTERNATIONAL SPORTS FEDERATION.

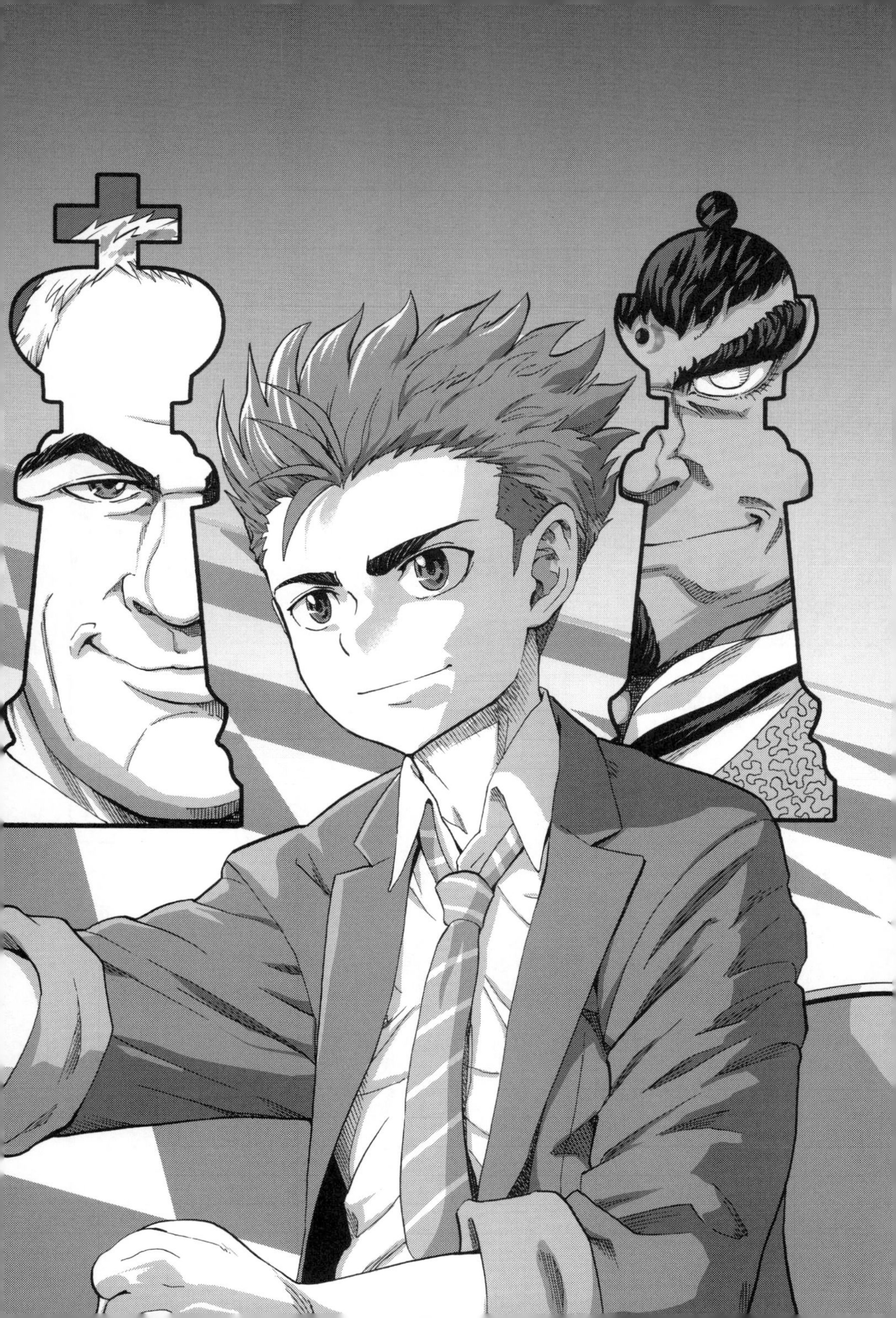

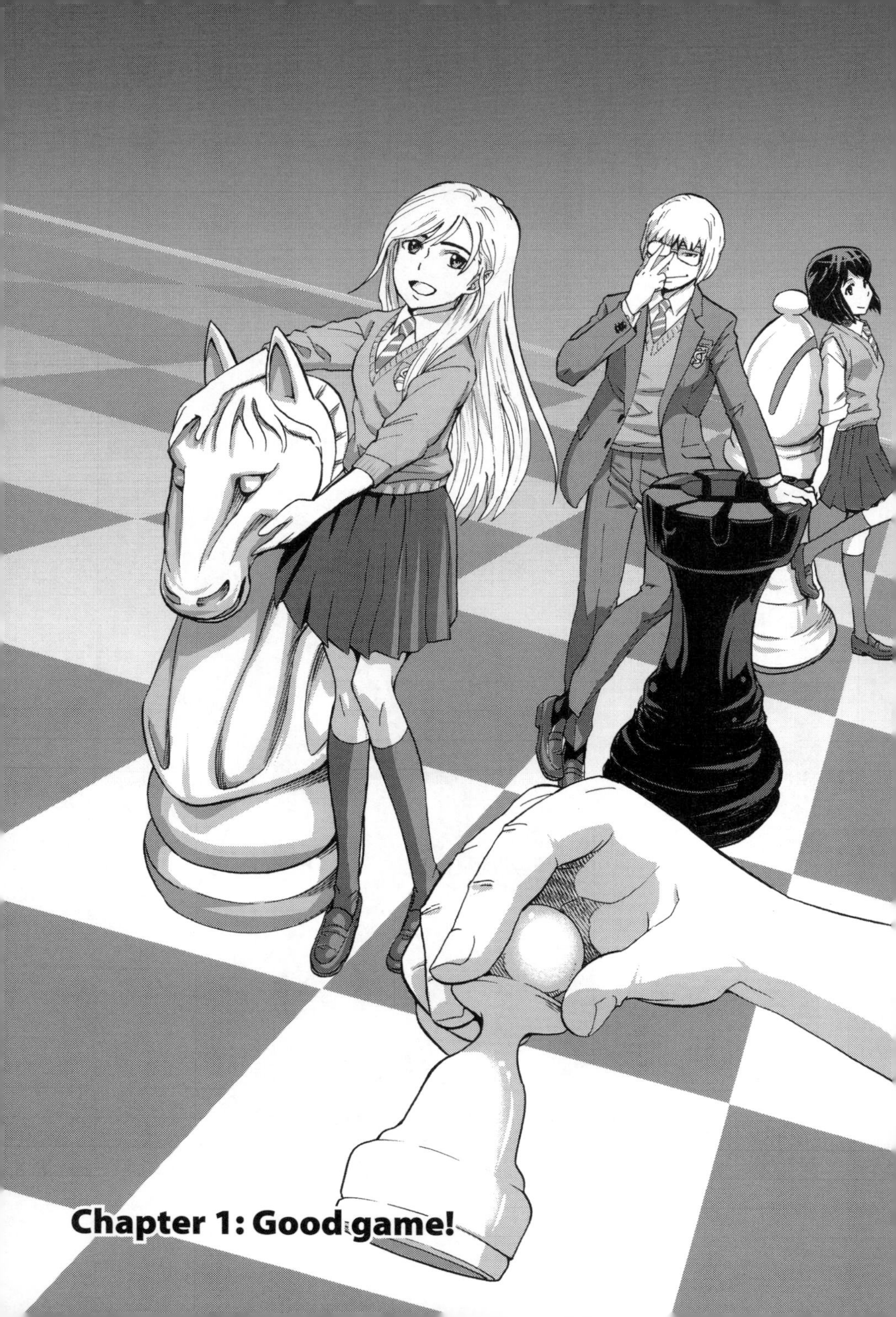

Chapter 1: Good game!

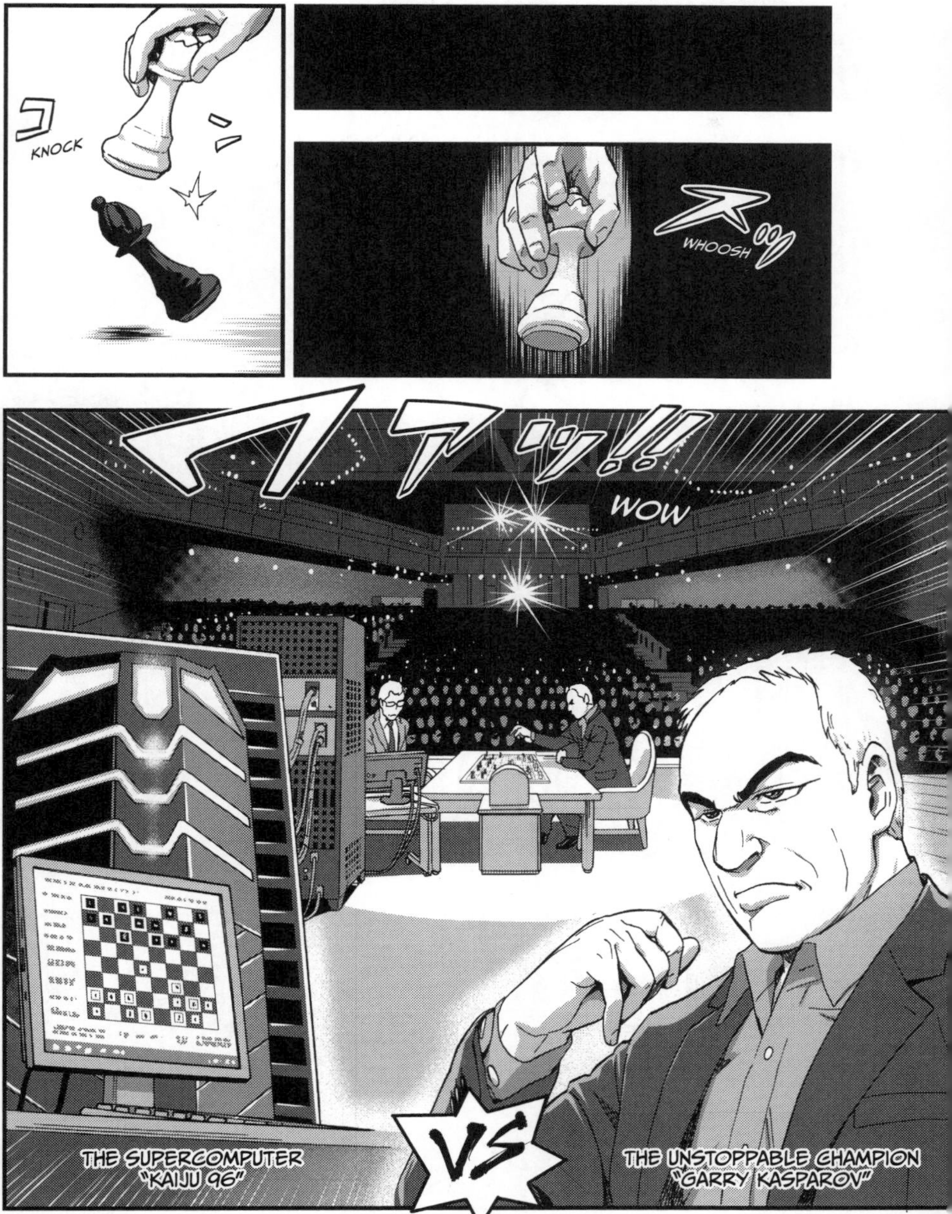
WHOOSH
KNOCK
WOW
THE UNSTOPPABLE CHAMPION "GARRY KASPAROV"
VS
THE SUPERCOMPUTER "KAIJU 96"

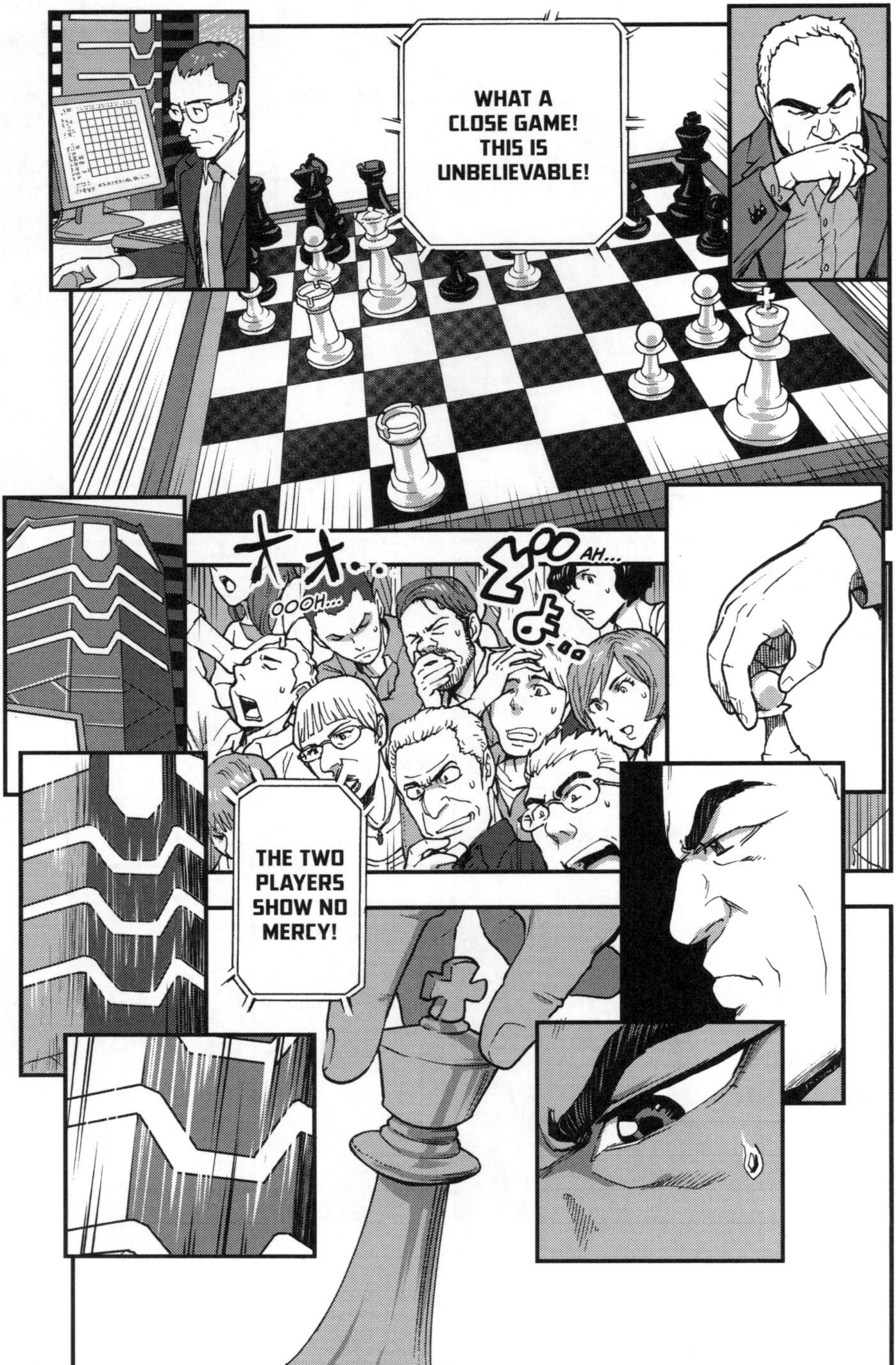
WHAT A CLOSE GAME! THIS IS UNBELIEVABLE!
どよ..
AH...
オオ..
OOOH...
THE TWO PLAYERS SHOW NO MERCY!

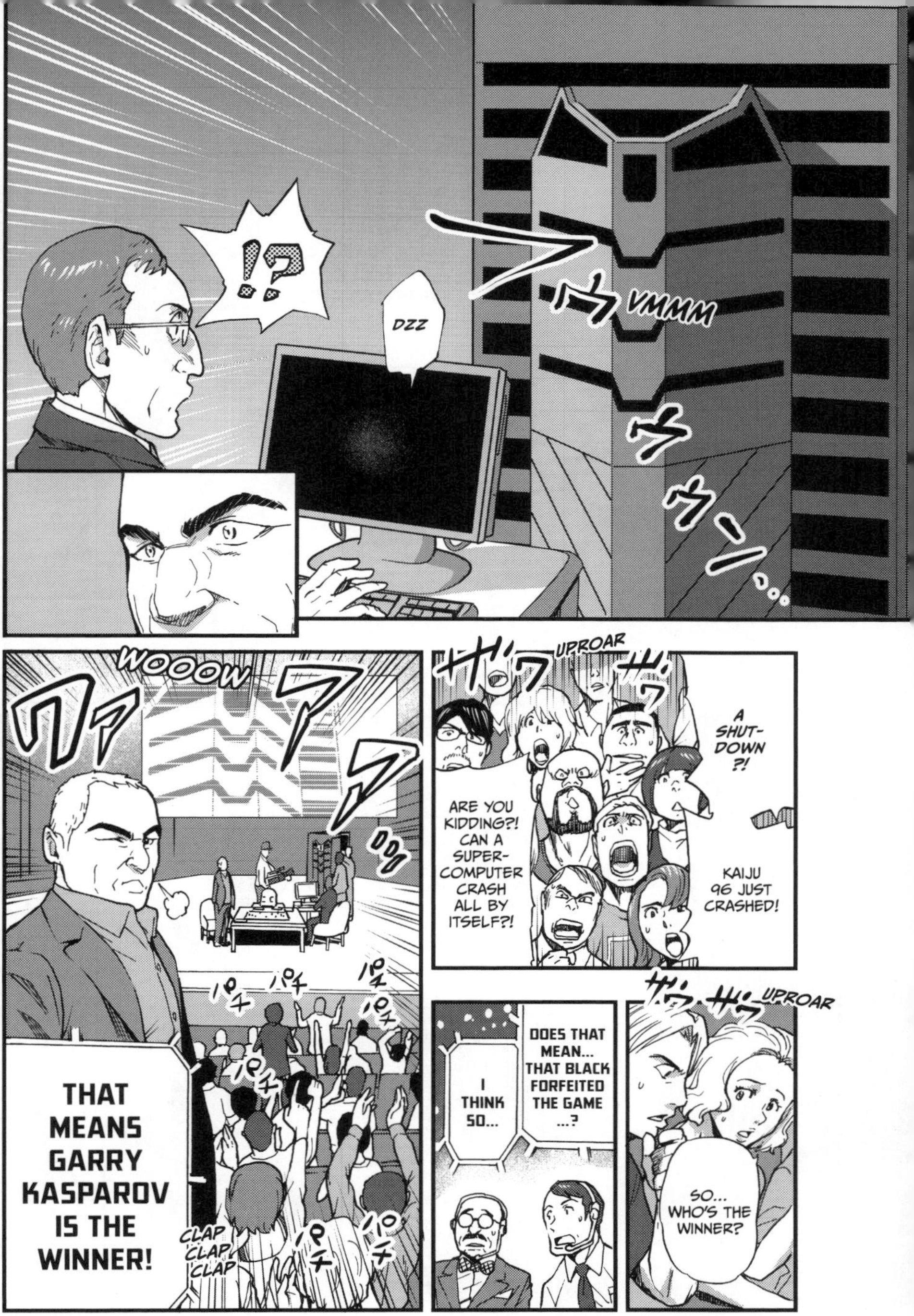
VMMM
DZZ
!?
UPROAR
A SHUT-DOWN?!
KAIJU 96 JUST CRASHED!
ARE YOU KIDDING?! CAN A SUPER-COMPUTER CRASH ALL BY ITSELF?!
UPROAR
SO... WHO'S THE WINNER?
DOES THAT MEAN... THAT BLACK FORFEITED THE GAME ...?
I THINK SO...
WOOOOW
THAT MEANS GARRY KASPAROV IS THE WINNER!
CLAP CLAP CLAP

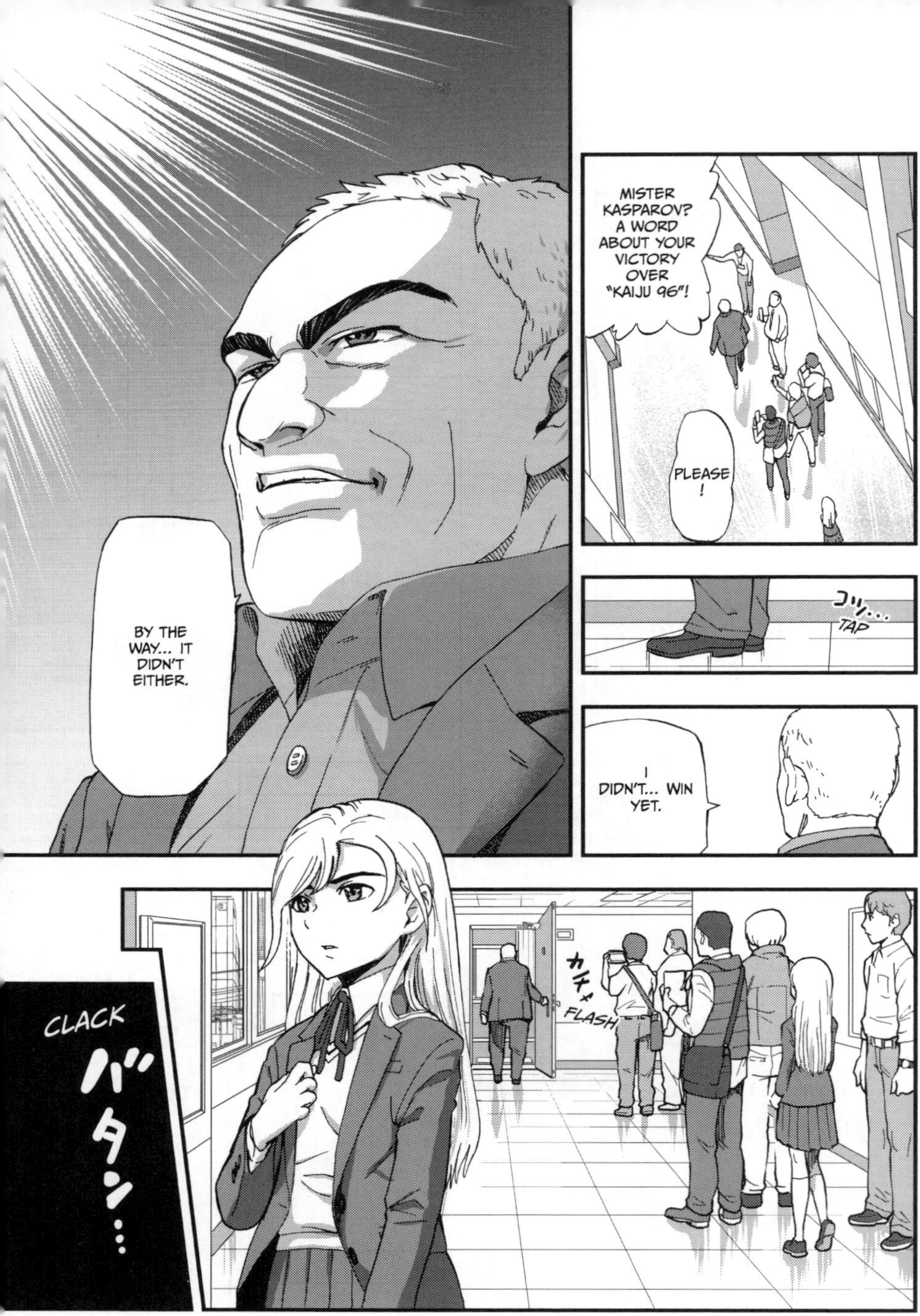
MISTER KASPAROV? A WORD ABOUT YOUR VICTORY OVER "KAIJU 96"!
PLEASE!
コツ…
TAP
I DIDN'T... WIN YET.
BY THE WAY... IT DIDN'T EITHER.
カチャ
FLASH
CLACK
バタン…

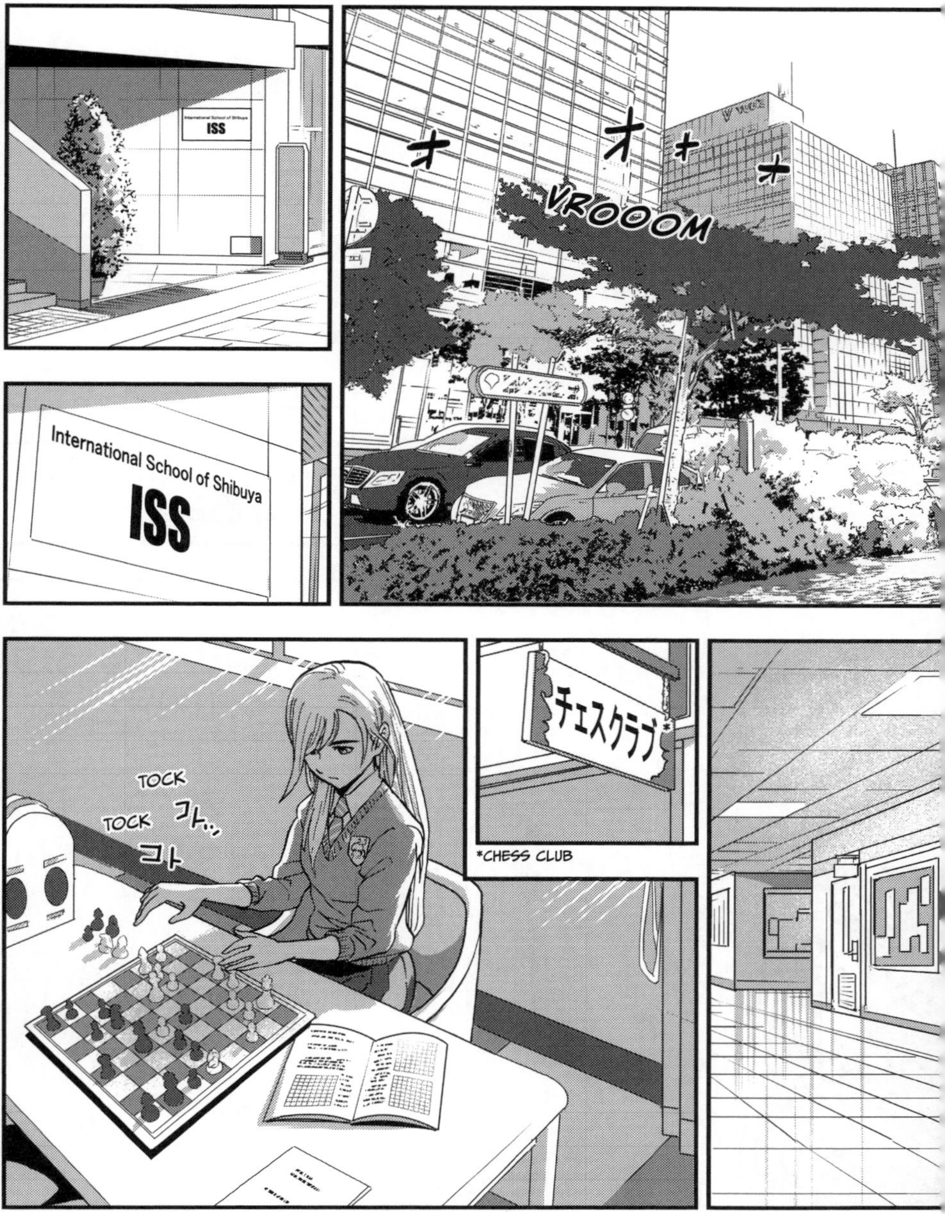
オ
オ
オ
オ
VROOOM
International School of Shibuya
ISS
International School of Shibuya
ISS
チェスクラブ*
*CHESS CLUB
TOCK
コト..
TOCK
コト

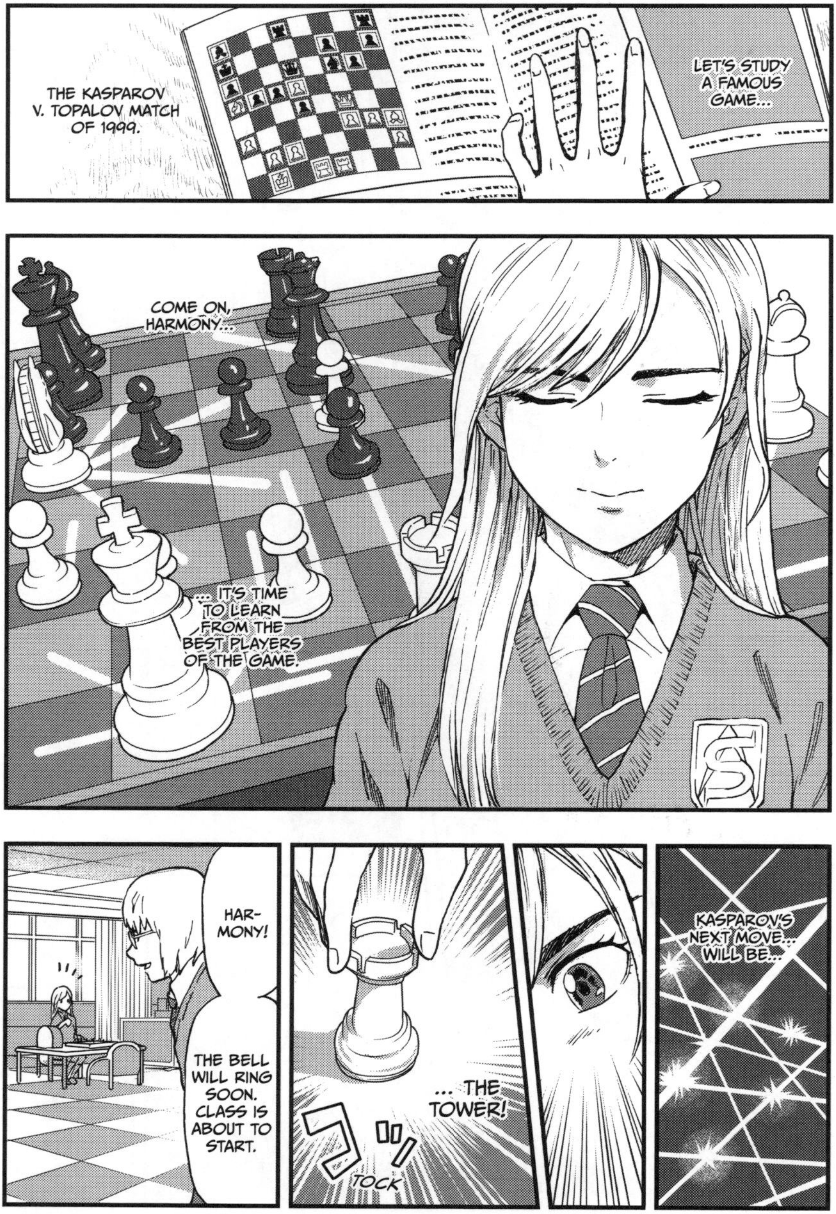
LET'S STUDY A FAMOUS GAME...
THE KASPAROV V. TOPALOV MATCH OF 1999.
COME ON, HARMONY...
... IT'S TIME TO LEARN FROM THE BEST PLAYERS OF THE GAME.
KASPAROV'S NEXT MOVE... WILL BE...
... THE TOWER!
TOCK
HAR-MONY!
THE BELL WILL RING SOON. CLASS IS ABOUT TO START.

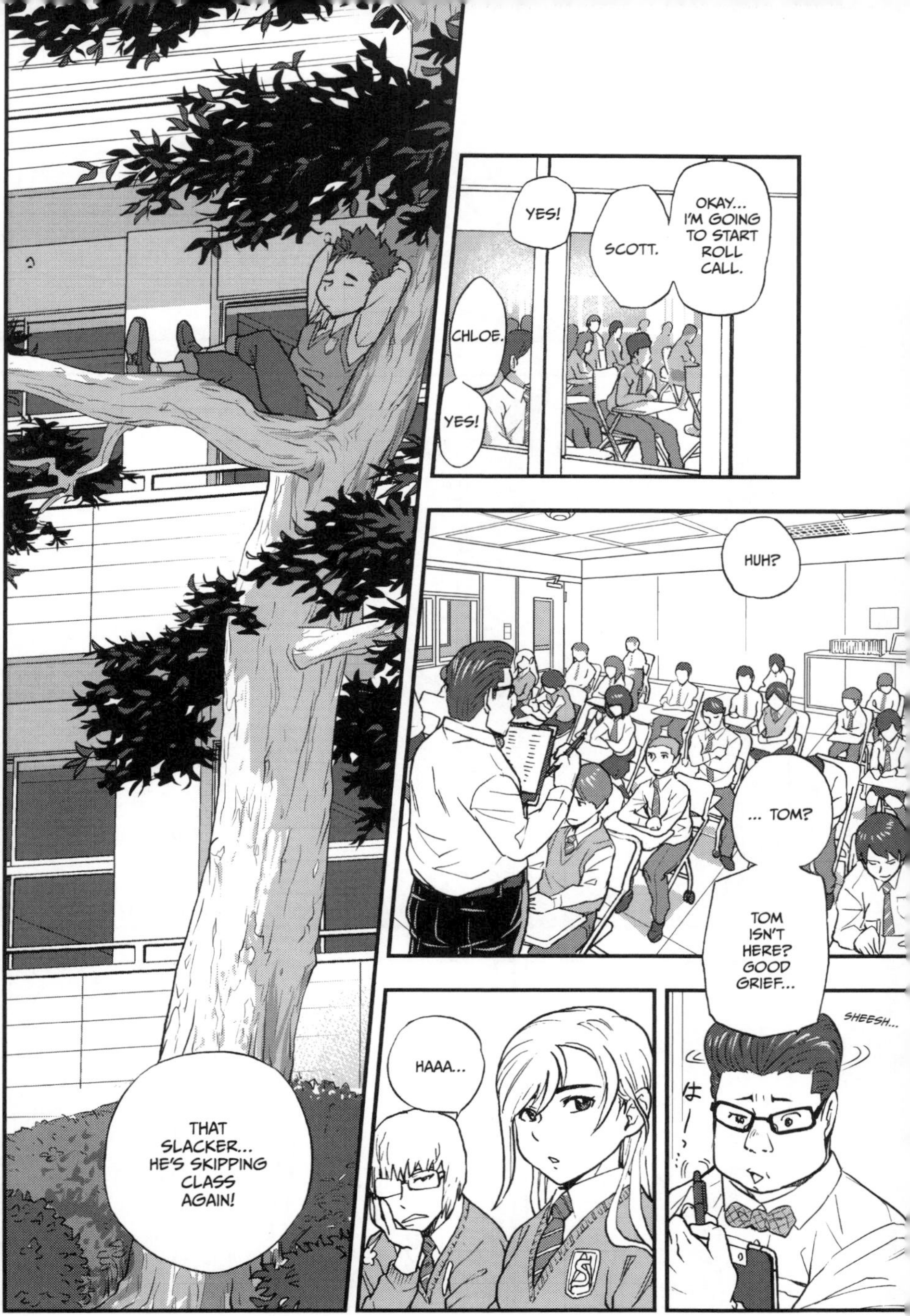
OKAY... I'M GOING TO START ROLL CALL.
SCOTT.
YES!
CHLOE.
YES!
HUH?
... TOM?
TOM ISN'T HERE? GOOD GRIEF...
SHEESH...
はー
HAAA...
THAT SLACKER... HE'S SKIPPING CLASS AGAIN!

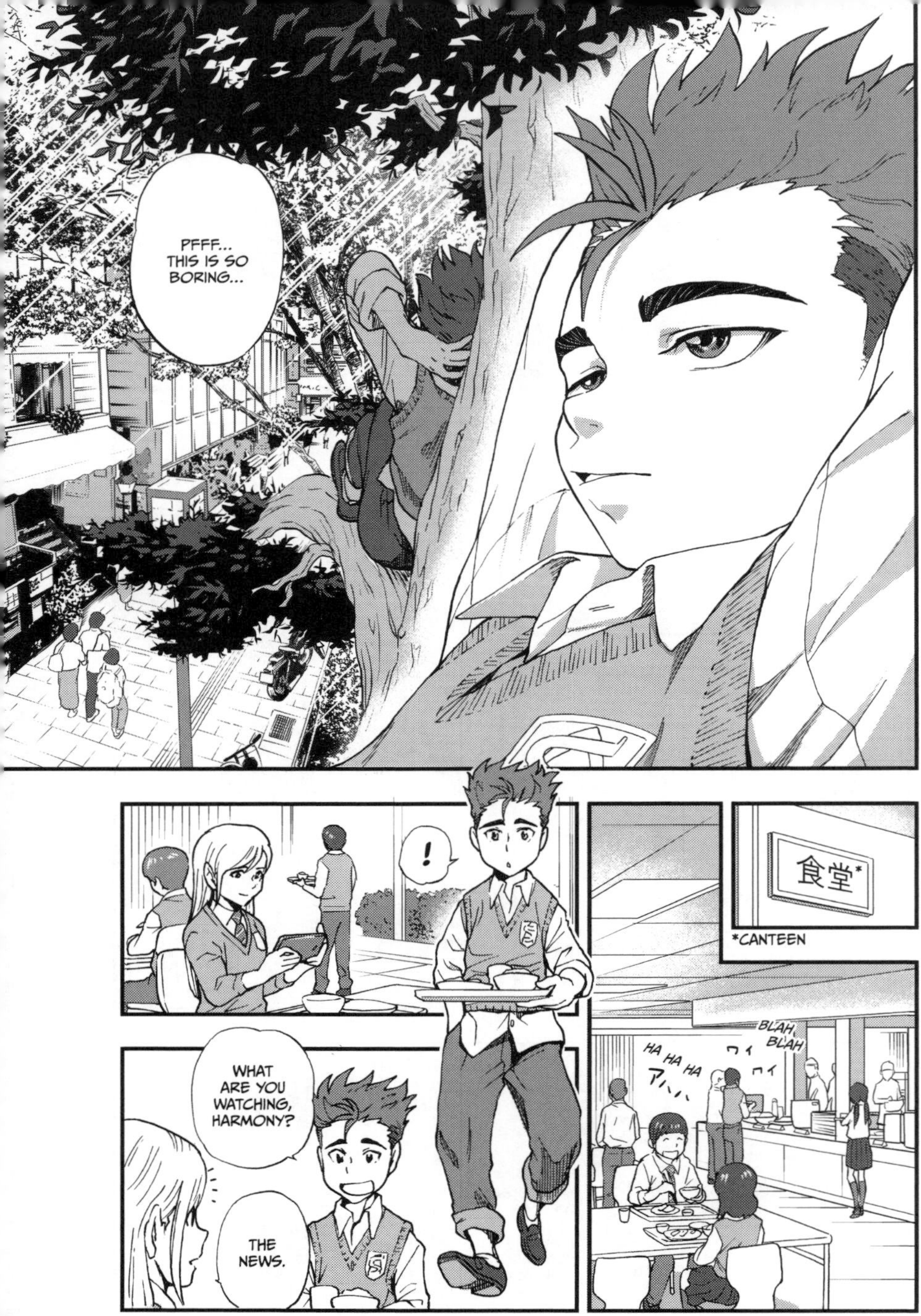
PFFF... THIS IS SO BORING...
食堂*
*CANTEEN
BLAH BLAH
HA HA HA
ワイワイ
アハハ
!
WHAT ARE YOU WATCHING, HARMONY?
THE NEWS.

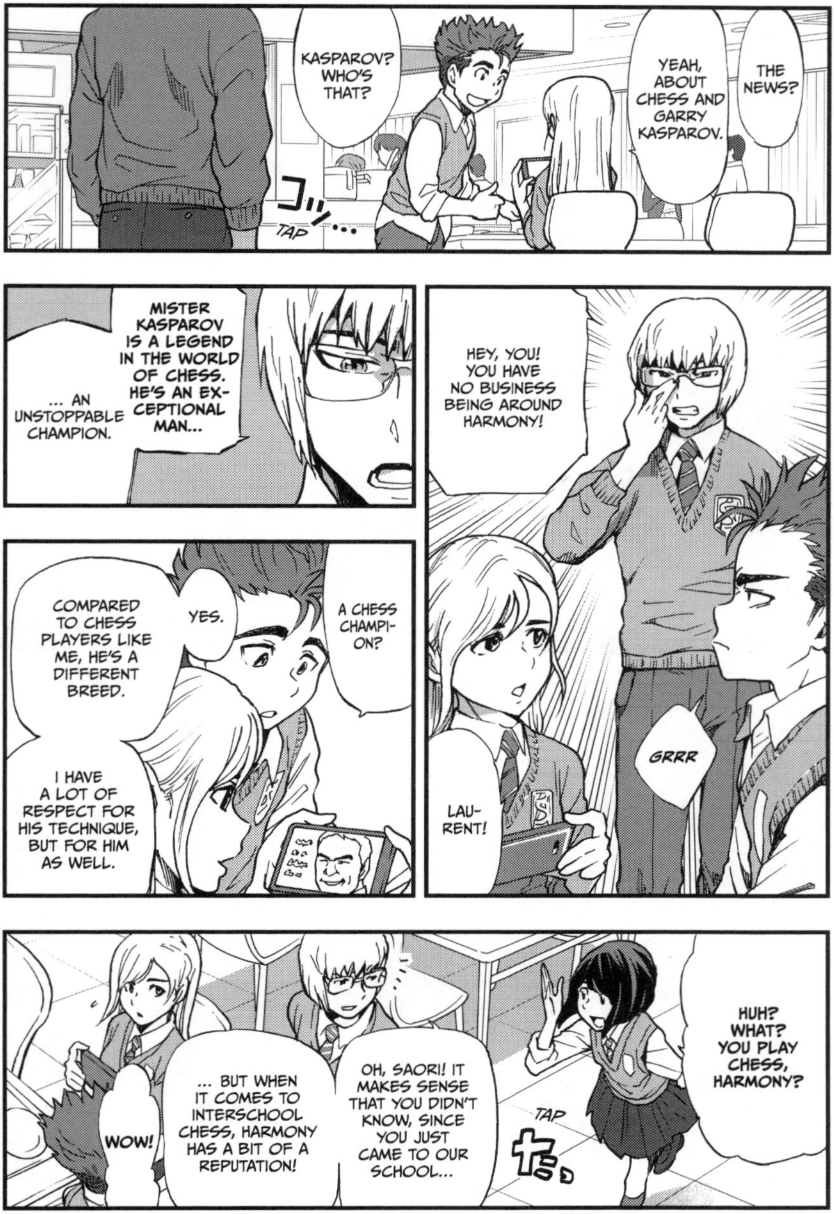
THE NEWS?
YEAH, ABOUT CHESS AND GARRY KASPAROV.
KASPAROV? WHO'S THAT?
TAP
HEY, YOU! YOU HAVE NO BUSINESS BEING AROUND HARMONY!
GRRR
LAU-RENT!
MISTER KASPAROV IS A LEGEND IN THE WORLD OF CHESS. HE'S AN EX-CEPTIONAL MAN...
... AN UNSTOPPABLE CHAMPION.
A CHESS CHAMPI-ON?
YES.
COMPARED TO CHESS PLAYERS LIKE ME, HE'S A DIFFERENT BREED.
I HAVE A LOT OF RESPECT FOR HIS TECHNIQUE, BUT FOR HIM AS WELL.
HUH? WHAT? YOU PLAY CHESS, HARMONY?
TAP
OH, SAORI! IT MAKES SENSE THAT YOU DIDN'T KNOW, SINCE YOU JUST CAME TO OUR SCHOOL...
... BUT WHEN IT COMES TO INTERSCHOOL CHESS, HARMONY HAS A BIT OF A REPUTATION!
WOW!

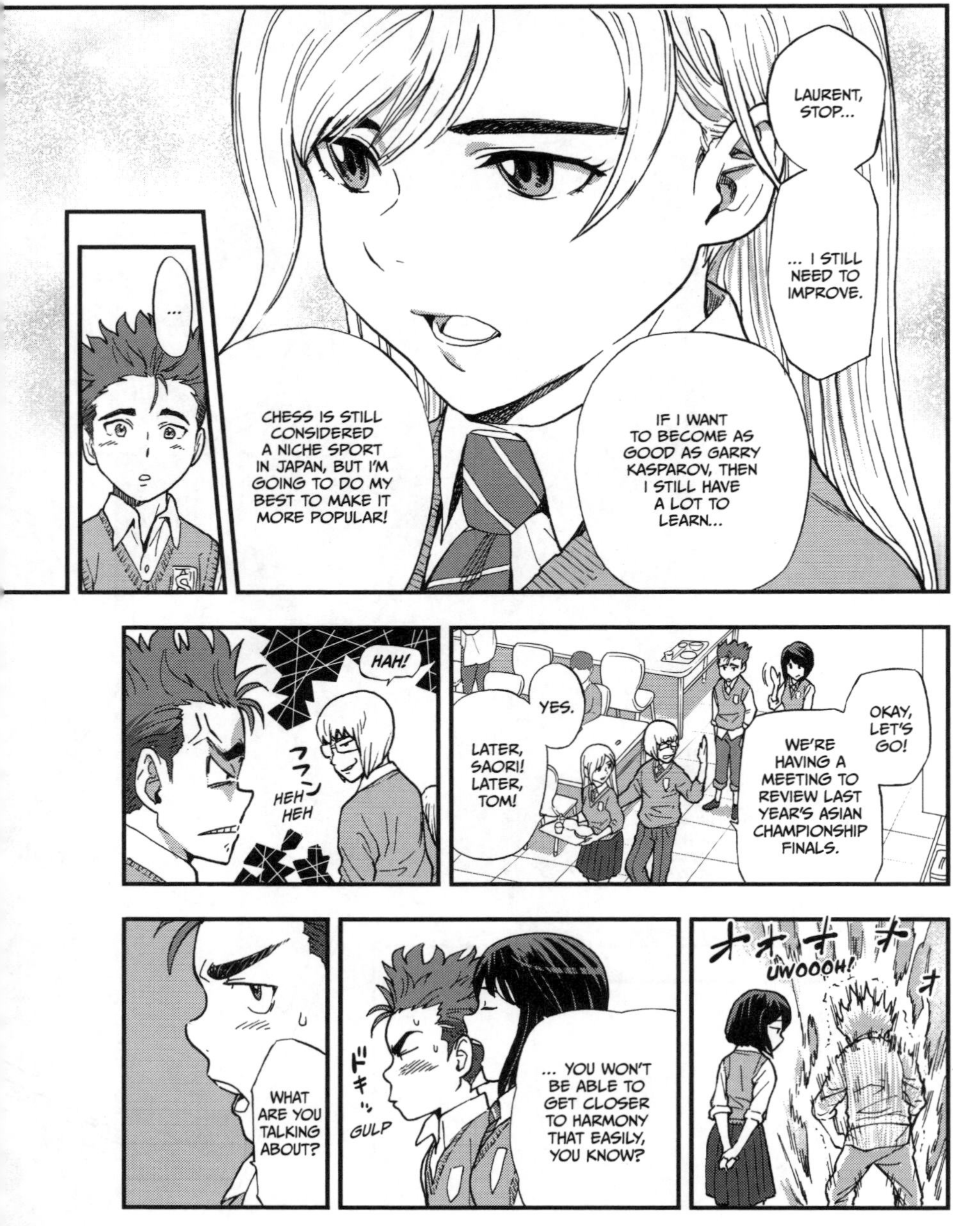
LAURENT, STOP...
... I STILL NEED TO IMPROVE.
IF I WANT TO BECOME AS GOOD AS GARRY KASPAROV, THEN I STILL HAVE A LOT TO LEARN...
CHESS IS STILL CONSIDERED A NICHE SPORT IN JAPAN, BUT I'M GOING TO DO MY BEST TO MAKE IT MORE POPULAR!
...
OKAY, LET'S GO!
WE'RE HAVING A MEETING TO REVIEW LAST YEAR'S ASIAN CHAMPIONSHIP FINALS.
YES.
LATER, SAORI! LATER, TOM!
HAH!
フフン
HEH HEH
UWOOOH!
... YOU WON'T BE ABLE TO GET CLOSER TO HARMONY THAT EASILY, YOU KNOW?
ドキッ
GULP
WHAT ARE YOU TALKING ABOUT?

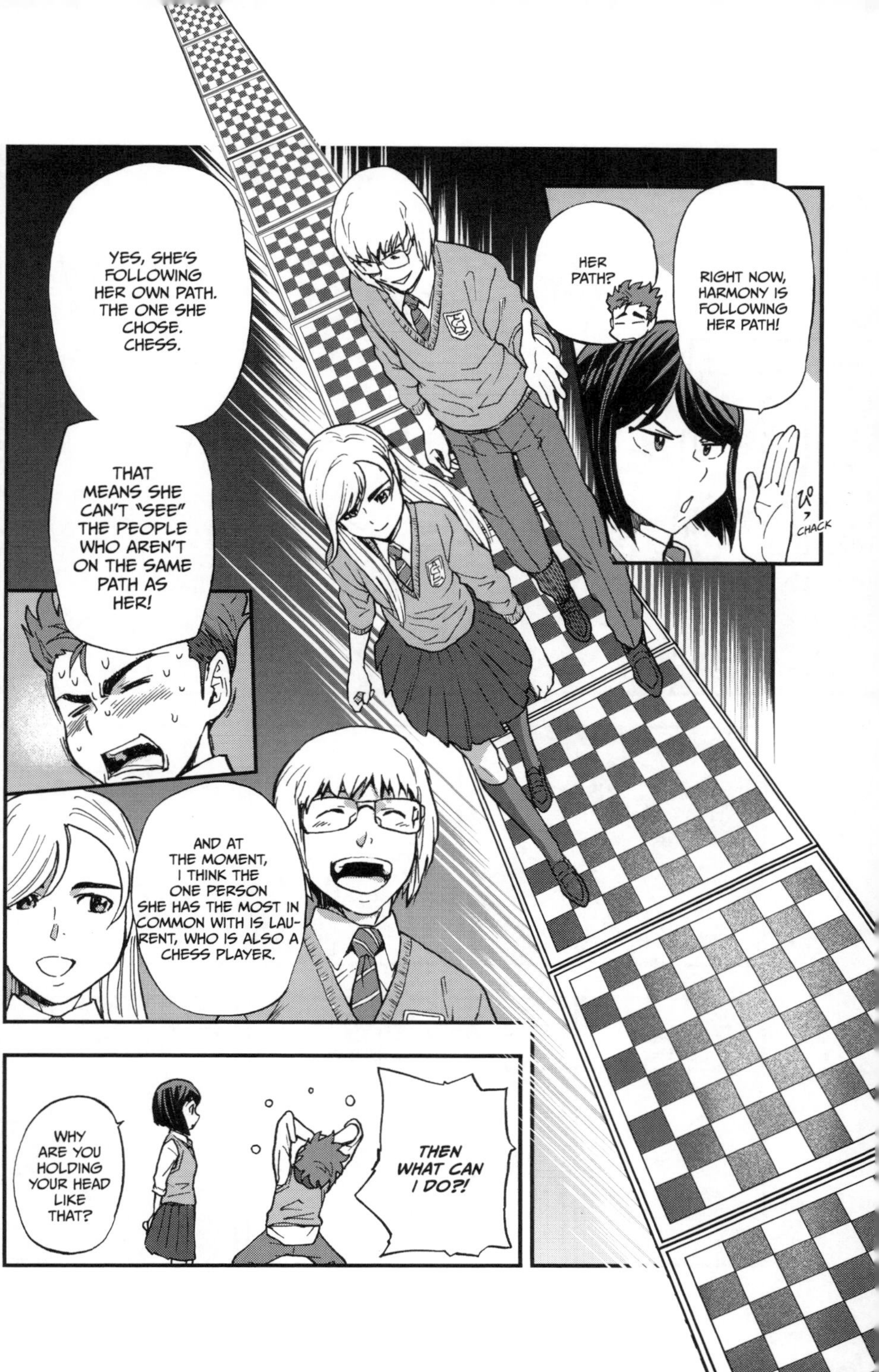
RIGHT NOW, HARMONY IS FOLLOWING HER PATH!
HER PATH?
CHACK
YES, SHE'S FOLLOWING HER OWN PATH. THE ONE SHE CHOSE. CHESS.
THAT MEANS SHE CAN'T "SEE" THE PEOPLE WHO AREN'T ON THE SAME PATH AS HER!
AND AT THE MOMENT, I THINK THE ONE PERSON SHE HAS THE MOST IN COMMON WITH IS LAURENT, WHO IS ALSO A CHESS PLAYER.
THEN WHAT CAN I DO?!
WHY ARE YOU HOLDING YOUR HEAD LIKE THAT?

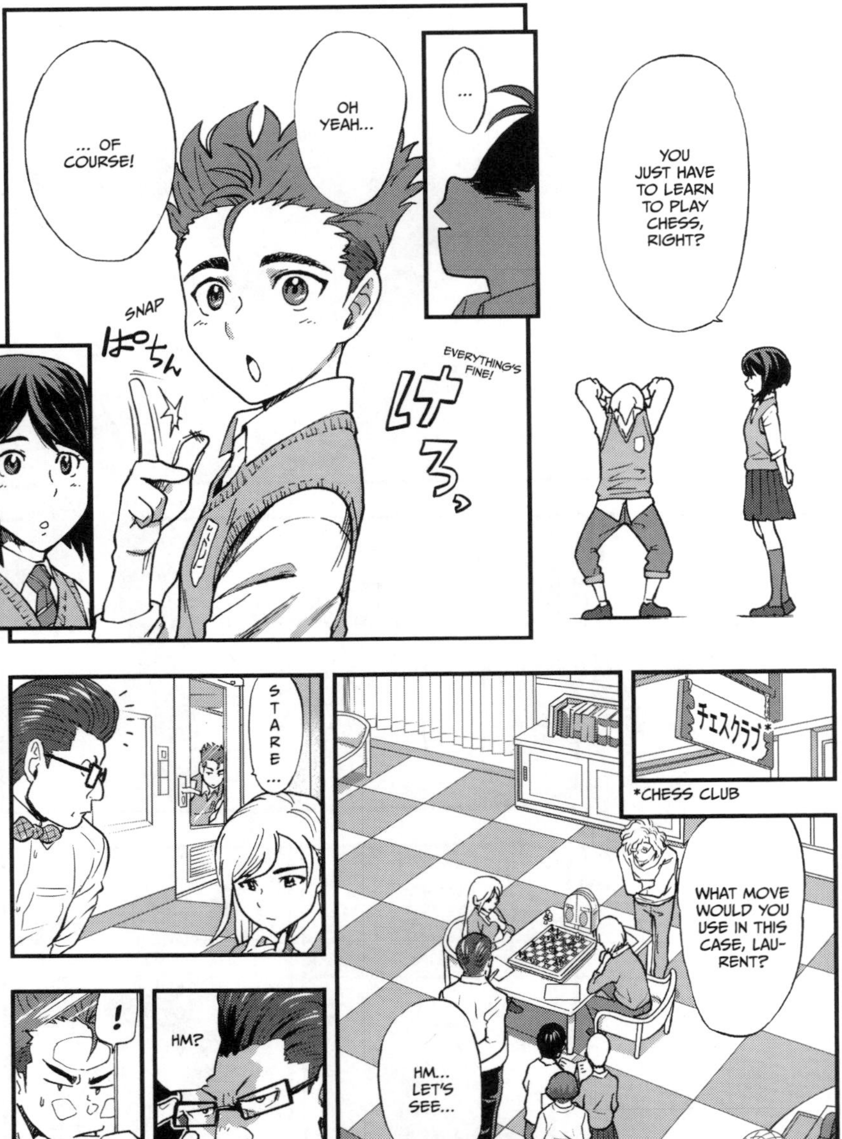
YOU JUST HAVE TO LEARN TO PLAY CHESS, RIGHT?
...
OH YEAH...
... OF COURSE!
SNAP
ぱちん
EVERYTHING'S FINE!
チェスクラブ*
*CHESS CLUB
WHAT MOVE WOULD YOU USE IN THIS CASE, LAURENT?
HM... LET'S SEE...
STARE ...
HM?
!
DAMN!

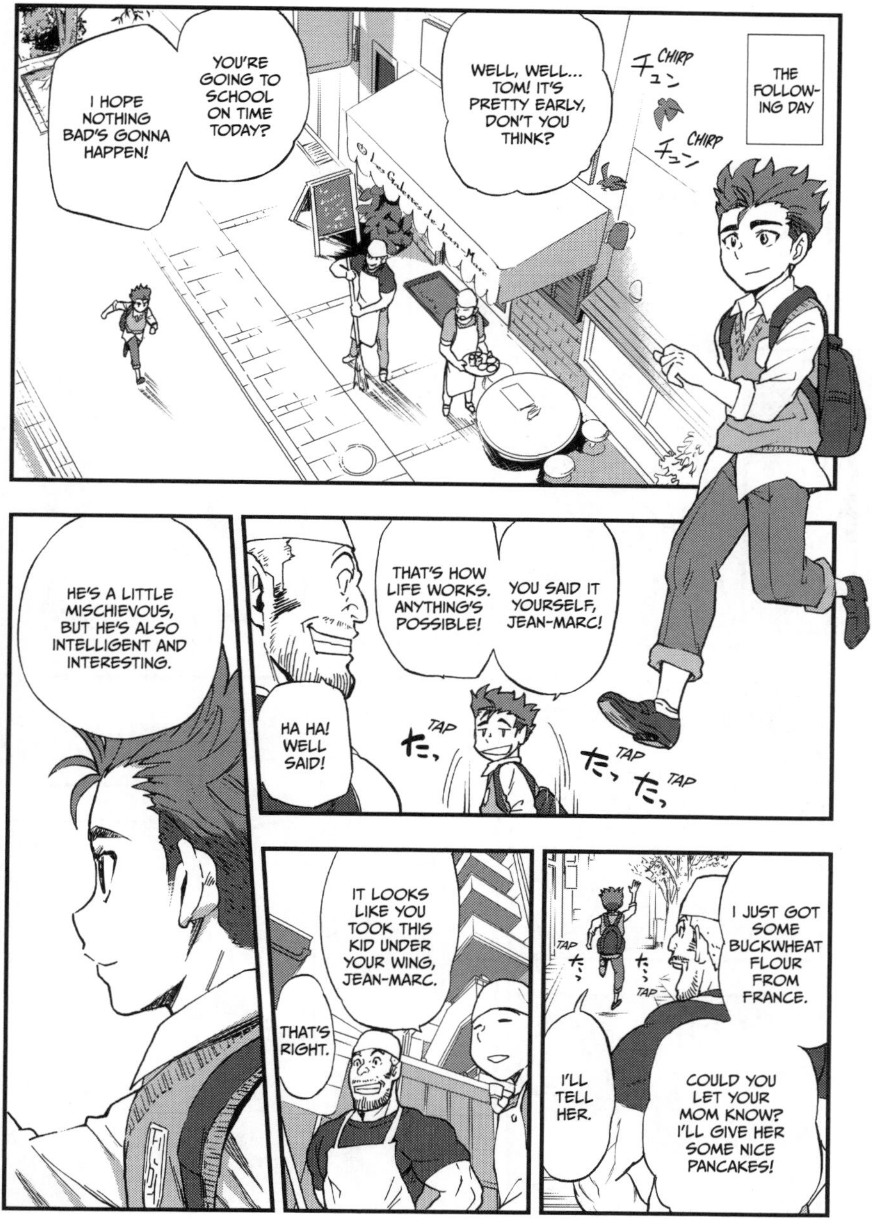
THE FOLLOW-ING DAY
CHIRP チュン
CHIRP チュン
WELL, WELL... TOM! IT'S PRETTY EARLY, DON'T YOU THINK?
Les Galettes de Jean-Marc
YOU'RE GOING TO SCHOOL ON TIME TODAY?
I HOPE NOTHING BAD'S GONNA HAPPEN!
YOU SAID IT YOURSELF, JEAN-MARC!
THAT'S HOW LIFE WORKS. ANYTHING'S POSSIBLE!
TAP たっ
TAP たっ
HA HA! WELL SAID!
TAP たっ
I JUST GOT SOME BUCKWHEAT FLOUR FROM FRANCE.
COULD YOU LET YOUR MOM KNOW? I'LL GIVE HER SOME NICE PANCAKES!
I'LL TELL HER.
TAP たっ
TAP たっ
IT LOOKS LIKE YOU TOOK THIS KID UNDER YOUR WING, JEAN-MARC.
THAT'S RIGHT.
HE'S A LITTLE MISCHIEVOUS, BUT HE'S ALSO INTELLIGENT AND INTERESTING.

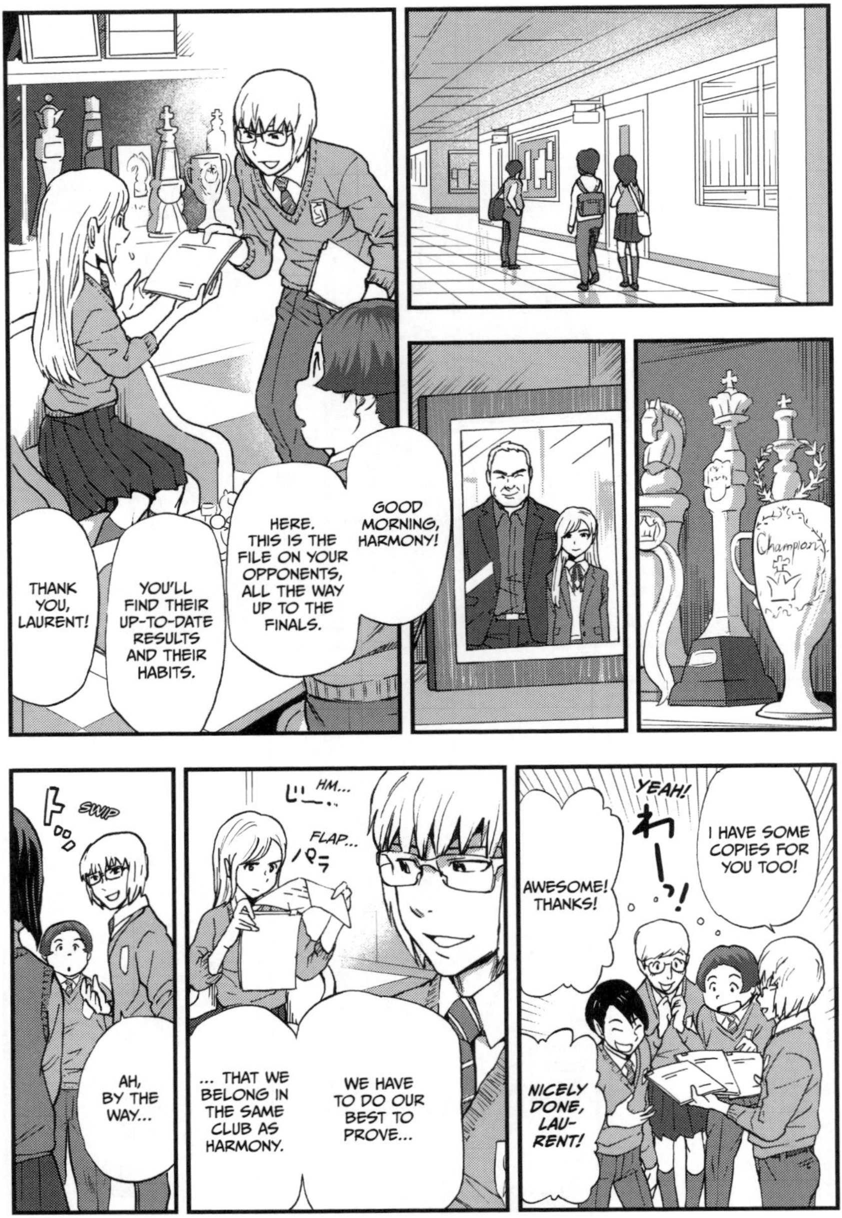
Champion
GOOD MORNING, HARMONY!
HERE. THIS IS THE FILE ON YOUR OPPONENTS, ALL THE WAY UP TO THE FINALS.
YOU'LL FIND THEIR UP-TO-DATE RESULTS AND THEIR HABITS.
THANK YOU, LAURENT!
I HAVE SOME COPIES FOR YOU TOO!
YEAH!
AWESOME! THANKS!
NICELY DONE, LAU-RENT!
HM...
FLAP...
WE HAVE TO DO OUR BEST TO PROVE...
... THAT WE BELONG IN THE SAME CLUB AS HARMONY.
SWIP
AH, BY THE WAY...

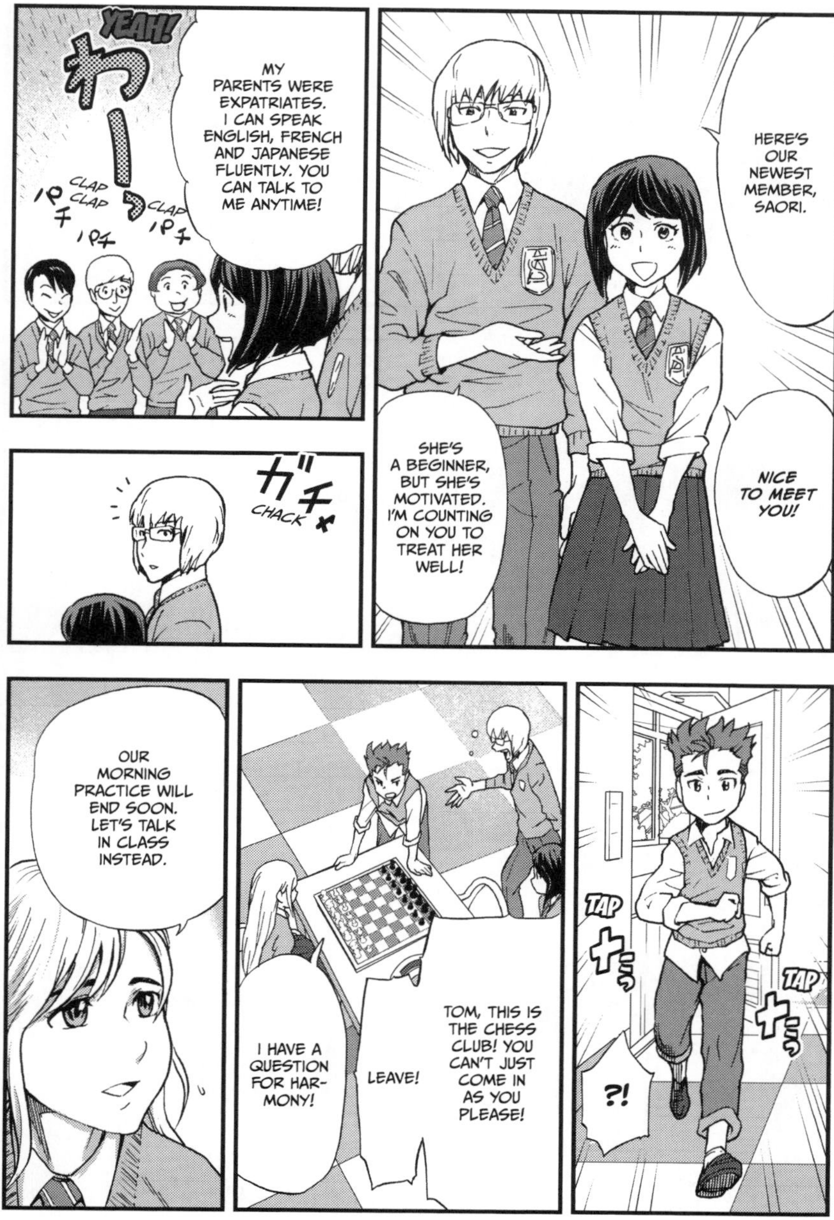
HERE'S OUR NEWEST MEMBER, SAORI.
NICE TO MEET YOU!
SHE'S A BEGINNER, BUT SHE'S MOTIVATED. I'M COUNTING ON YOU TO TREAT HER WELL!
MY PARENTS WERE EXPATRIATES. I CAN SPEAK ENGLISH, FRENCH AND JAPANESE FLUENTLY. YOU CAN TALK TO ME ANYTIME!
YEAH!
わーっ
CLAP CLAP
パチ
パチ
CLAP
パチ
ガチャ
CHACK
TAP
TAP
?!
TOM, THIS IS THE CHESS CLUB! YOU CAN'T JUST COME IN AS YOU PLEASE!
LEAVE!
I HAVE A QUESTION FOR HAR-MONY!
OUR MORNING PRACTICE WILL END SOON. LET'S TALK IN CLASS INSTEAD.

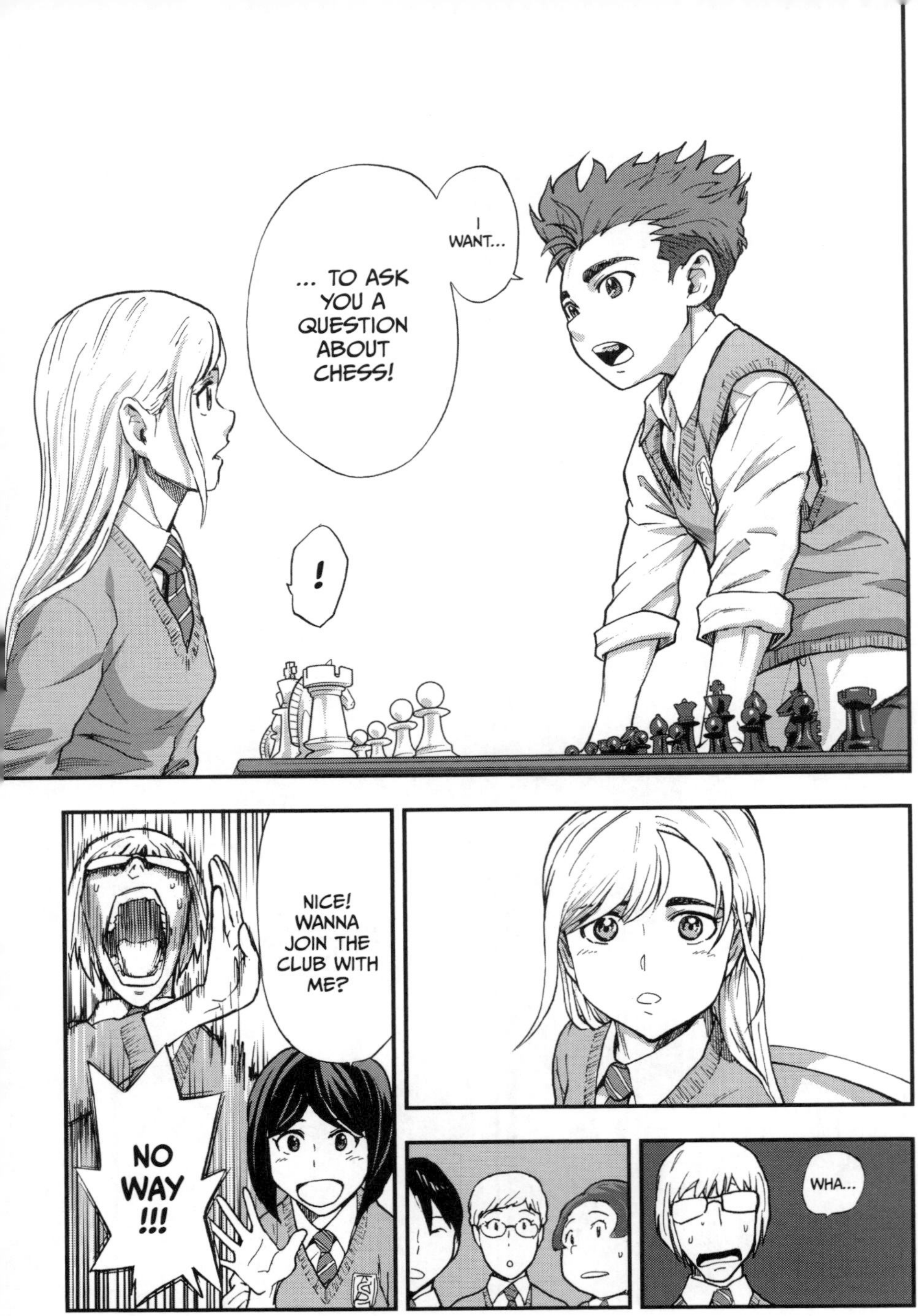
I WANT...
... TO ASK YOU A QUESTION ABOUT CHESS!
!
WHA...
NICE! WANNA JOIN THE CLUB WITH ME?
NO WAY !!!

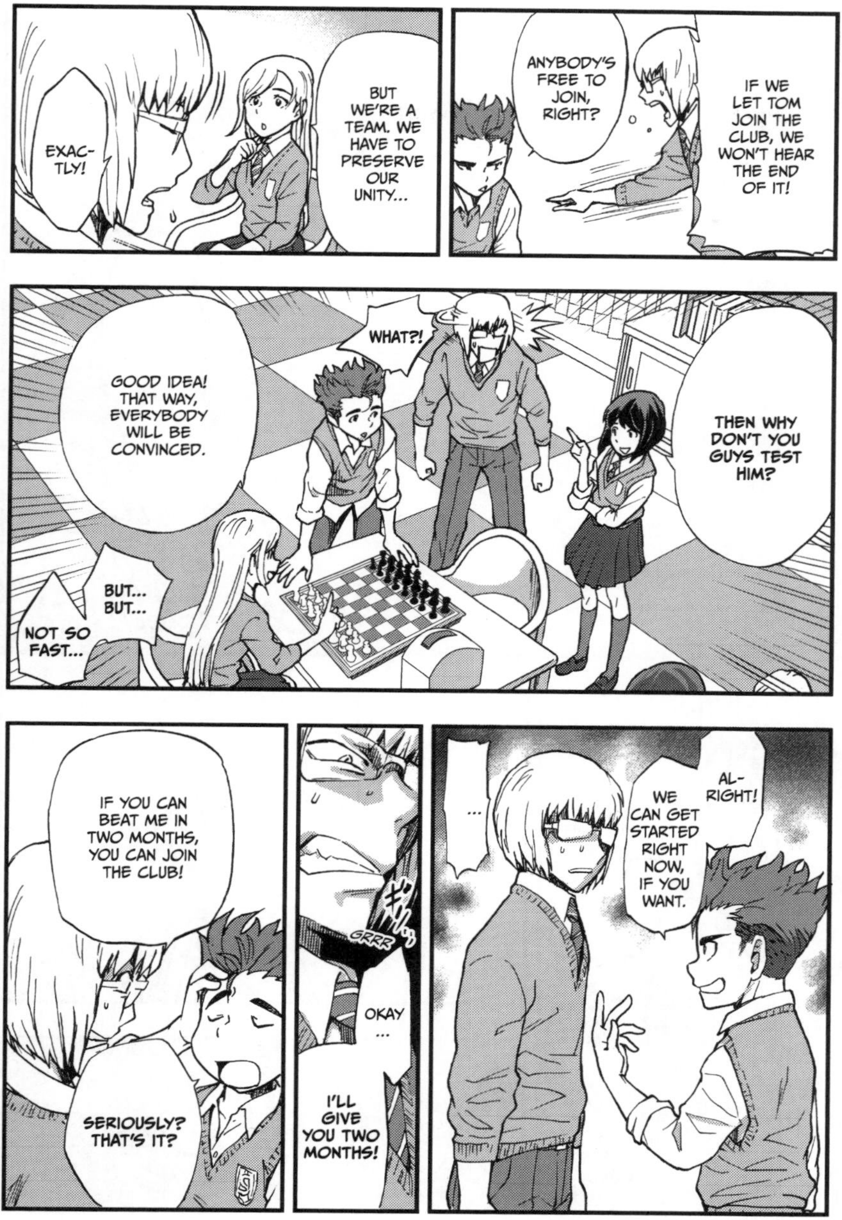
IF WE LET TOM JOIN THE CLUB, WE WON'T HEAR THE END OF IT!
ANYBODY'S FREE TO JOIN, RIGHT?
BUT WE'RE A TEAM. WE HAVE TO PRESERVE OUR UNITY...
EXACTLY!
THEN WHY DON'T YOU GUYS TEST HIM?
WHAT?!
GOOD IDEA! THAT WAY, EVERYBODY WILL BE CONVINCED.
BUT... BUT...
NOT SO FAST...
AL-RIGHT!
WE CAN GET STARTED RIGHT NOW, IF YOU WANT.
...
GRRR
OKAY ...
I'LL GIVE YOU TWO MONTHS!
IF YOU CAN BEAT ME IN TWO MONTHS, YOU CAN JOIN THE CLUB!
SERIOUSLY? THAT'S IT?

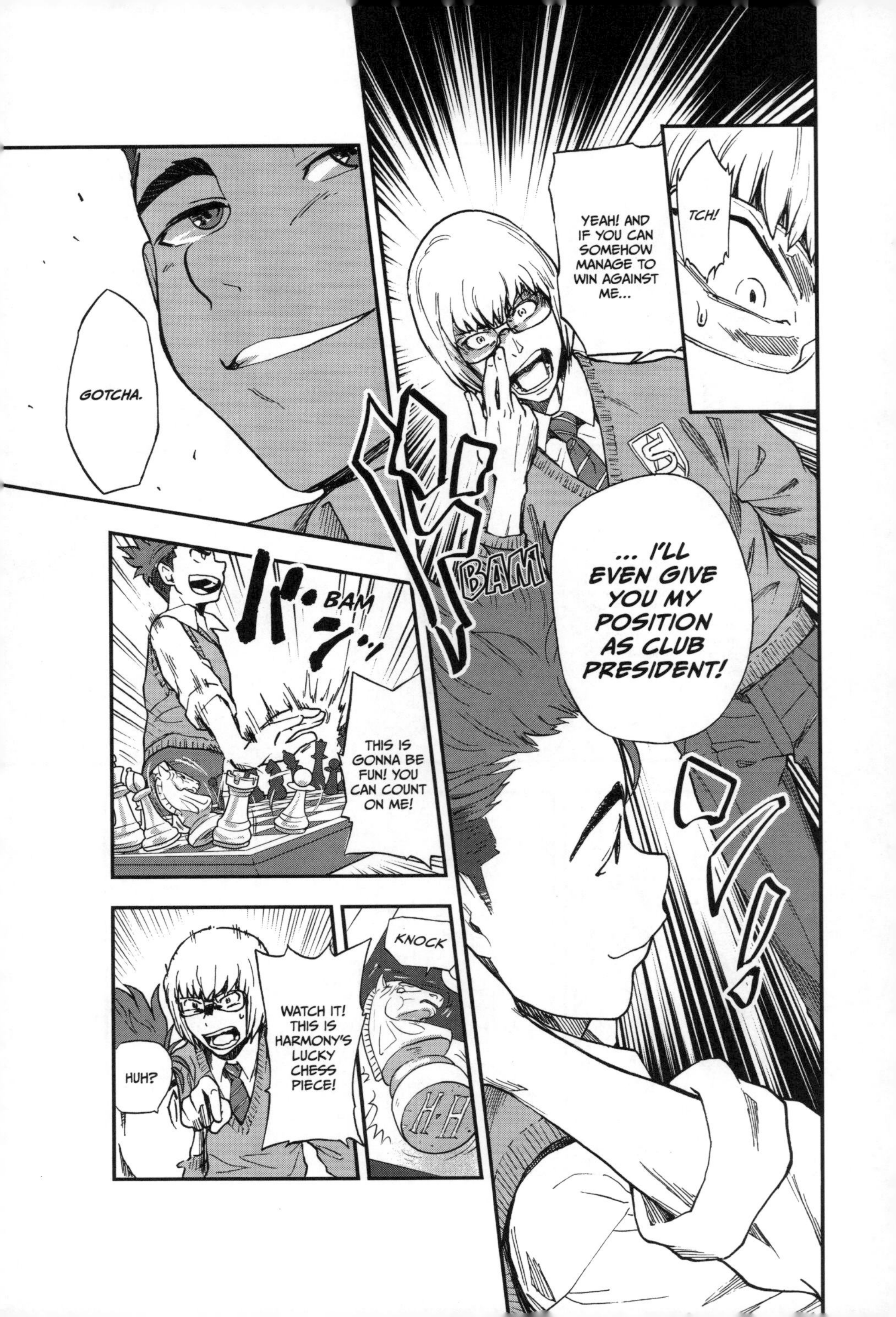
TCH!
YEAH! AND IF YOU CAN SOMEHOW MANAGE TO WIN AGAINST ME...
BAM
... I'LL EVEN GIVE YOU MY POSITION AS CLUB PRESIDENT!
GOTCHA.
BAM
THIS IS GONNA BE FUN! YOU CAN COUNT ON ME!
KNOCK
WATCH IT! THIS IS HARMONY'S LUCKY CHESS PIECE!
HUH?

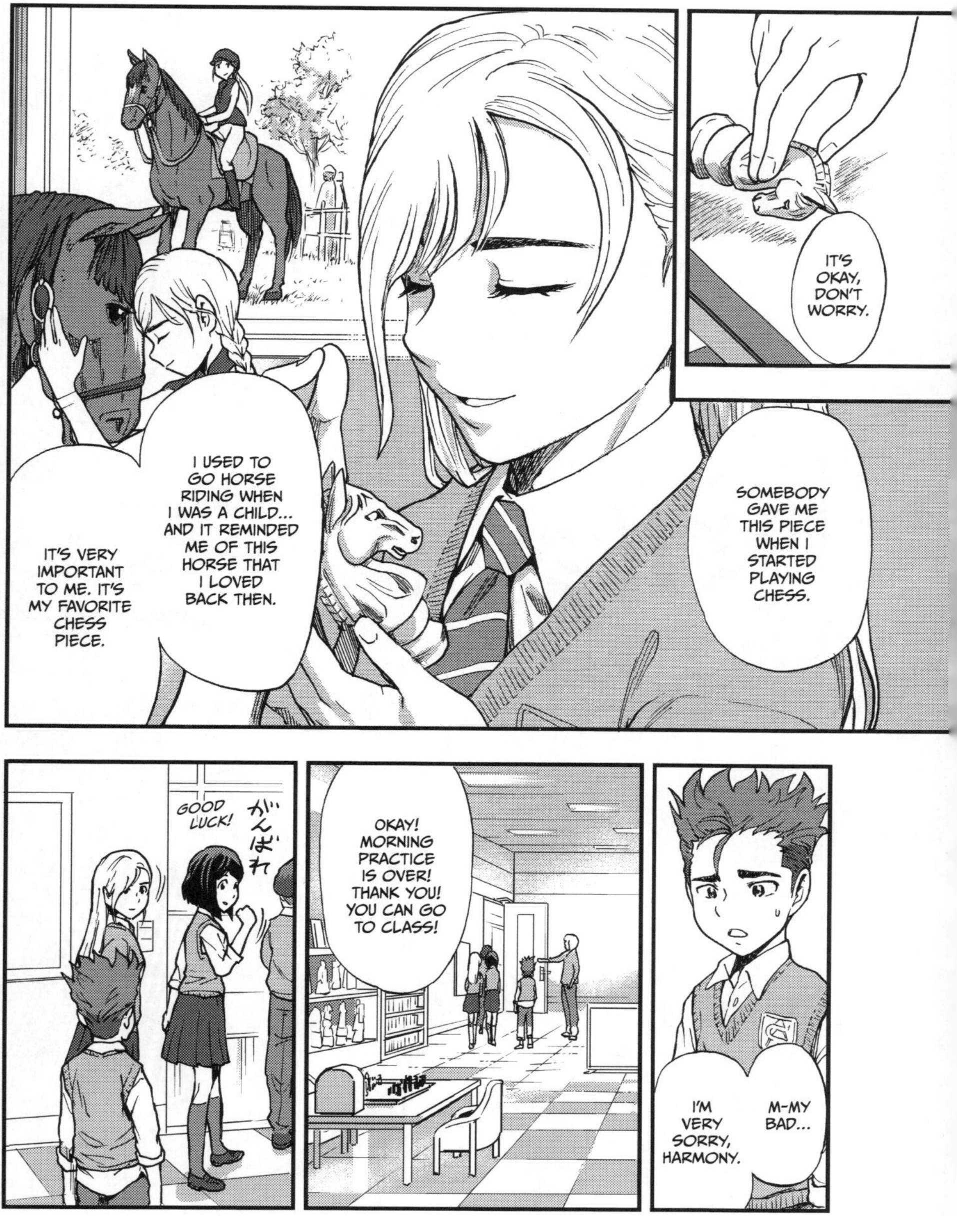
IT'S OKAY, DON'T WORRY.
SOMEBODY GAVE ME THIS PIECE WHEN I STARTED PLAYING CHESS.
I USED TO GO HORSE RIDING WHEN I WAS A CHILD... AND IT REMINDED ME OF THIS HORSE THAT I LOVED BACK THEN.
IT'S VERY IMPORTANT TO ME. IT'S MY FAVORITE CHESS PIECE.
M-MY BAD...
I'M VERY SORRY, HARMONY.
OKAY! MORNING PRACTICE IS OVER! THANK YOU! YOU CAN GO TO CLASS!
がんばれ
GOOD LUCK!

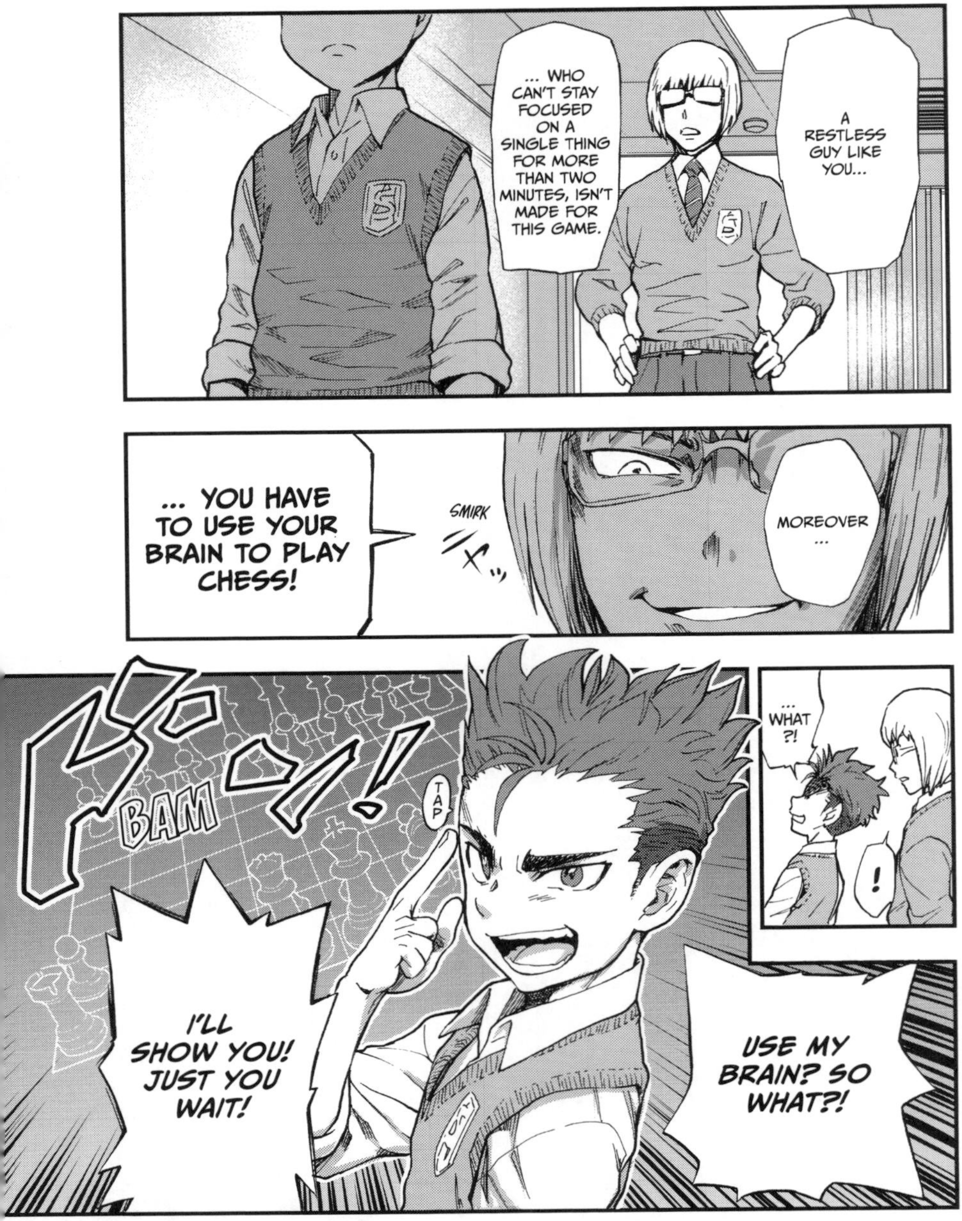
A RESTLESS GUY LIKE YOU...
... WHO CAN'T STAY FOCUSED ON A SINGLE THING FOR MORE THAN TWO MINUTES, ISN'T MADE FOR THIS GAME.
MOREOVER ...
SMIRK
... YOU HAVE TO USE YOUR BRAIN TO PLAY CHESS!
... WHAT ?!
!
USE MY BRAIN? SO WHAT?!
TAP
BAM
I'LL SHOW YOU! JUST YOU WAIT!

BLiTZ

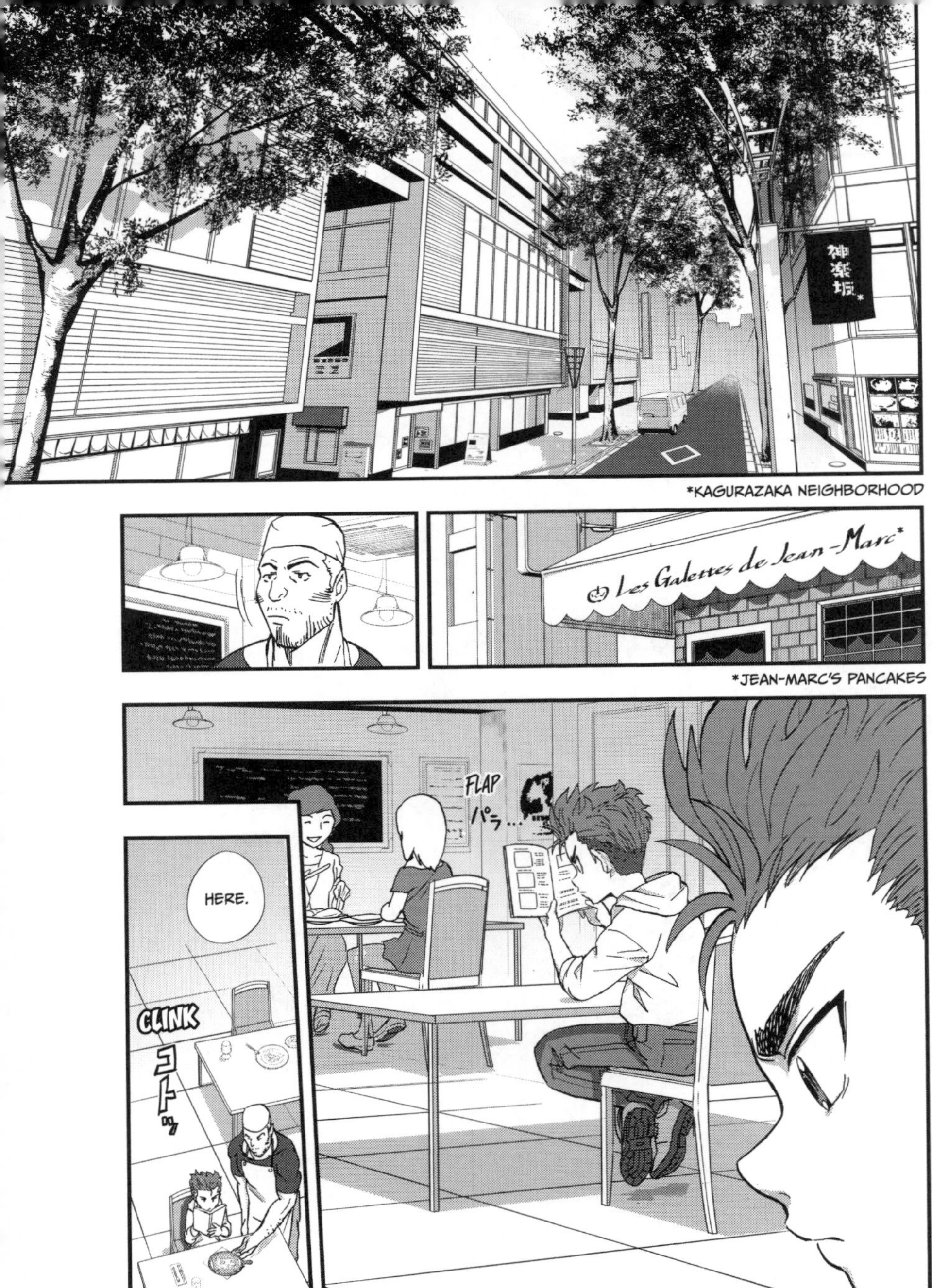

神楽坂*
*KAGURAZAKA NEIGHBORHOOD
Les Galettes de Jean-Marc*
*JEAN-MARC'S PANCAKES
FLAP
パラ…
HERE.
CLINK
コトッ

Chapter 2: I'm a pawn

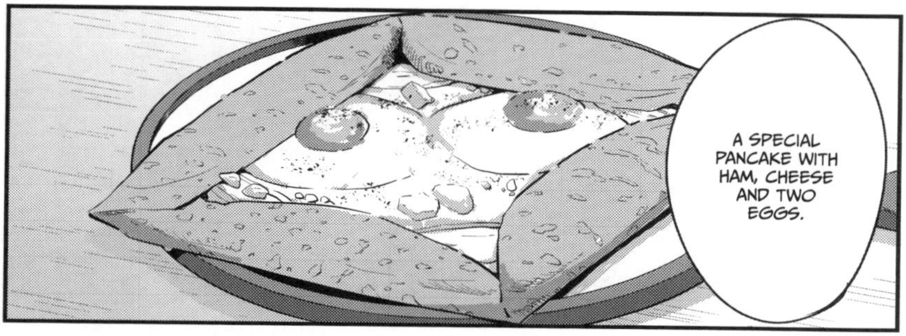
A SPECIAL PANCAKE WITH HAM, CHEESE AND TWO EGGS.

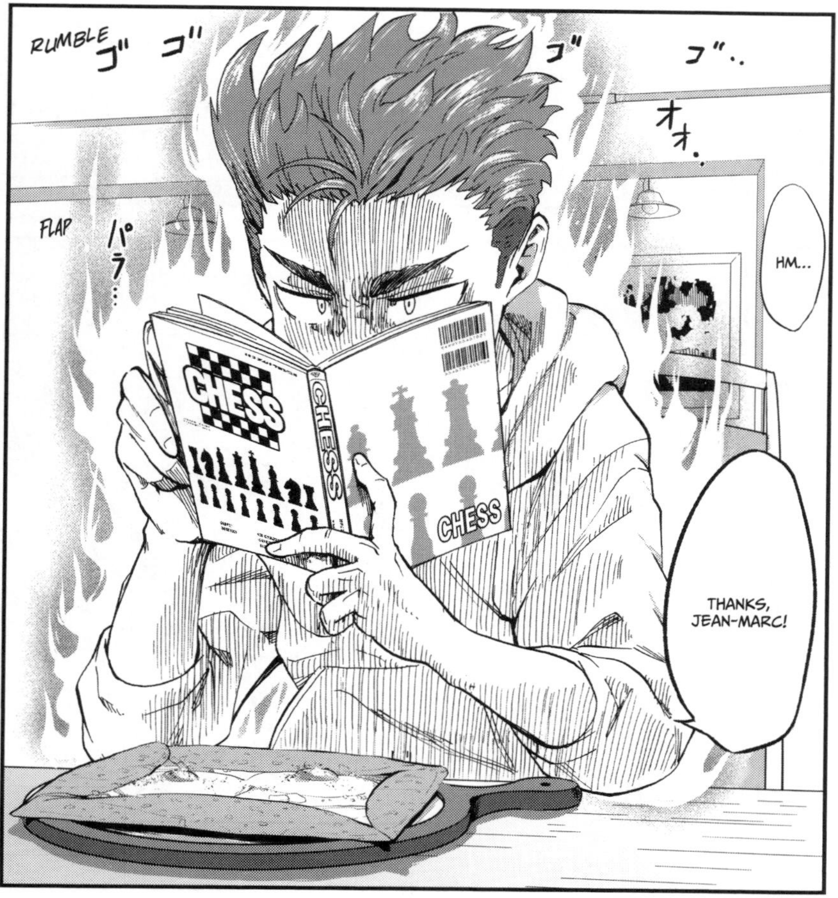
ゴ ゴ..
オオ..
RUMBLE ゴゴ
HM...
FLAP パラ...
CHESS
CHESS
CHESS
THANKS, JEAN-MARC!

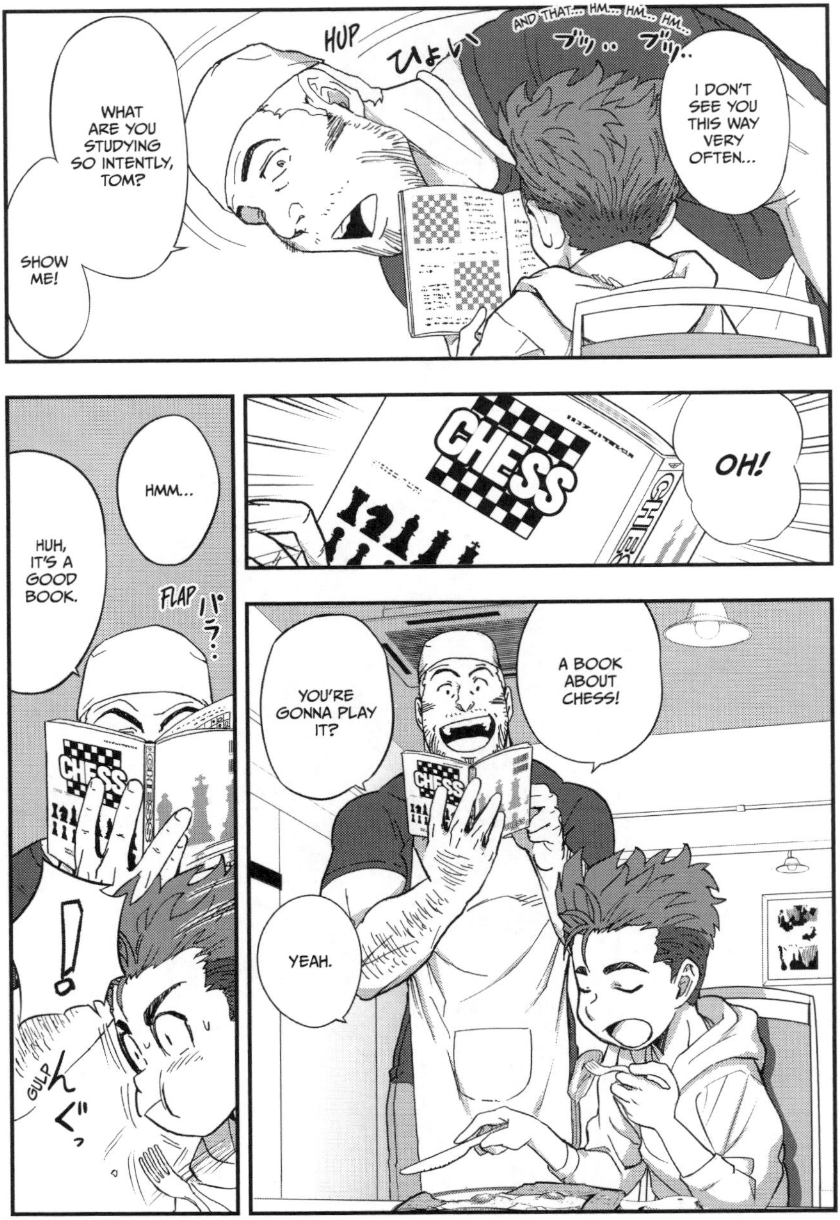
AND THAT... HM... HM... HM...
ブツ.. ブツ..
I DON'T SEE YOU THIS WAY VERY OFTEN...
HUP
ひょい
WHAT ARE YOU STUDYING SO INTENTLY, TOM?
SHOW ME!
CHESS
OH!
A BOOK ABOUT CHESS!
YOU'RE GONNA PLAY IT?
CHESS
YEAH.
HMM...
HUH, IT'S A GOOD BOOK.
FLAP
パラ..
CHESS
!
GULP
んぐっ

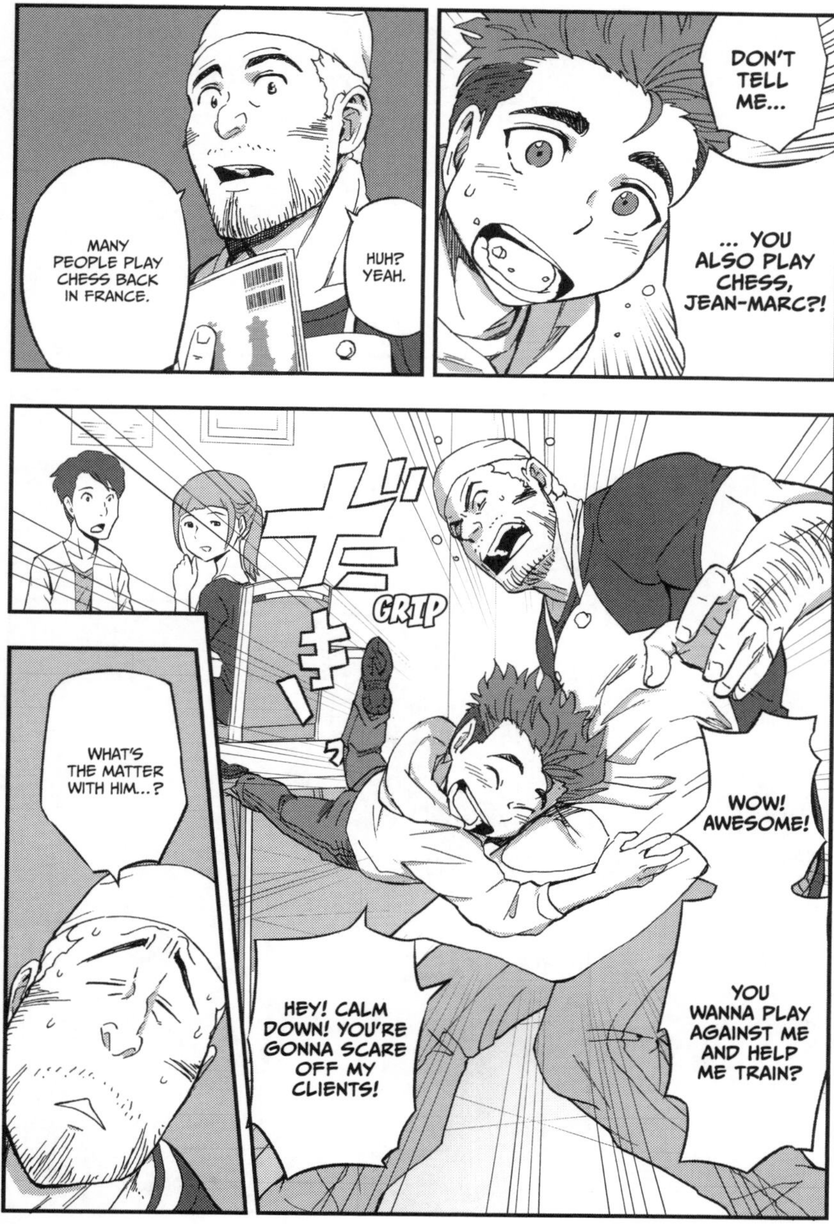
DON'T TELL ME...
... YOU ALSO PLAY CHESS, JEAN-MARC?!
HUH? YEAH.
MANY PEOPLE PLAY CHESS BACK IN FRANCE.
GRIP
WOW! AWESOME!
YOU WANNA PLAY AGAINST ME AND HELP ME TRAIN?
HEY! CALM DOWN! YOU'RE GONNA SCARE OFF MY CLIENTS!
WHAT'S THE MATTER WITH HIM...?

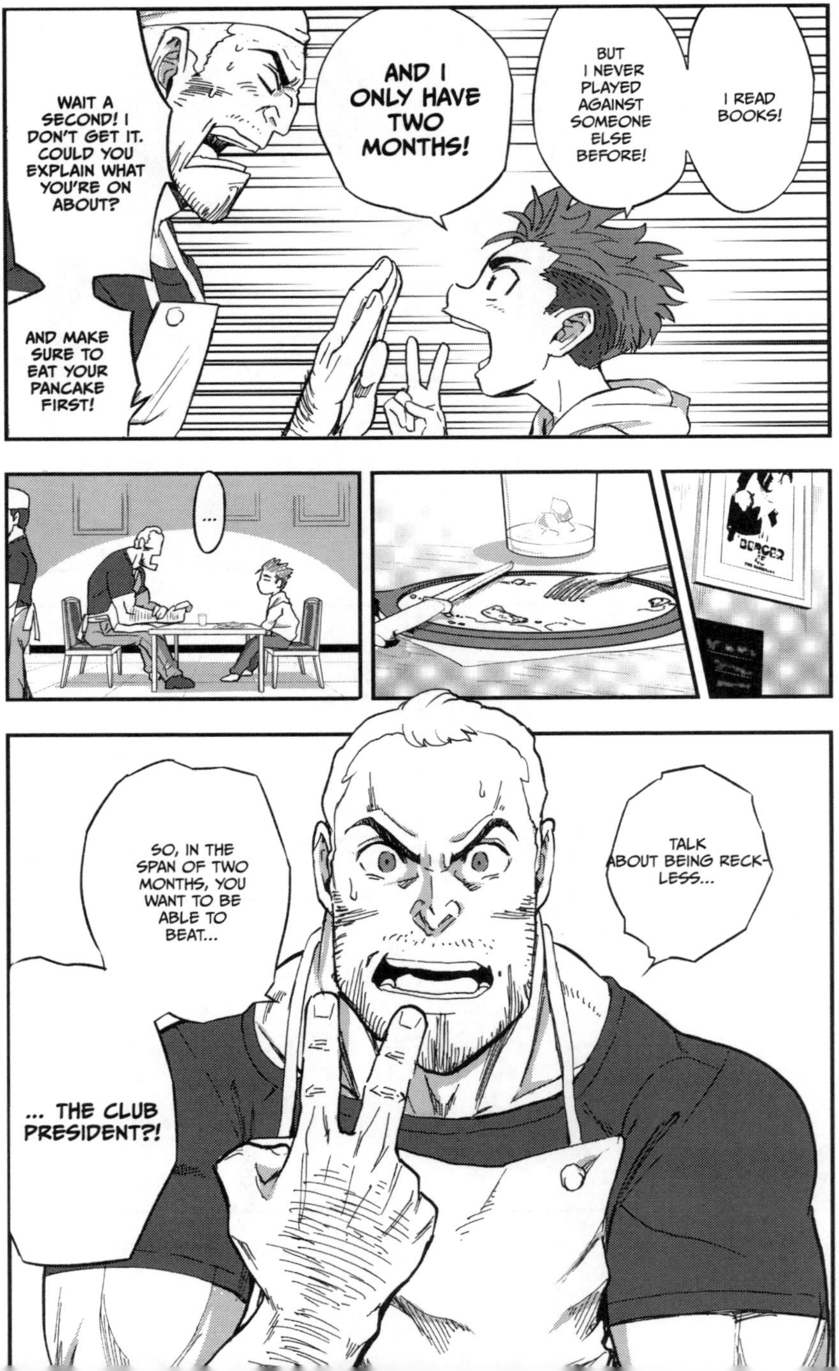
I READ BOOKS!
BUT I NEVER PLAYED AGAINST SOMEONE ELSE BEFORE!
AND I ONLY HAVE TWO MONTHS!
WAIT A SECOND! I DON'T GET IT. COULD YOU EXPLAIN WHAT YOU'RE ON ABOUT?
AND MAKE SURE TO EAT YOUR PANCAKE FIRST!
...
TALK ABOUT BEING RECK-LESS...
SO, IN THE SPAN OF TWO MONTHS, YOU WANT TO BE ABLE TO BEAT...
... THE CLUB PRESIDENT?!

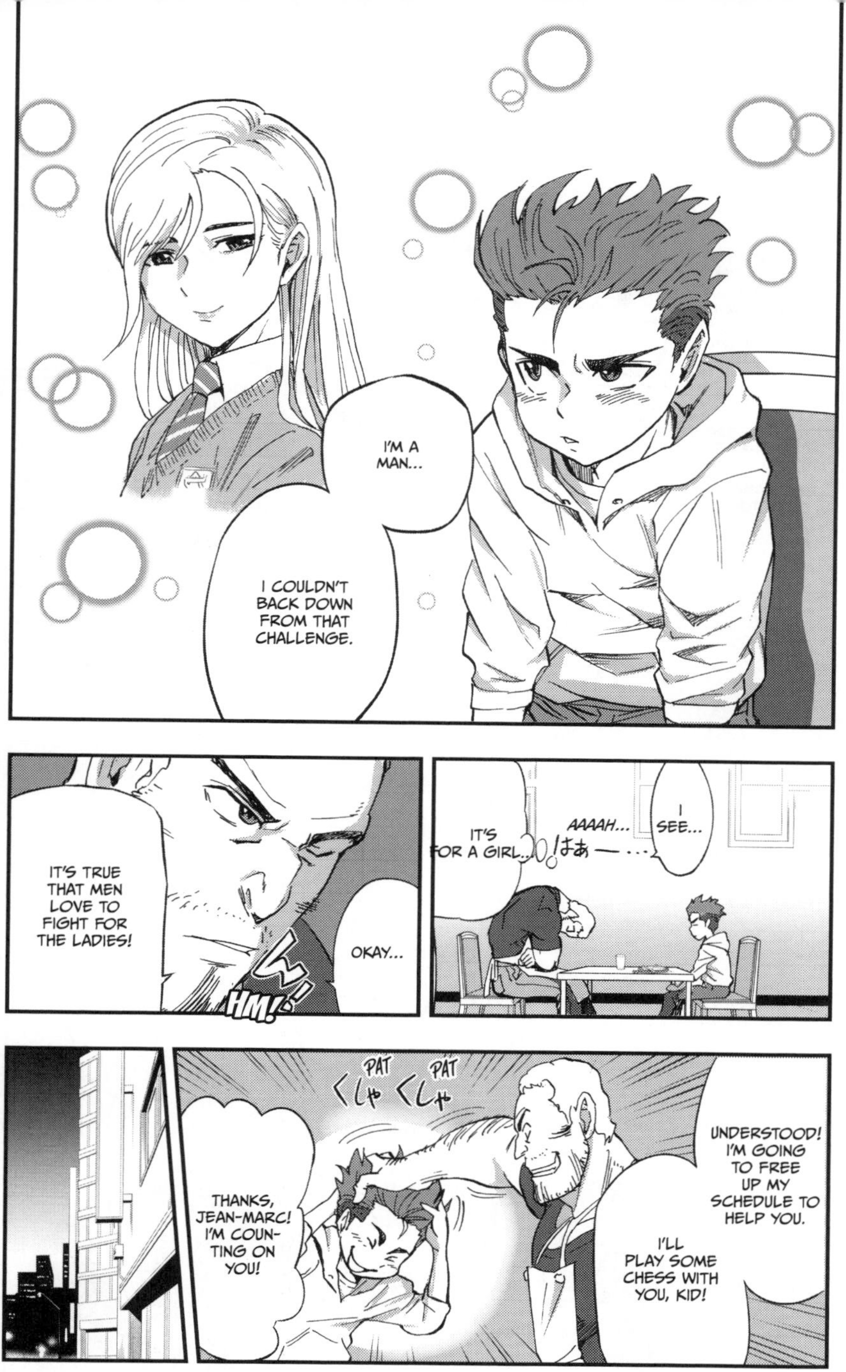
I'M A MAN...
I COULDN'T BACK DOWN FROM THAT CHALLENGE.
I SEE...
AAAAH...
はあー・・・
IT'S FOR A GIRL...
OKAY...
IT'S TRUE THAT MEN LOVE TO FIGHT FOR THE LADIES!
HM!
PAT PAT
くしゃくしゃ
UNDERSTOOD! I'M GOING TO FREE UP MY SCHEDULE TO HELP YOU.
I'LL PLAY SOME CHESS WITH YOU, KID!
THANKS, JEAN-MARC! I'M COUNTING ON YOU!

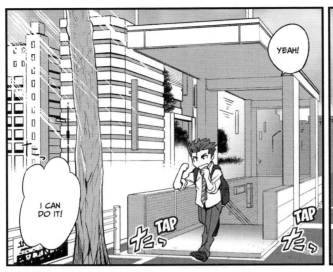

YEAH!
TAP
I CAN DO IT!
TAP
THAT'S NOT POSSIBLE.
THE RULES SAY SO, YOU KNOW!
HUH?
"TOUCH AND MOVE". WHEN YOU TOUCH A PIECE, YOU HAVE TO MOVE IT.
TAP
WHAT IF IT'S NOT IN THE RIGHT PLACE?

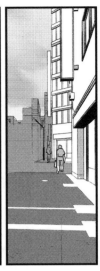

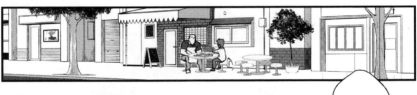

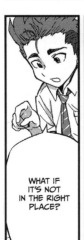

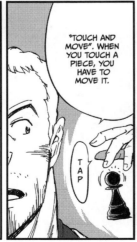

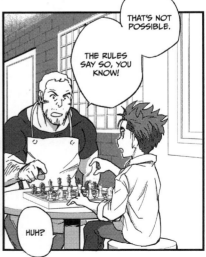

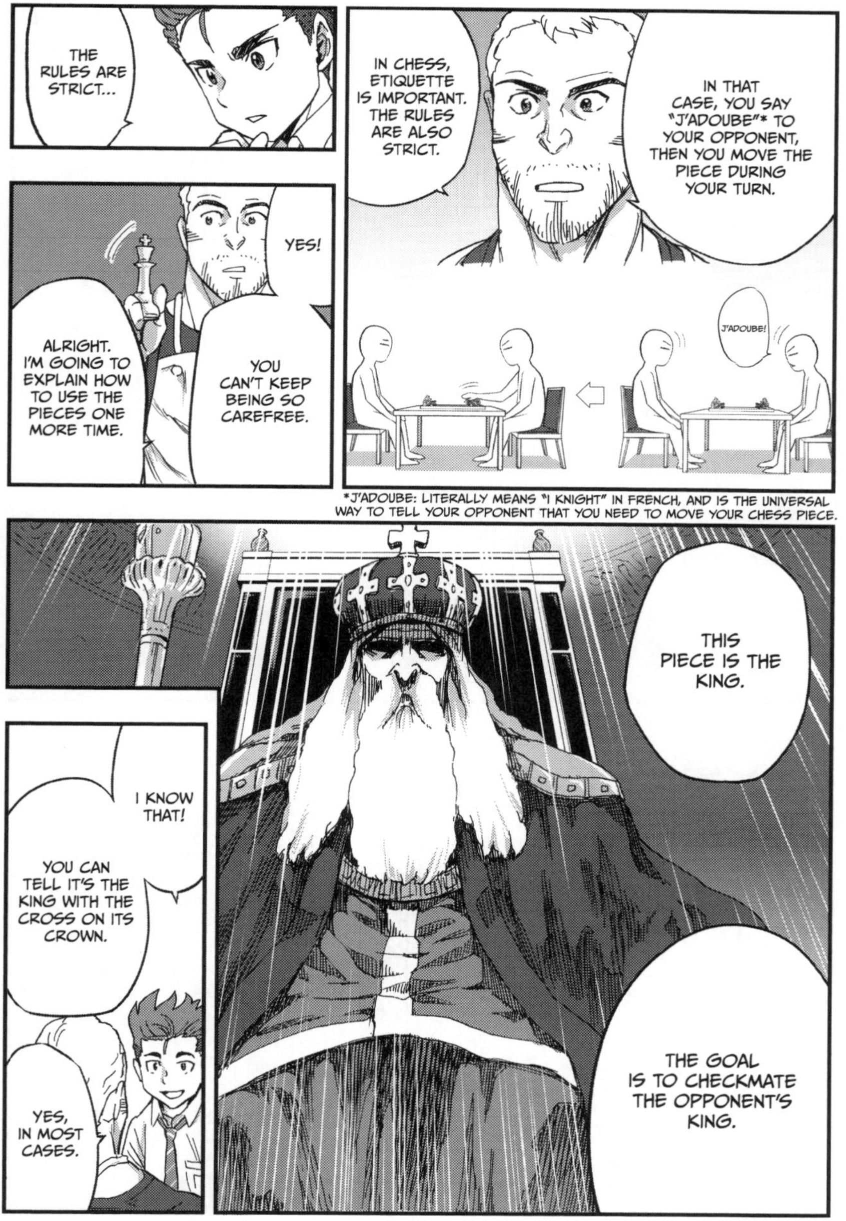
IN CHESS, ETIQUETTE IS IMPORTANT. THE RULES ARE ALSO STRICT.
IN THAT CASE, YOU SAY "J'ADOUBE"* TO YOUR OPPONENT, THEN YOU MOVE THE PIECE DURING YOUR TURN.
THE RULES ARE STRICT...
J'ADOUBE!
YES!
YOU CAN'T KEEP BEING SO CAREFREE.
ALRIGHT. I'M GOING TO EXPLAIN HOW TO USE THE PIECES ONE MORE TIME.
THIS PIECE IS THE KING.
I KNOW THAT!
YOU CAN TELL IT'S THE KING WITH THE CROSS ON ITS CROWN.
THE GOAL IS TO CHECKMATE THE OPPONENT'S KING.
YES, IN MOST CASES.

*J'ADOUBE: LITERALLY MEANS "I KNIGHT" IN FRENCH, AND IS THE UNIVERSAL WAY TO TELL YOUR OPPONENT THAT YOU NEED TO MOVE YOUR CHESS PIECE.

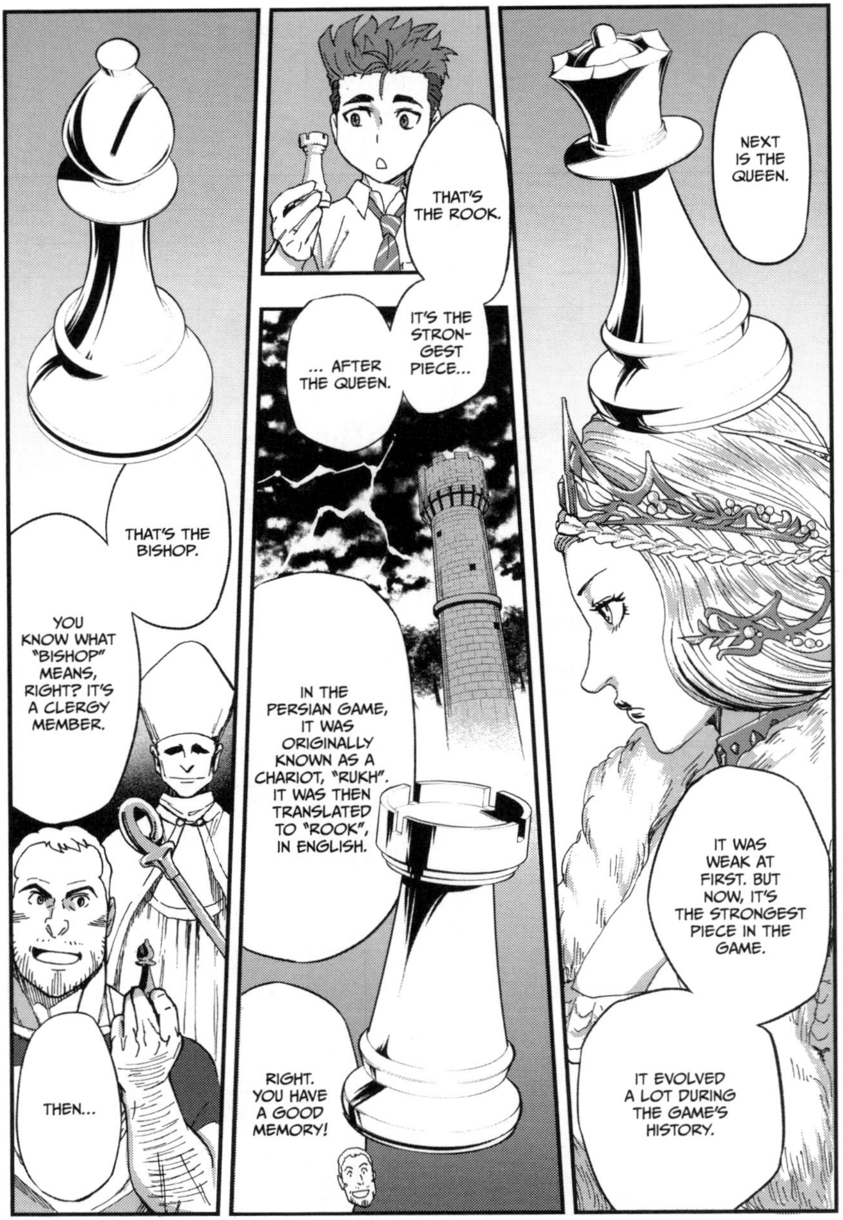
THAT'S THE BISHOP.
YOU KNOW WHAT "BISHOP" MEANS, RIGHT? IT'S A CLERGY MEMBER.
THEN...
THAT'S THE ROOK.
IT'S THE STRONGEST PIECE...
... AFTER THE QUEEN.
IN THE PERSIAN GAME, IT WAS ORIGINALLY KNOWN AS A CHARIOT, "RUKH". IT WAS THEN TRANSLATED TO "ROOK", IN ENGLISH.
RIGHT. YOU HAVE A GOOD MEMORY!
NEXT IS THE QUEEN.
IT WAS WEAK AT FIRST. BUT NOW, IT'S THE STRONGEST PIECE IN THE GAME.
IT EVOLVED A LOT DURING THE GAME'S HISTORY.

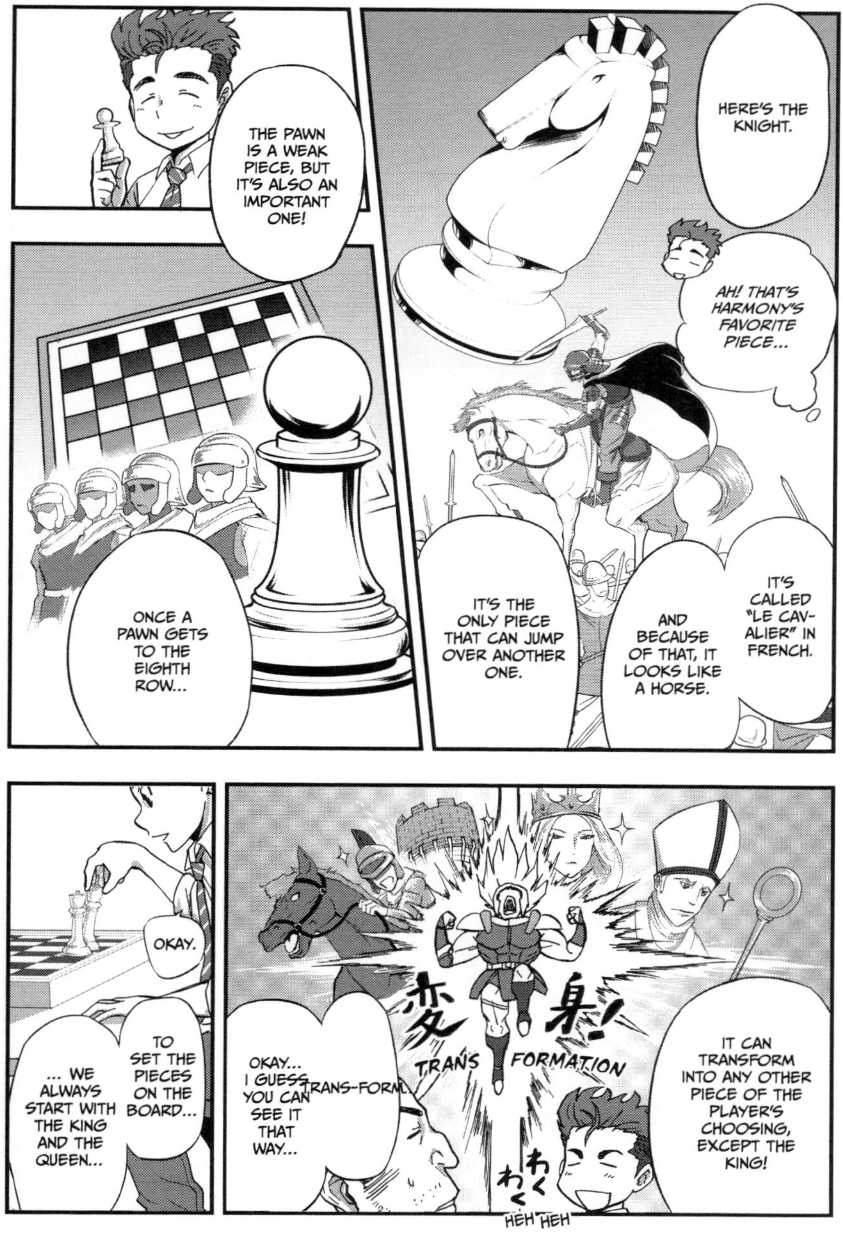
HERE'S THE KNIGHT.
AH! THAT'S HARMONY'S FAVORITE PIECE...
IT'S CALLED "LE CAVALIER" IN FRENCH.
AND BECAUSE OF THAT, IT LOOKS LIKE A HORSE.
IT'S THE ONLY PIECE THAT CAN JUMP OVER ANOTHER ONE.
THE PAWN IS A WEAK PIECE, BUT IT'S ALSO AN IMPORTANT ONE!
ONCE A PAWN GETS TO THE EIGHTH ROW...
IT CAN TRANSFORM INTO ANY OTHER PIECE OF THE PLAYER'S CHOOSING, EXCEPT THE KING!
変身!
TRANS FORMATION
わくわく
HEH HEH
TRANS-FORM...
OKAY... I GUESS YOU CAN SEE IT THAT WAY...
OKAY.
TO SET THE PIECES ON THE BOARD...
... WE ALWAYS START WITH THE KING AND THE QUEEN...

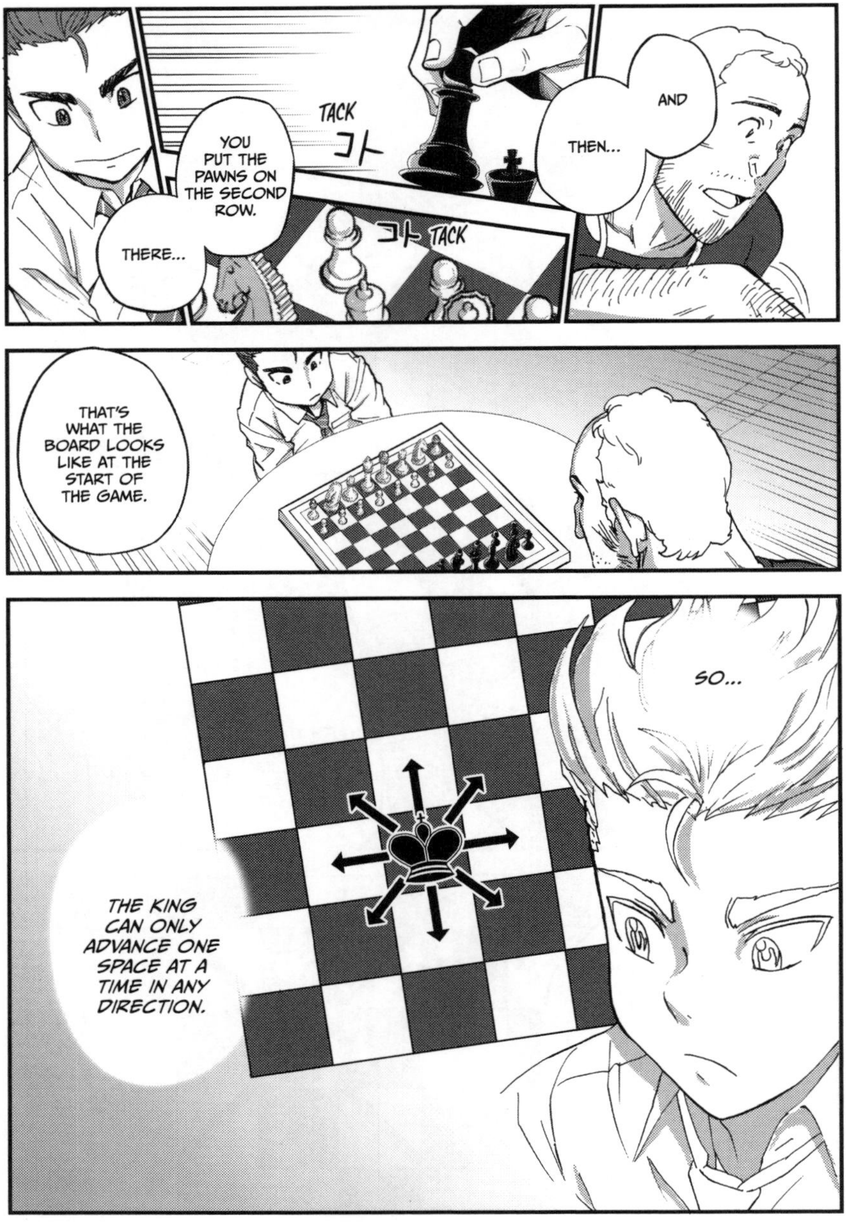
AND THEN...
TACK
コト
YOU PUT THE PAWNS ON THE SECOND ROW.
コト TACK
THERE...
THAT'S WHAT THE BOARD LOOKS LIKE AT THE START OF THE GAME.
SO...
THE KING CAN ONLY ADVANCE ONE SPACE AT A TIME IN ANY DIRECTION.

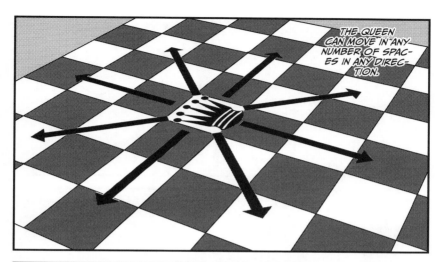

THE QUEEN CAN MOVE IN ANY NUMBER OF SPACES IN ANY DIRECTION.
THE ROOK CAN MOVE IN ANY NUMBER OF SPACES TOO, BUT ONLY HORIZONTALLY OR VERTICALLY.
IT'S THE STRONGEST PIECE AFTER THE QUEEN, REMEMBER?
AND THE BISHOP CAN MOVE AS FAR AS POSSIBLE DIAGONALLY.

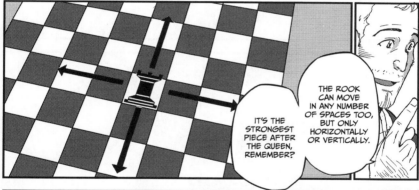

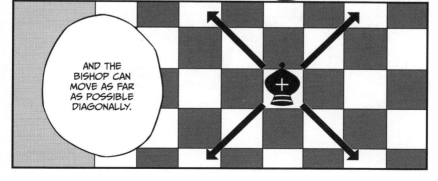

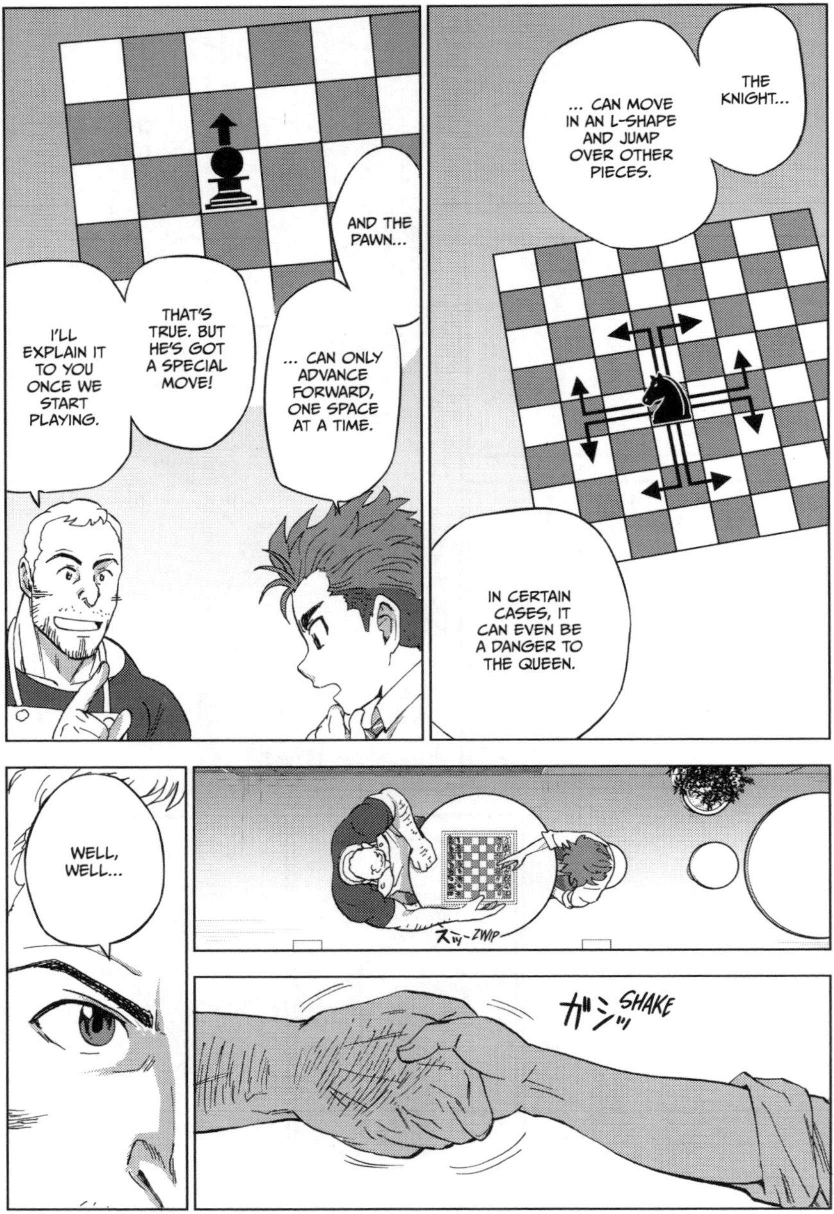
THE KNIGHT...
... CAN MOVE IN AN L-SHAPE AND JUMP OVER OTHER PIECES.
IN CERTAIN CASES, IT CAN EVEN BE A DANGER TO THE QUEEN.
AND THE PAWN...
... CAN ONLY ADVANCE FORWARD, ONE SPACE AT A TIME.
THAT'S TRUE. BUT HE'S GOT A SPECIAL MOVE!
I'LL EXPLAIN IT TO YOU ONCE WE START PLAYING.
スッ ZWIP
ガシッ SHAKE
WELL, WELL...

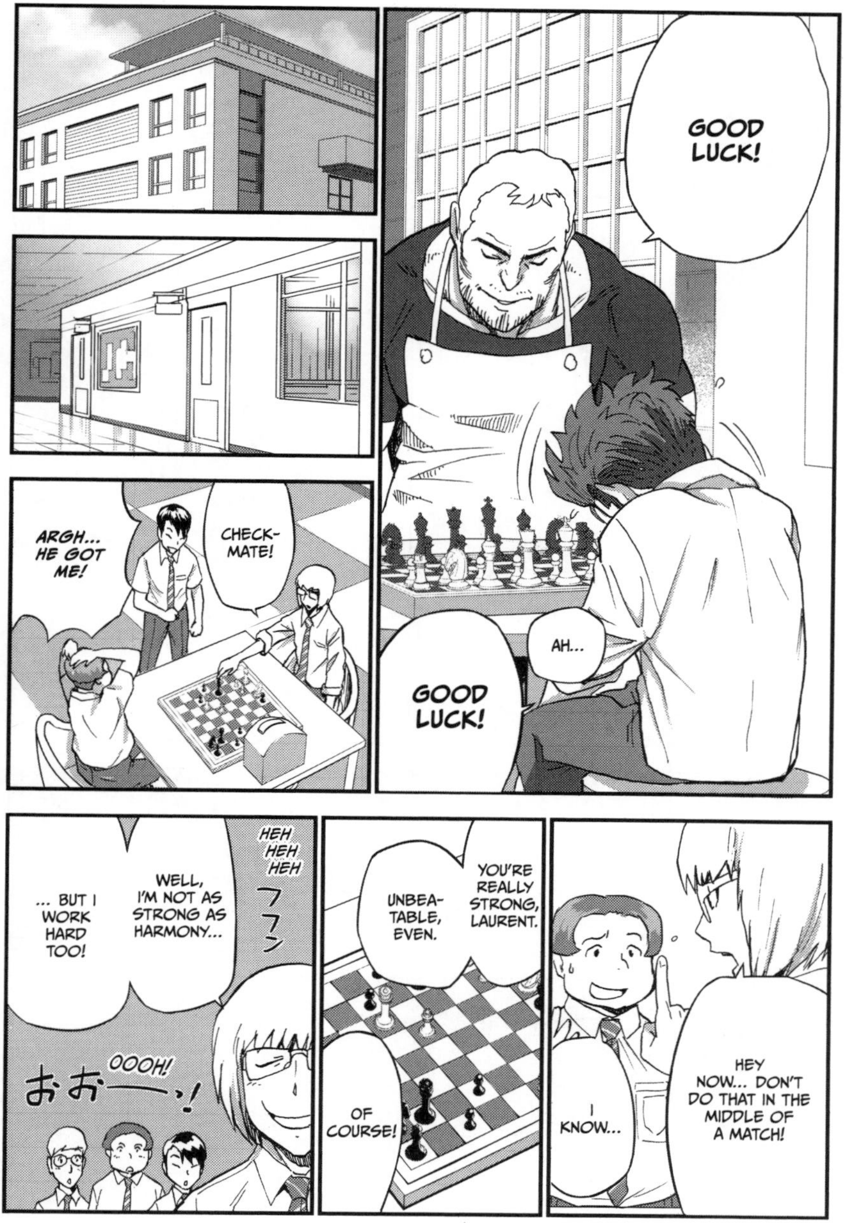
GOOD LUCK!
AH...
GOOD LUCK!
CHECK-MATE!
ARGH... HE GOT ME!
HEY NOW... DON'T DO THAT IN THE MIDDLE OF A MATCH!
I KNOW...
YOU'RE REALLY STRONG, LAURENT.
UNBEA-TABLE, EVEN.
OF COURSE!
HEH HEH HEH
フフン
WELL, I'M NOT AS STRONG AS HARMONY...
... BUT I WORK HARD TOO!
OOOH!
おおーっ!

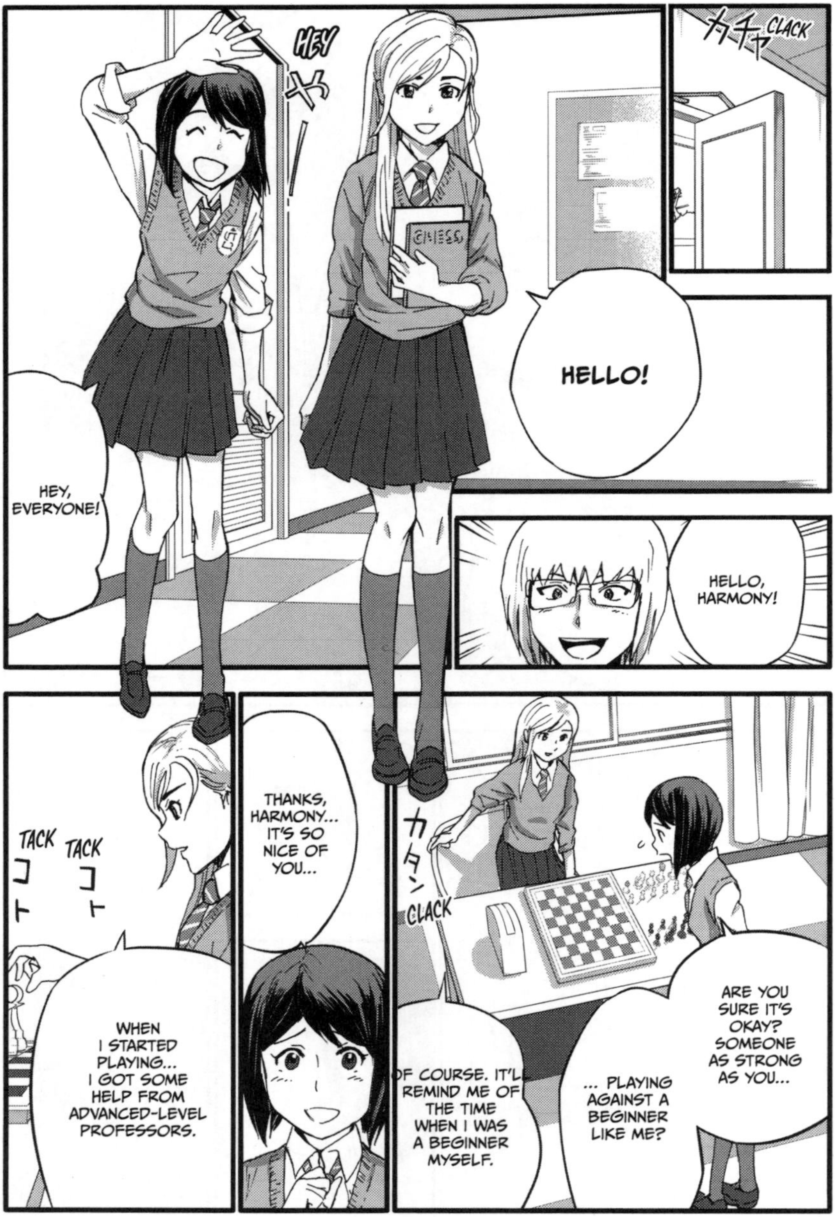

カチャ CLACK
HELLO!
HELLO, HARMONY!
HEY や
HEY, EVERYONE!
カタン CLACK
ARE YOU SURE IT'S OKAY? SOMEONE AS STRONG AS YOU...
... PLAYING AGAINST A BEGINNER LIKE ME?
OF COURSE. IT'LL REMIND ME OF THE TIME WHEN I WAS A BEGINNER MYSELF.
THANKS, HARMONY... IT'S SO NICE OF YOU...
TACK コト TACK コト
WHEN I STARTED PLAYING... I GOT SOME HELP FROM ADVANCED-LEVEL PROFESSORS.

I WAS LUCKY ENOUGH TO GET HELP FROM VARIOUS MASTERS. PROFESSIONALS RECOGNIZED BY THE ICF*.

I ALSO GOT HELP FROM THE GREAT GARRY KASPAROV... HE SAID IT WAS...

... "FOR THE FUTURE OF CHESS".

*ICF: INTERNATIONAL CHESS FEDERATION

GOOD LUCK.

GOOD LUCK.

SWISH

YES!

WOW! THAT'S SO COOL!

WOOOW

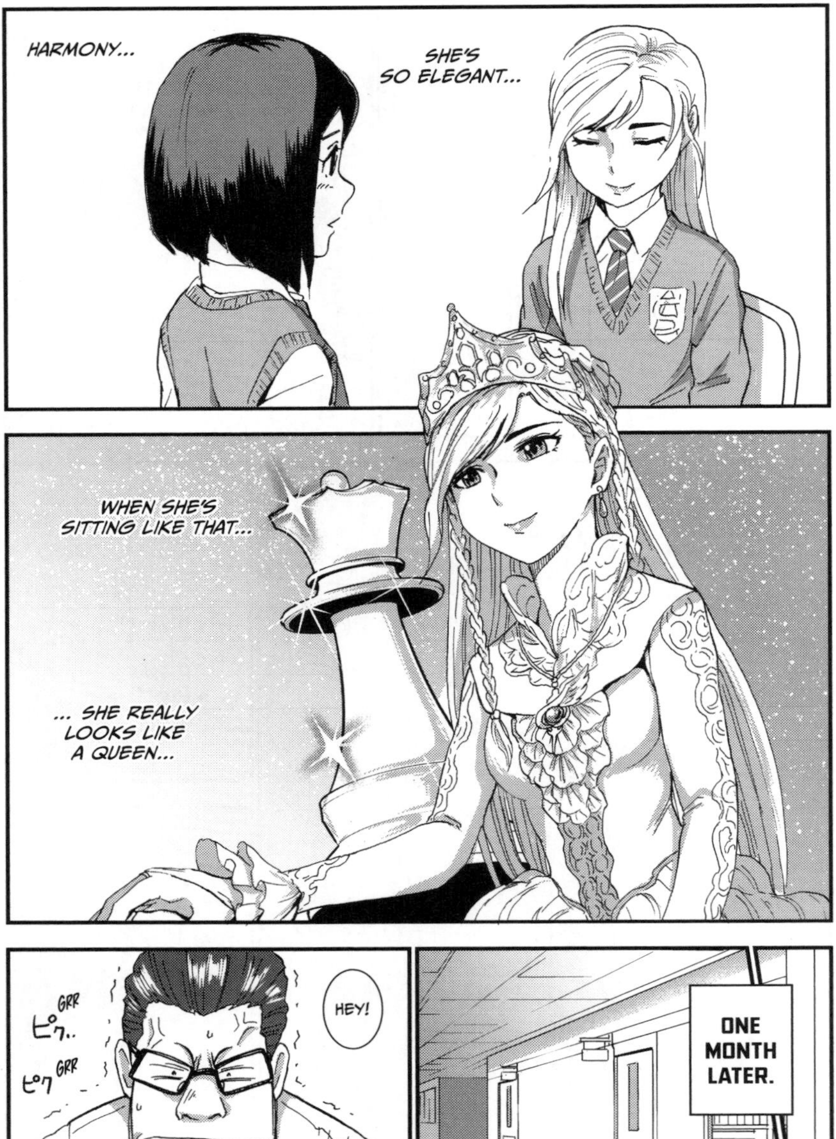
SHE'S SO ELEGANT...
HARMONY...
WHEN SHE'S SITTING LIKE THAT...
... SHE REALLY LOOKS LIKE A QUEEN...
ONE MONTH LATER.
HEY!
ピク.. GRR
ピク GRR

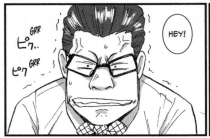

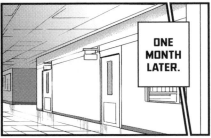

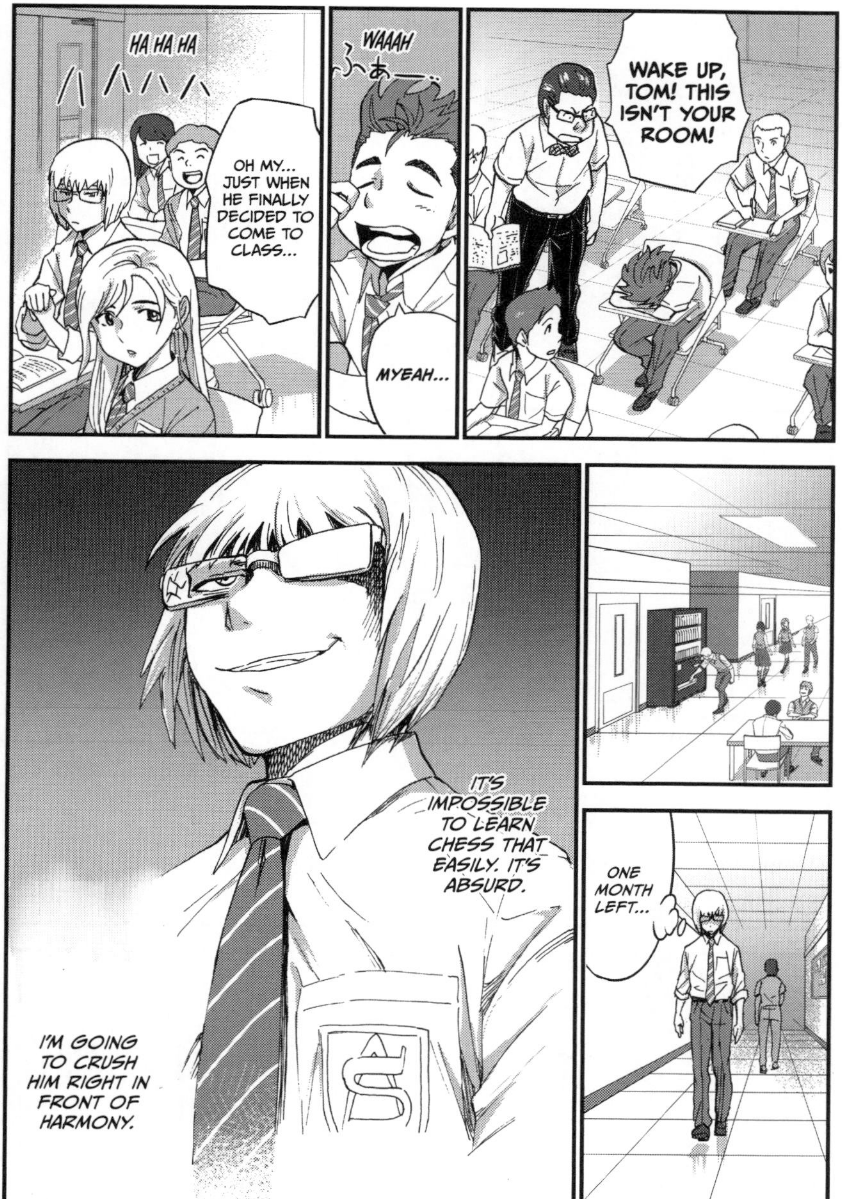
WAKE UP, TOM! THIS ISN'T YOUR ROOM!
WAAAH
ふあー
MYEAH...
HA HA HA
ハハハハ
OH MY... JUST WHEN HE FINALLY DECIDED TO COME TO CLASS...
ONE MONTH LEFT...
IT'S IMPOSSIBLE TO LEARN CHESS THAT EASILY. IT'S ABSURD.
I'M GOING TO CRUSH HIM RIGHT IN FRONT OF HARMONY.

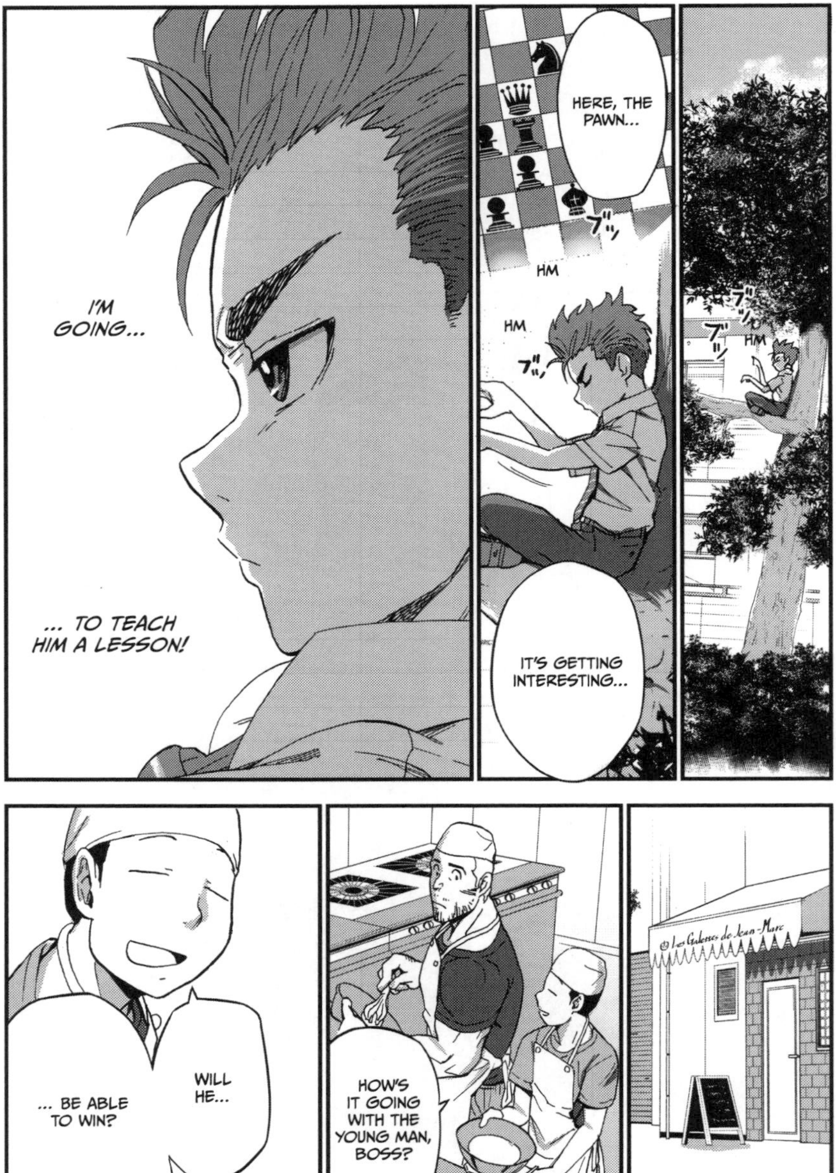
HM
HERE, THE PAWN...
HM
HM
IT'S GETTING INTERESTING...
I'M GOING...
... TO TEACH HIM A LESSON!
Les Galettes de Jean-Marc
HOW'S IT GOING WITH THE YOUNG MAN, BOSS?
WILL HE...
... BE ABLE TO WIN?

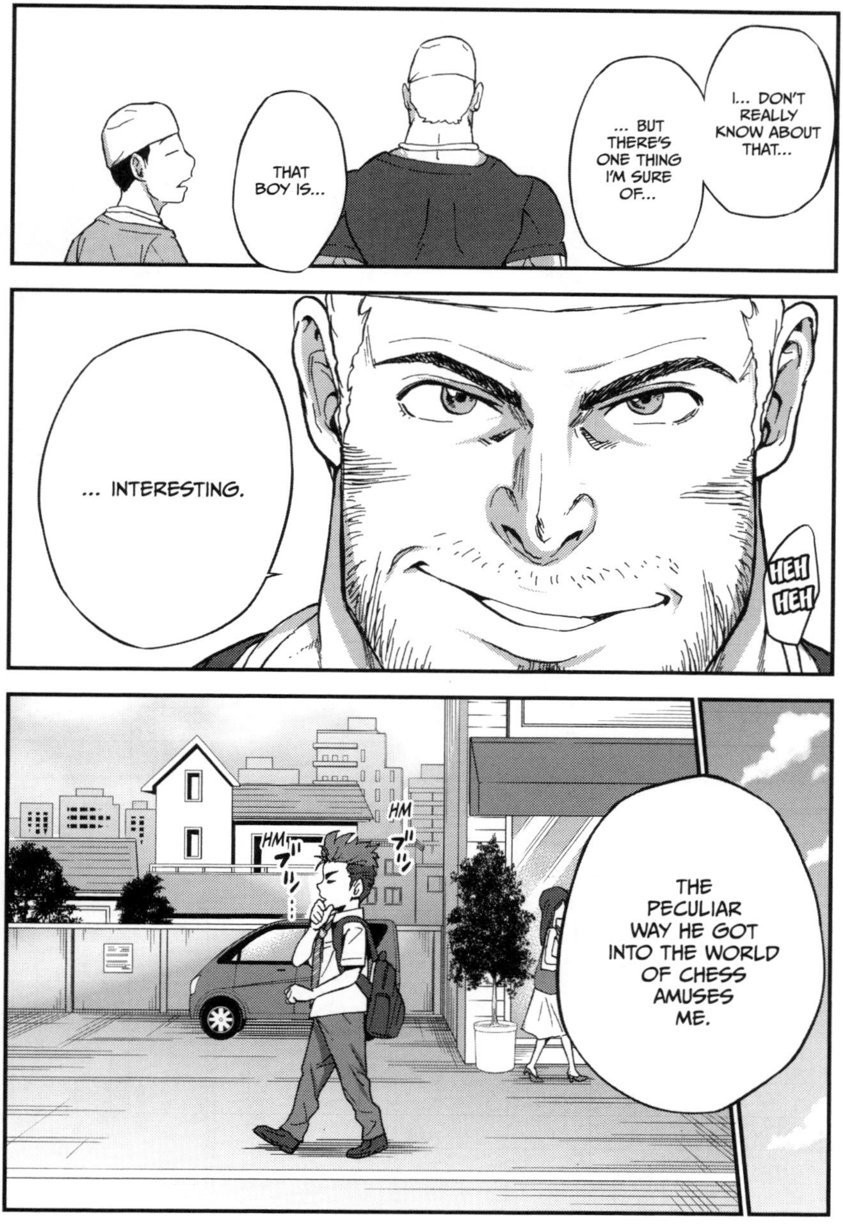
I... DON'T REALLY KNOW ABOUT THAT...
... BUT THERE'S ONE THING I'M SURE OF...
THAT BOY IS...
... INTERESTING.
HEH HEH
THE PECULIAR WAY HE GOT INTO THE WORLD OF CHESS AMUSES ME.
HM
ブツ
HM
ブツ…

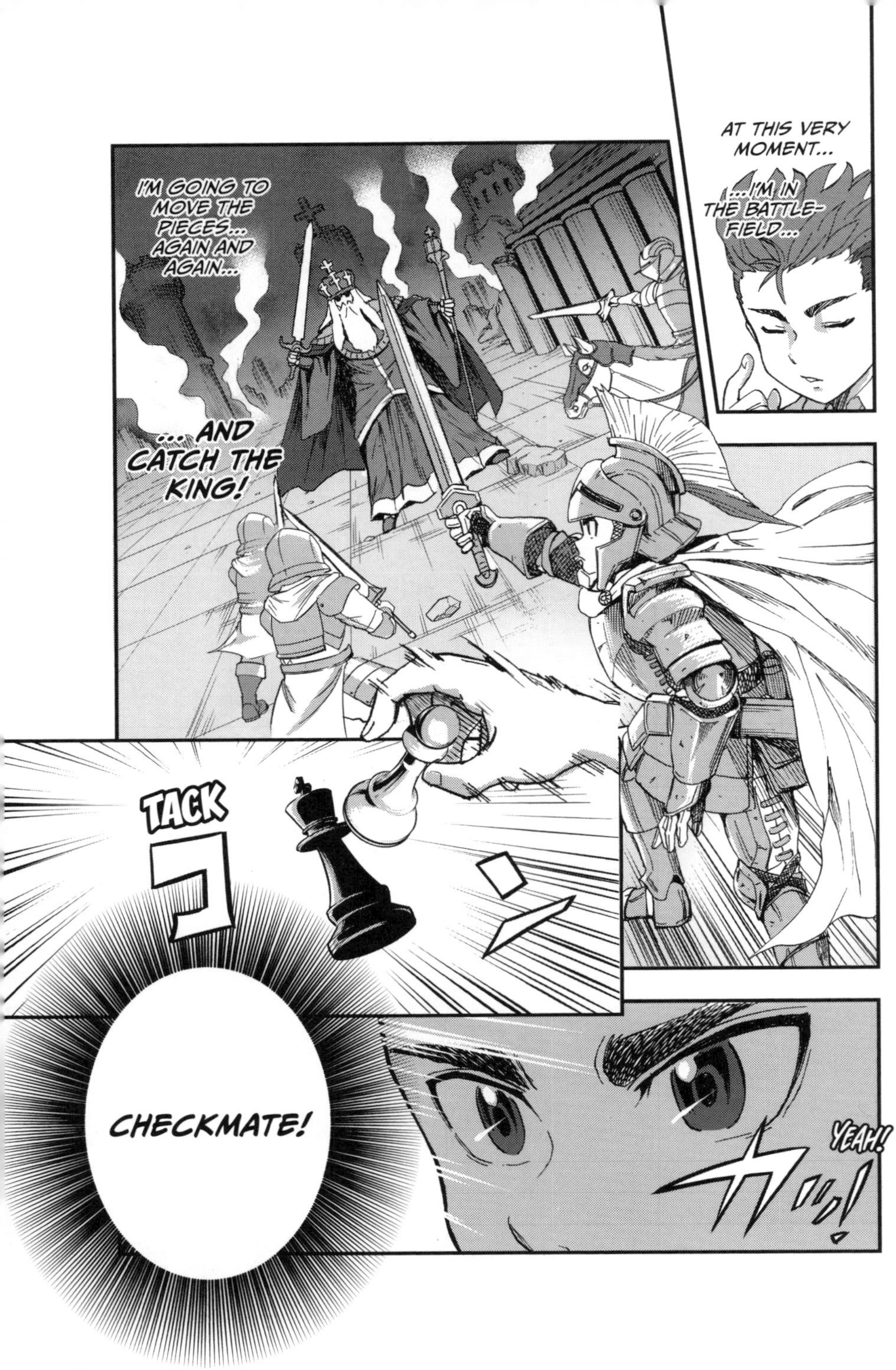
AT THIS VERY MOMENT...
...I'M IN THE BATTLE-FIELD...
I'M GOING TO MOVE THE PIECES... AGAIN AND AGAIN...
...AND CATCH THE KING!
TACK
CHECKMATE!
YEAH!

BLITZ

Chapter 3: The pawn's fight

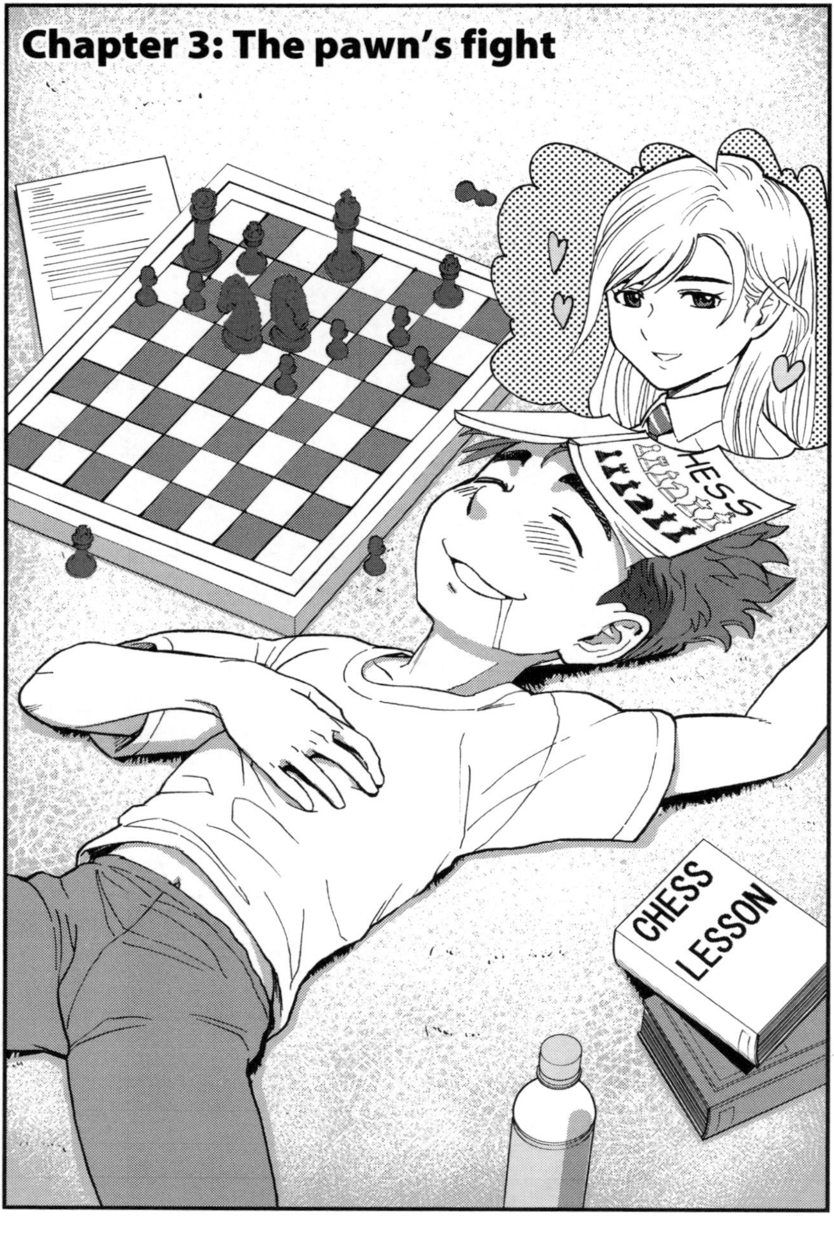
CHESS
LESSON

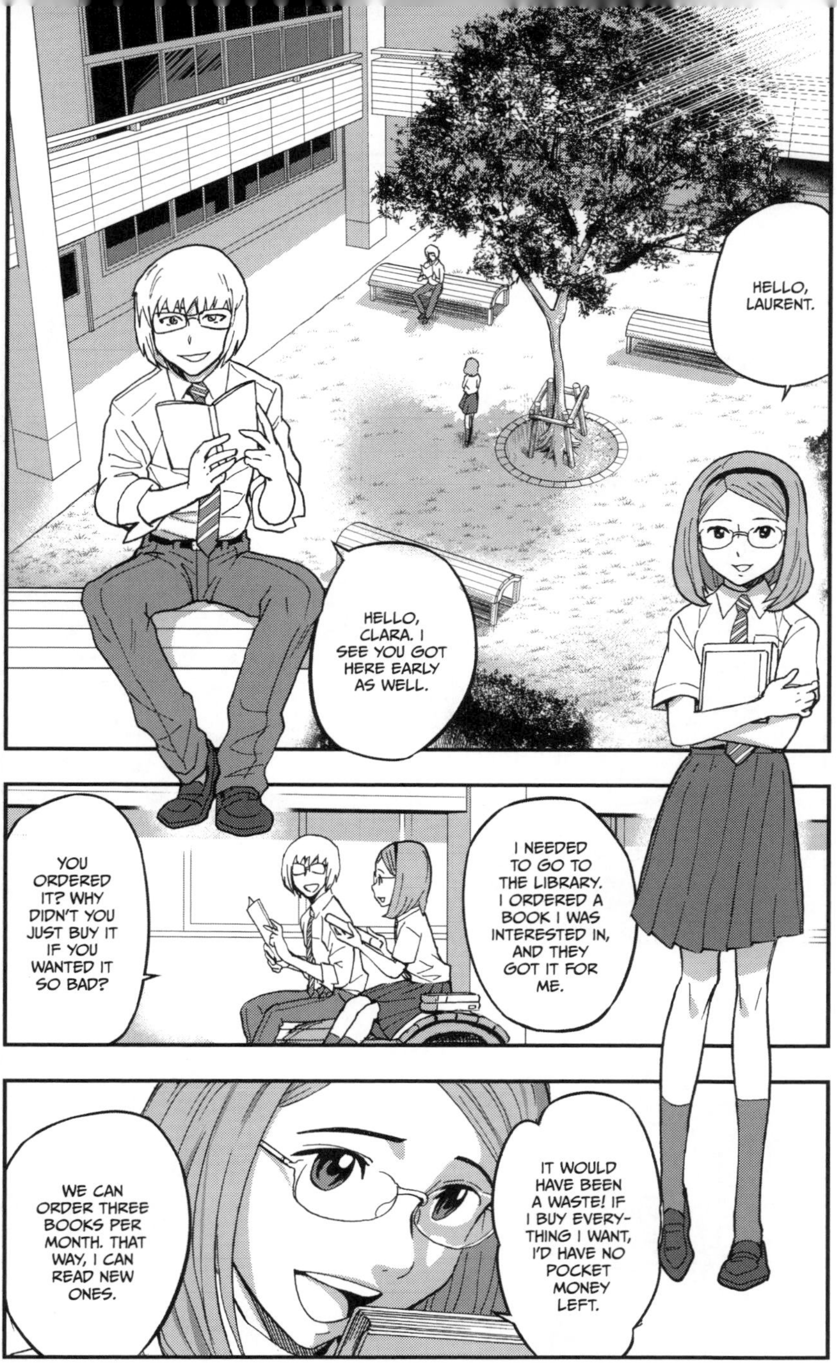
HELLO, LAURENT.
HELLO, CLARA. I SEE YOU GOT HERE EARLY AS WELL.
I NEEDED TO GO TO THE LIBRARY. I ORDERED A BOOK I WAS INTERESTED IN, AND THEY GOT IT FOR ME.
YOU ORDERED IT? WHY DIDN'T YOU JUST BUY IT IF YOU WANTED IT SO BAD?
IT WOULD HAVE BEEN A WASTE! IF I BUY EVERY-THING I WANT, I'D HAVE NO POCKET MONEY LEFT.
WE CAN ORDER THREE BOOKS PER MONTH. THAT WAY, I CAN READ NEW ONES.

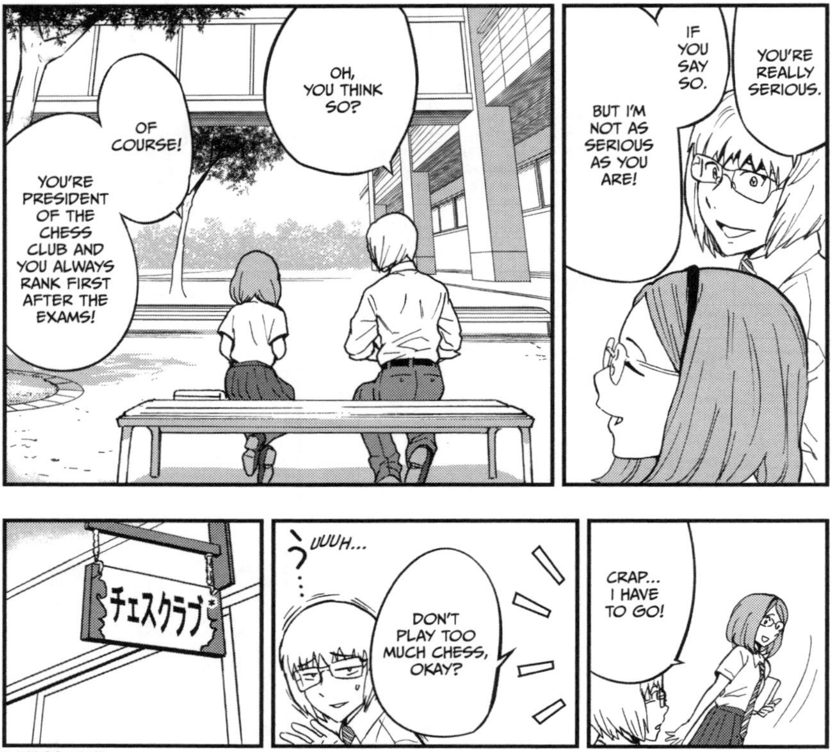
YOU'RE REALLY SERIOUS.
IF YOU SAY SO.
BUT I'M NOT AS SERIOUS AS YOU ARE!
OH, YOU THINK SO?
OF COURSE!
YOU'RE PRESIDENT OF THE CHESS CLUB AND YOU ALWAYS RANK FIRST AFTER THE EXAMS!
CRAP... I HAVE TO GO!
UUUH...
DON'T PLAY TOO MUCH CHESS, OKAY?
チェスクラブ*

*CHESS CLUB

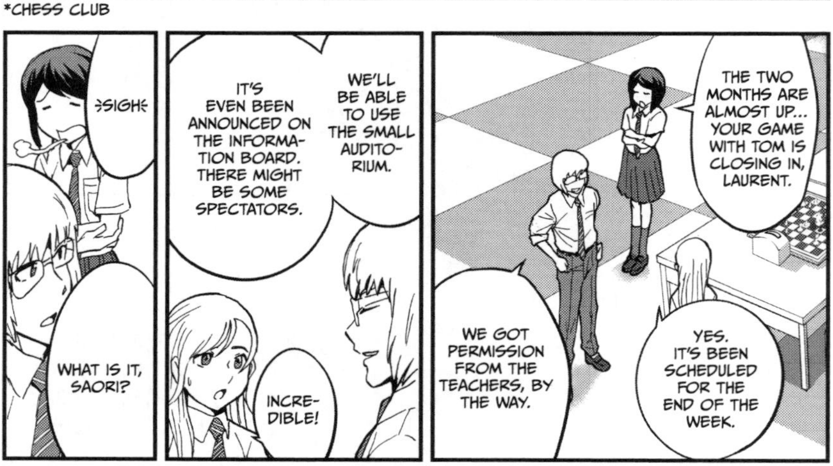
THE TWO MONTHS ARE ALMOST UP... YOUR GAME WITH TOM IS CLOSING IN, LAURENT.
YES. IT'S BEEN SCHEDULED FOR THE END OF THE WEEK.
WE GOT PERMISSION FROM THE TEACHERS, BY THE WAY.
WE'LL BE ABLE TO USE THE SMALL AUDITO-RIUM.
IT'S EVEN BEEN ANNOUNCED ON THE INFORMA-TION BOARD. THERE MIGHT BE SOME SPECTATORS.
INCRE-DIBLE!
SIGH
WHAT IS IT, SAORI?

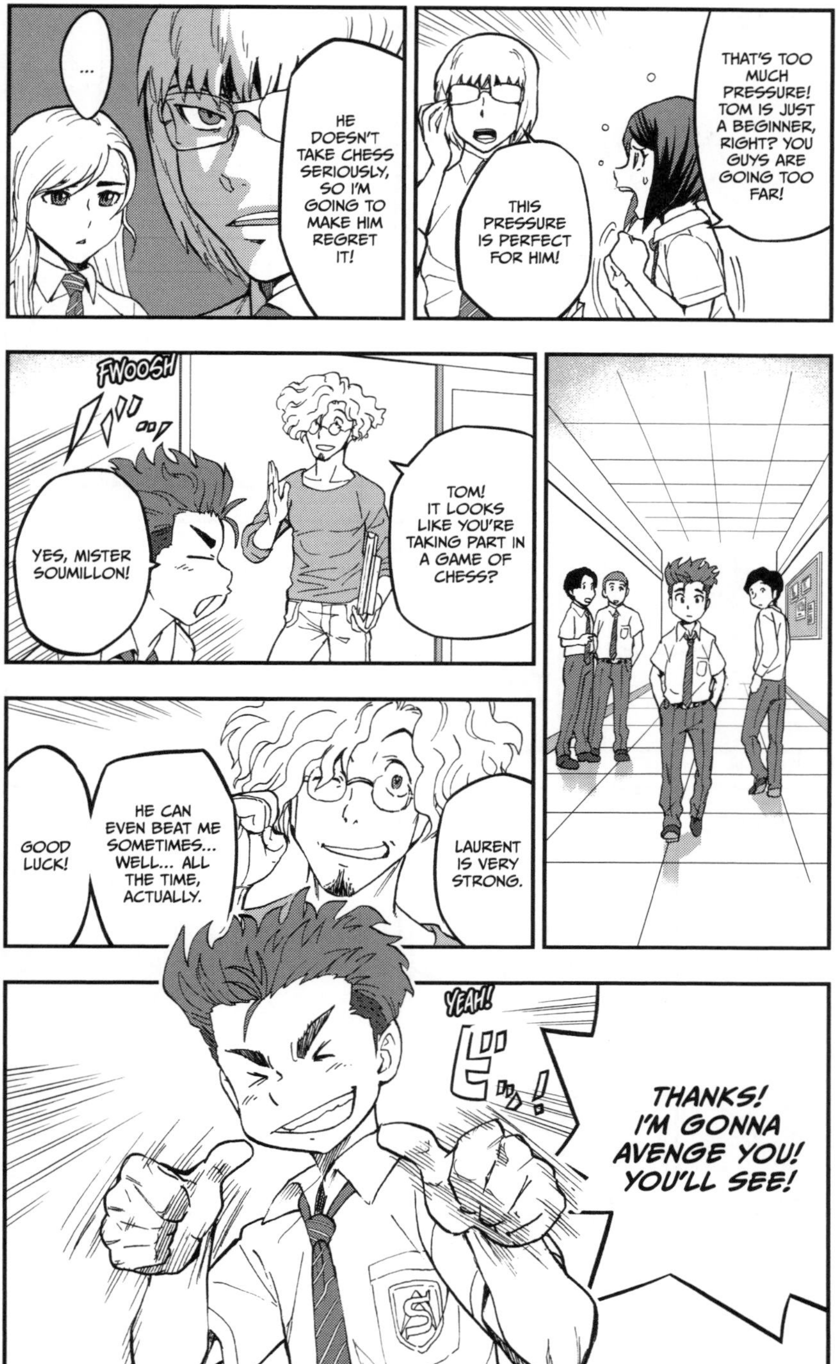
THAT'S TOO MUCH PRESSURE! TOM IS JUST A BEGINNER, RIGHT? YOU GUYS ARE GOING TOO FAR!
THIS PRESSURE IS PERFECT FOR HIM!
HE DOESN'T TAKE CHESS SERIOUSLY, SO I'M GOING TO MAKE HIM REGRET IT!
...
TOM! IT LOOKS LIKE YOU'RE TAKING PART IN A GAME OF CHESS?
FWOOSH
YES, MISTER SOUMILLON!
LAURENT IS VERY STRONG.
HE CAN EVEN BEAT ME SOMETIMES... WELL... ALL THE TIME, ACTUALLY.
GOOD LUCK!
YEAH!
THANKS! I'M GONNA AVENGE YOU! YOU'LL SEE!

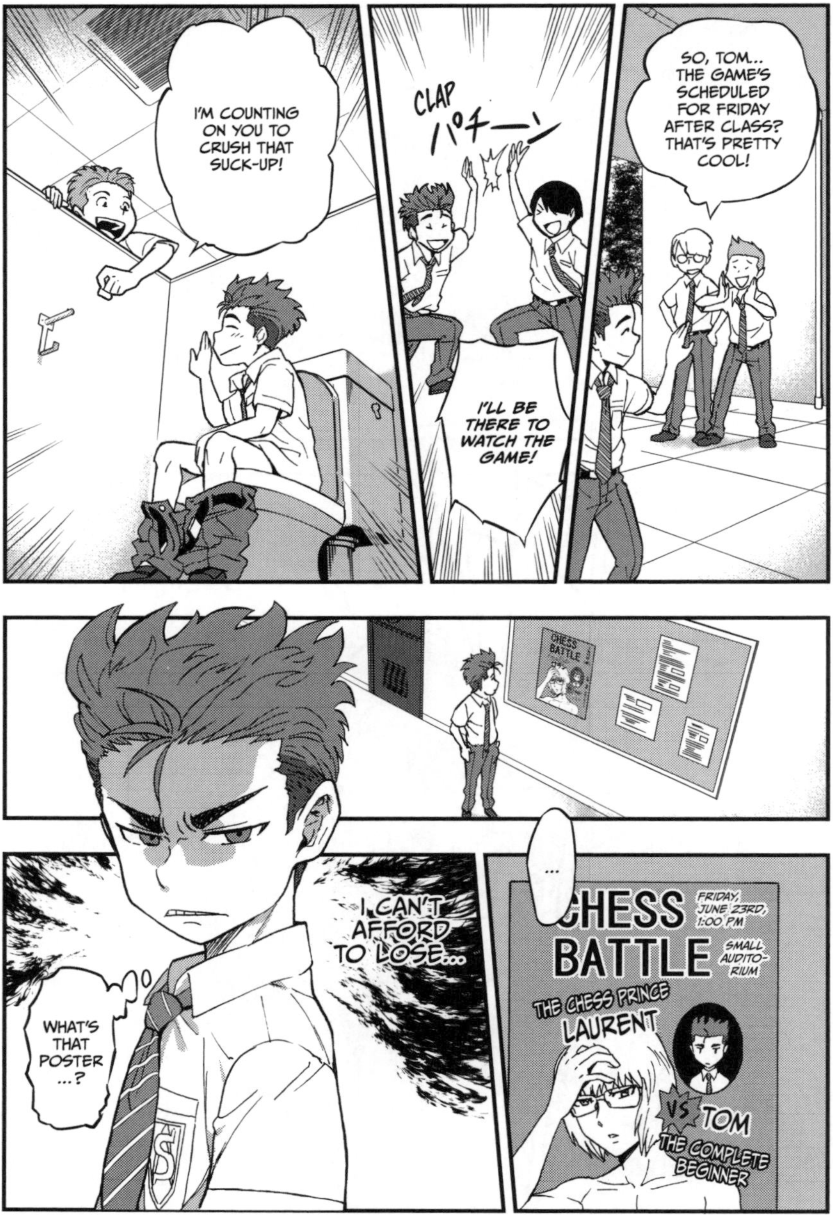
SO, TOM... THE GAME'S SCHEDULED FOR FRIDAY AFTER CLASS? THAT'S PRETTY COOL!
CLAP
パチーン
I'LL BE THERE TO WATCH THE GAME!
I'M COUNTING ON YOU TO CRUSH THAT SUCK-UP!
...
CHESS BATTLE
FRIDAY, JUNE 23RD, 1:00 PM
SMALL AUDITO-RIUM
THE CHESS PRINCE LAURENT
VS TOM
THE COMPLETE BEGINNER
I CAN'T AFFORD TO LOSE...
WHAT'S THAT POSTER ...?

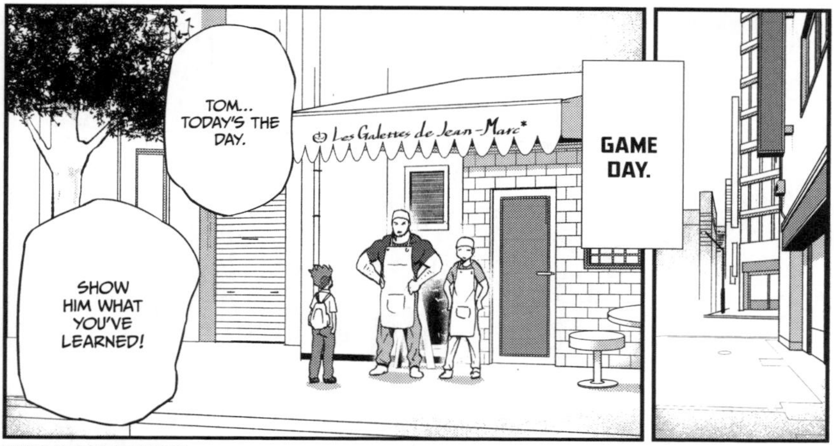
GAME DAY.
Les Galettes de Jean-Marc*
TOM... TODAY'S THE DAY.
SHOW HIM WHAT YOU'VE LEARNED!

*JEAN-MARC'S PANCAKES

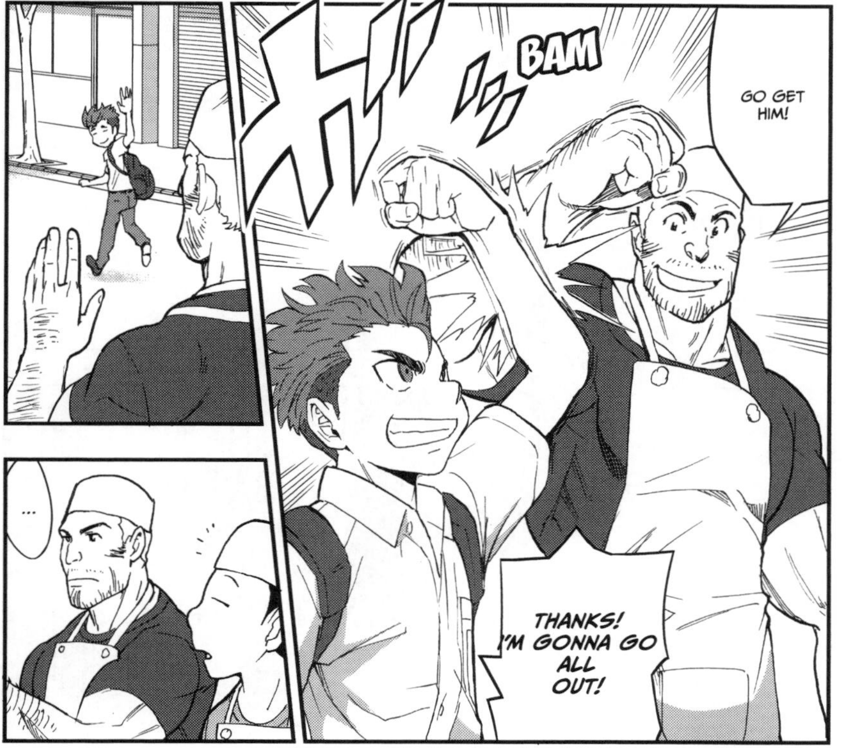
BAM
GO GET HIM!
THANKS! I'M GONNA GO ALL OUT!
...

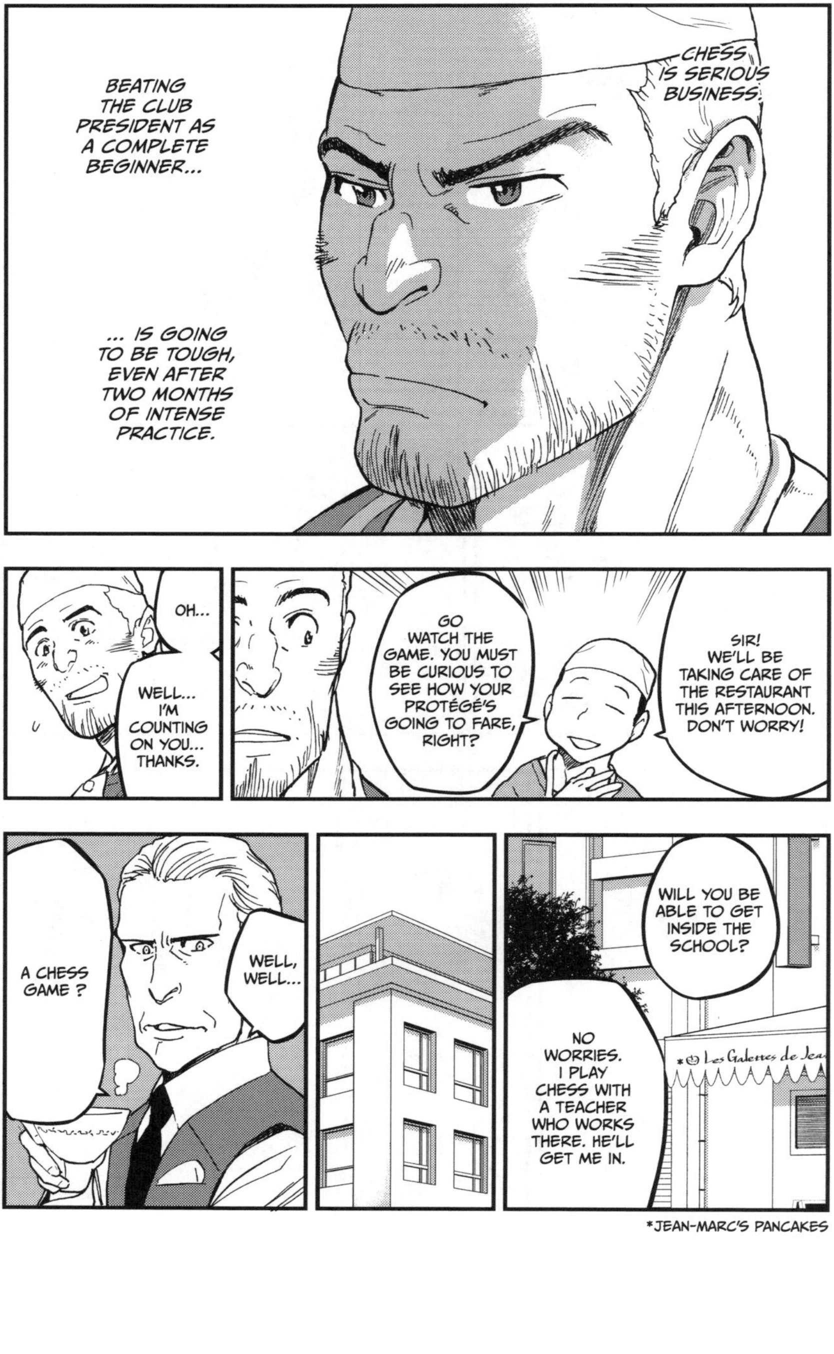
CHESS IS SERIOUS BUSINESS.
BEATING THE CLUB PRESIDENT AS A COMPLETE BEGINNER...
... IS GOING TO BE TOUGH, EVEN AFTER TWO MONTHS OF INTENSE PRACTICE.
SIR! WE'LL BE TAKING CARE OF THE RESTAURANT THIS AFTERNOON. DON'T WORRY!
GO WATCH THE GAME. YOU MUST BE CURIOUS TO SEE HOW YOUR PROTÉGÉ'S GOING TO FARE, RIGHT?
OH...
WELL... I'M COUNTING ON YOU... THANKS.
WILL YOU BE ABLE TO GET INSIDE THE SCHOOL?
* Les Galettes de Jea
NO WORRIES. I PLAY CHESS WITH A TEACHER WHO WORKS THERE. HE'LL GET ME IN.
WELL, WELL...
A CHESS GAME ?

*JEAN-MARC'S PANCAKES

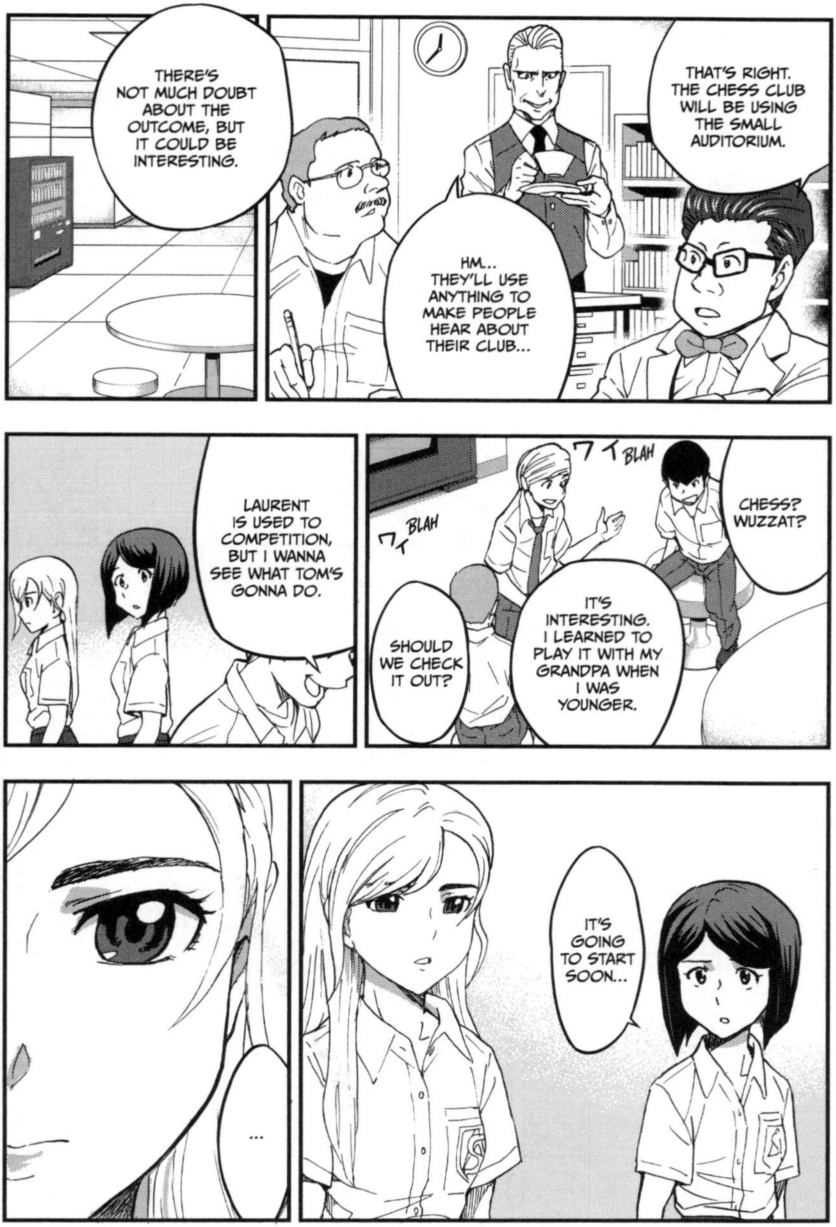
THAT'S RIGHT. THE CHESS CLUB WILL BE USING THE SMALL AUDITORIUM.
HM... THEY'LL USE ANYTHING TO MAKE PEOPLE HEAR ABOUT THEIR CLUB...
THERE'S NOT MUCH DOUBT ABOUT THE OUTCOME, BUT IT COULD BE INTERESTING.
ワイ BLAH
CHESS? WUZZAT?
IT'S INTERESTING. I LEARNED TO PLAY IT WITH MY GRANDPA WHEN I WAS YOUNGER.
ワイ BLAH
SHOULD WE CHECK IT OUT?
LAURENT IS USED TO COMPETITION, BUT I WANNA SEE WHAT TOM'S GONNA DO.
IT'S GOING TO START SOON...
...

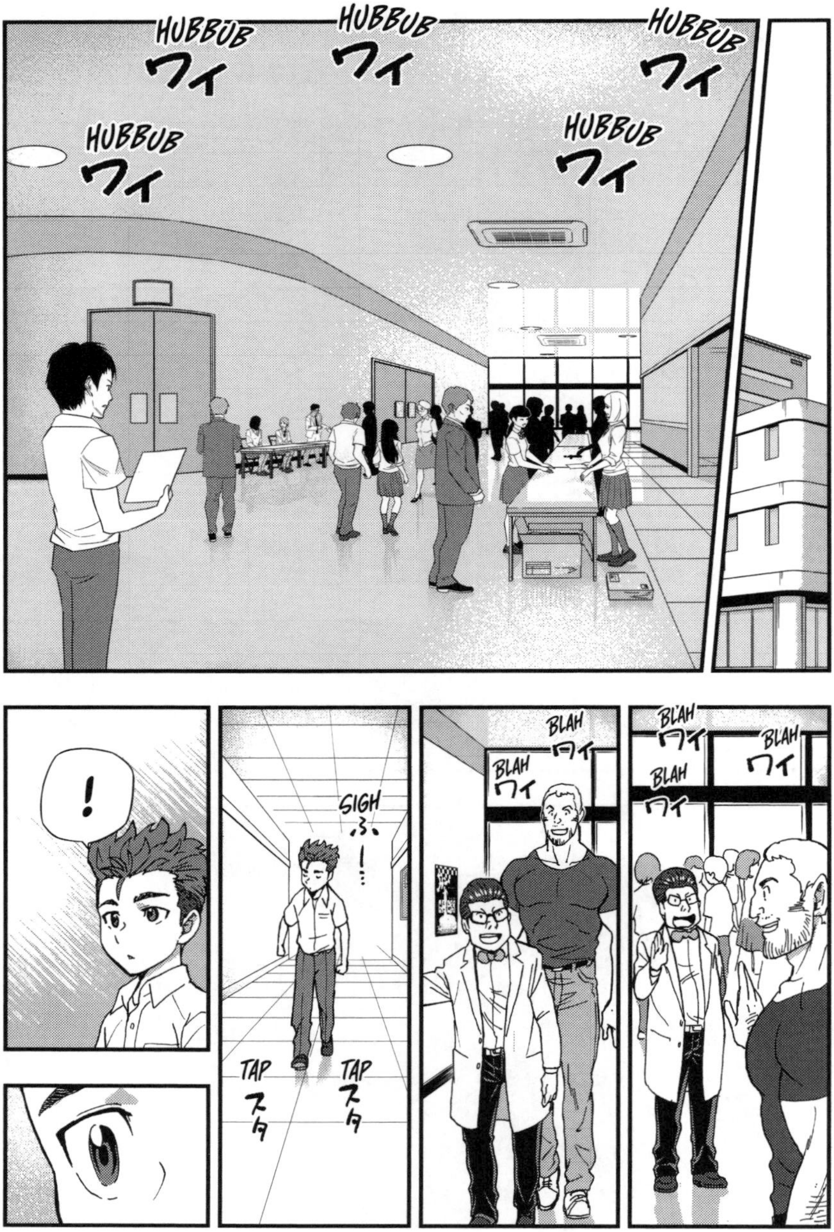
HUBBUB ワイ
HUBBUB ワイ
HUBBUB ワイ
HUBBUB ワイ
HUBBUB ワイ
BLAH ワイ
BLAH ワイ
BLAH ワイ
BLAH ワイ
BLAH ワイ
SIGH ふー…
TAP スタ
TAP スタ
!

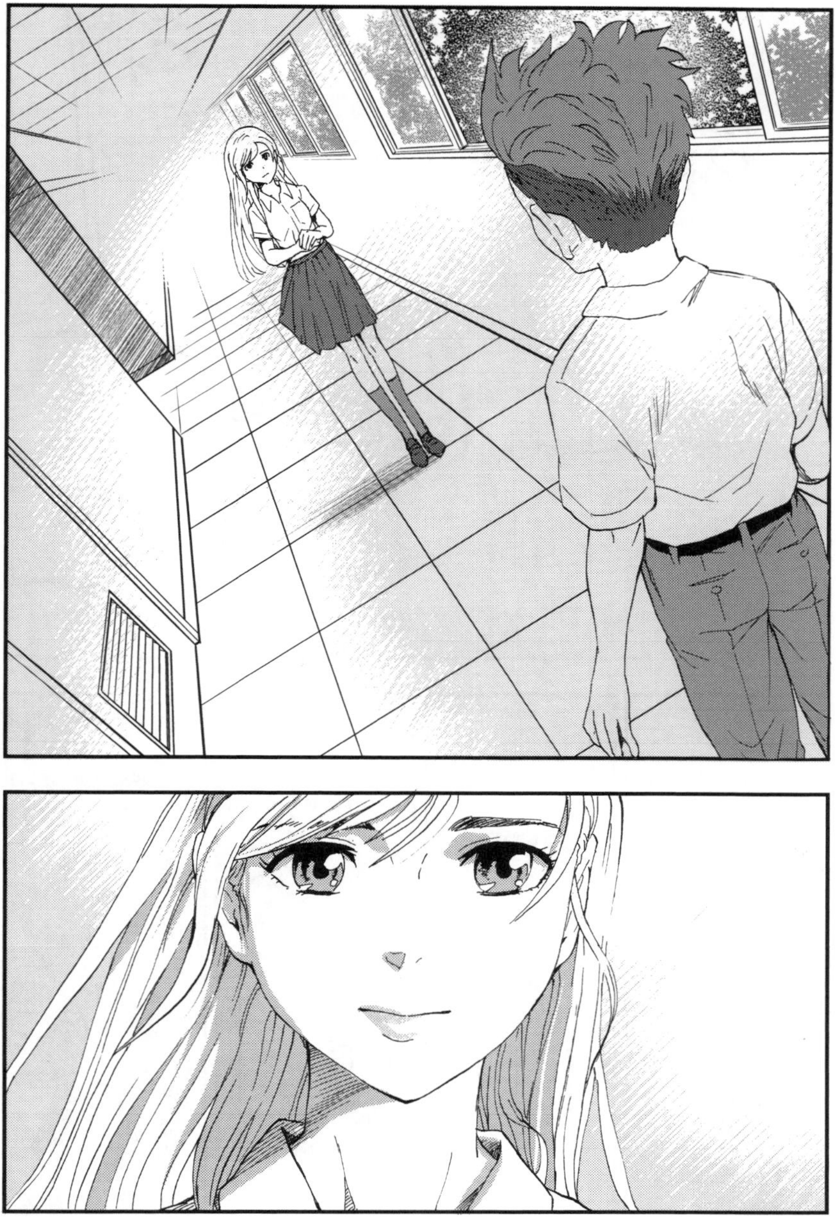

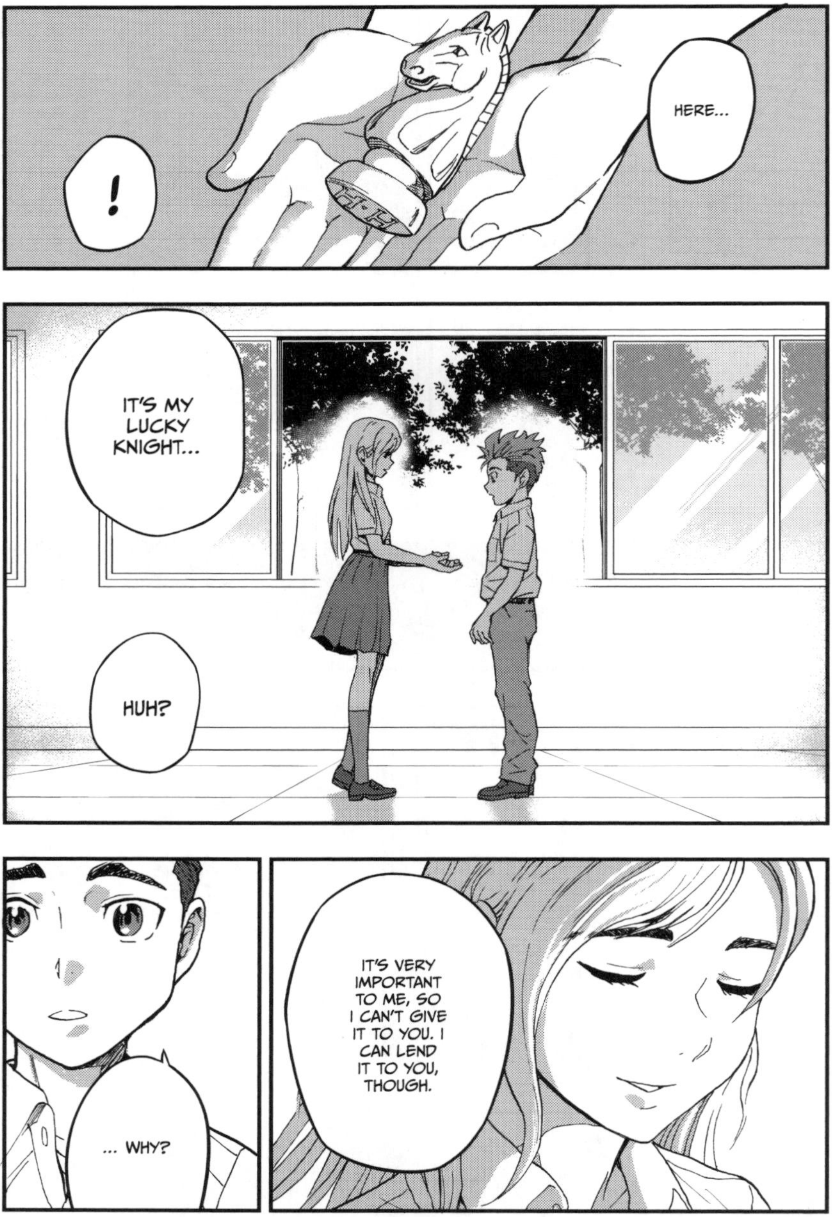
HERE...
!
IT'S MY LUCKY KNIGHT...
HUH?
IT'S VERY IMPORTANT TO ME, SO I CAN'T GIVE IT TO YOU. I CAN LEND IT TO YOU, THOUGH.
... WHY?

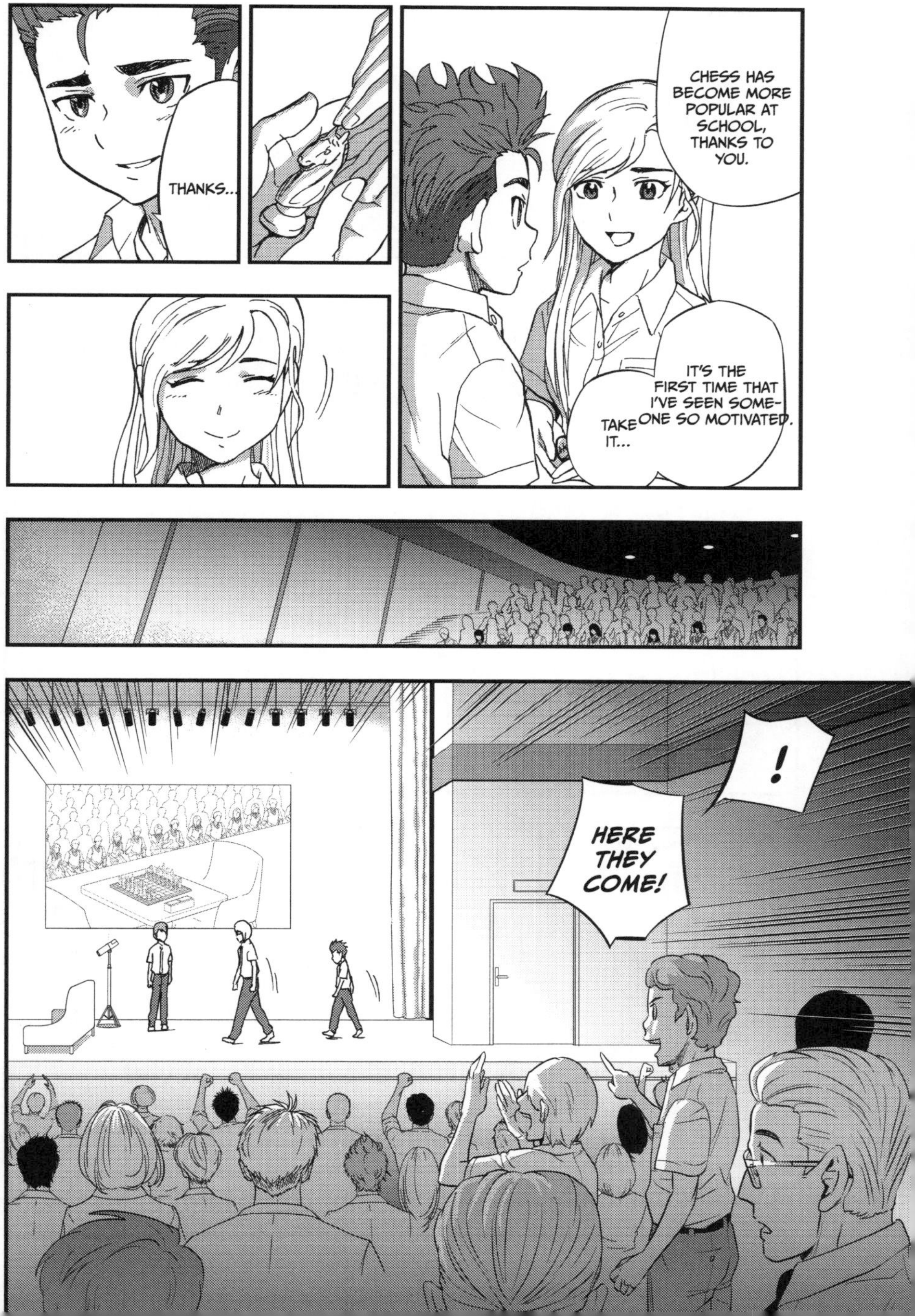
CHESS HAS BECOME MORE POPULAR AT SCHOOL, THANKS TO YOU.
IT'S THE FIRST TIME THAT I'VE SEEN SOME-ONE SO MOTIVATED.
TAKE IT...
THANKS...
!
HERE THEY COME!

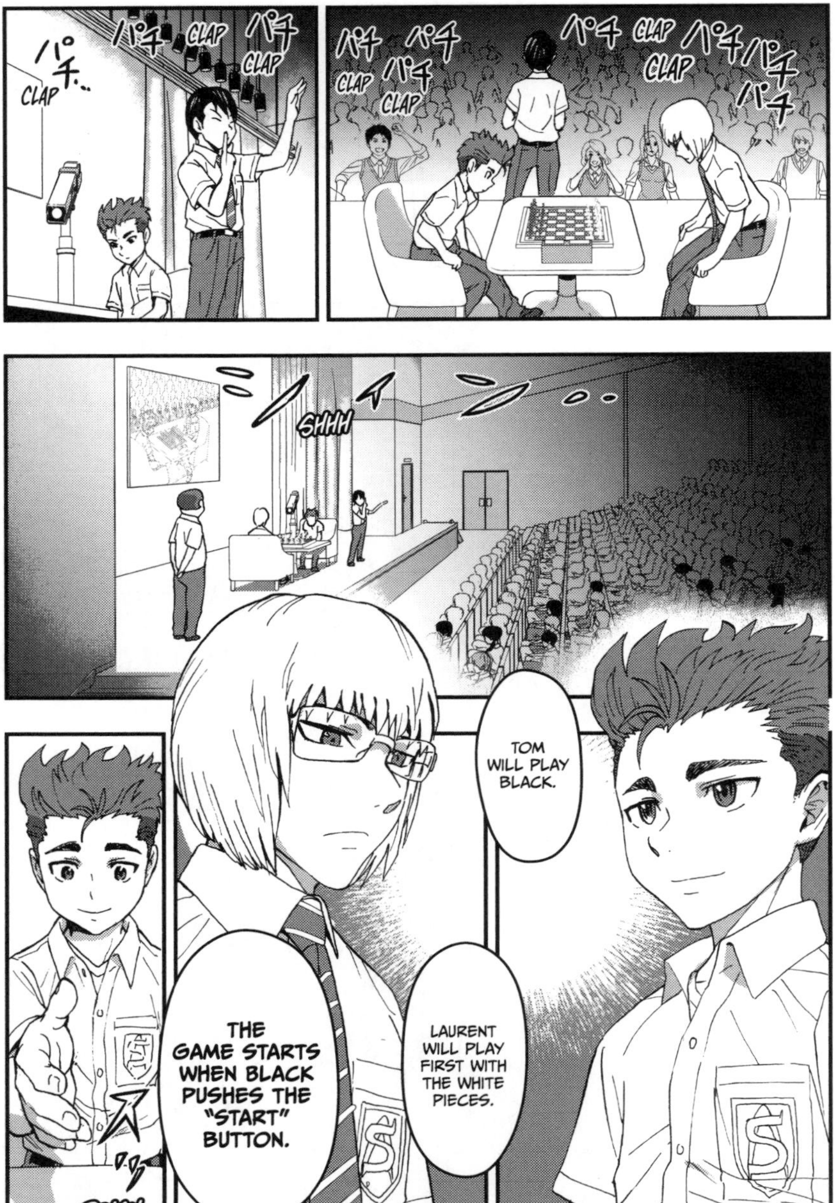
パチ CLAP パチ CLAP パチパチパチ
パチ パチ CLAP パチ CLAP パチ CLAP
パチ CLAP パチ CLAP
パチ... CLAP
SHHH
TOM WILL PLAY BLACK.
LAURENT WILL PLAY FIRST WITH THE WHITE PIECES.
THE GAME STARTS WHEN BLACK PUSHES THE "START" BUTTON.
REACH

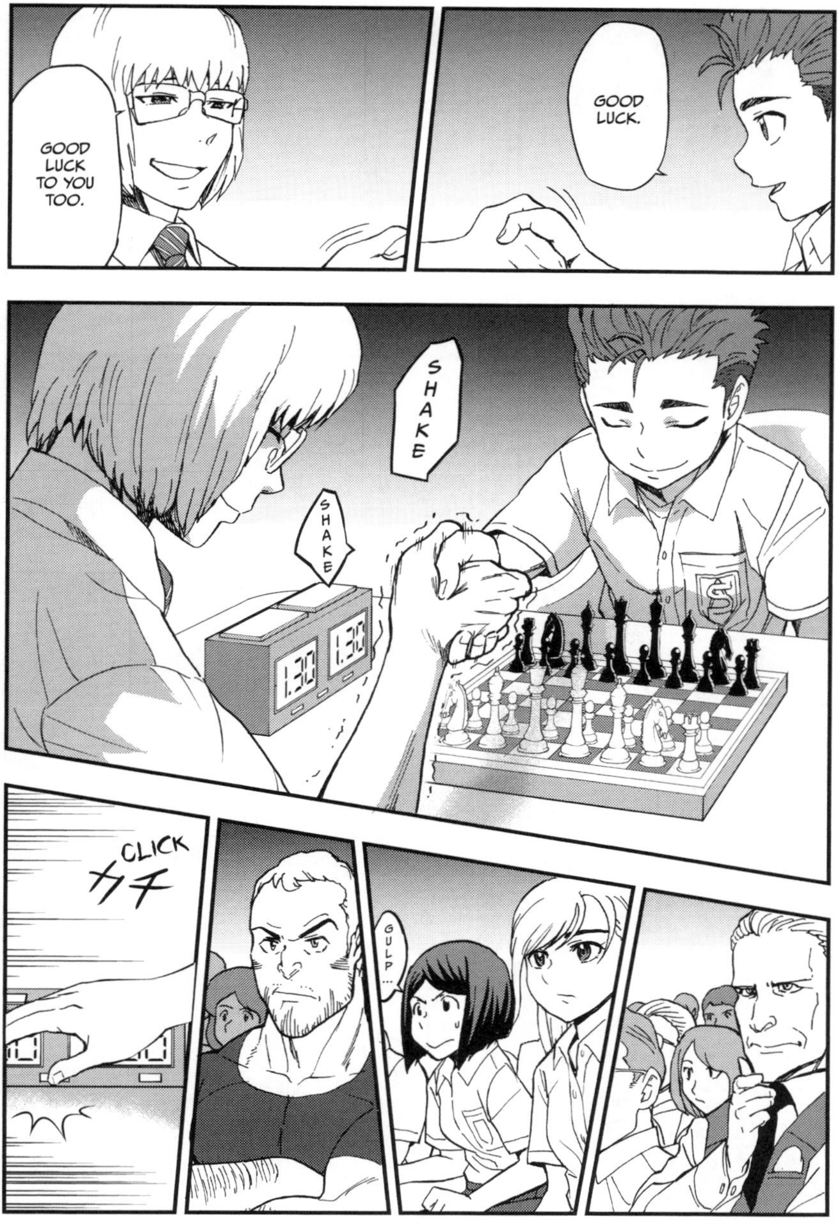
GOOD LUCK.
GOOD LUCK TO YOU TOO.
SHAKE
SHAKE
GULP...
CLICK
カチ

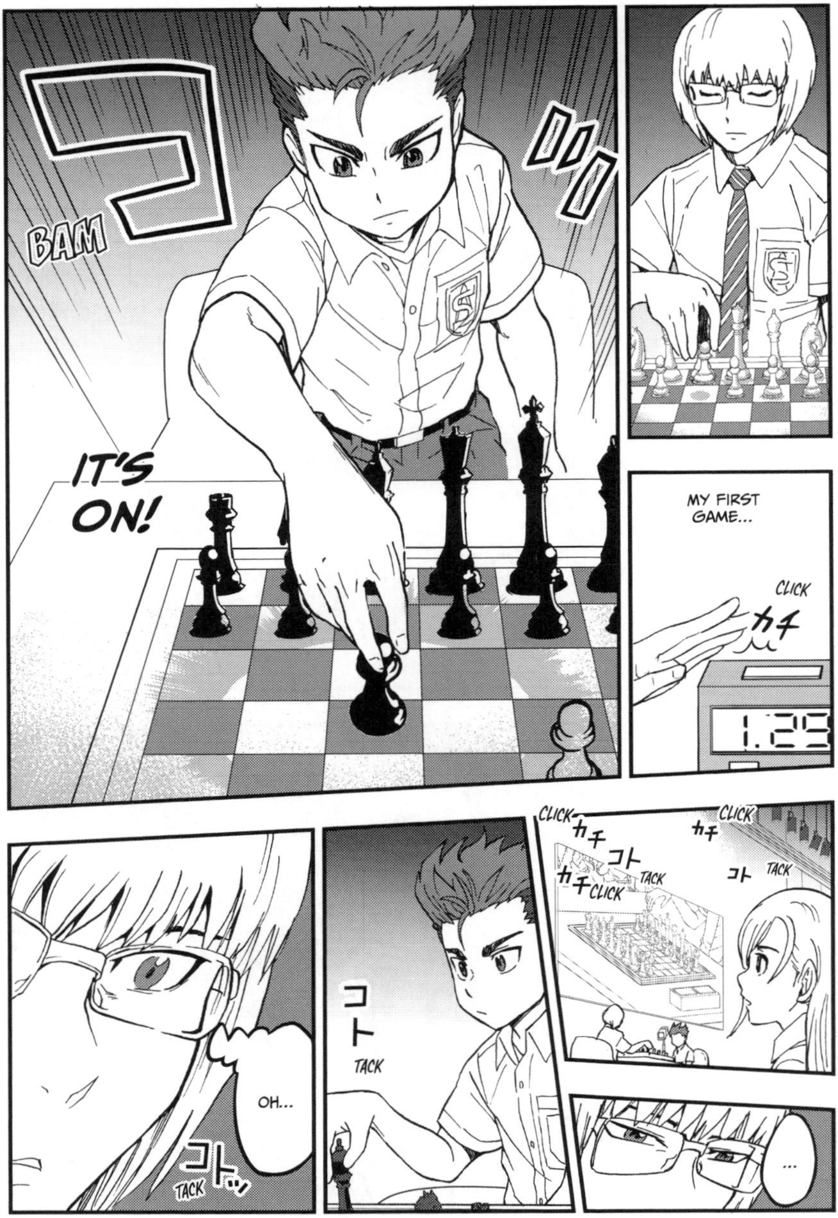
MY FIRST GAME...
CLICK
カチ
1.25
BAM
IT'S ON!
CLICK
カチ
CLICK
カチ
コト
TACK
コト
TACK
カチ
CLICK
...
コト
TACK
OH...
コトッ
TACK

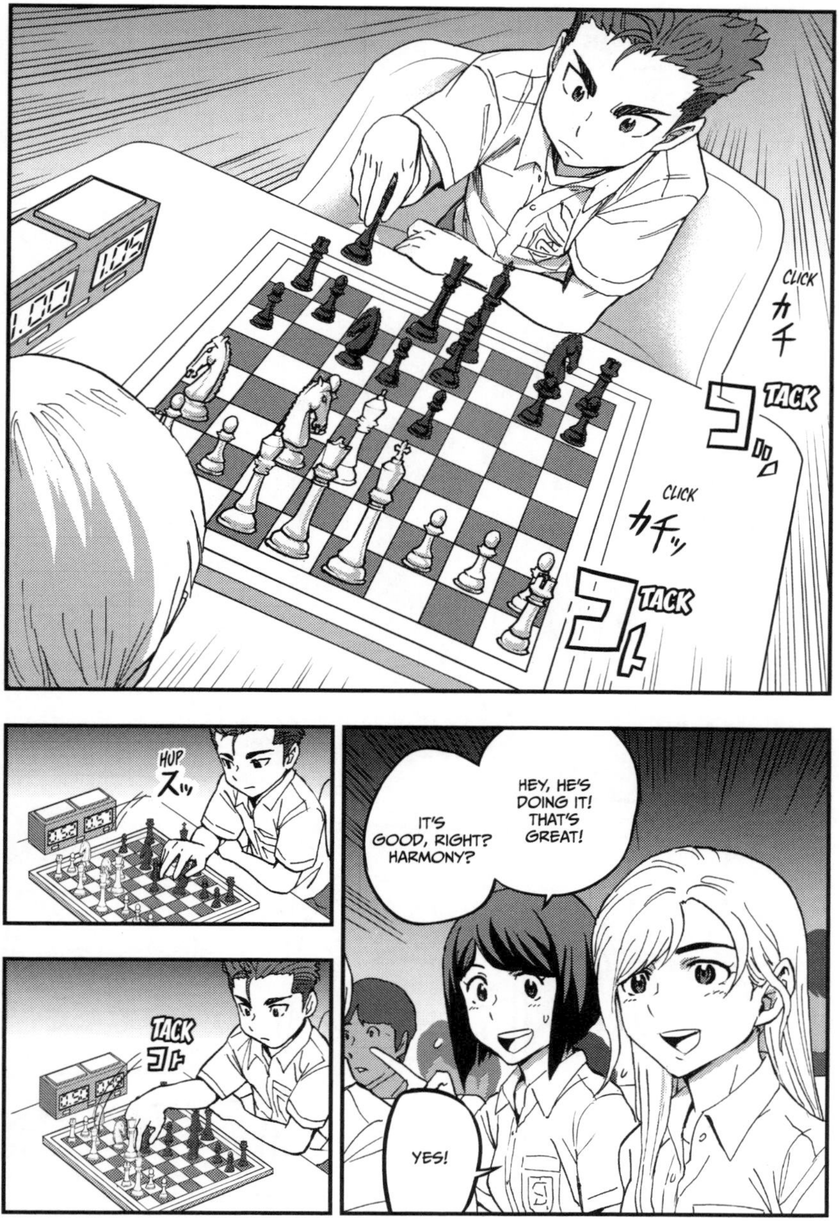
CLICK
カチ
TACK
コッ
CLICK
カチッ
TACK
コト
HEY, HE'S DOING IT! THAT'S GREAT!
IT'S GOOD, RIGHT? HARMONY?
YES!
HUP
スッ
TACK
コト

COME ON...!

コトッ
TACK

TACK
コト

GOOD!

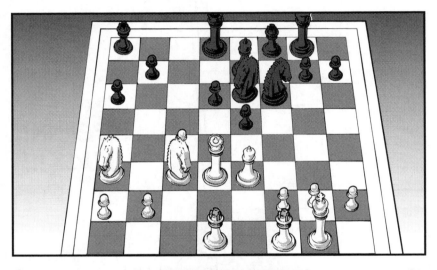

BUT...

ス
HUP

HE LEARNED TO PLAY, AT LEAST...

HE EVEN LOOKS CONFIDENT...

HMM...

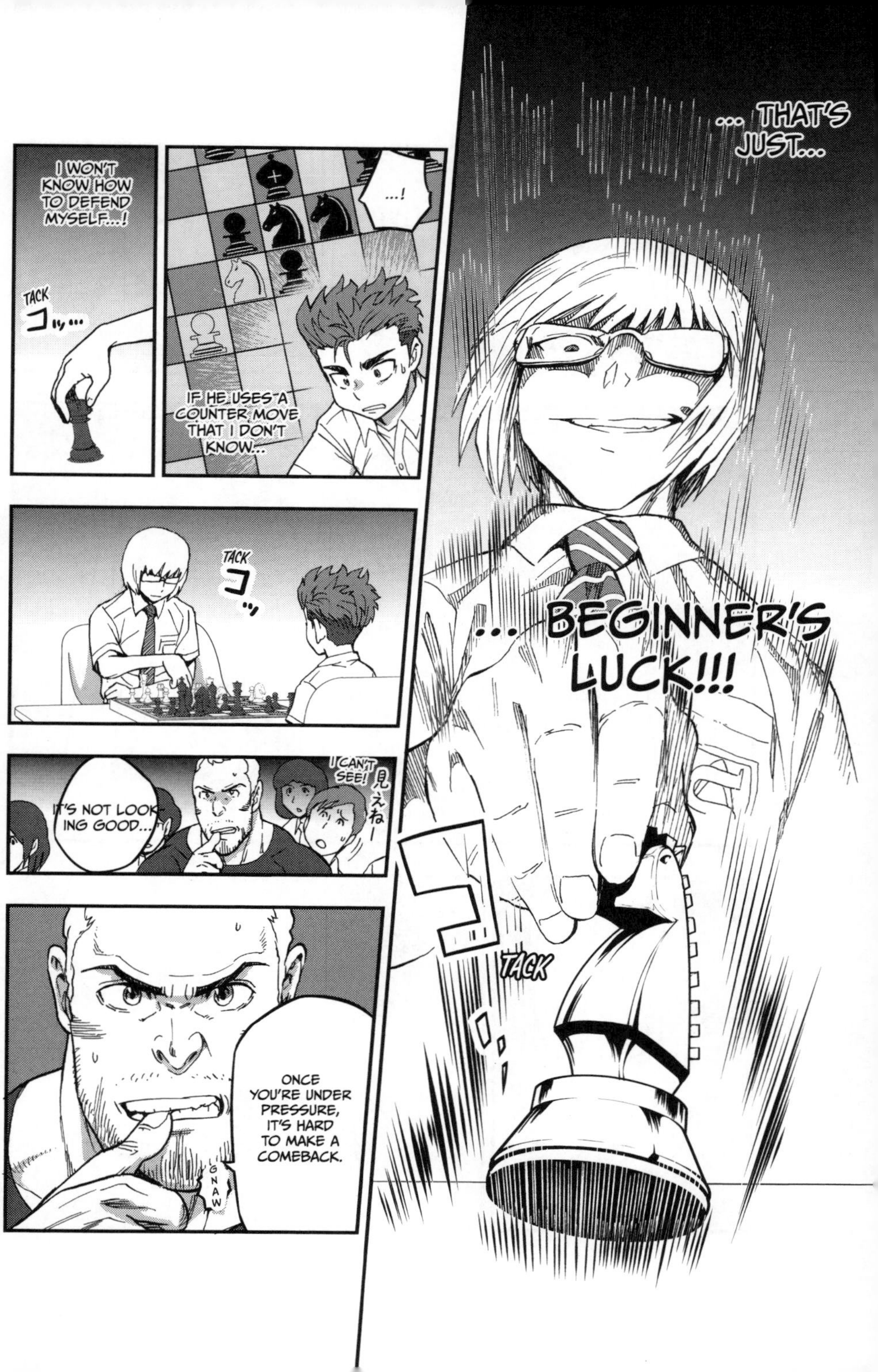
... THAT'S JUST...
... BEGINNER'S LUCK!!!
TACK
...!
IF HE USES A COUNTER MOVE THAT I DON'T KNOW...
I WON'T KNOW HOW TO DEFEND MYSELF...!
TACK
TACK
I CAN'T SEE!
見えねー
IT'S NOT LOOKING GOOD...
ONCE YOU'RE UNDER PRESSURE, IT'S HARD TO MAKE A COMEBACK.
GNAW

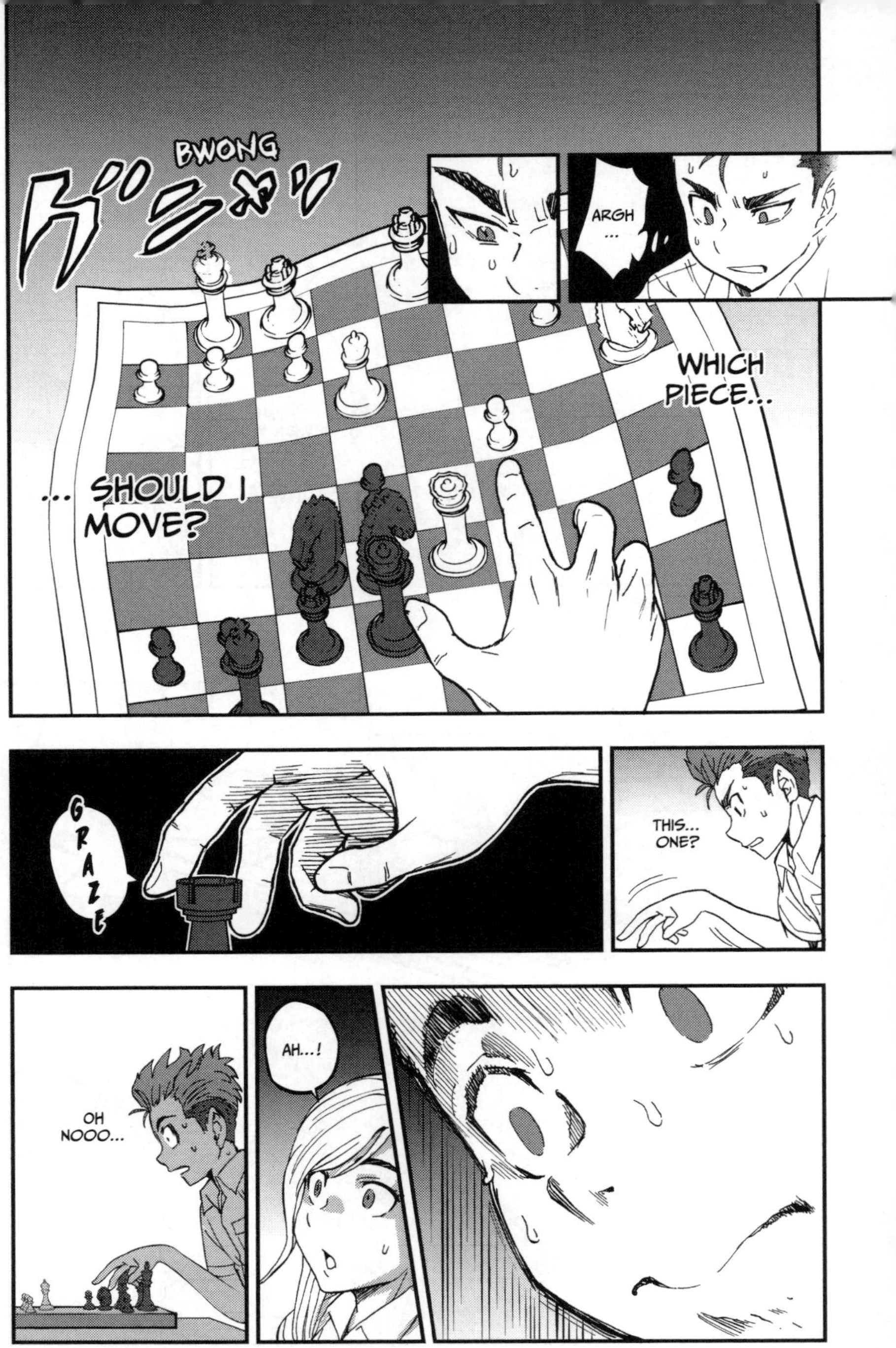
ARGH ...
BWONG
WHICH PIECE...
... SHOULD I MOVE?
THIS... ONE?
GRAZE
AH...!
OH NOOO...

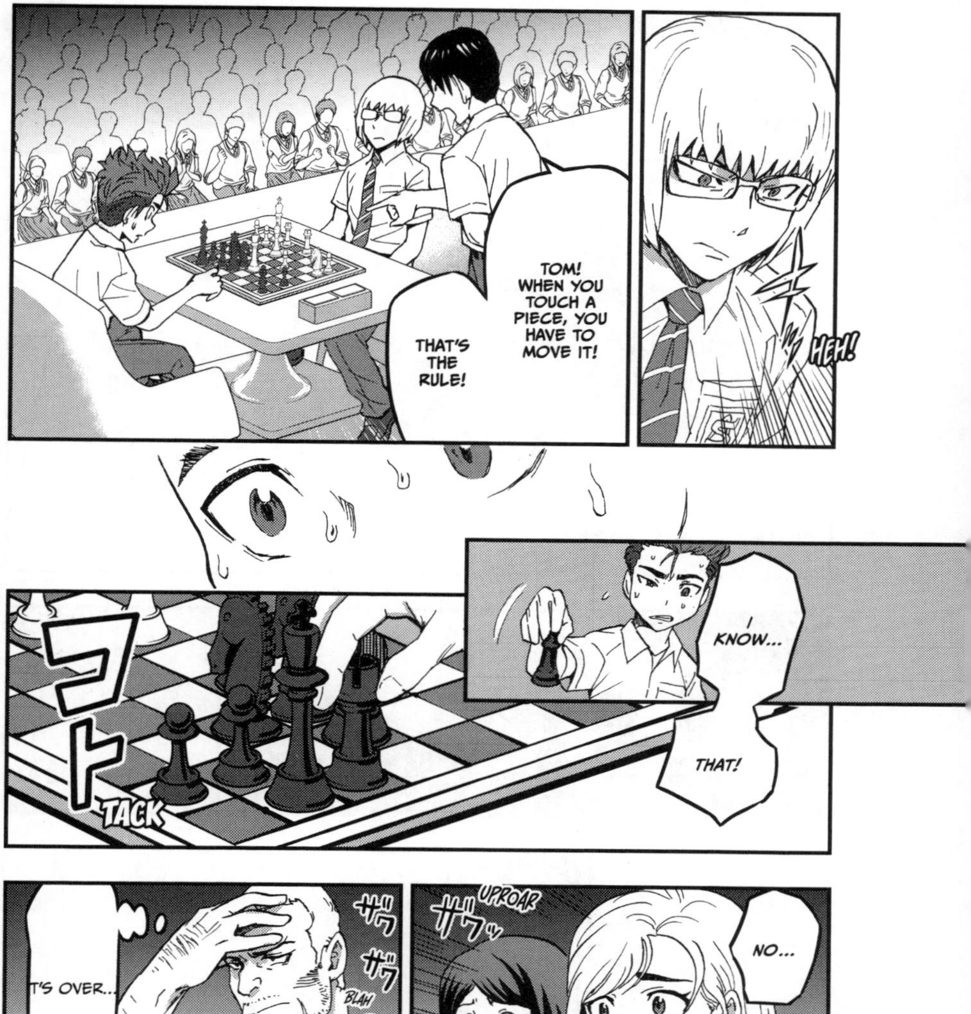
HEH!
TOM! WHEN YOU TOUCH A PIECE, YOU HAVE TO MOVE IT!
THAT'S THE RULE!
I KNOW...
THAT!
コト
TACK
ザワッ
UPROAR
NO...
NOT THAT PIECE...
ザワ
ザワ
BLAH
BLAH
T'S OVER...

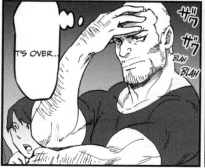

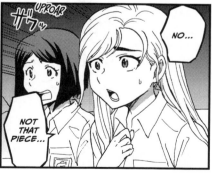

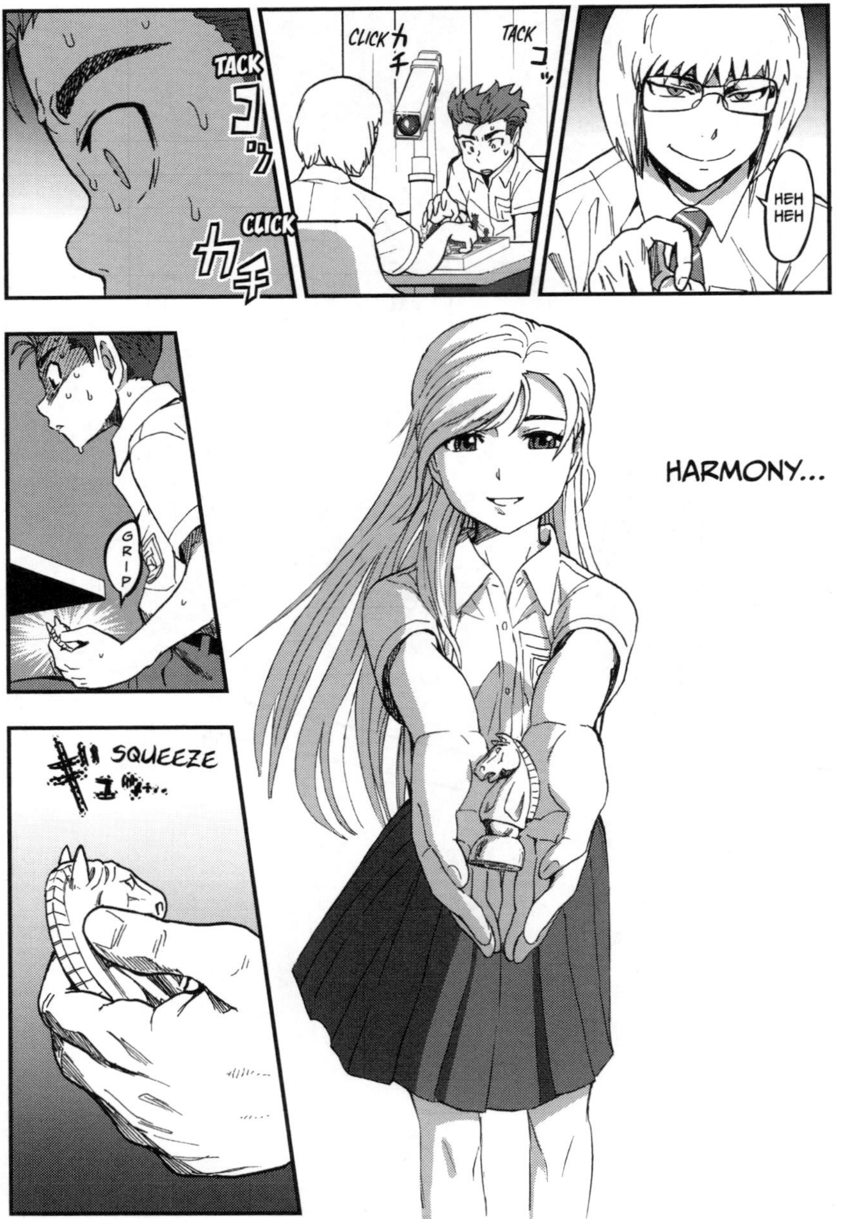
HEH HEH
TACK
コッ
CLICK
カチ
TACK
コッ
CLICK
カチ
HARMONY...
GRIP
SQUEEZE

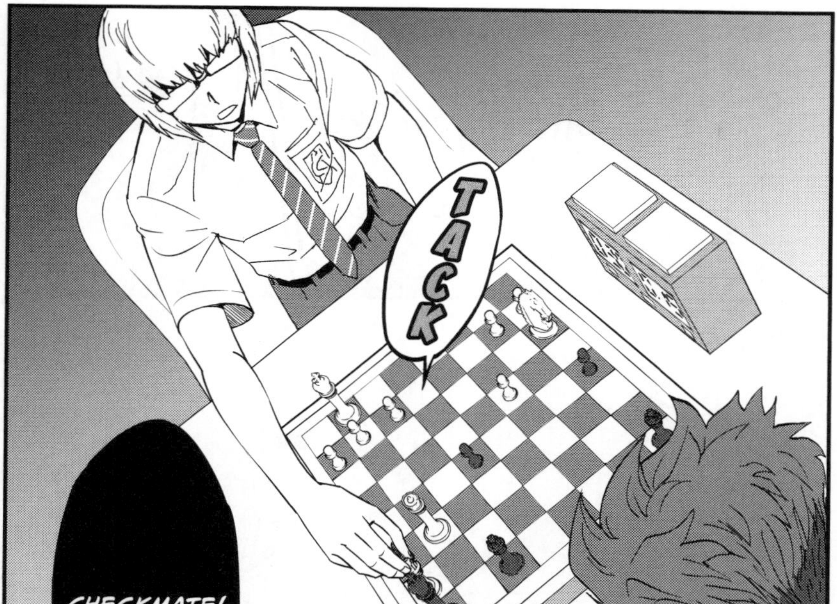
TACK
CHECKMATE!
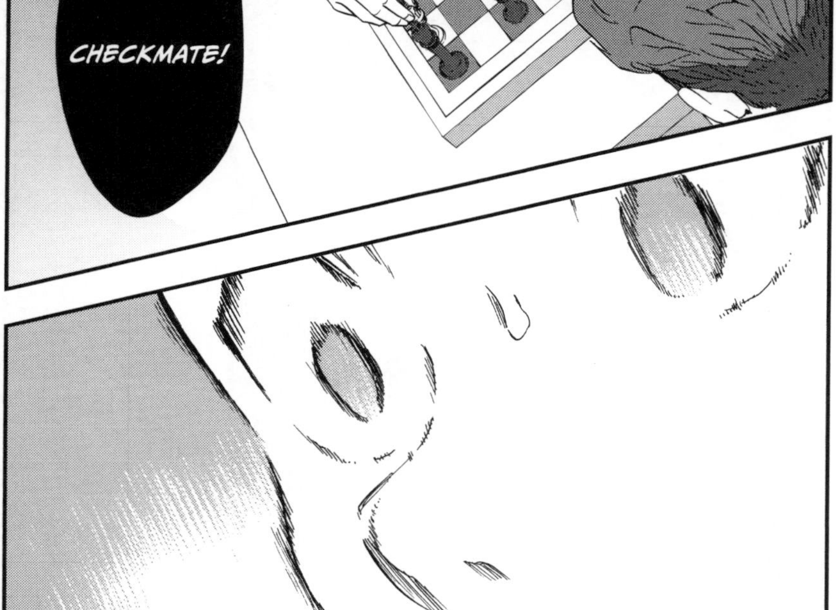

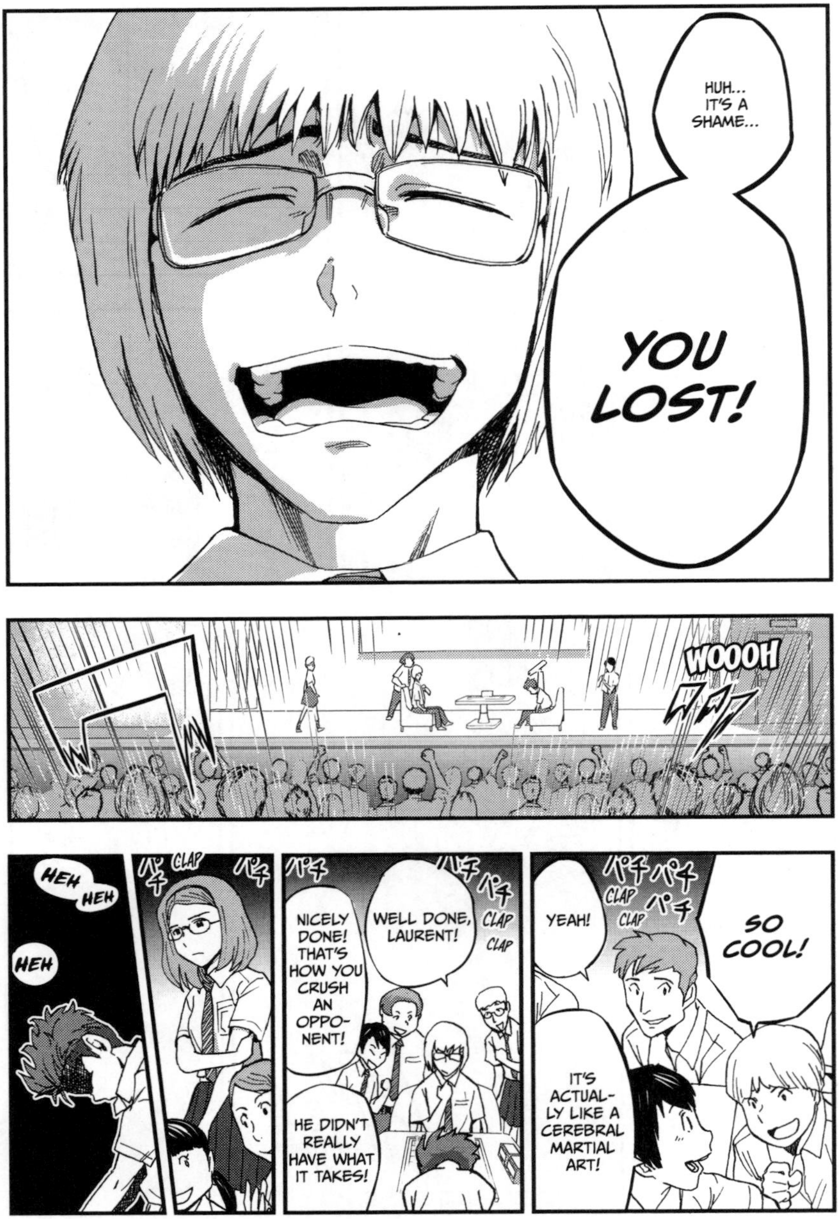
HUH... IT'S A SHAME...
YOU LOST!
WOOOH
ワァ
パチ パチ パチ
CLAP CLAP
SO COOL!
YEAH!
IT'S ACTUALLY LIKE A CEREBRAL MARTIAL ART!
パチ パチ
CLAP CLAP
WELL DONE, LAURENT!
NICELY DONE! THAT'S HOW YOU CRUSH AN OPPONENT!
HE DIDN'T REALLY HAVE WHAT IT TAKES!
パチ
パチ CLAP パチ
HEH HEH
HEH

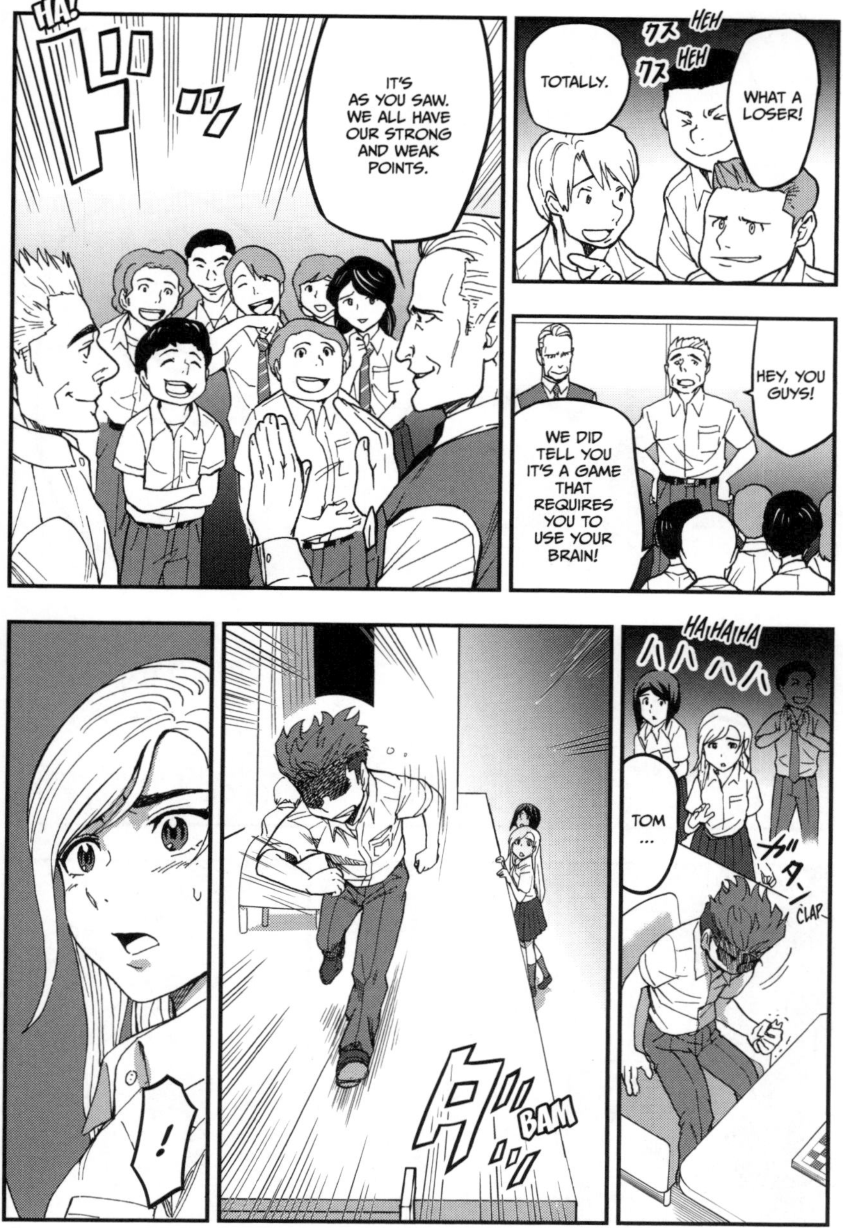
WHAT A LOSER!
HEH
クス
HEH
クス
TOTALLY.
HEY, YOU GUYS!
WE DID TELL YOU IT'S A GAME THAT REQUIRES YOU TO USE YOUR BRAIN!
IT'S AS YOU SAW. WE ALL HAVE OUR STRONG AND WEAK POINTS.
HA!
ドッ
HA HA HA
ハハハハ
TOM ...
ガタッ
CLAP
タッ
BAM
!

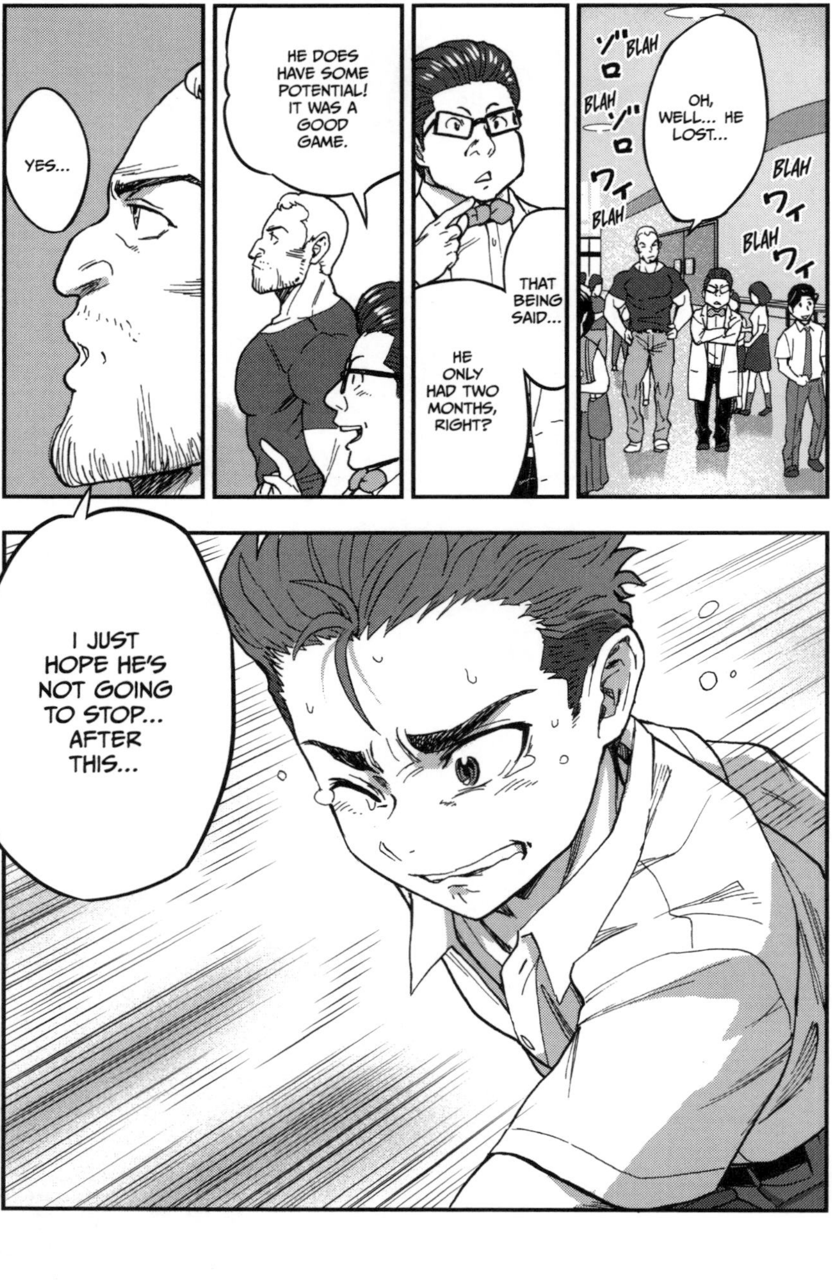
ゾロ BLAH
BLAH ゾロ
ワイ BLAH
BLAH ワイ
BLAH ワイ
OH, WELL... HE LOST...
THAT BEING SAID...
HE ONLY HAD TWO MONTHS, RIGHT?
HE DOES HAVE SOME POTENTIAL! IT WAS A GOOD GAME.
YES...
I JUST HOPE HE'S NOT GOING TO STOP... AFTER THIS...

BLiTZ

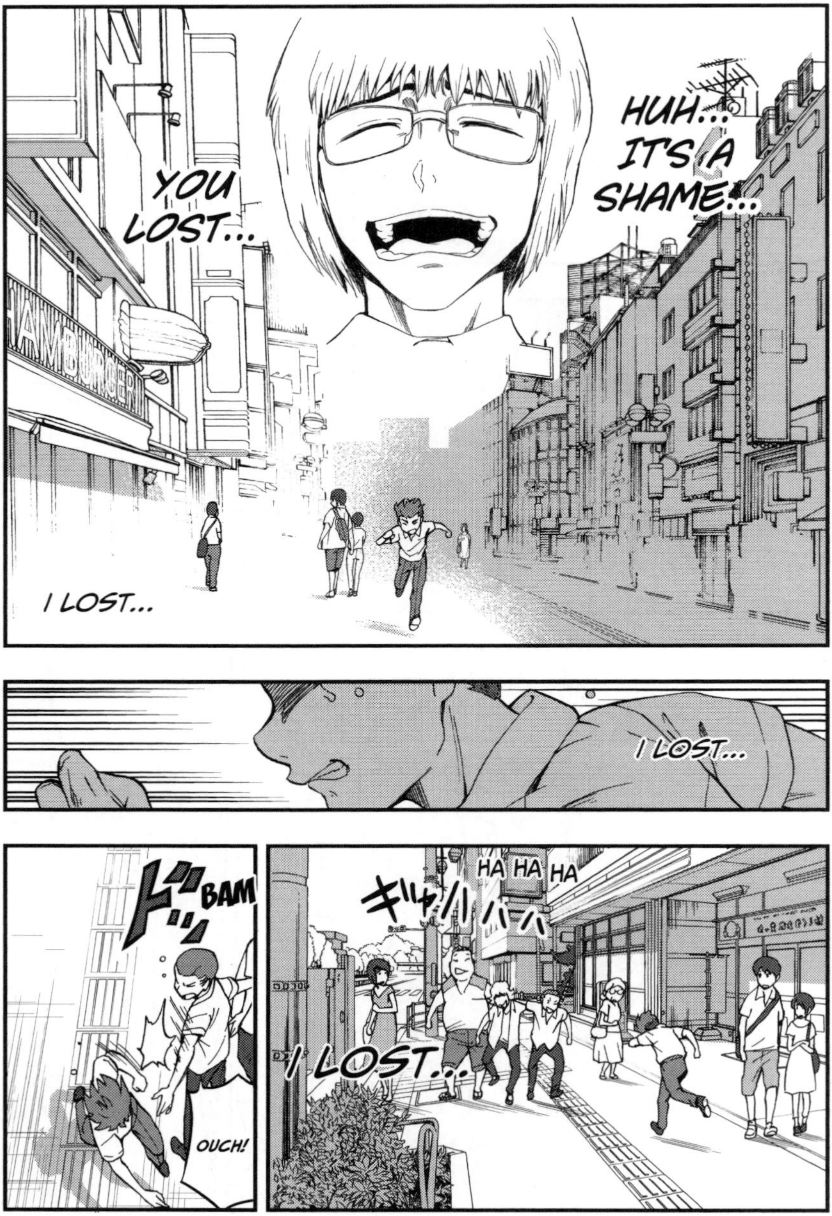
HUH... IT'S A SHAME...
YOU LOST...
I LOST...
I LOST...
HA HA HA
キャハハハ
I LOST...
ドッ
BAM
OUCH!

Chapter 4: The knight's path

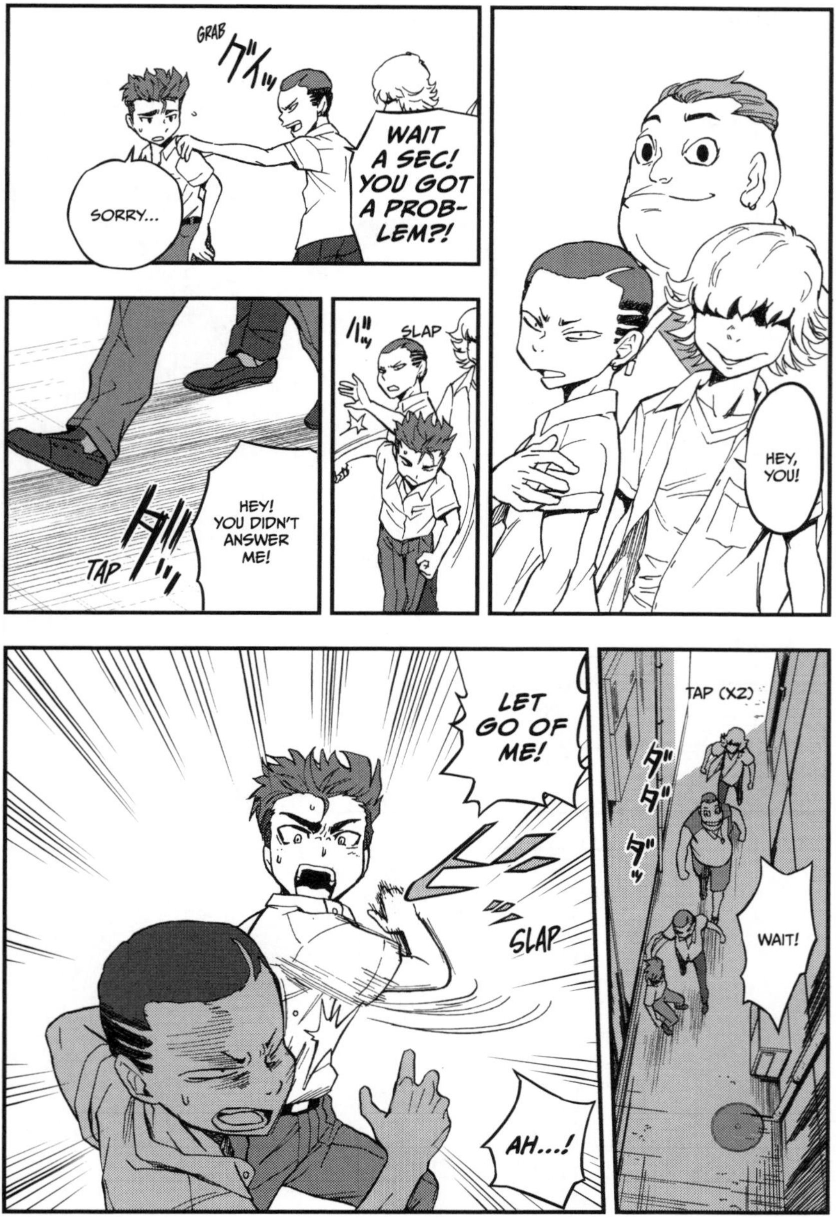
HEY, YOU!
GRAB
グイッ
WAIT A SEC! YOU GOT A PROB-LEM?!
SORRY...
SLAP
バッ
HEY! YOU DIDN'T ANSWER ME!
ダッ
TAP
TAP (X2)
ダダダッ
WAIT!
LET GO OF ME!
SLAP
AH...!

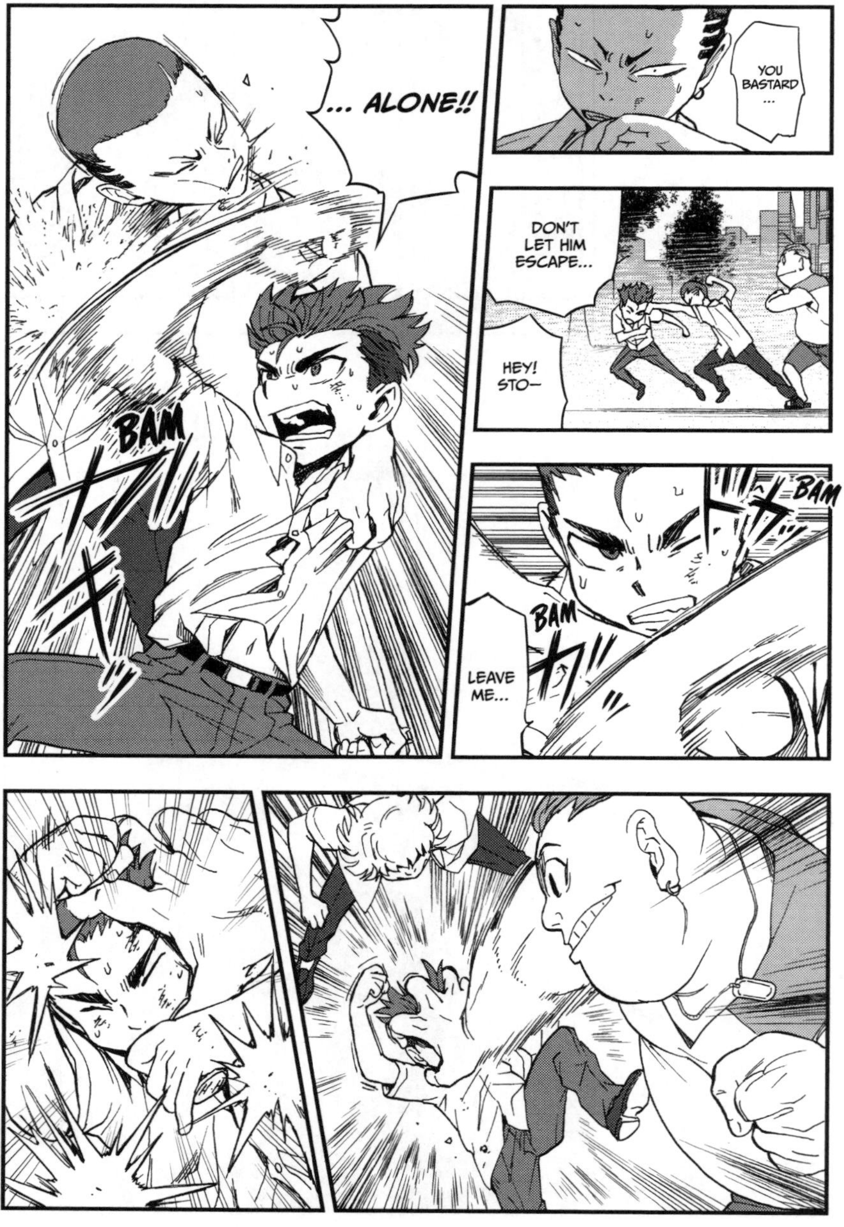
YOU BASTARD ...
DON'T LET HIM ESCAPE...
HEY! STO—
BAM
BAM
LEAVE ME...
... ALONE!!
BAM

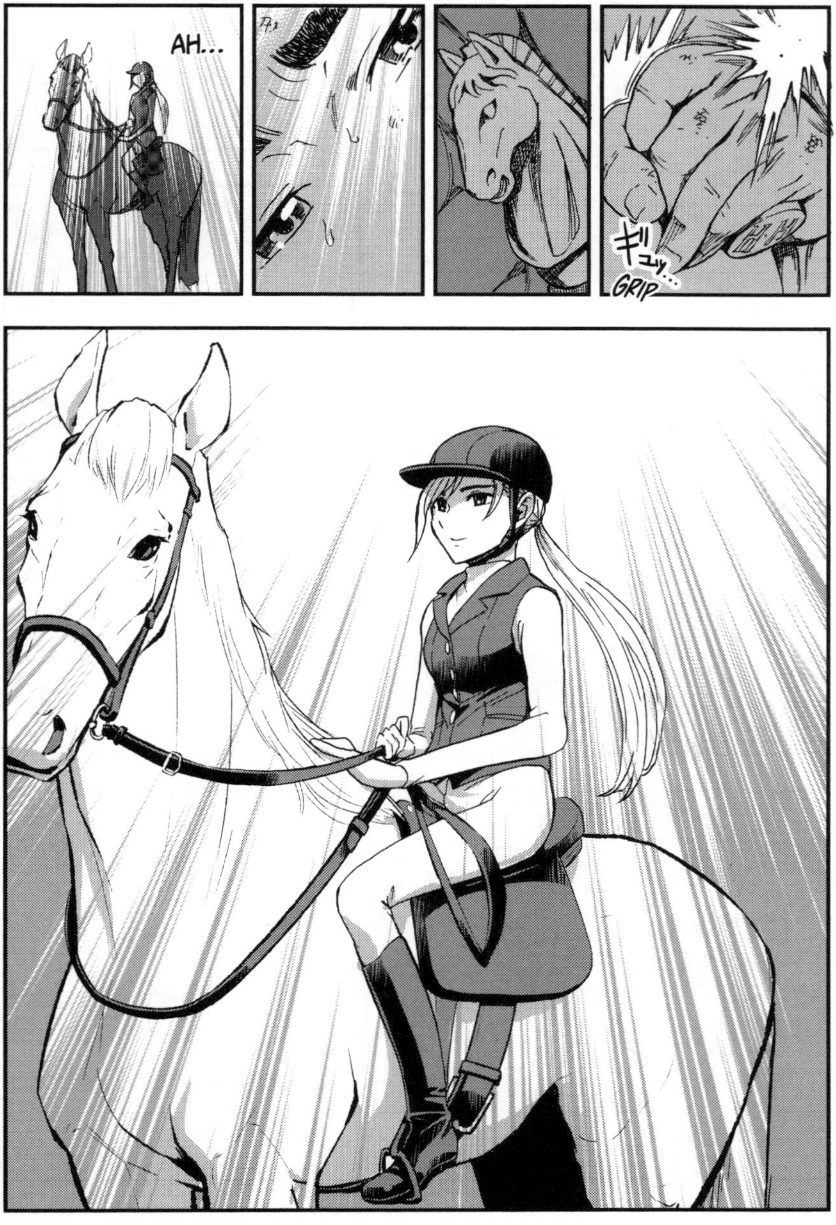
ギュッ…
GRIP
AH...

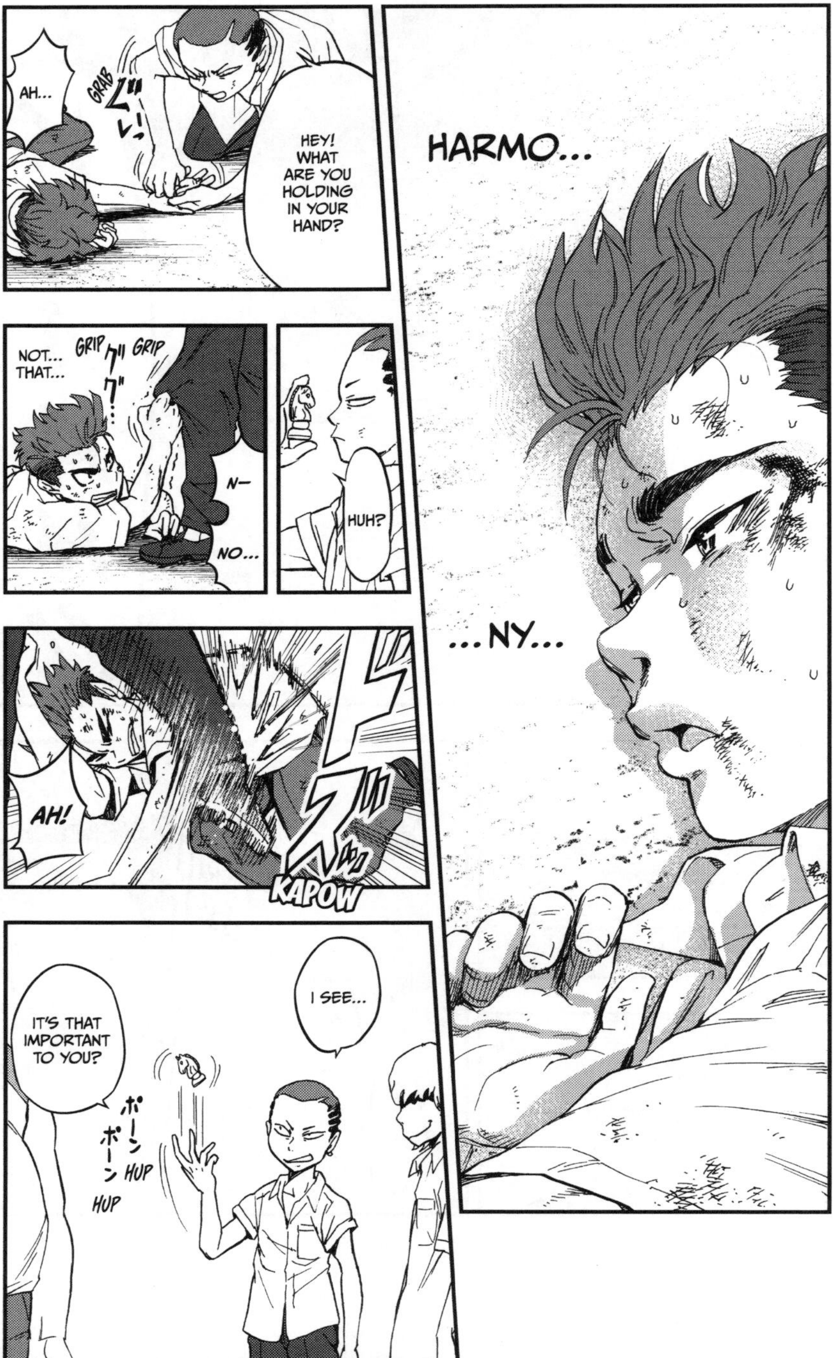
HARMO...
...NY...
HEY! WHAT ARE YOU HOLDING IN YOUR HAND?
GRAB
AH...
HUH?
GRIP GRIP
NOT... THAT...
N–
NO...
KAPOW
AH!
I SEE...
IT'S THAT IMPORTANT TO YOU?
ポーン ポーン
HUP HUP

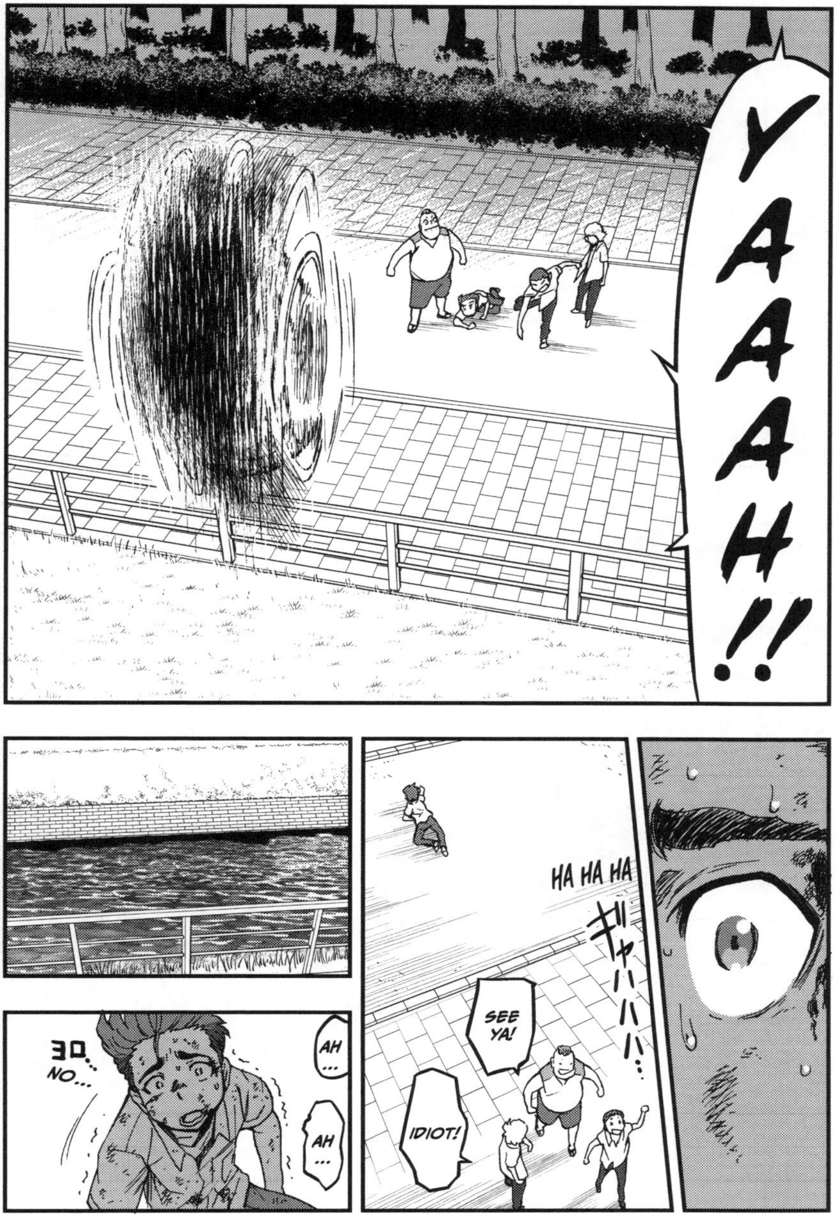
YAAAAH!!
HA HA HA
ギャハハハ…
SEE YA!
IDIOT!
AH…
AH…
ヨロ…
NO…

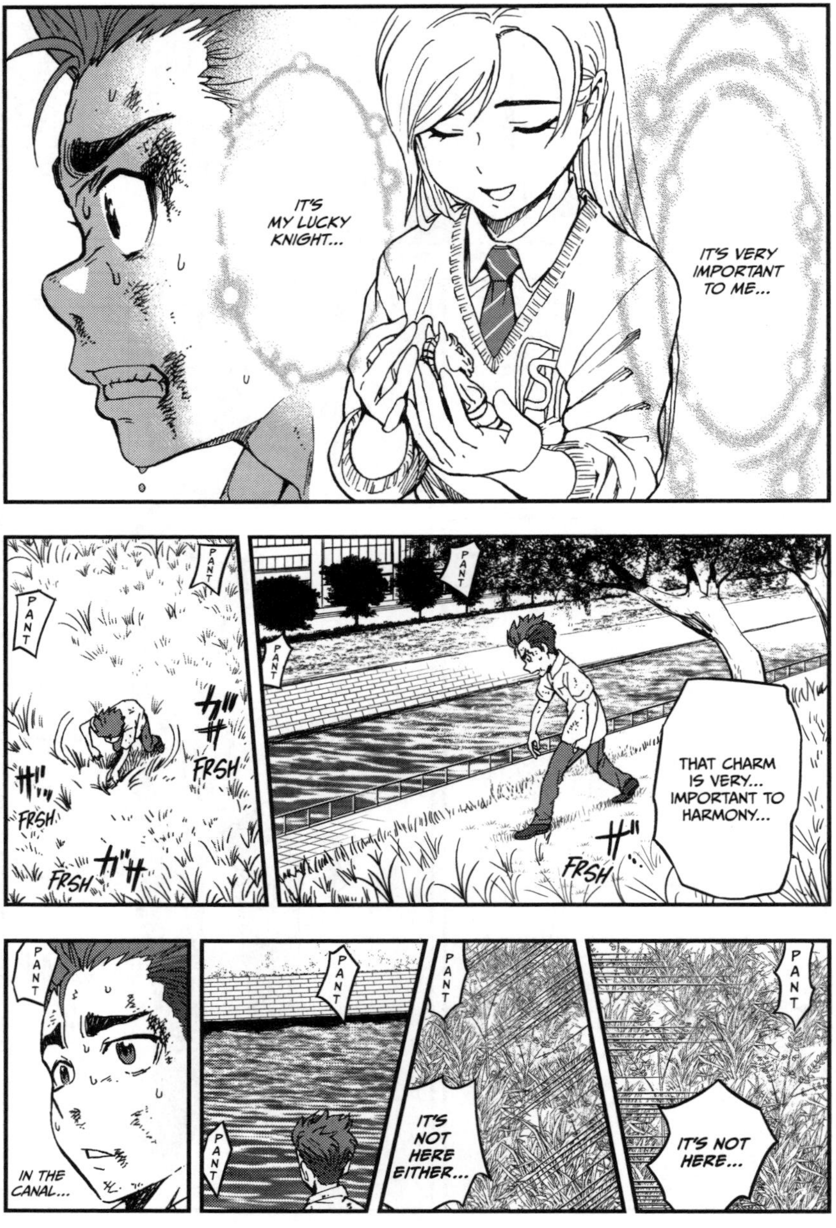
IT'S MY LUCKY KNIGHT...
IT'S VERY IMPORTANT TO ME...
PANT
PANT
THAT CHARM IS VERY... IMPORTANT TO HARMONY...
FRSH
PANT
PANT
FRSH
FRSH
FRSH
PANT
IT'S NOT HERE...
PANT
IT'S NOT HERE EITHER...
PANT
PANT
PANT
IN THE CANAL...

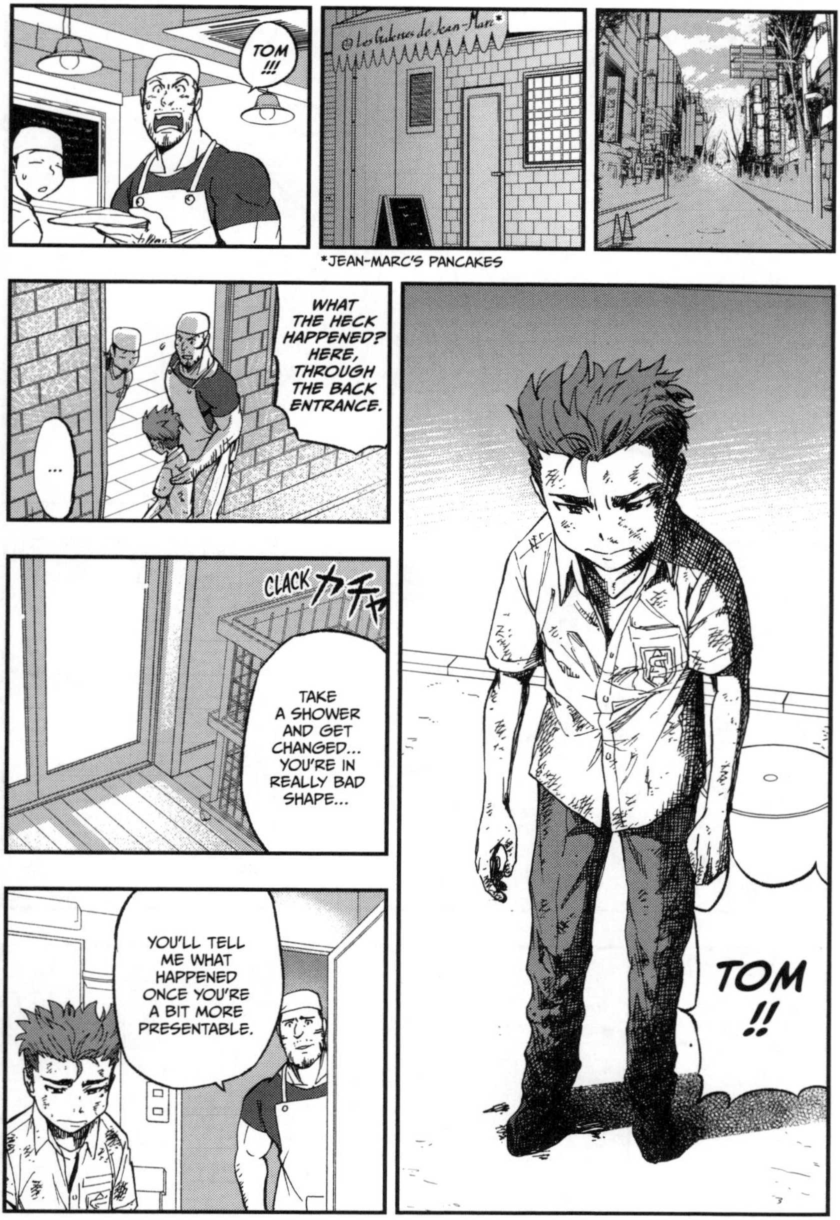
Les Galettes de Jean-Marc*
TOM !!!
*JEAN-MARC'S PANCAKES
TOM !!
WHAT THE HECK HAPPENED? HERE, THROUGH THE BACK ENTRANCE.
...
CLACK
TAKE A SHOWER AND GET CHANGED... YOU'RE IN REALLY BAD SHAPE...
YOU'LL TELL ME WHAT HAPPENED ONCE YOU'RE A BIT MORE PRESENTABLE.

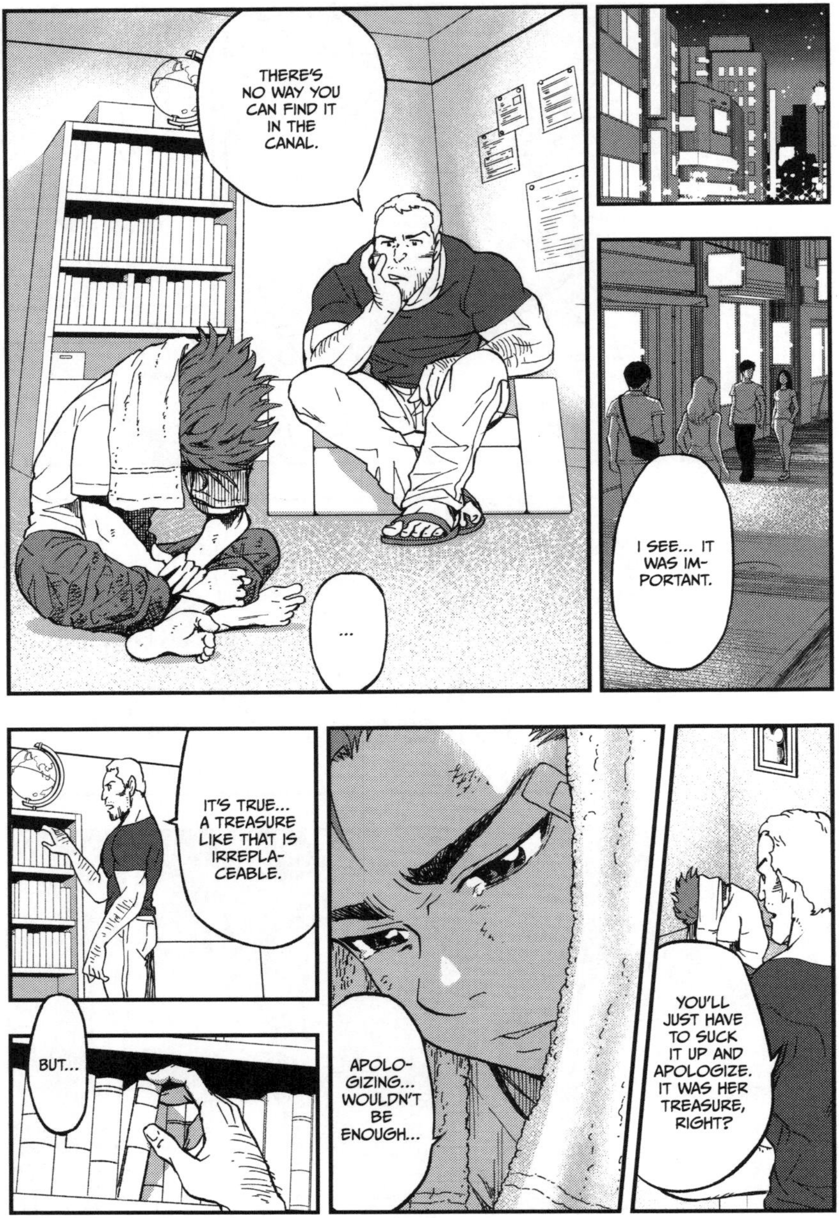

I SEE... IT WAS IMPORTANT.
THERE'S NO WAY YOU CAN FIND IT IN THE CANAL.
...
YOU'LL JUST HAVE TO SUCK IT UP AND APOLOGIZE. IT WAS HER TREASURE, RIGHT?
APOLOGIZING... WOULDN'T BE ENOUGH...
IT'S TRUE... A TREASURE LIKE THAT IS IRREPLACEABLE.
BUT...

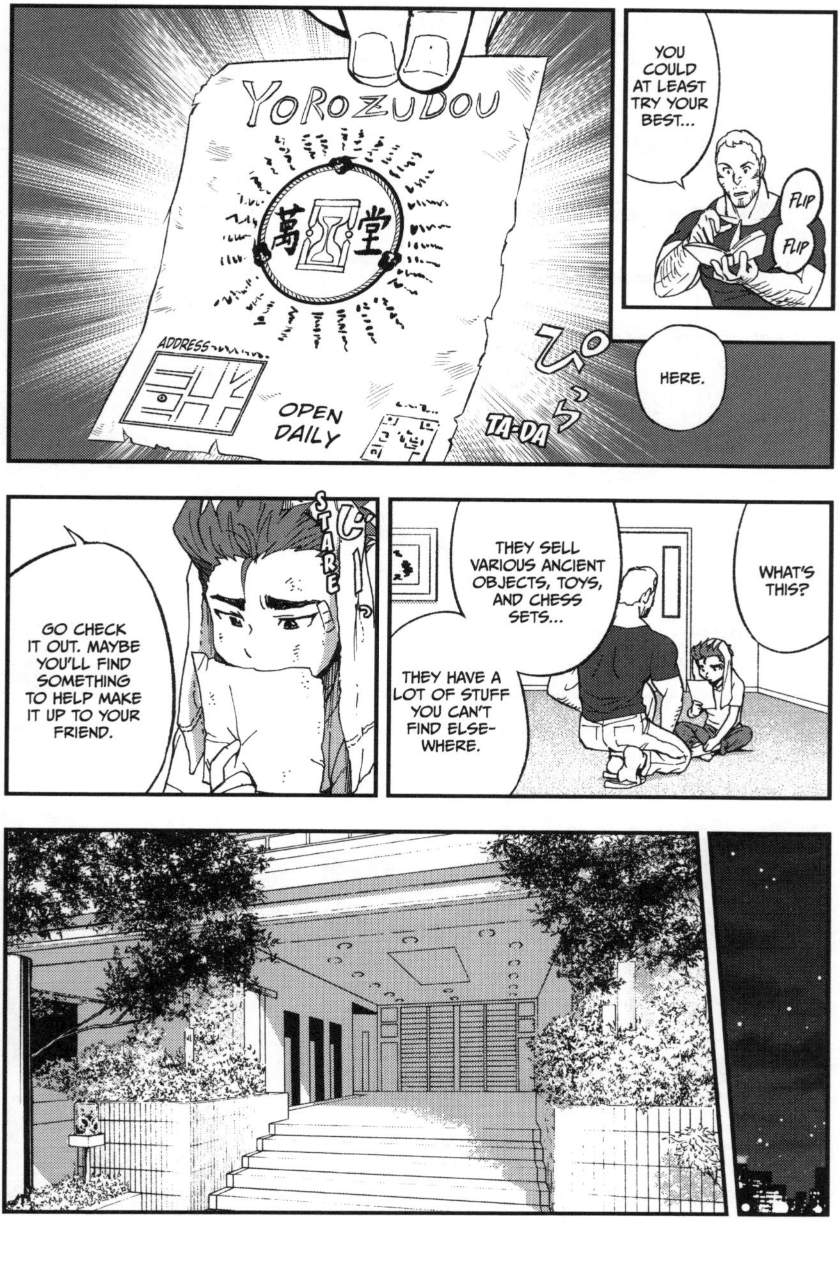
YOU COULD AT LEAST TRY YOUR BEST...
FLIP
FLIP
HERE.
YOROZUDOU
萬堂
ADDRESS
OPEN DAILY
TA-DA
WHAT'S THIS?
THEY SELL VARIOUS ANCIENT OBJECTS, TOYS, AND CHESS SETS...
THEY HAVE A LOT OF STUFF YOU CAN'T FIND ELSE-WHERE.
STARE
GO CHECK IT OUT. MAYBE YOU'LL FIND SOMETHING TO HELP MAKE IT UP TO YOUR FRIEND.

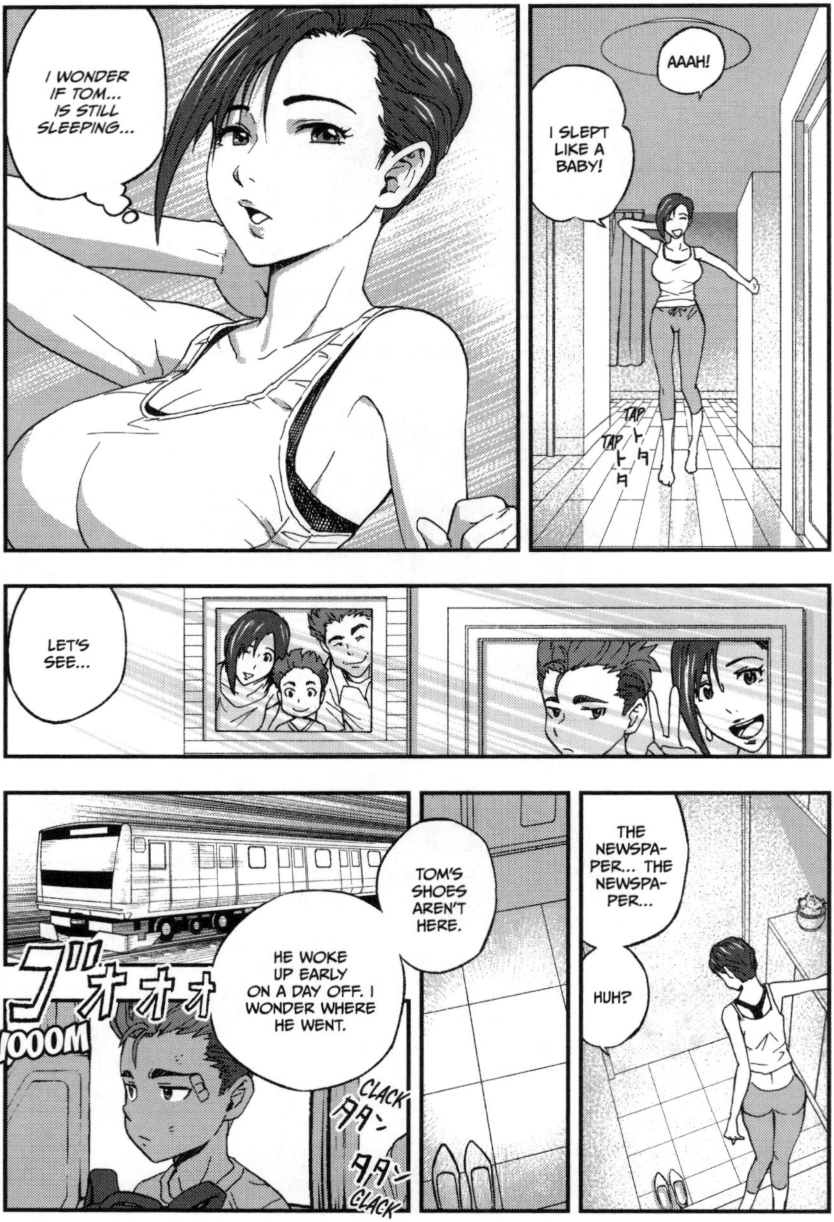
AAAH!
I SLEPT LIKE A BABY!
TAP トタ
TAP トタ
I WONDER IF TOM... IS STILL SLEEPING...
LET'S SEE...
THE NEWSPAPER... THE NEWSPAPER...
HUH?
TOM'S SHOES AREN'T HERE.
HE WOKE UP EARLY ON A DAY OFF. I WONDER WHERE HE WENT.
ゴォオオオ
VOOOM
CLACK タタン
タタン CLACK

水野
ジャリ..
TAP
萬堂
IS HE SERIOUS?
FWOOOOSH

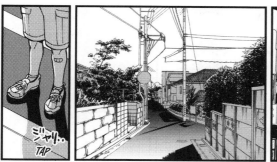

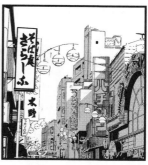

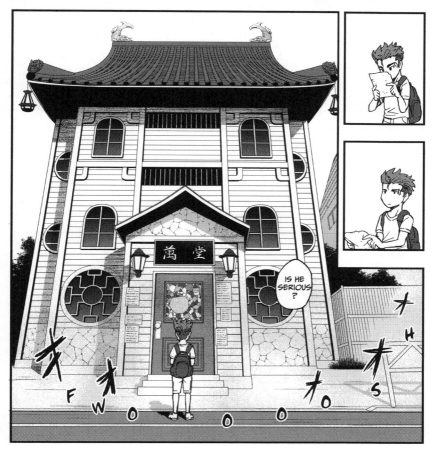

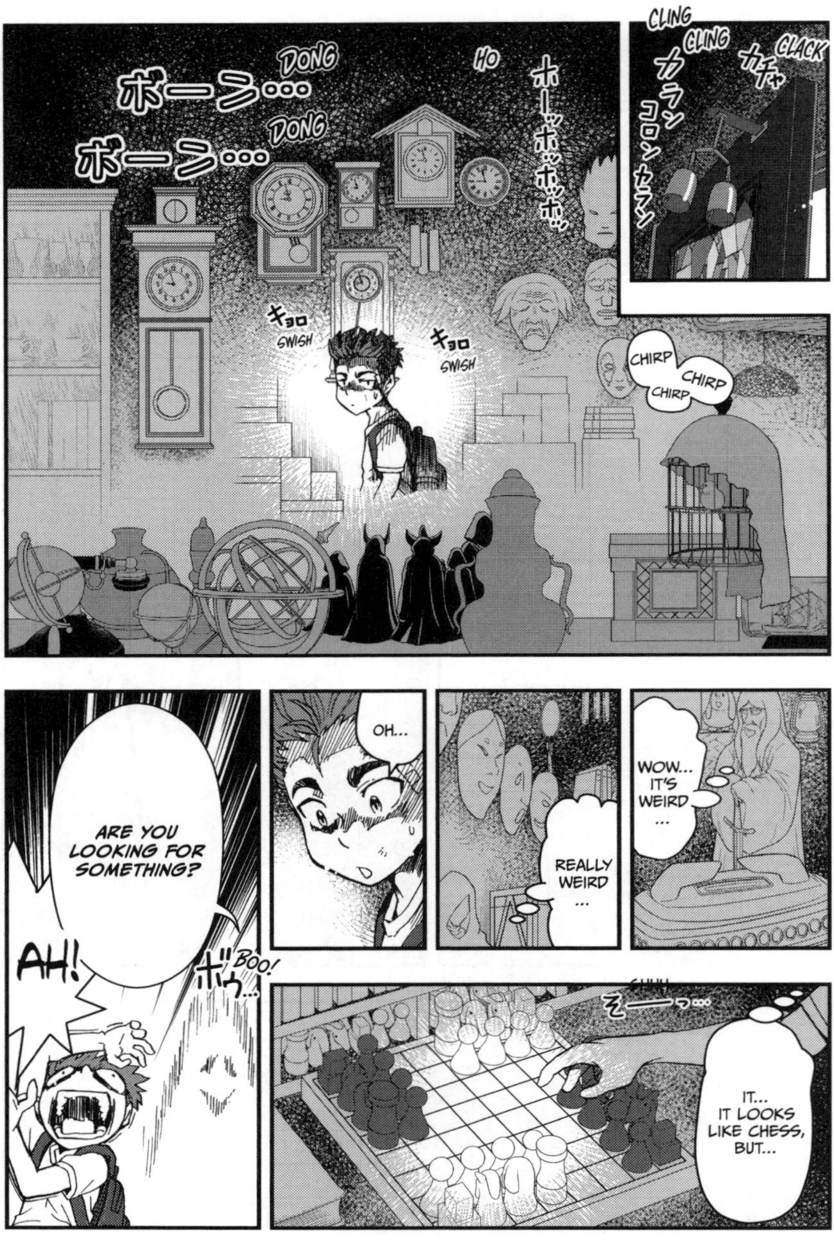
CLING
CLING
カランコロンカラン
CLACK
カチャ
ボーン…
DONG
ボーン…
DONG
HO
ホーッホッホッホッ
キョロ
SWISH
キョロ
SWISH
CHIRP
CHIRP
CHIRP
WOW... IT'S WEIRD ...
REALLY WEIRD ...
OH...
SHHH
そーっ…
IT... IT LOOKS LIKE CHESS, BUT...
ARE YOU LOOKING FOR SOMETHING?
ボウ…
BOO!
AH!

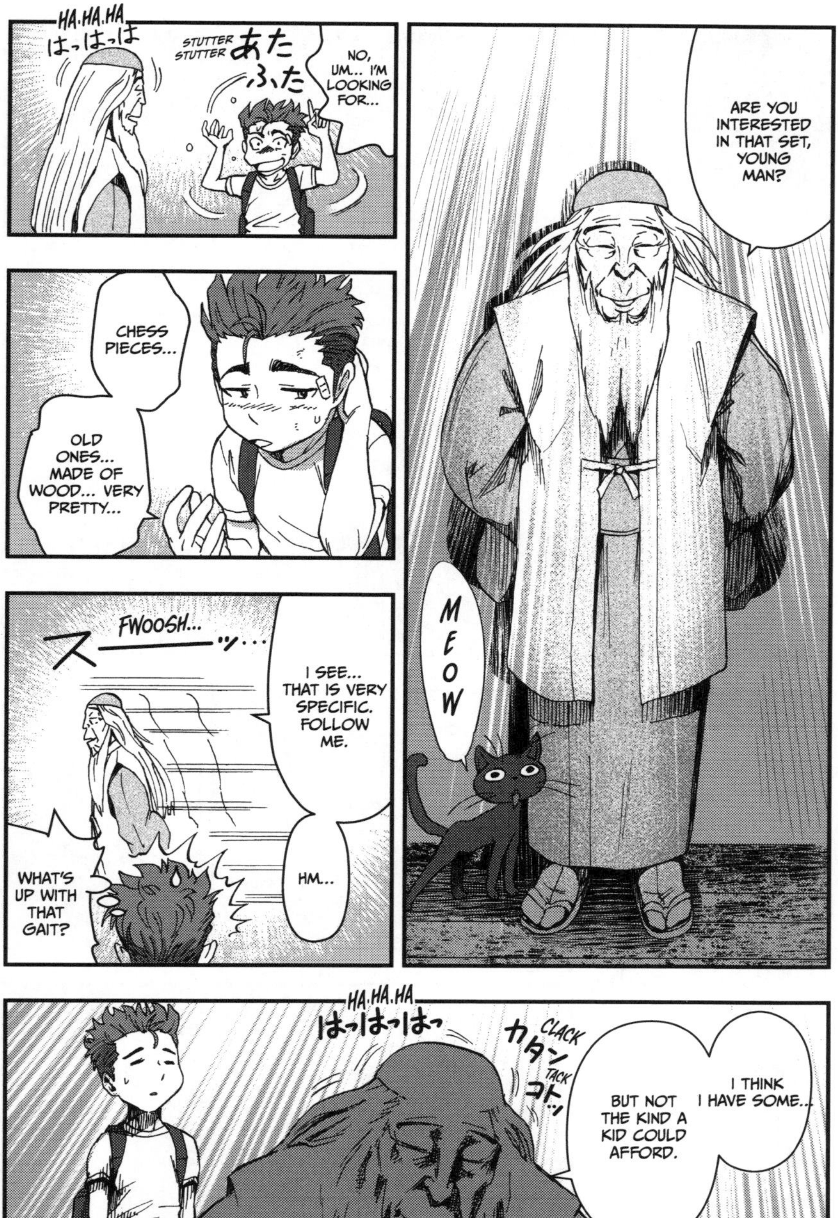
ARE YOU INTERESTED IN THAT SET, YOUNG MAN?
MEOW
NO, UM... I'M LOOKING FOR...
STUTTER STUTTER あたふた
HA HA HA はっはっは
CHESS PIECES...
OLD ONES... MADE OF WOOD... VERY PRETTY...
I SEE... THAT IS VERY SPECIFIC. FOLLOW ME.
HM...
FWOOSH... スーーッ...
WHAT'S UP WITH THAT GAIT?
I THINK I HAVE SOME...
BUT NOT THE KIND A KID COULD AFFORD.
CLACK カタン
TACK コトッ
HA HA HA はっはっはっ

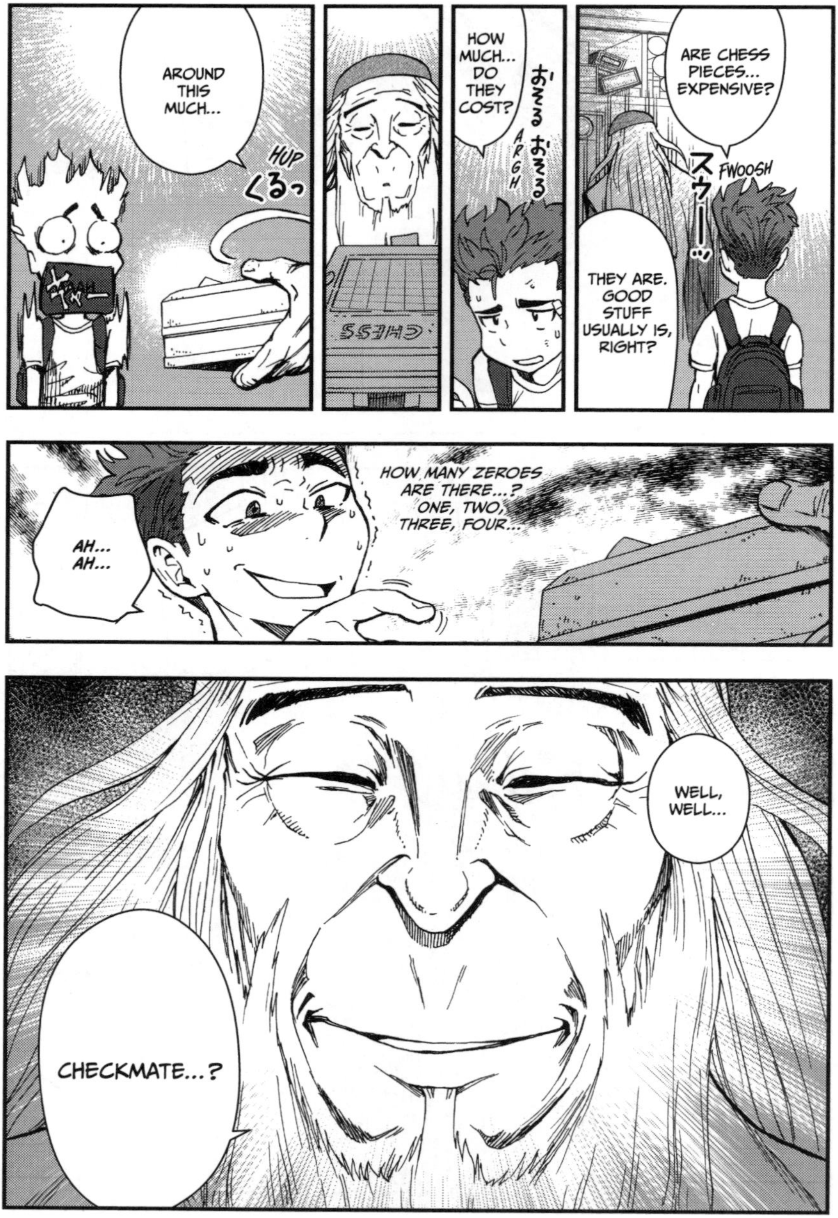
ARE CHESS PIECES... EXPENSIVE?
FWOOSH
スウーッ
THEY ARE. GOOD STUFF USUALLY IS, RIGHT?
HOW MUCH... DO THEY COST?
おそる おそる
ARGH
AROUND THIS MUCH...
HUP
くるっ
ギャー
HOW MANY ZEROES ARE THERE...? ONE, TWO, THREE, FOUR...
AH... AH...
WELL, WELL...
CHECKMATE...?

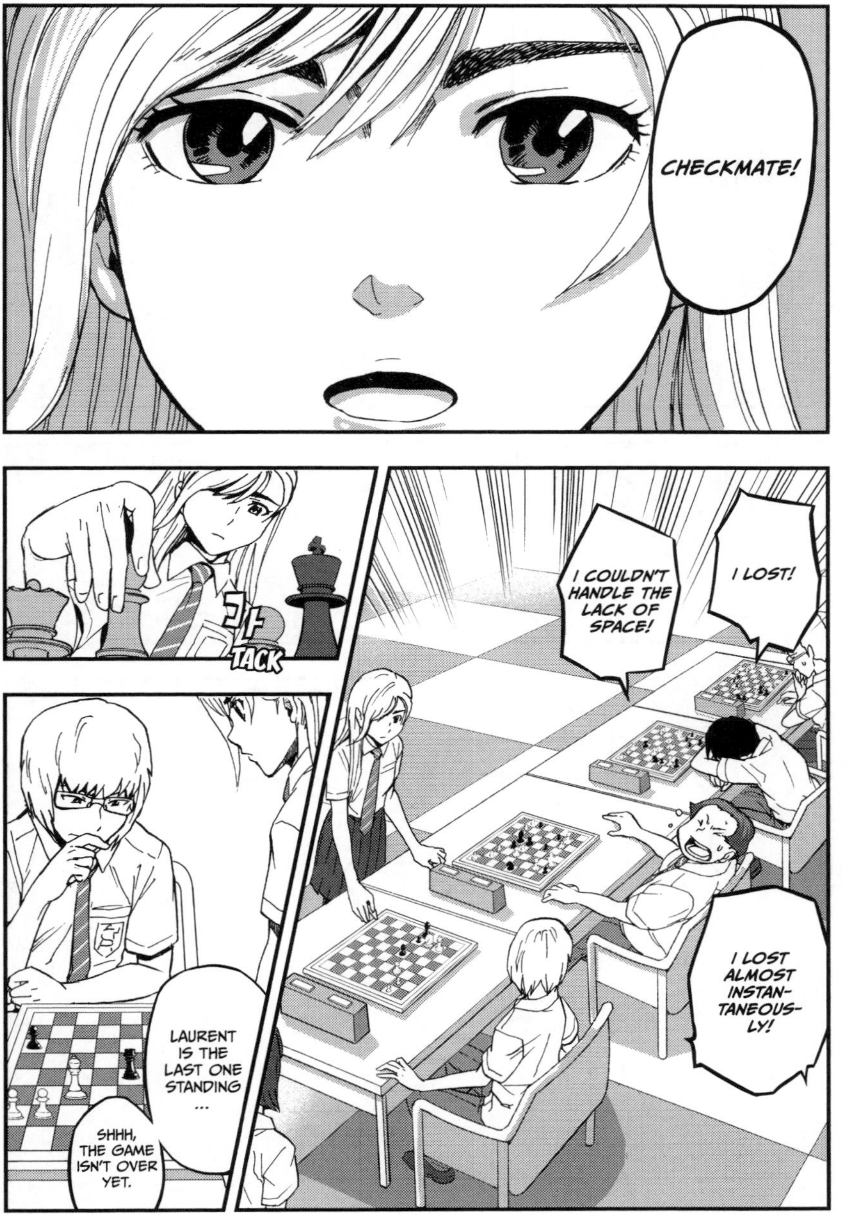
CHECKMATE!
I LOST!
I COULDN'T HANDLE THE LACK OF SPACE!
I LOST ALMOST INSTAN-TANEOUS-LY!
TACK
LAURENT IS THE LAST ONE STANDING ...
SHHH, THE GAME ISN'T OVER YET.

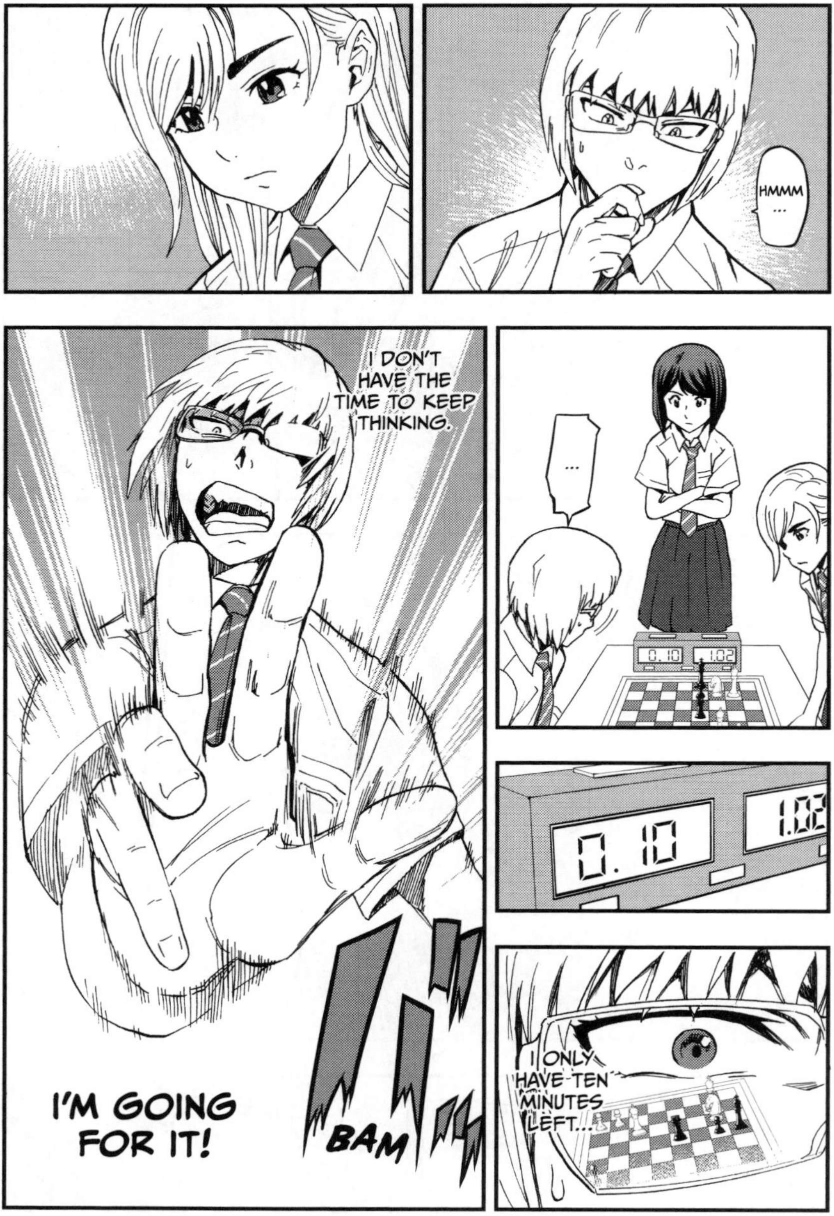
HMMM ...
...
I ONLY HAVE TEN MINUTES LEFT...
I DON'T HAVE THE TIME TO KEEP THINKING.
I'M GOING FOR IT!
BAM

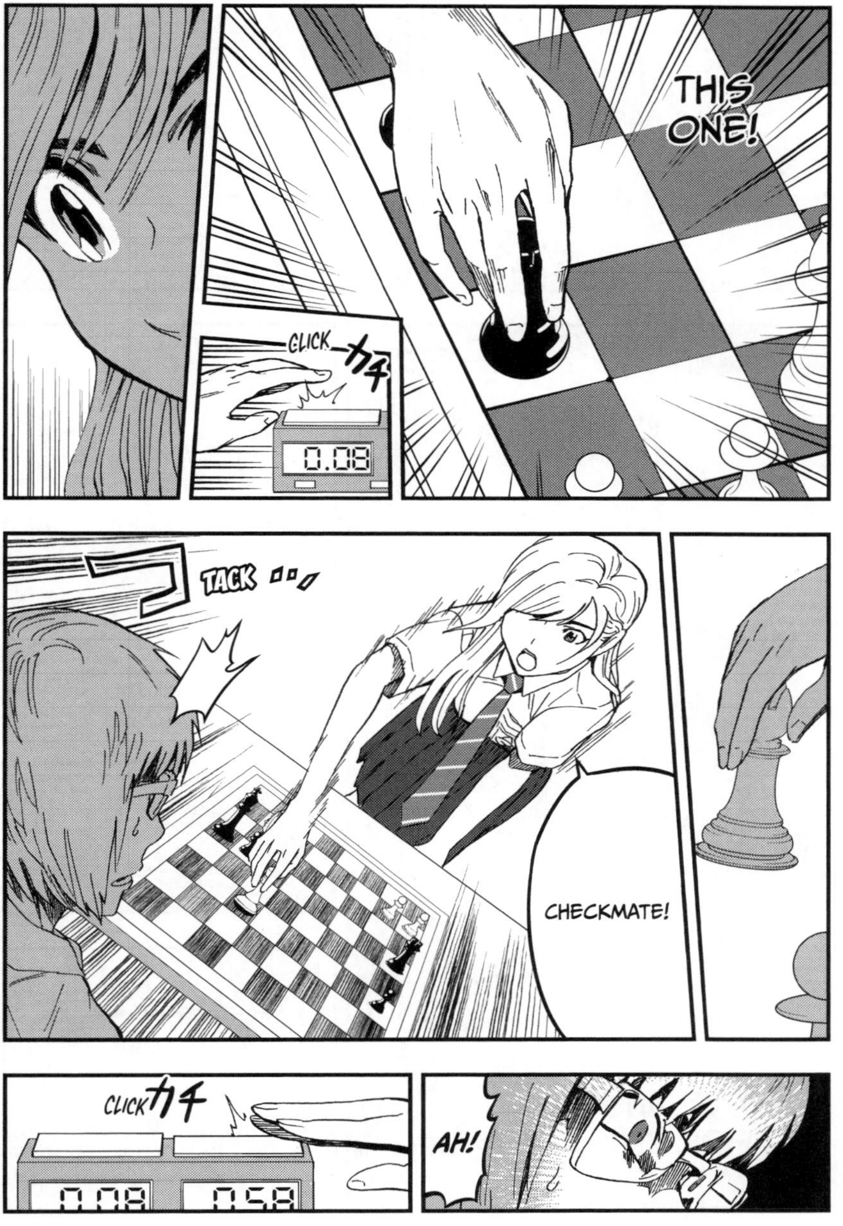
THIS ONE!
CLICK カチ
TACK
CHECKMATE!
AH!
CLICK カチ

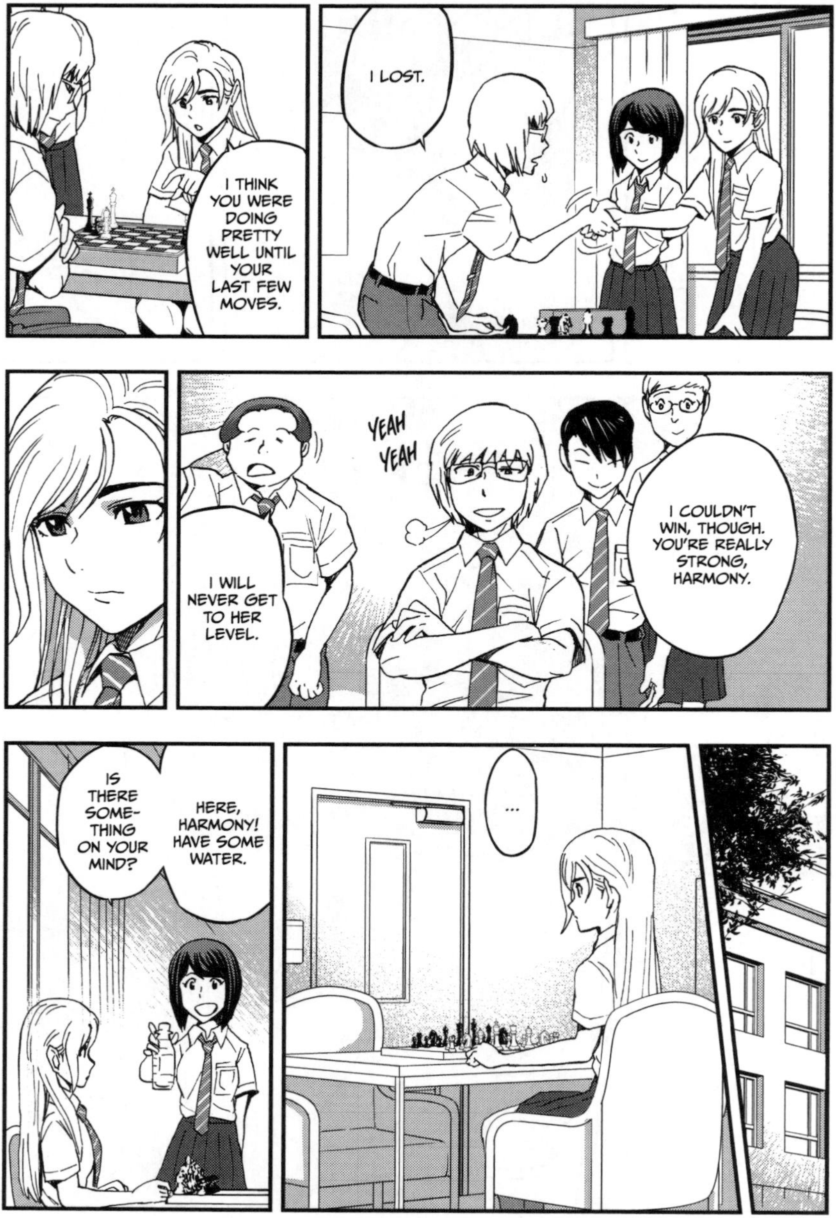
I LOST.
I THINK YOU WERE DOING PRETTY WELL UNTIL YOUR LAST FEW MOVES.
I COULDN'T WIN, THOUGH. YOU'RE REALLY STRONG, HARMONY.
YEAH YEAH
I WILL NEVER GET TO HER LEVEL.
...
HERE, HARMONY! HAVE SOME WATER.
IS THERE SOME-THING ON YOUR MIND?

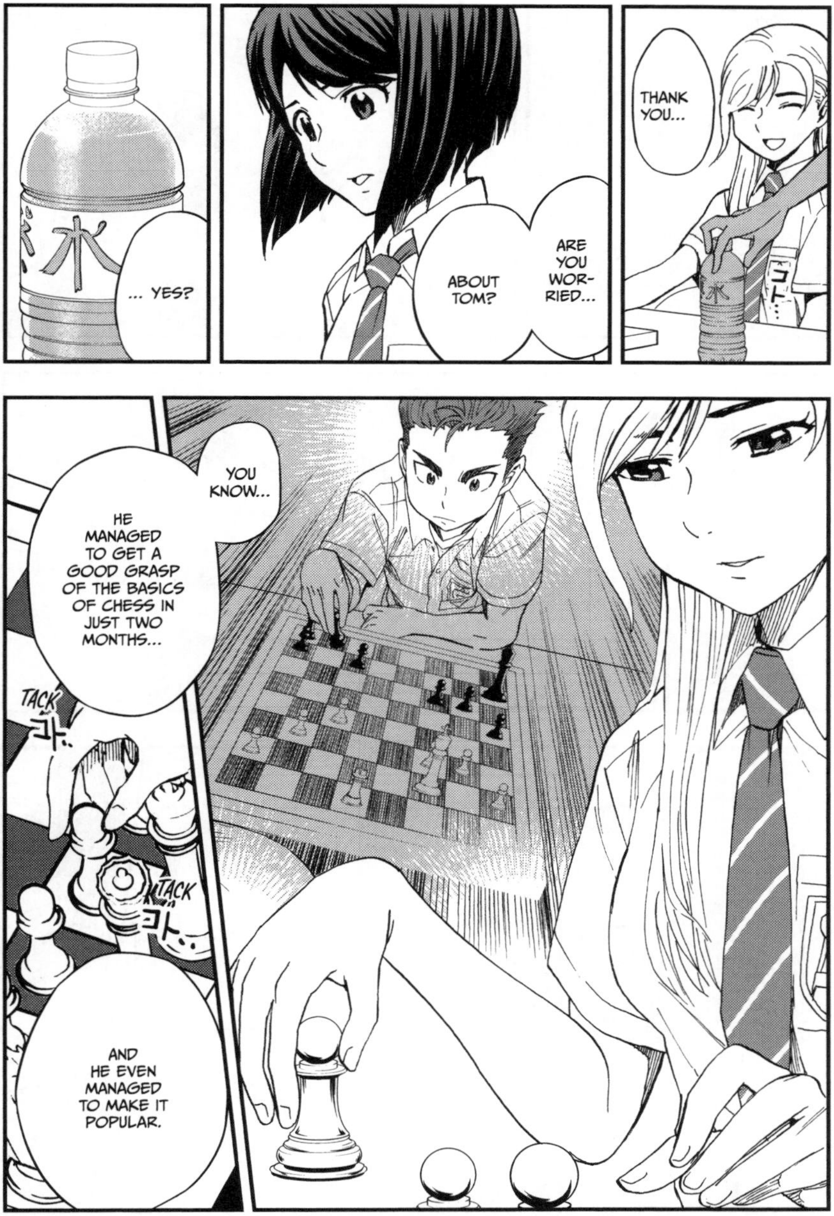
THANK YOU...
コト…
ARE YOU WOR-RIED...
ABOUT TOM?
... YES?
YOU KNOW...
HE MANAGED TO GET A GOOD GRASP OF THE BASICS OF CHESS IN JUST TWO MONTHS...
TACK
TACK
AND HE EVEN MANAGED TO MAKE IT POPULAR.

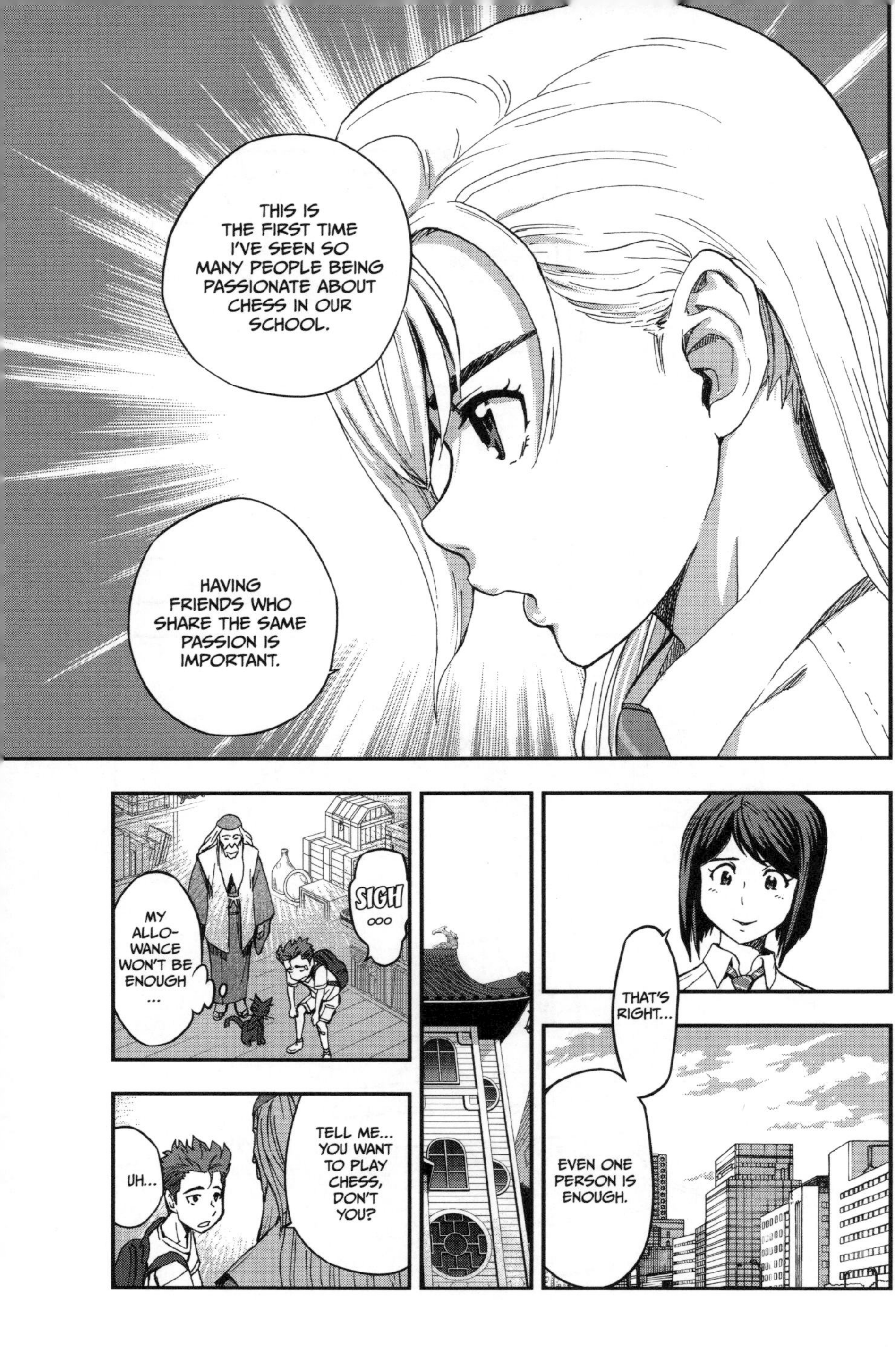
THIS IS THE FIRST TIME I'VE SEEN SO MANY PEOPLE BEING PASSIONATE ABOUT CHESS IN OUR SCHOOL.
HAVING FRIENDS WHO SHARE THE SAME PASSION IS IMPORTANT.
THAT'S RIGHT...
EVEN ONE PERSON IS ENOUGH.
SIGH
ooo
MY ALLO-WANCE WON'T BE ENOUGH ...
TELL ME... YOU WANT TO PLAY CHESS, DON'T YOU?
UH...

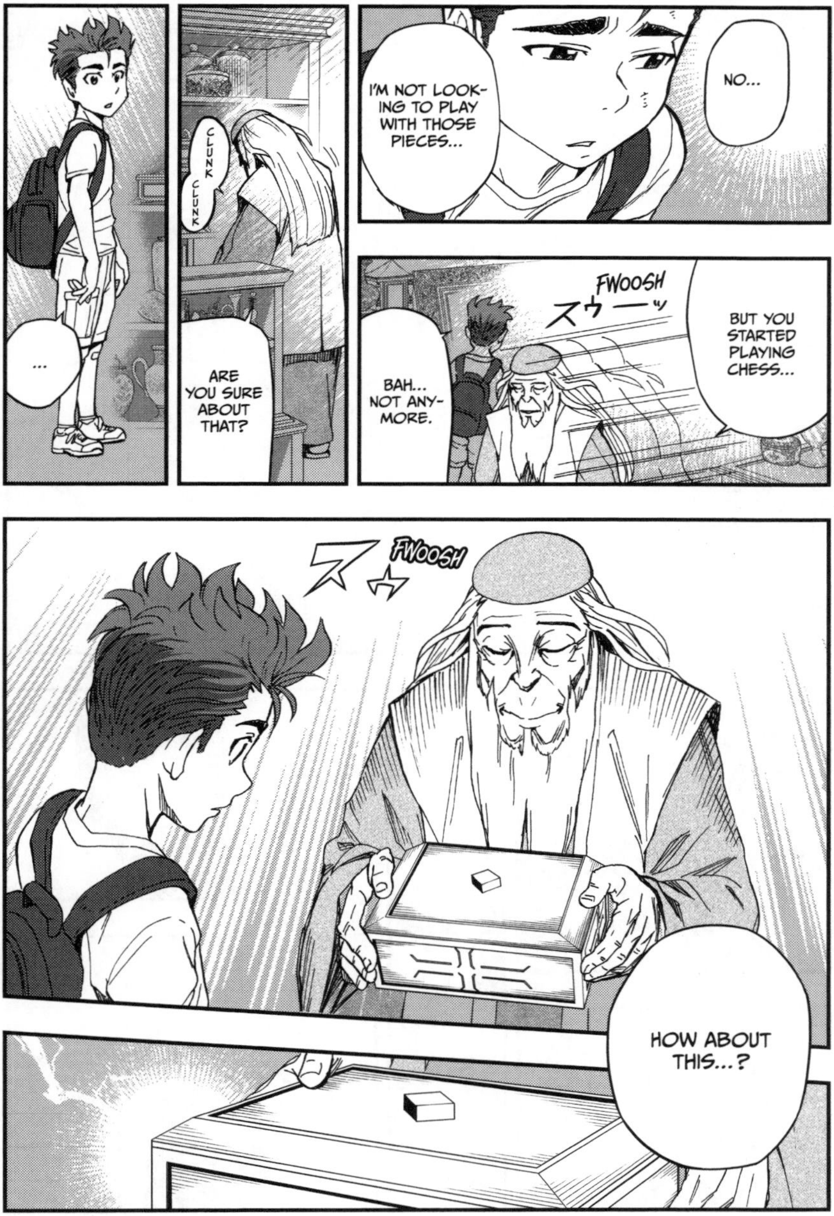
NO...
I'M NOT LOOK-ING TO PLAY WITH THOSE PIECES...
BUT YOU STARTED PLAYING CHESS...
FWOOSH
スウーッ
BAH... NOT ANY-MORE.
CLUNK CLUNK
ARE YOU SURE ABOUT THAT?
...
FWOOSH
スッ
HOW ABOUT THIS...?

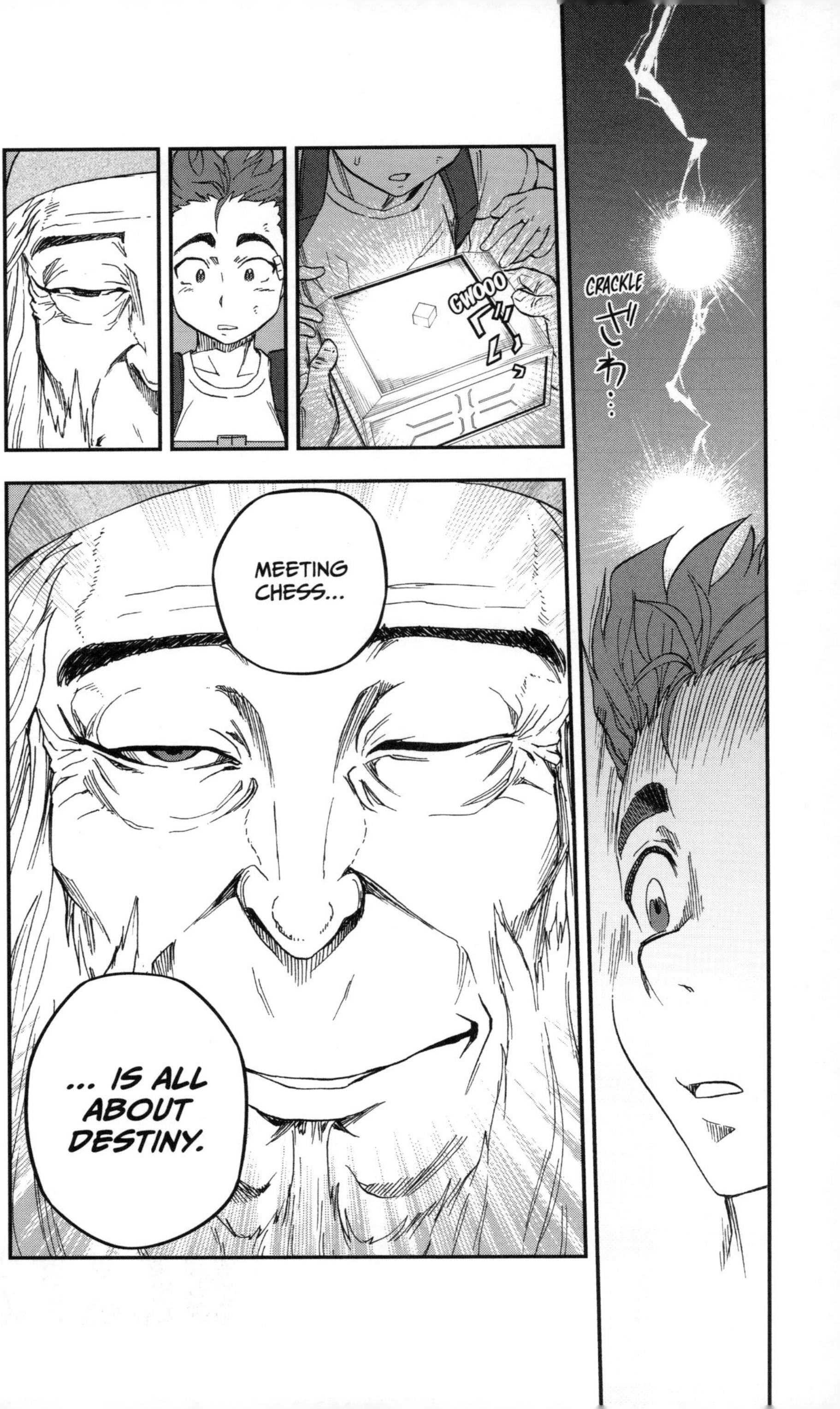
CRACKLE
ざわ…
GWOOO
MEETING CHESS...
... IS ALL ABOUT DESTINY.

BLITZ

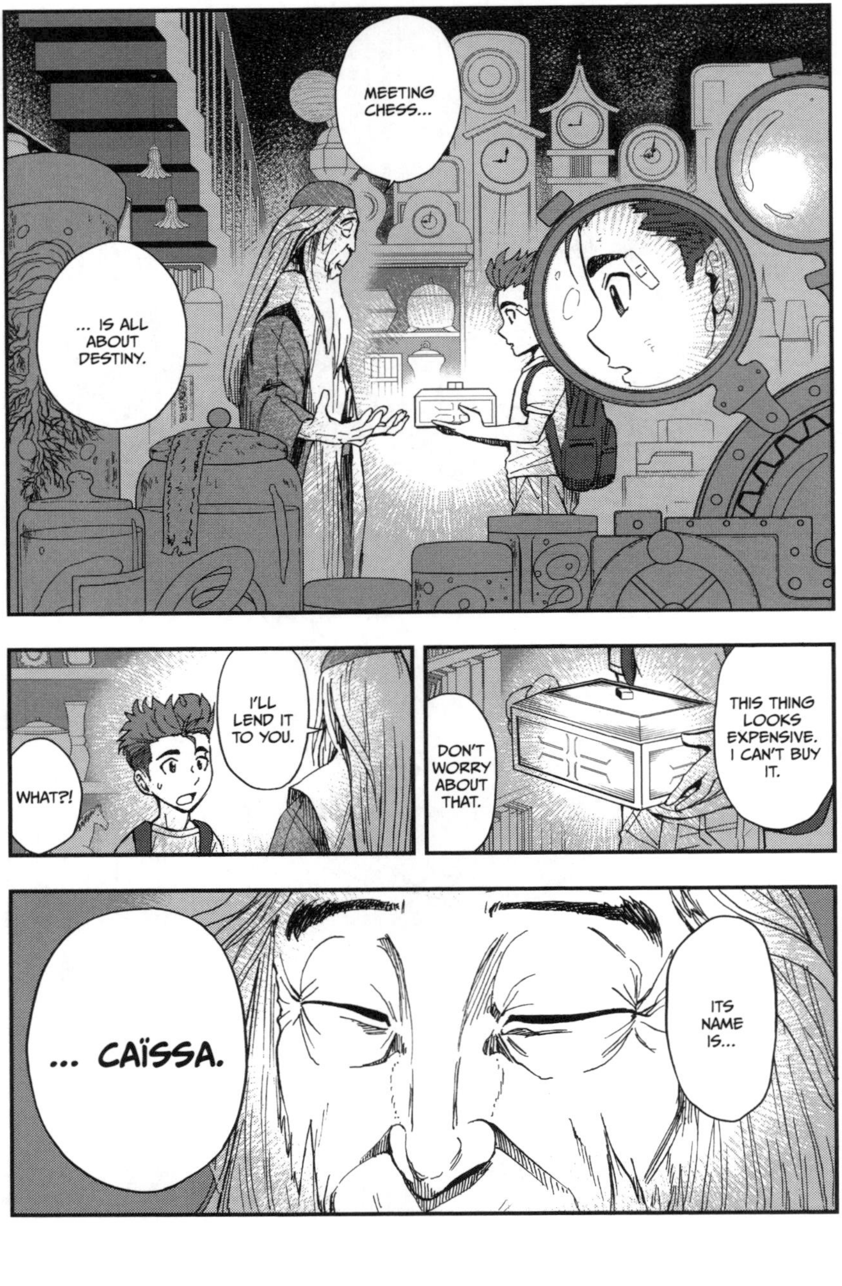
MEETING CHESS...
... IS ALL ABOUT DESTINY.
THIS THING LOOKS EXPENSIVE. I CAN'T BUY IT.
DON'T WORRY ABOUT THAT.
I'LL LEND IT TO YOU.
WHAT?!
ITS NAME IS...
... CAÏSSA.

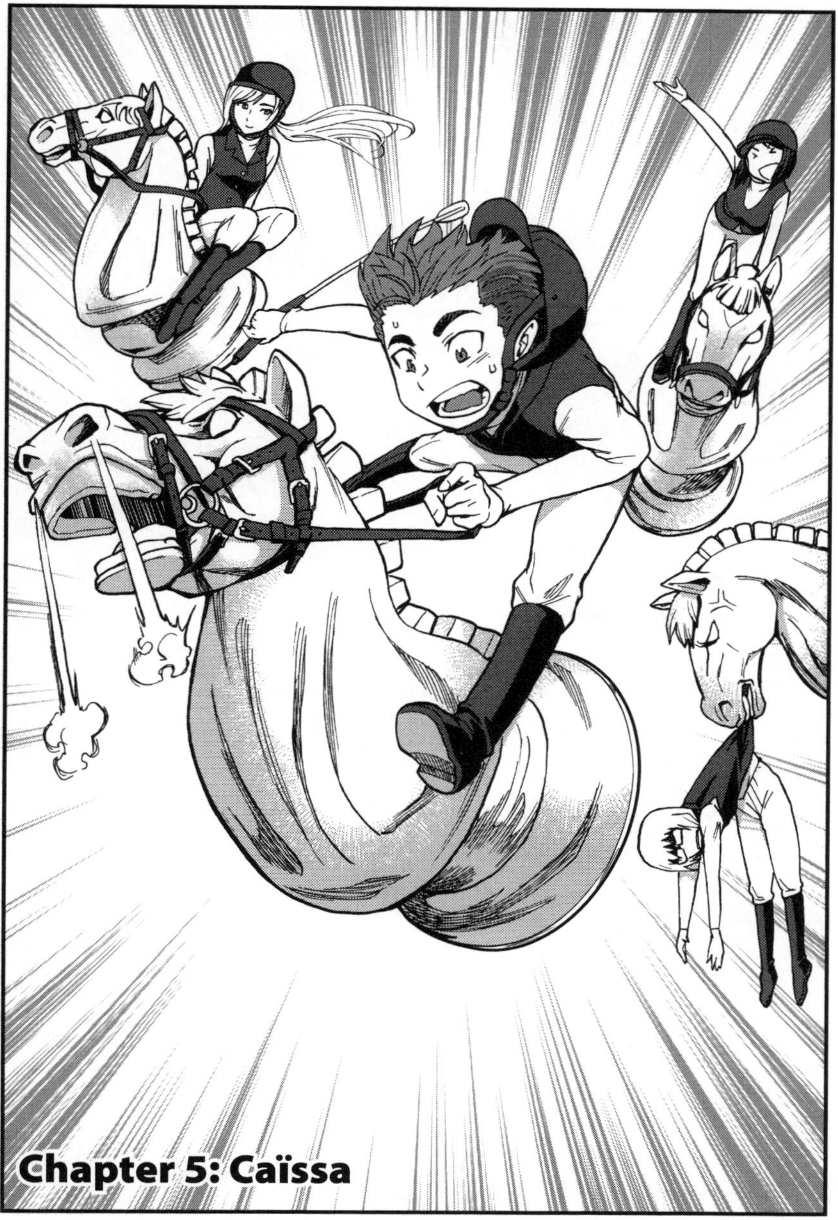

Chapter 5: Caïssa

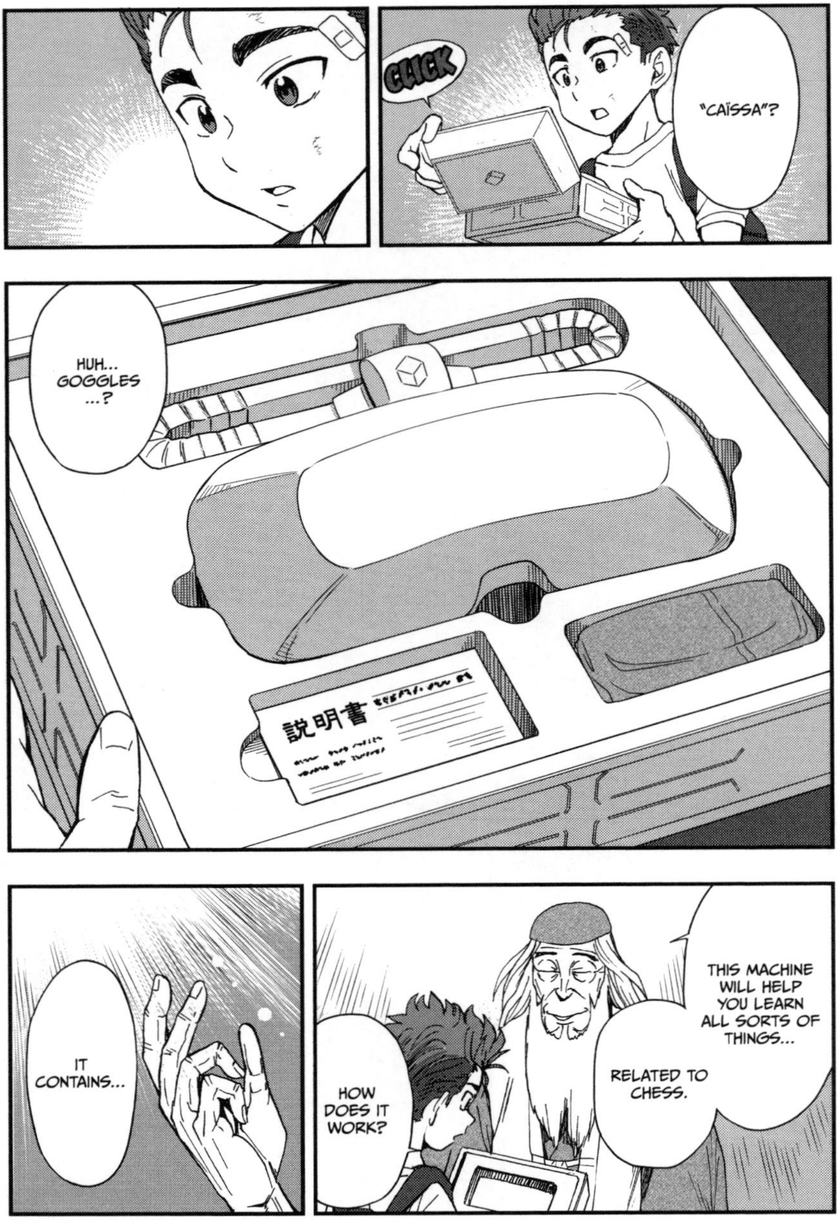
CLICK
"CAÏSSA"?
HUH... GOGGLES ...?
説明書
THIS MACHINE WILL HELP YOU LEARN ALL SORTS OF THINGS...
RELATED TO CHESS.
HOW DOES IT WORK?
IT CONTAINS...

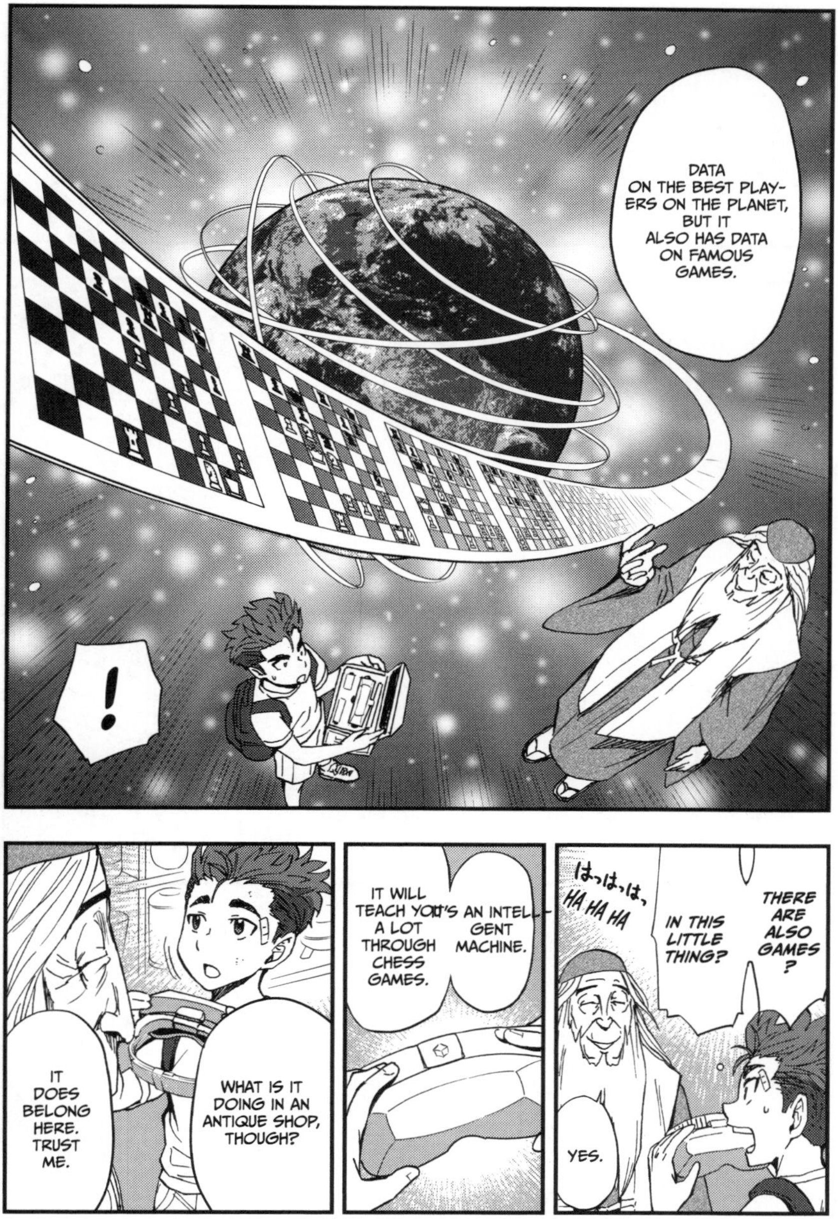
DATA ON THE BEST PLAYERS ON THE PLANET, BUT IT ALSO HAS DATA ON FAMOUS GAMES.
!
THERE ARE ALSO GAMES?
IN THIS LITTLE THING?
はっはっは、
HA HA HA
YES.
IT'S AN INTEL- GENT MACHINE.
IT WILL TEACH YOU A LOT THROUGH CHESS GAMES.
WHAT IS IT DOING IN AN ANTIQUE SHOP, THOUGH?
IT DOES BELONG HERE. TRUST ME.

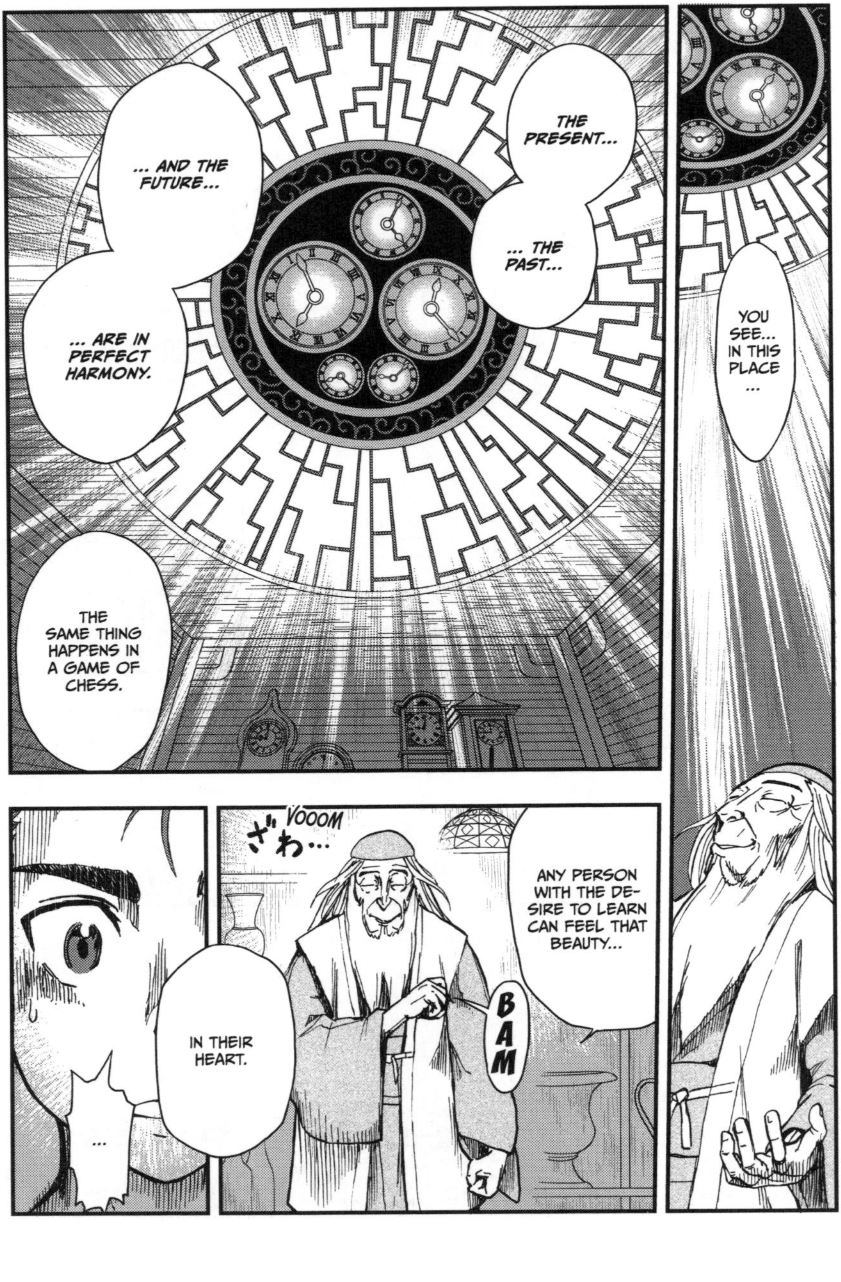
YOU SEE... IN THIS PLACE ...
THE PRESENT...
... THE PAST...
... AND THE FUTURE...
... ARE IN PERFECT HARMONY.
THE SAME THING HAPPENS IN A GAME OF CHESS.
ざわ...
VOOOM
ANY PERSON WITH THE DE- SIRE TO LEARN CAN FEEL THAT BEAUTY...
BAM
IN THEIR HEART.
...

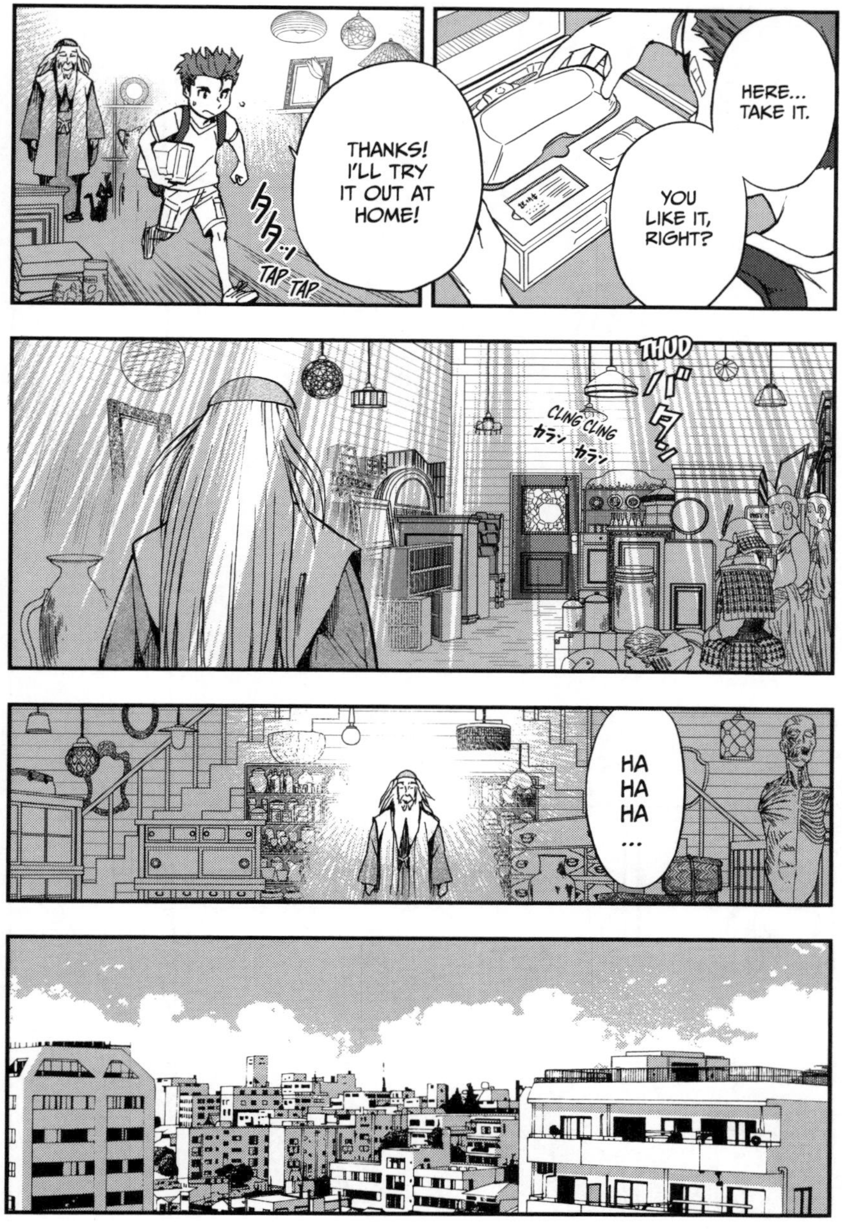
HERE... TAKE IT.
YOU LIKE IT, RIGHT?
THANKS! I'LL TRY IT OUT AT HOME!
タタッ
TAP TAP
THUD
バタン
CLING CLING
カラン
カラン
HA HA HA ...

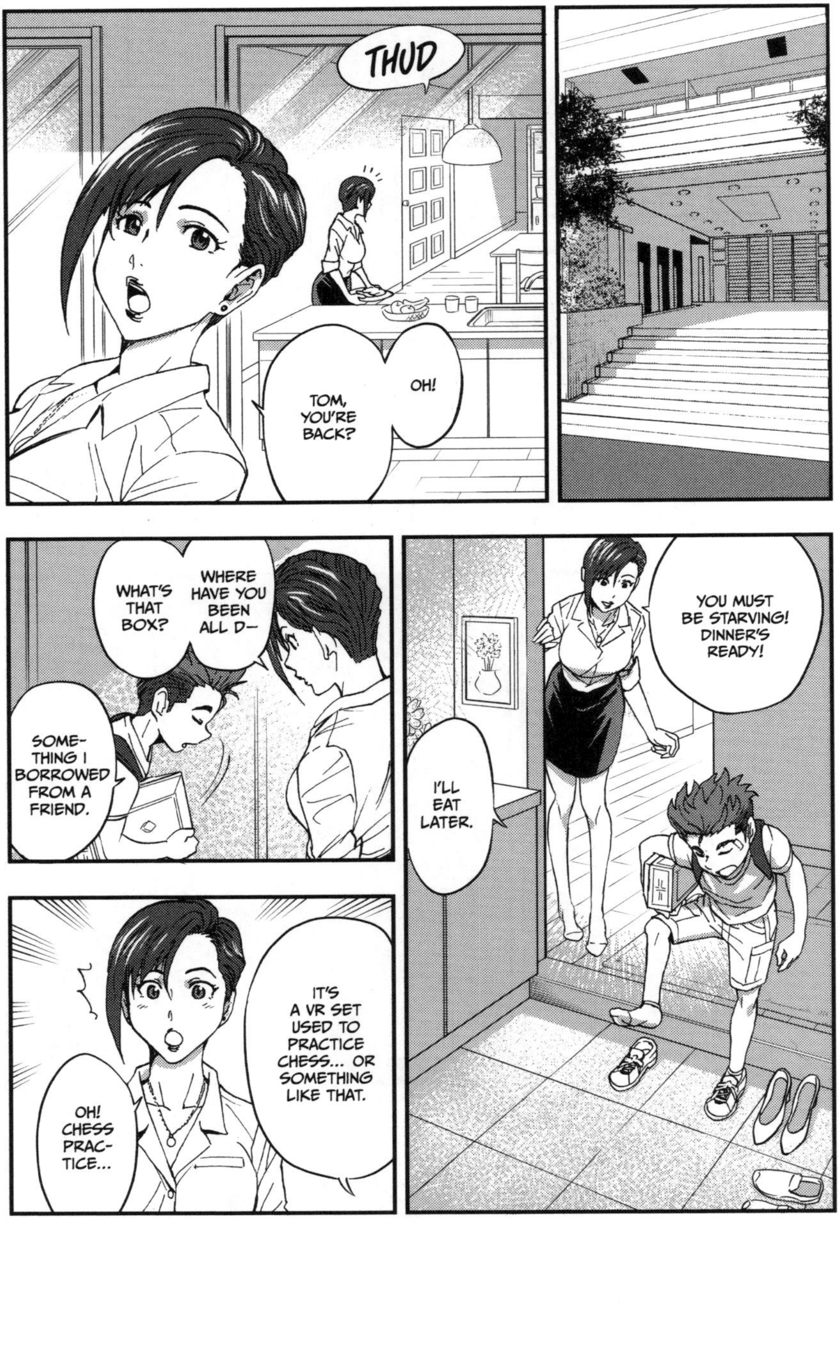
THUD
OH!
TOM, YOU'RE BACK?
YOU MUST BE STARVING! DINNER'S READY!
I'LL EAT LATER.
WHERE HAVE YOU BEEN ALL D—
WHAT'S THAT BOX?
SOME-THING I BORROWED FROM A FRIEND.
IT'S A VR SET USED TO PRACTICE CHESS... OR SOMETHING LIKE THAT.
OH! CHESS PRAC-TICE...

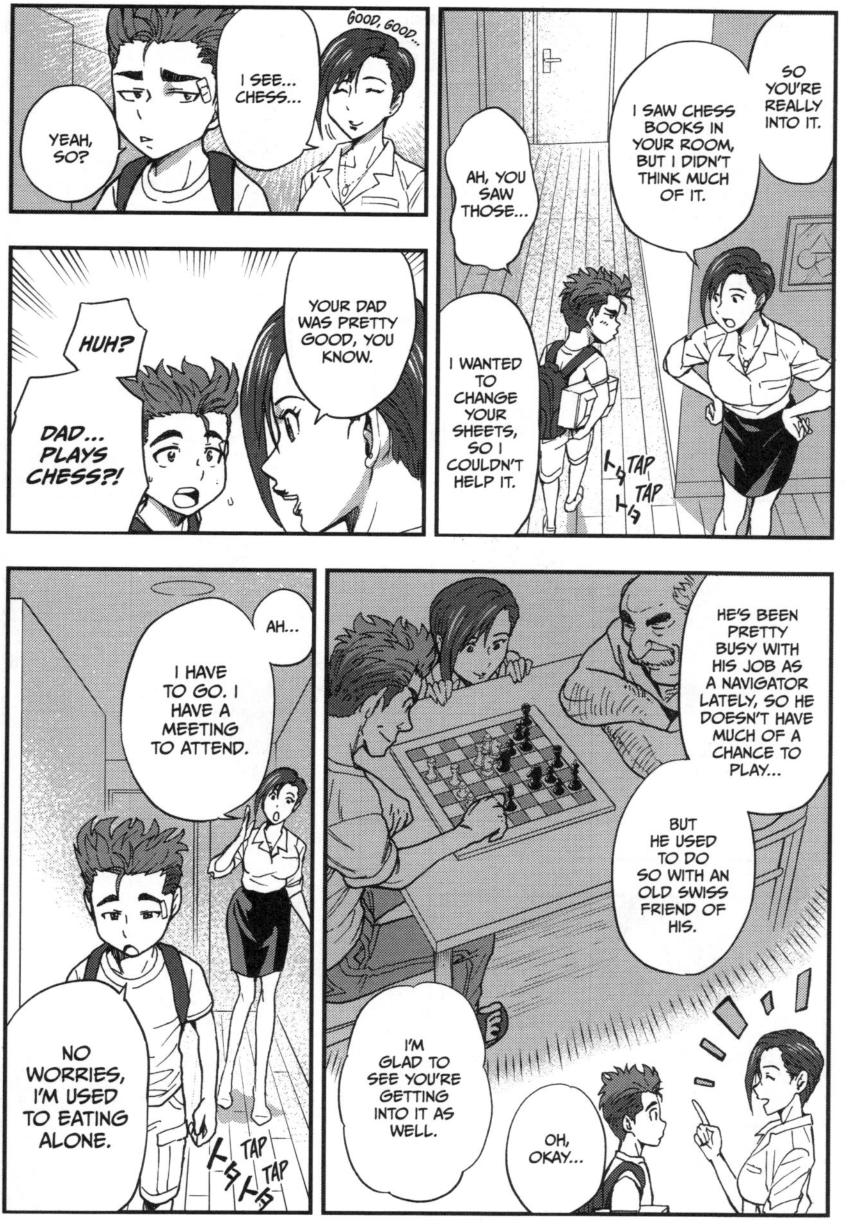
SO YOU'RE REALLY INTO IT.
I SAW CHESS BOOKS IN YOUR ROOM, BUT I DIDN'T THINK MUCH OF IT.
AH, YOU SAW THOSE...
I WANTED TO CHANGE YOUR SHEETS, SO I COULDN'T HELP IT.
TAP TAP
GOOD, GOOD...
I SEE... CHESS...
YEAH, SO?
YOUR DAD WAS PRETTY GOOD, YOU KNOW.
HUH?
DAD... PLAYS CHESS?!
HE'S BEEN PRETTY BUSY WITH HIS JOB AS A NAVIGATOR LATELY, SO HE DOESN'T HAVE MUCH OF A CHANCE TO PLAY...
BUT HE USED TO DO SO WITH AN OLD SWISS FRIEND OF HIS.
I'M GLAD TO SEE YOU'RE GETTING INTO IT AS WELL.
OH, OKAY...
AH...
I HAVE TO GO. I HAVE A MEETING TO ATTEND.
NO WORRIES, I'M USED TO EATING ALONE.
TAP TAP

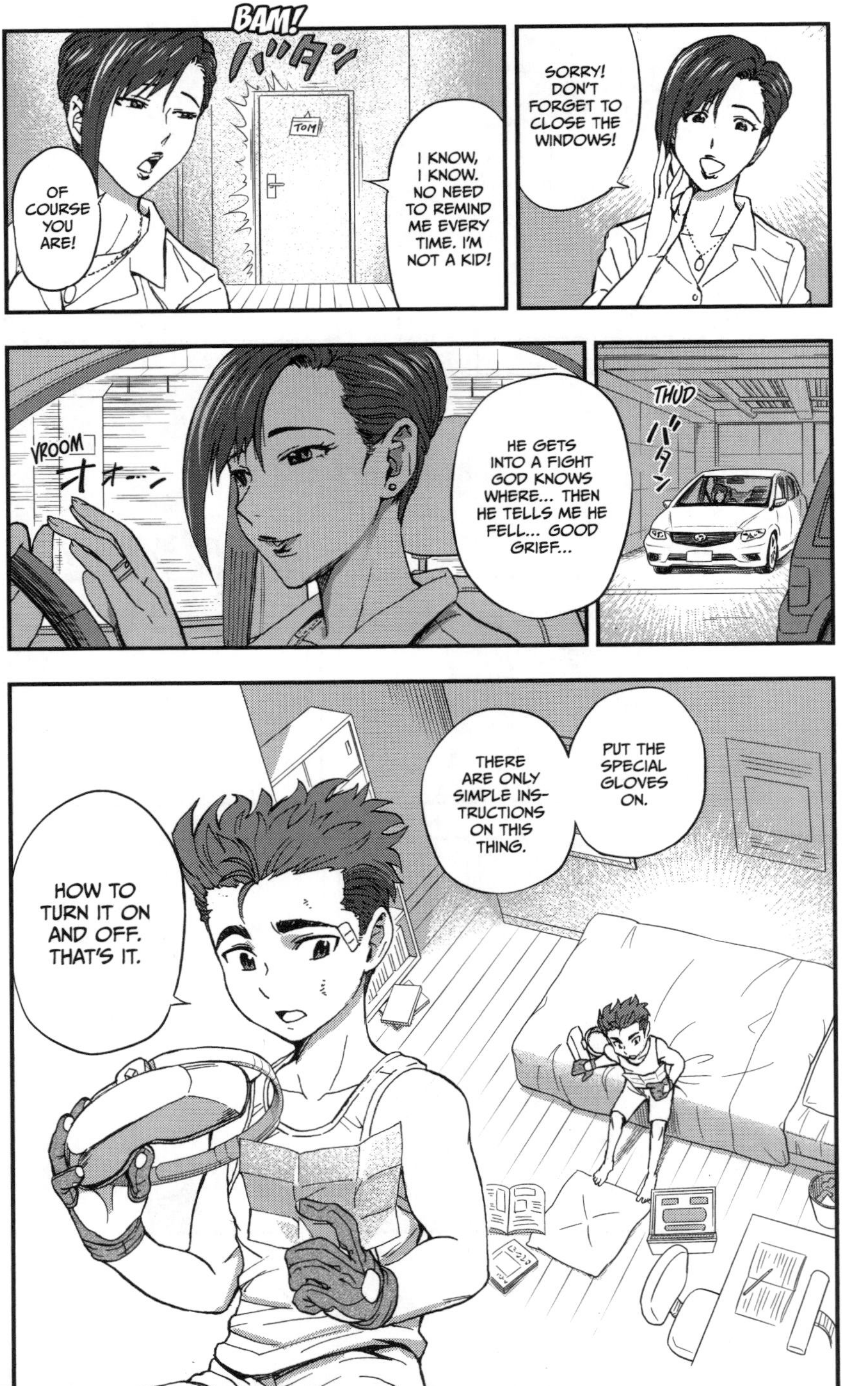
SORRY! DON'T FORGET TO CLOSE THE WINDOWS!
BAM!
バタン
I KNOW, I KNOW. NO NEED TO REMIND ME EVERY TIME. I'M NOT A KID!
TOM
OF COURSE YOU ARE!
THUD
バタン
HE GETS INTO A FIGHT GOD KNOWS WHERE... THEN HE TELLS ME HE FELL... GOOD GRIEF...
VROOM
オォーン
PUT THE SPECIAL GLOVES ON.
THERE ARE ONLY SIMPLE INS-TRUCTIONS ON THIS THING.
HOW TO TURN IT ON AND OFF. THAT'S IT.

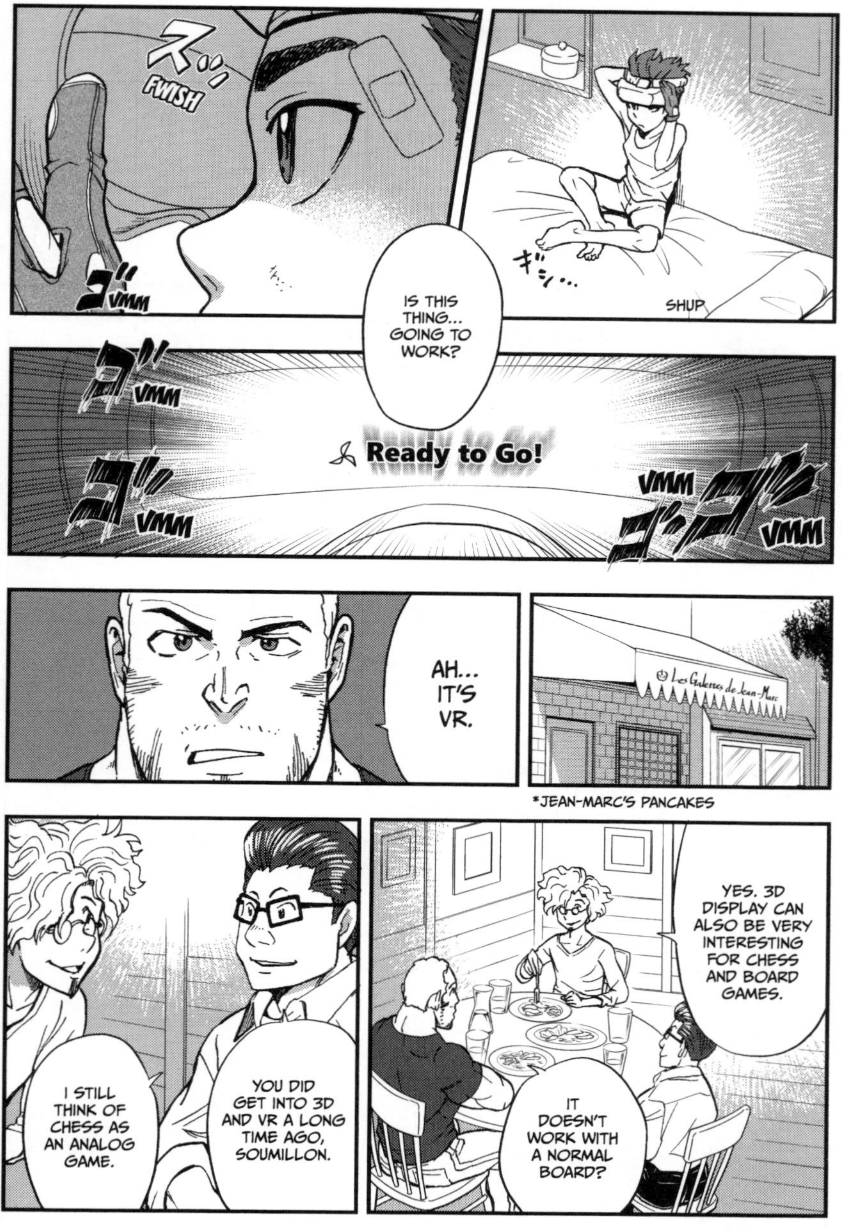
SHUP
IS THIS THING... GOING TO WORK?
FWISH
VMM
Ready to Go!
VMM
VMM
VMM
VMM
Les Galettes de Jean-Marc
AH... IT'S VR.
YES. 3D DISPLAY CAN ALSO BE VERY INTERESTING FOR CHESS AND BOARD GAMES.
IT DOESN'T WORK WITH A NORMAL BOARD?
YOU DID GET INTO 3D AND VR A LONG TIME AGO, SOUMILLON.
I STILL THINK OF CHESS AS AN ANALOG GAME.

*JEAN-MARC'S PANCAKES

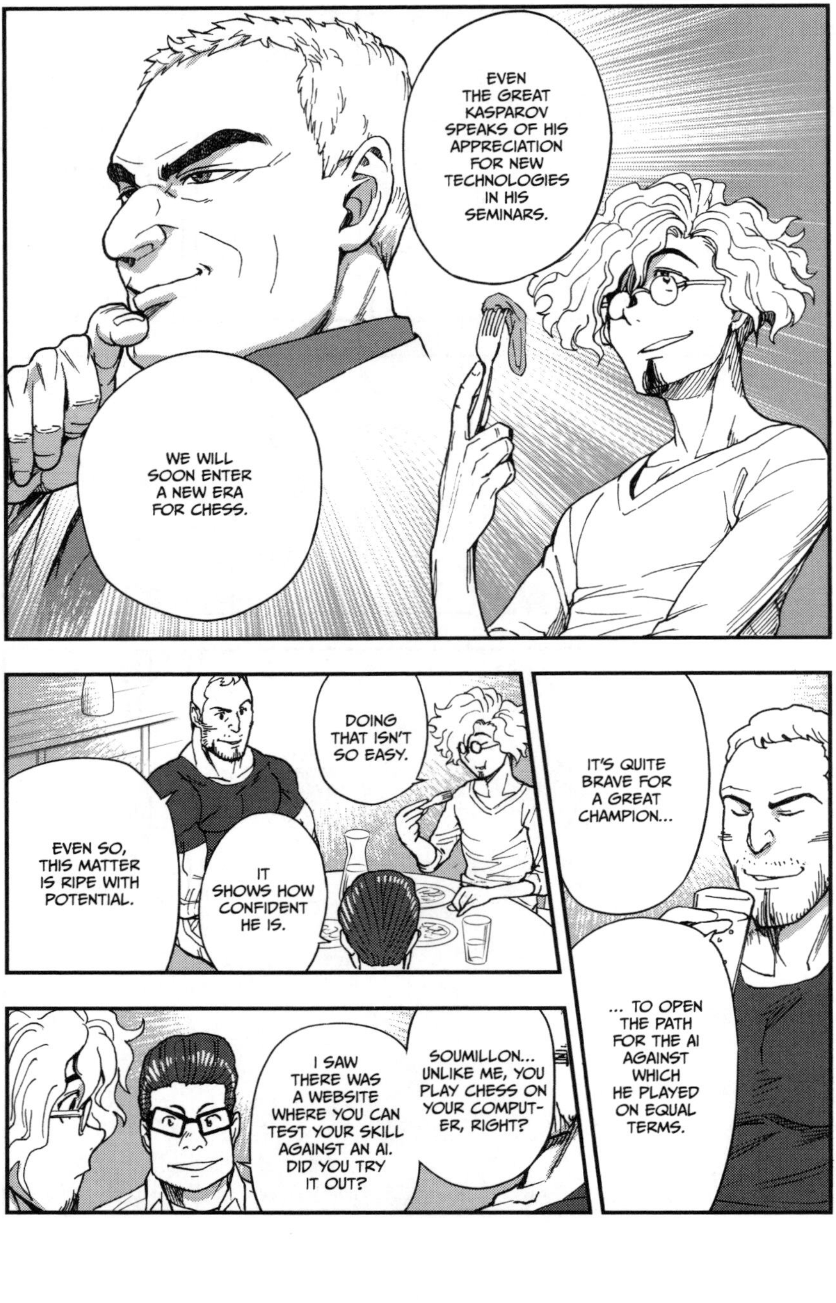
EVEN THE GREAT KASPAROV SPEAKS OF HIS APPRECIATION FOR NEW TECHNOLOGIES IN HIS SEMINARS.
WE WILL SOON ENTER A NEW ERA FOR CHESS.
IT'S QUITE BRAVE FOR A GREAT CHAMPION...
... TO OPEN THE PATH FOR THE AI AGAINST WHICH HE PLAYED ON EQUAL TERMS.
DOING THAT ISN'T SO EASY.
IT SHOWS HOW CONFIDENT HE IS.
EVEN SO, THIS MATTER IS RIPE WITH POTENTIAL.
SOUMILLON... UNLIKE ME, YOU PLAY CHESS ON YOUR COMPUTER, RIGHT?
I SAW THERE WAS A WEBSITE WHERE YOU CAN TEST YOUR SKILL AGAINST AN AI. DID YOU TRY IT OUT?

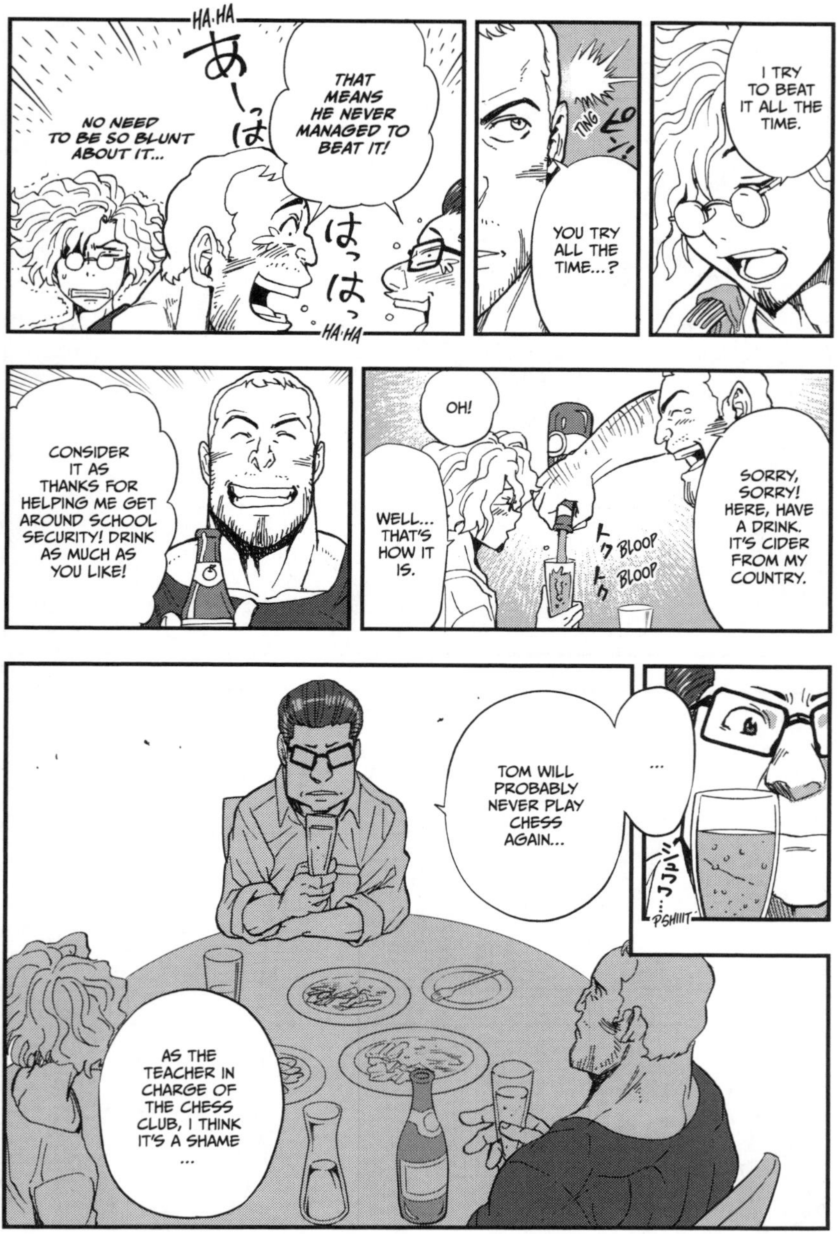
I TRY TO BEAT IT ALL THE TIME.
TING
YOU TRY ALL THE TIME...?
HA HA
THAT MEANS HE NEVER MANAGED TO BEAT IT!
NO NEED TO BE SO BLUNT ABOUT IT...
HA HA
OH!
SORRY, SORRY! HERE, HAVE A DRINK. IT'S CIDER FROM MY COUNTRY.
BLOOP BLOOP
WELL... THAT'S HOW IT IS.
CONSIDER IT AS THANKS FOR HELPING ME GET AROUND SCHOOL SECURITY! DRINK AS MUCH AS YOU LIKE!
...
...PSHIIIT
TOM WILL PROBABLY NEVER PLAY CHESS AGAIN...
AS THE TEACHER IN CHARGE OF THE CHESS CLUB, I THINK IT'S A SHAME ...

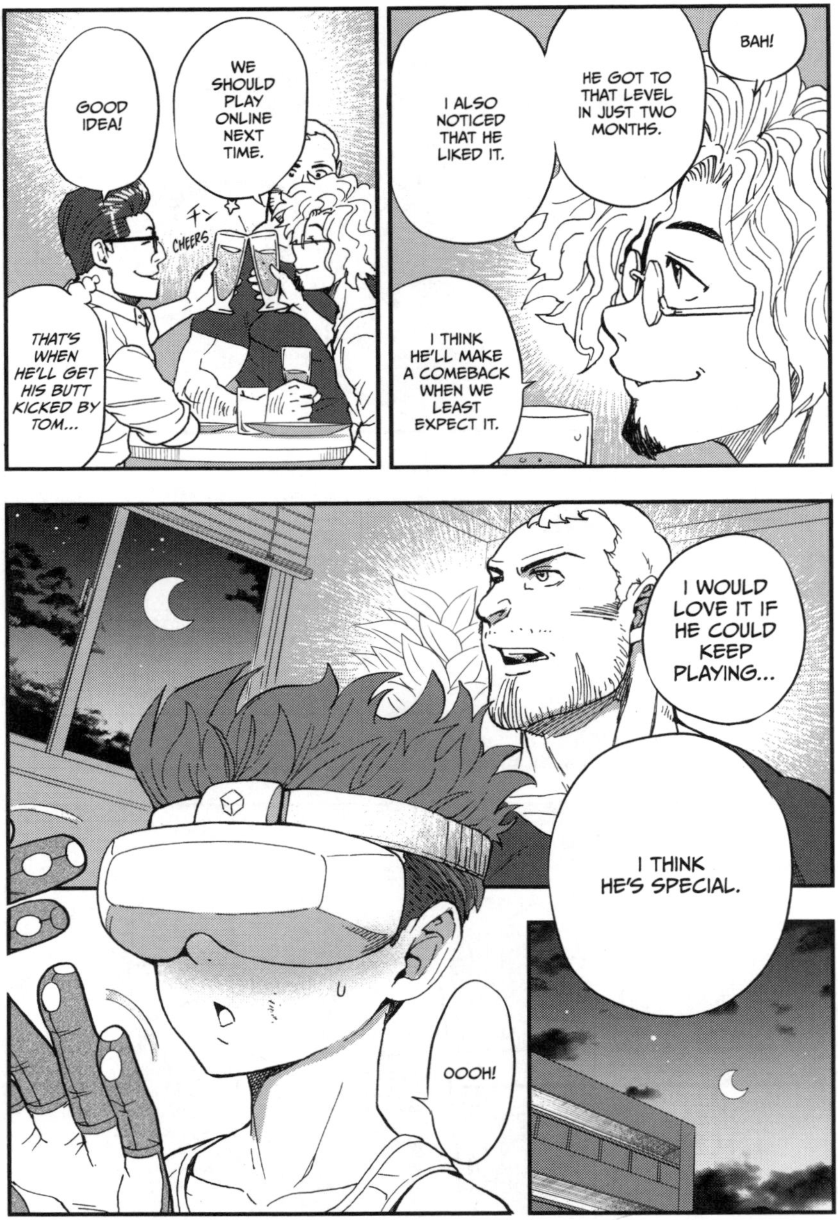
BAH!
HE GOT TO THAT LEVEL IN JUST TWO MONTHS.
I ALSO NOTICED THAT HE LIKED IT.
I THINK HE'LL MAKE A COMEBACK WHEN WE LEAST EXPECT IT.
WE SHOULD PLAY ONLINE NEXT TIME.
GOOD IDEA!
チン
CHEERS
THAT'S WHEN HE'LL GET HIS BUTT KICKED BY TOM...
I WOULD LOVE IT IF HE COULD KEEP PLAYING...
I THINK HE'S SPECIAL.
OOOH!

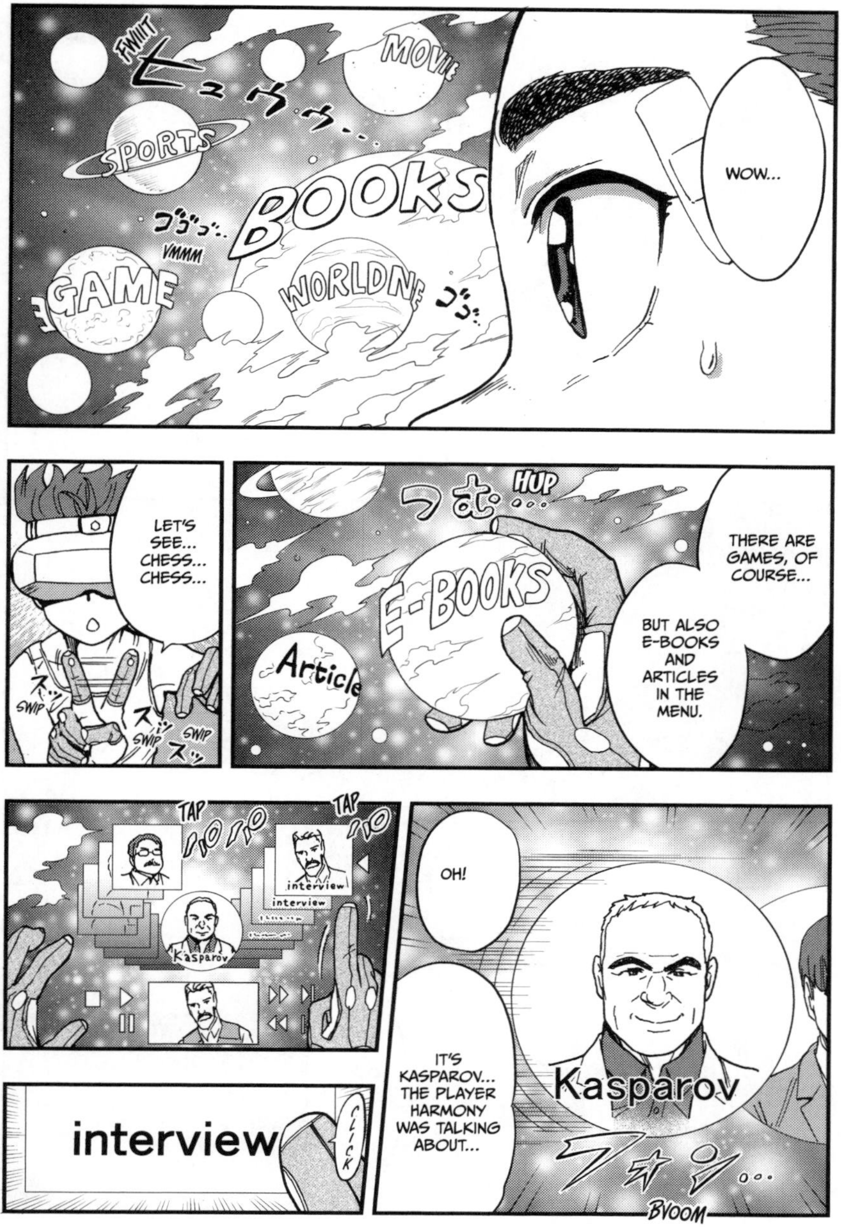
WOW...
MOVIE
FWIIIT
SPORTS
BOOKS
VMMM
GAME
WORLDNE
THERE ARE GAMES, OF COURSE...
BUT ALSO E-BOOKS AND ARTICLES IN THE MENU.
HUP
E-BOOKS
Article
LET'S SEE... CHESS... CHESS...
SWIP
SWIP
SWIP
OH!
IT'S KASPAROV... THE PLAYER HARMONY WAS TALKING ABOUT...
Kasparov
BVOOM
TAP
TAP
interview
interview
Kasparov
interview
CLICK

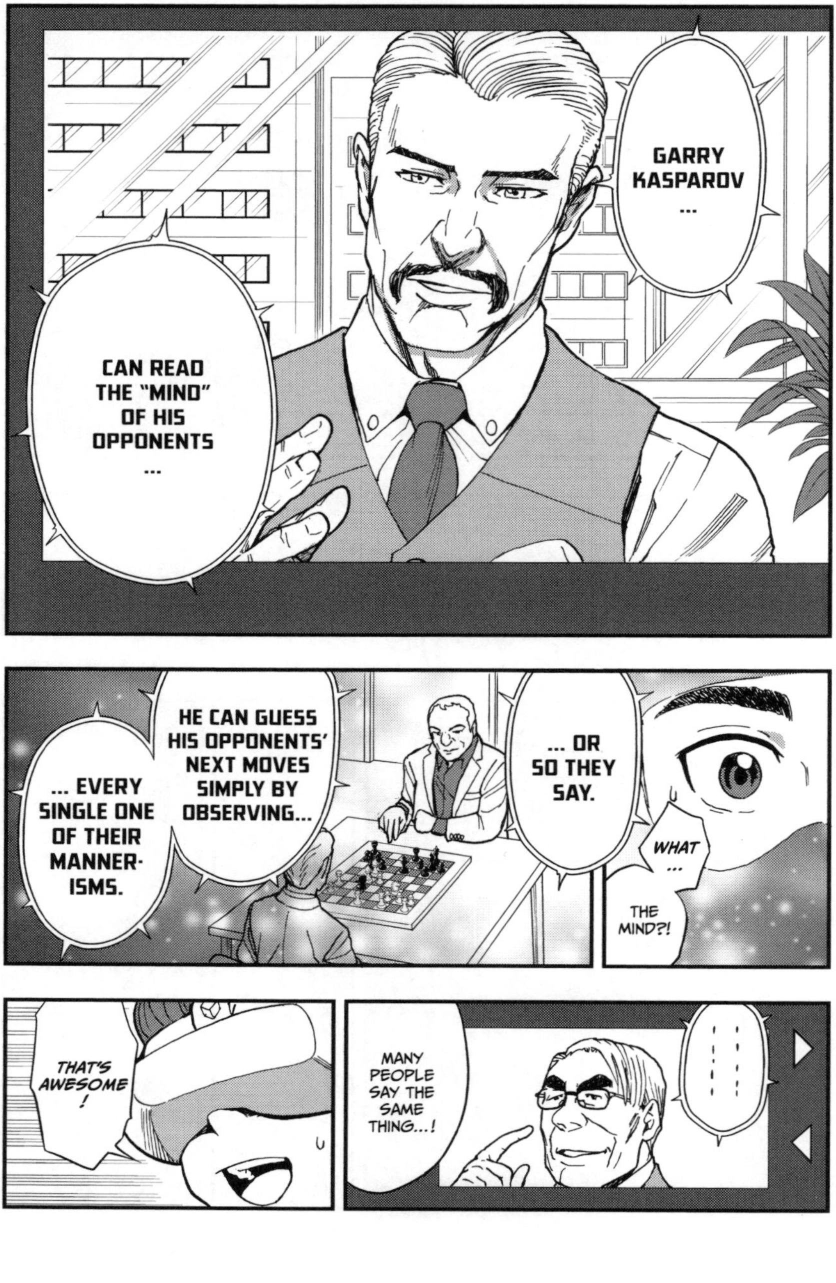
GARRY KASPAROV ...
CAN READ THE "MIND" OF HIS OPPONENTS ...
WHAT ...
THE MIND?!
... OR SO THEY SAY.
HE CAN GUESS HIS OPPONENTS' NEXT MOVES SIMPLY BY OBSERVING...
... EVERY SINGLE ONE OF THEIR MANNER-ISMS.
......
MANY PEOPLE SAY THE SAME THING...!
THAT'S AWESOME!

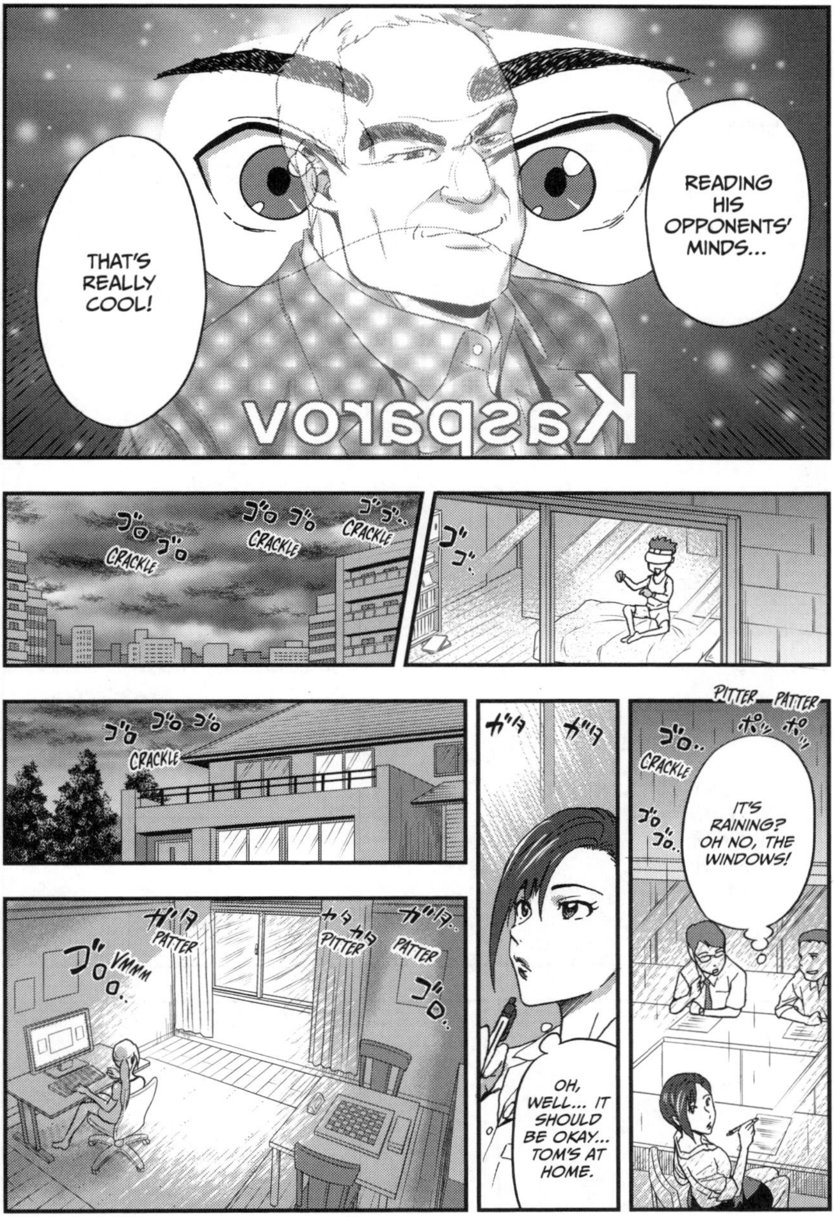
READING HIS OPPONENTS' MINDS...
THAT'S REALLY COOL!
Kasparov
ゴゴ...
ゴロ ゴロ CRACKLE
ゴロ ゴロ CRACKLE
ゴゴ... CRACKLE
PITTER PATTER
ポツ ポツ
ゴロ.. CRACKLE
IT'S RAINING? OH NO, THE WINDOWS!
ゴロゴロ..
ガタ ガタ
OH, WELL... IT SHOULD BE OKAY... TOM'S AT HOME.
ゴロ ゴロ ゴロ CRACKLE
ガタ.. PATTER
カタ カタ PITTER
ガタ PATTER
ゴロ..
VMMM
ゴロロ..

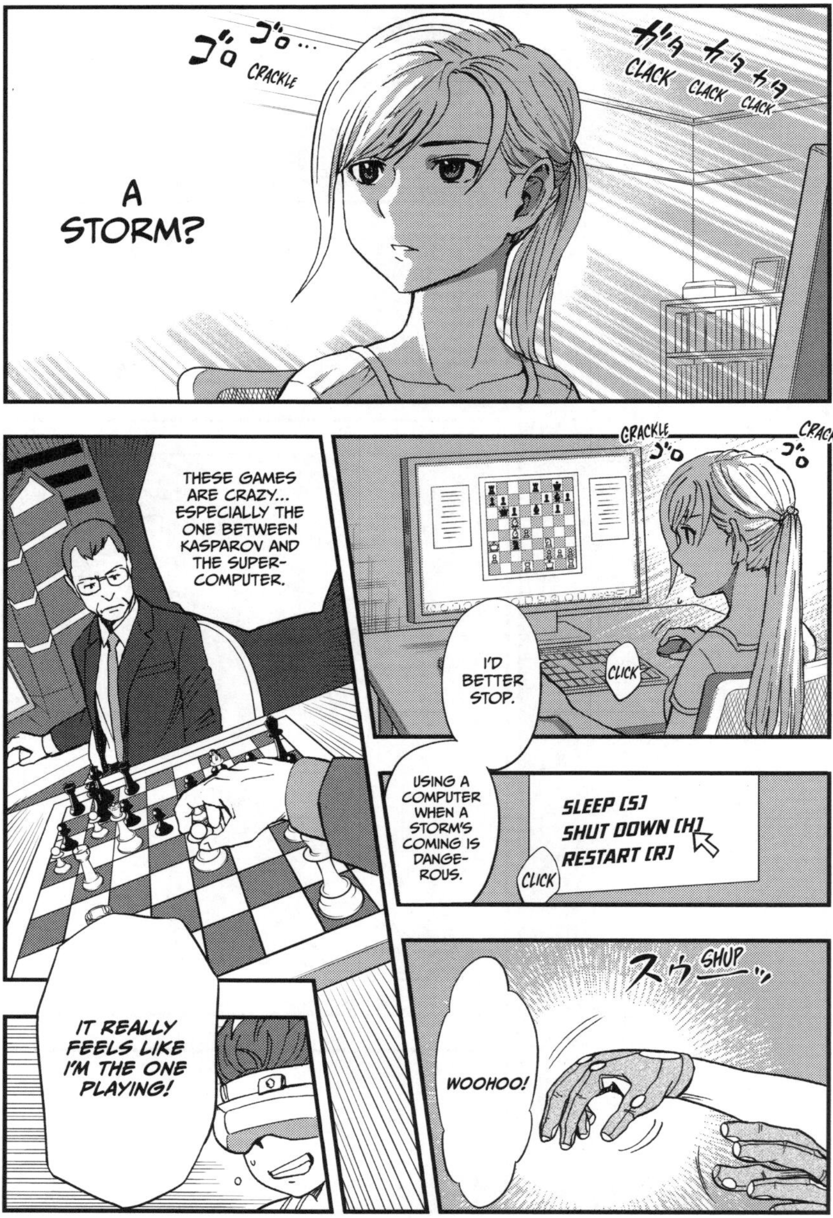
ガタ カタカタ
CLACK CLACK CLACK
ゴロ ゴロ…
CRACKLE
A STORM?
CRACKLE
ゴロ
CRACKLE
ゴロ
I'D BETTER STOP.
CLICK
USING A COMPUTER WHEN A STORM'S COMING IS DANGE-ROUS.
SLEEP [S]
SHUT DOWN [H]
RESTART [R]
CLICK
スウー
SHUP
WOOHOO!
THESE GAMES ARE CRAZY... ESPECIALLY THE ONE BETWEEN KASPAROV AND THE SUPER-COMPUTER.
IT REALLY FEELS LIKE I'M THE ONE PLAYING!

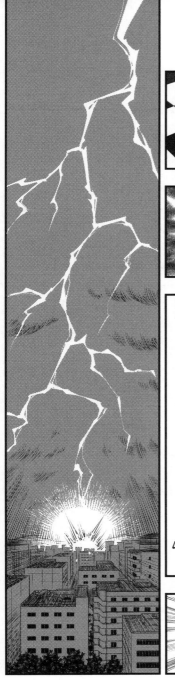

THE MORE OF HIS MATCHES I WATCH...

... THE MORE I UNDERSTAND HOW GREAT HE IS...

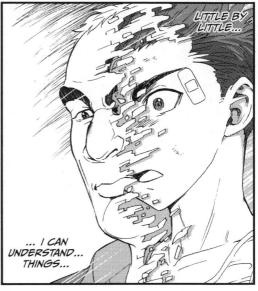

LITTLE BY LITTLE...

... I CAN UNDERSTAND... THINGS...

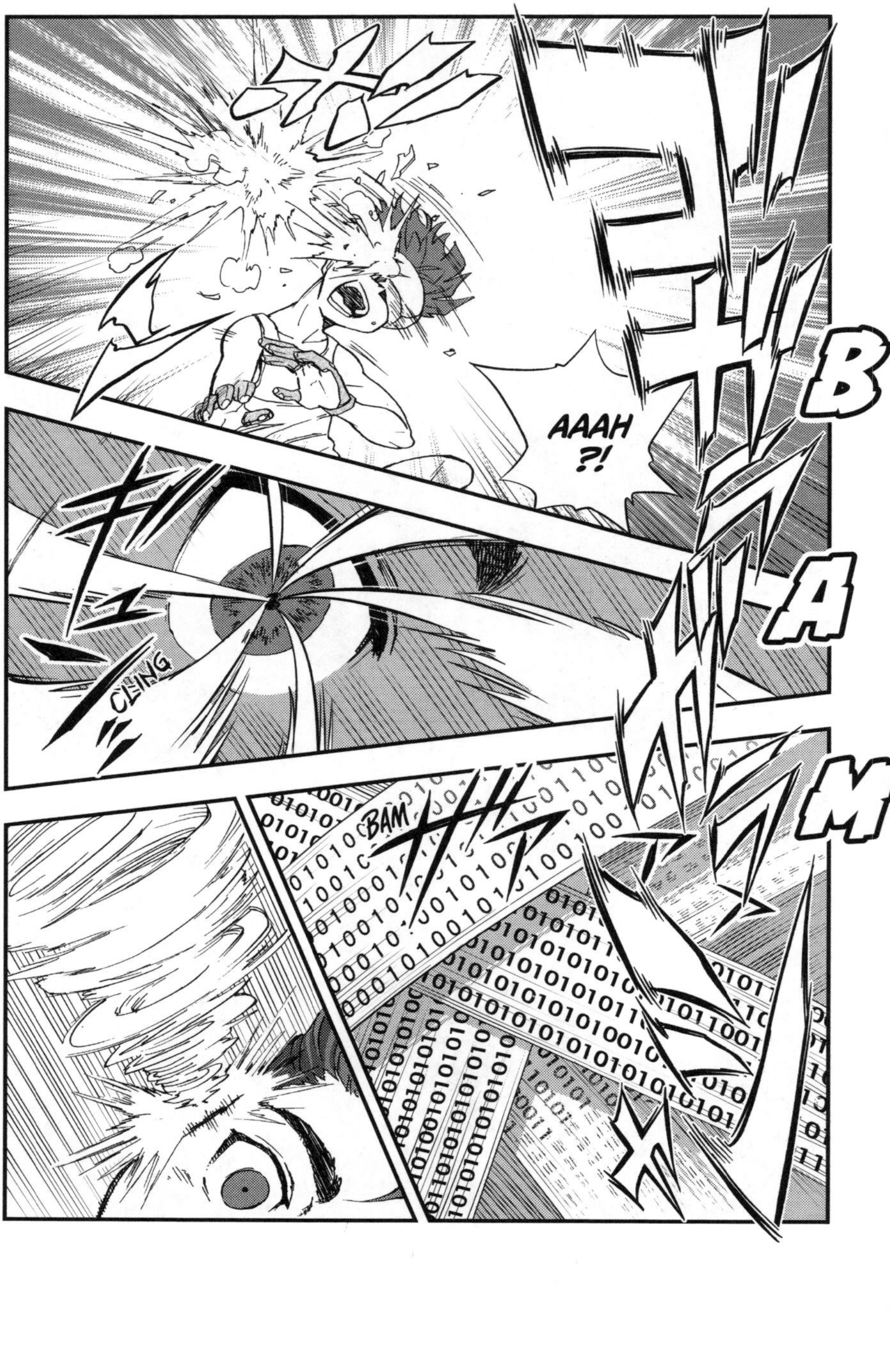
BAM
AAAH ?!
CLING
BAM

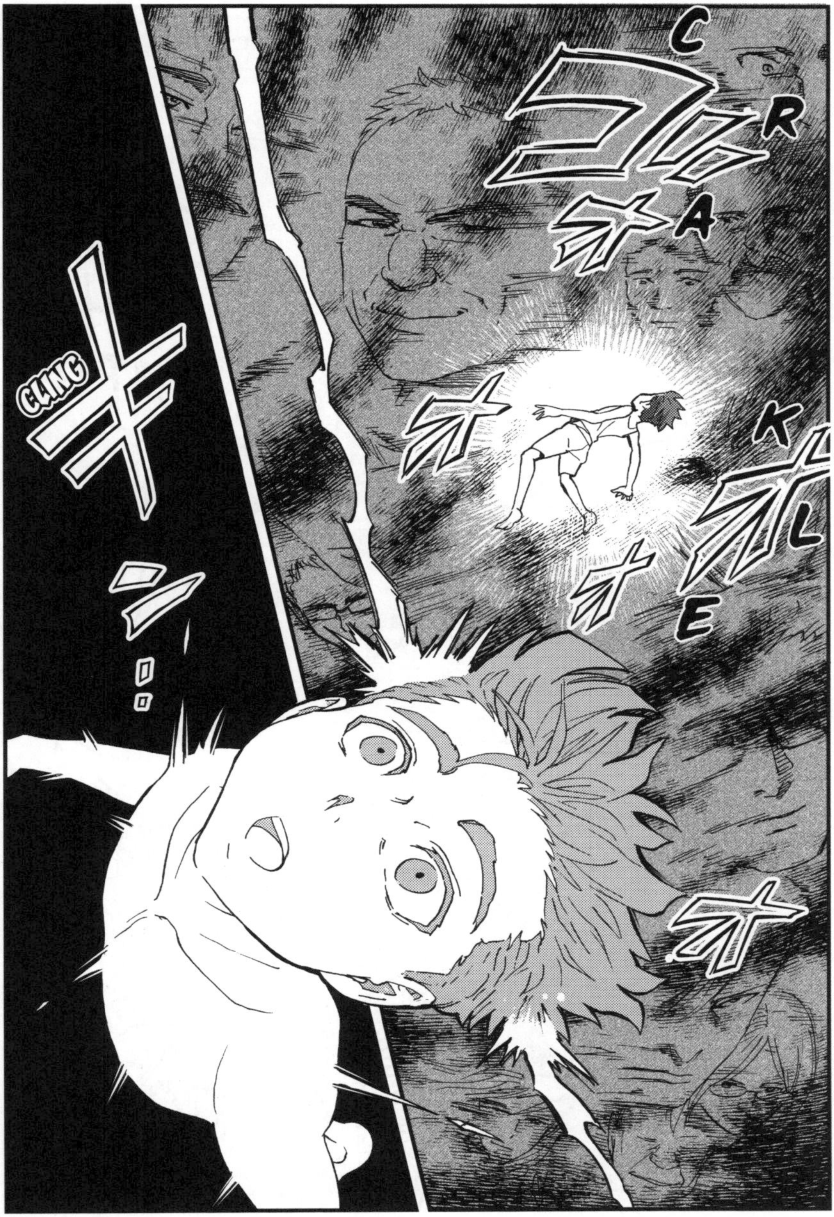
C R A K L E
CLING

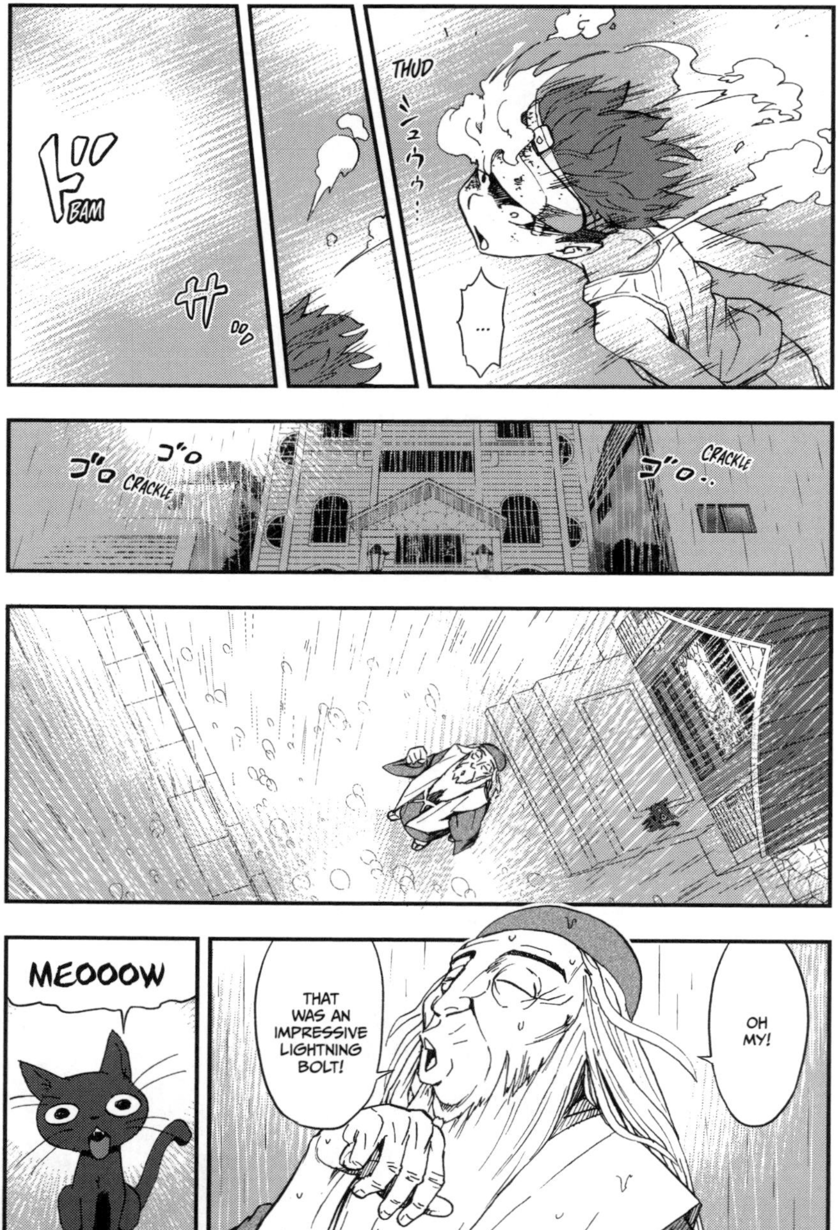
THUD
シュウゥ…
…
ドッ
BAM
サッ
CRACKLE
ゴロ…
ゴロ
ゴロ
CRACKLE
OH MY!
THAT WAS AN IMPRESSIVE LIGHTNING BOLT!
MEOOOW

BLITZ

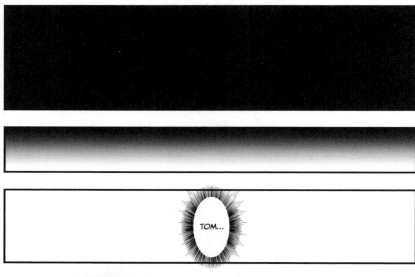

TOM...

TOM
!

!!!
!!!

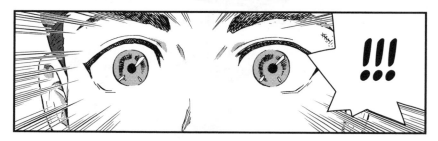

Chapter 6: Pawn 2.0

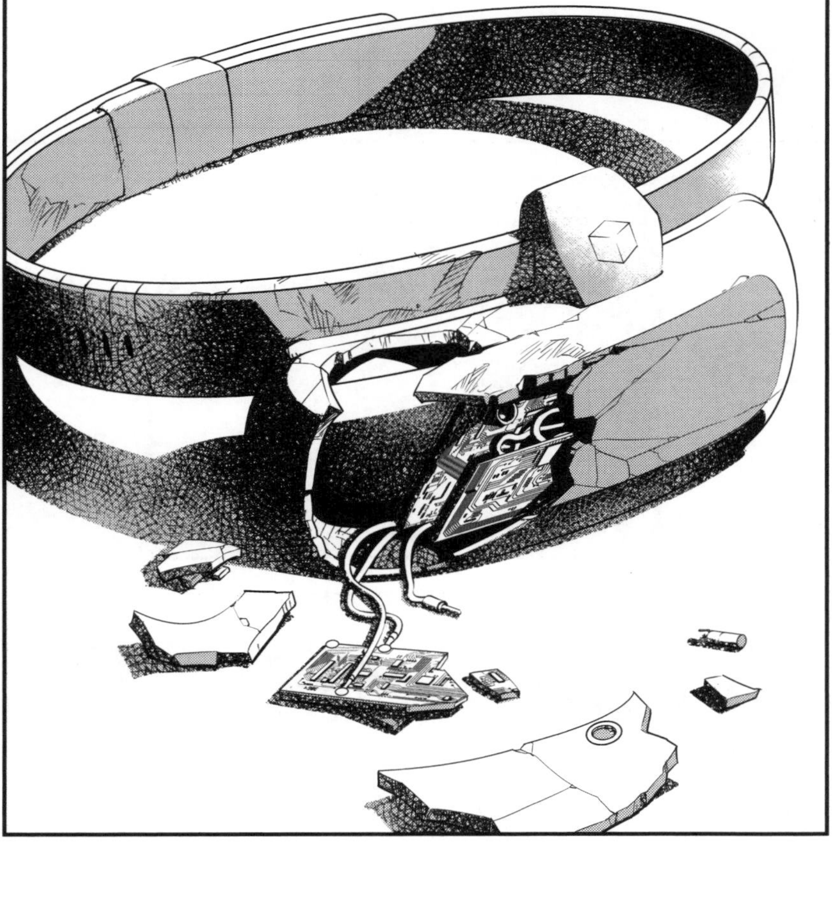

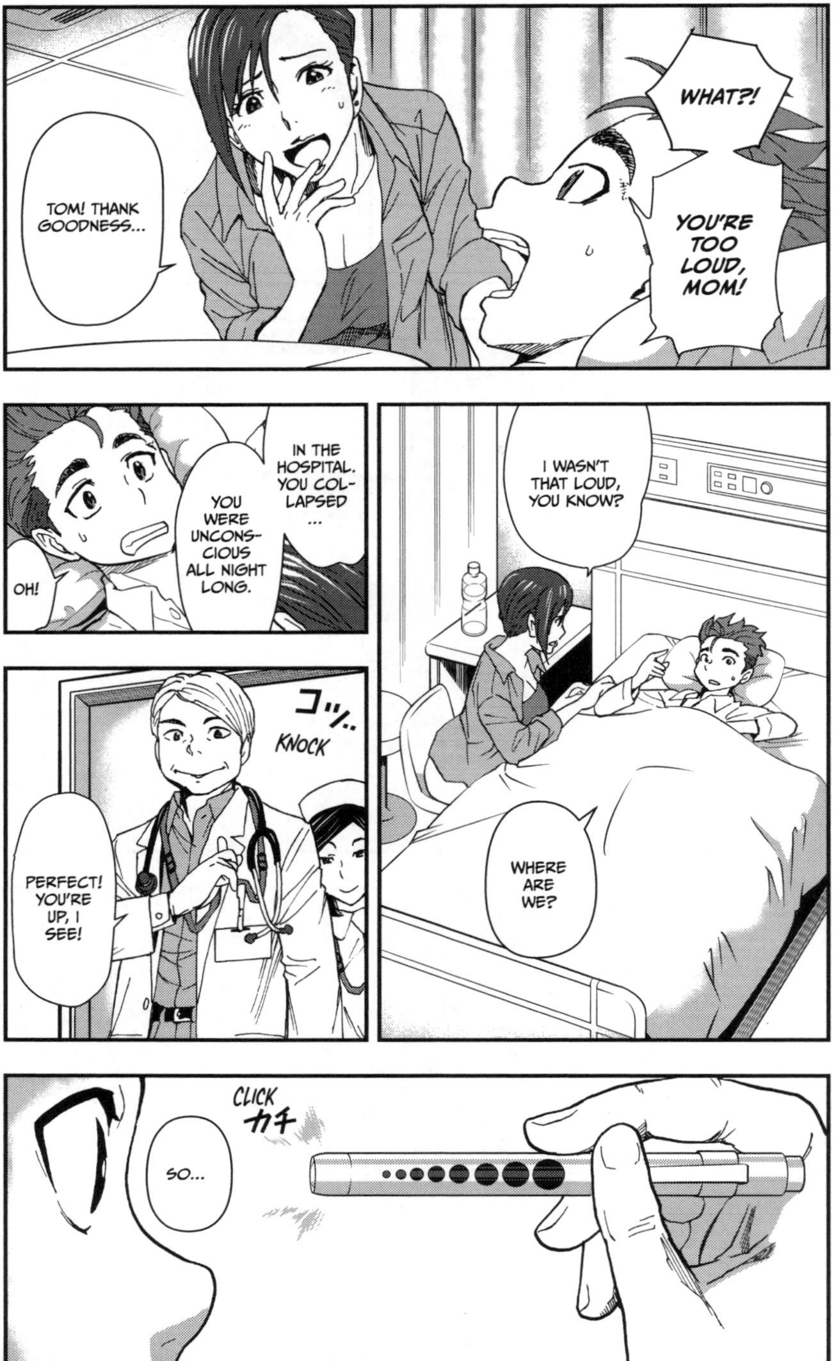
WHAT?!
YOU'RE TOO LOUD, MOM!
TOM! THANK GOODNESS...
I WASN'T THAT LOUD, YOU KNOW?
WHERE ARE WE?
IN THE HOSPITAL. YOU COLLAPSED ...
YOU WERE UNCONSCIOUS ALL NIGHT LONG.
OH!
コッ..
KNOCK
PERFECT! YOU'RE UP, I SEE!
CLICK
カチ
SO...

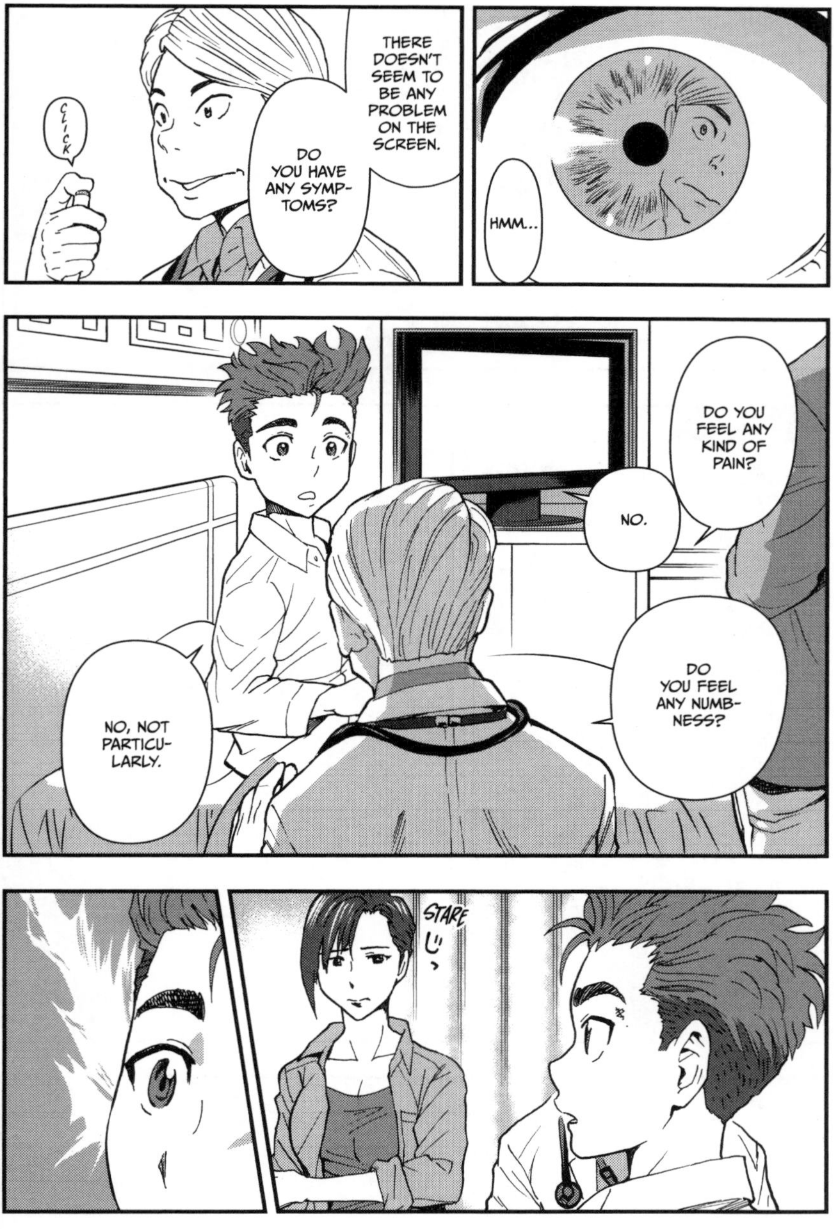
HMM...
THERE DOESN'T SEEM TO BE ANY PROBLEM ON THE SCREEN.
DO YOU HAVE ANY SYMP-TOMS?
CLICK
DO YOU FEEL ANY KIND OF PAIN?
NO.
DO YOU FEEL ANY NUMB-NESS?
NO, NOT PARTICU-LARLY.
STARE
じっ

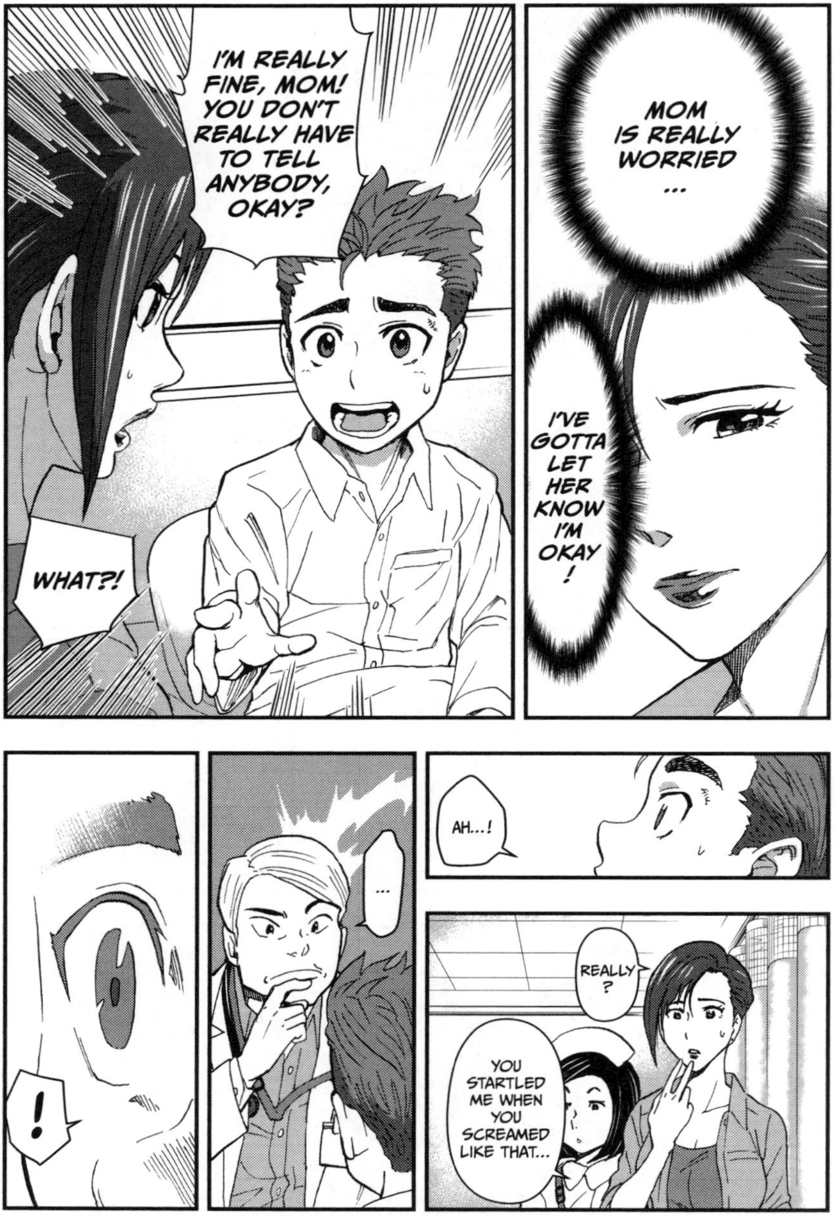
MOM IS REALLY WORRIED ...
I'VE GOTTA LET HER KNOW I'M OKAY!
I'M REALLY FINE, MOM! YOU DON'T REALLY HAVE TO TELL ANYBODY, OKAY?
WHAT?!
AH...!
REALLY?
YOU STARTLED ME WHEN YOU SCREAMED LIKE THAT...
...
!

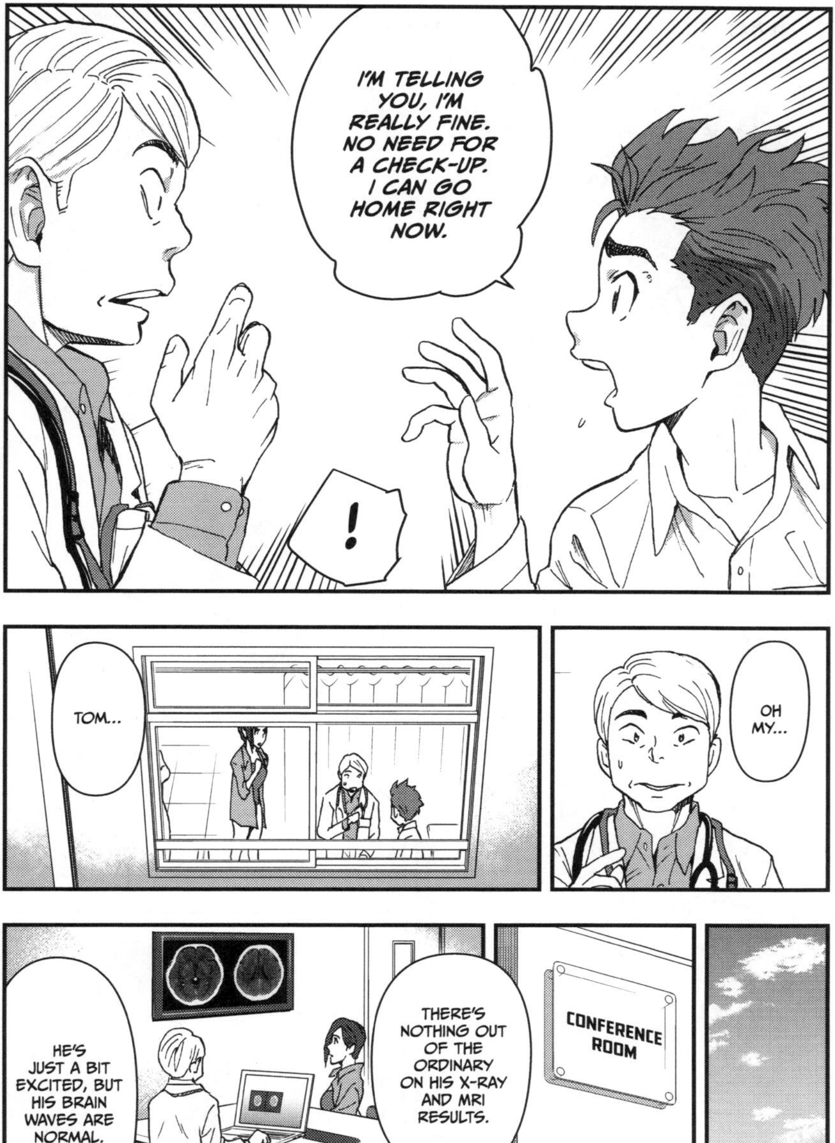
I'M TELLING YOU, I'M REALLY FINE. NO NEED FOR A CHECK-UP. I CAN GO HOME RIGHT NOW.
!
OH MY...
TOM...
CONFERENCE ROOM
THERE'S NOTHING OUT OF THE ORDINARY ON HIS X-RAY AND MRI RESULTS.
HE'S JUST A BIT EXCITED, BUT HIS BRAIN WAVES ARE NORMAL.

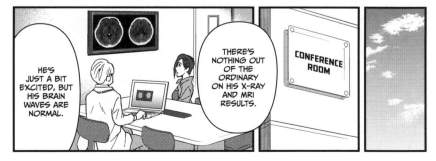

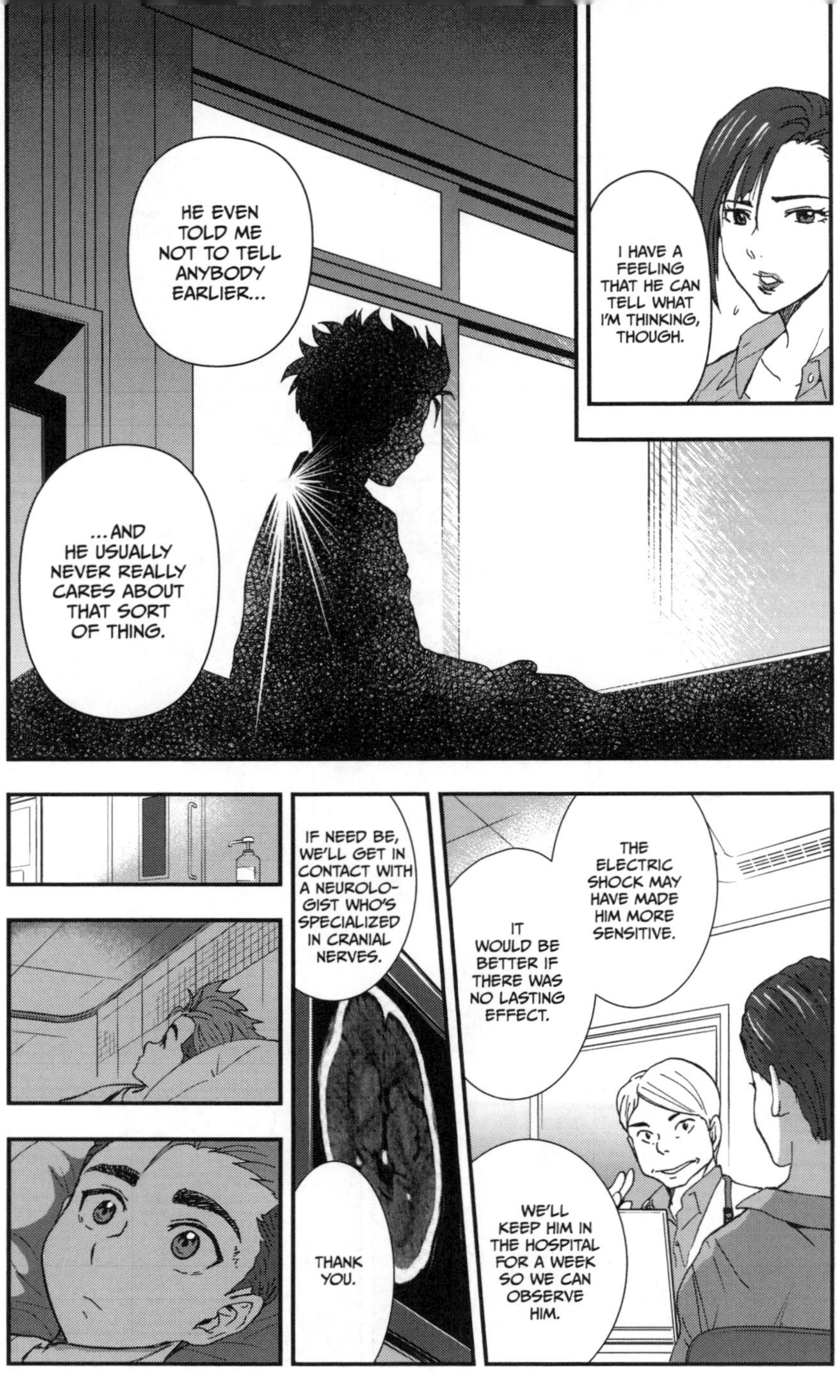
I HAVE A FEELING THAT HE CAN TELL WHAT I'M THINKING, THOUGH.
HE EVEN TOLD ME NOT TO TELL ANYBODY EARLIER...
...AND HE USUALLY NEVER REALLY CARES ABOUT THAT SORT OF THING.
THE ELECTRIC SHOCK MAY HAVE MADE HIM MORE SENSITIVE.
IT WOULD BE BETTER IF THERE WAS NO LASTING EFFECT.
WE'LL KEEP HIM IN THE HOSPITAL FOR A WEEK SO WE CAN OBSERVE HIM.
IF NEED BE, WE'LL GET IN CONTACT WITH A NEUROLO-GIST WHO'S SPECIALIZED IN CRANIAL NERVES.
THANK YOU.

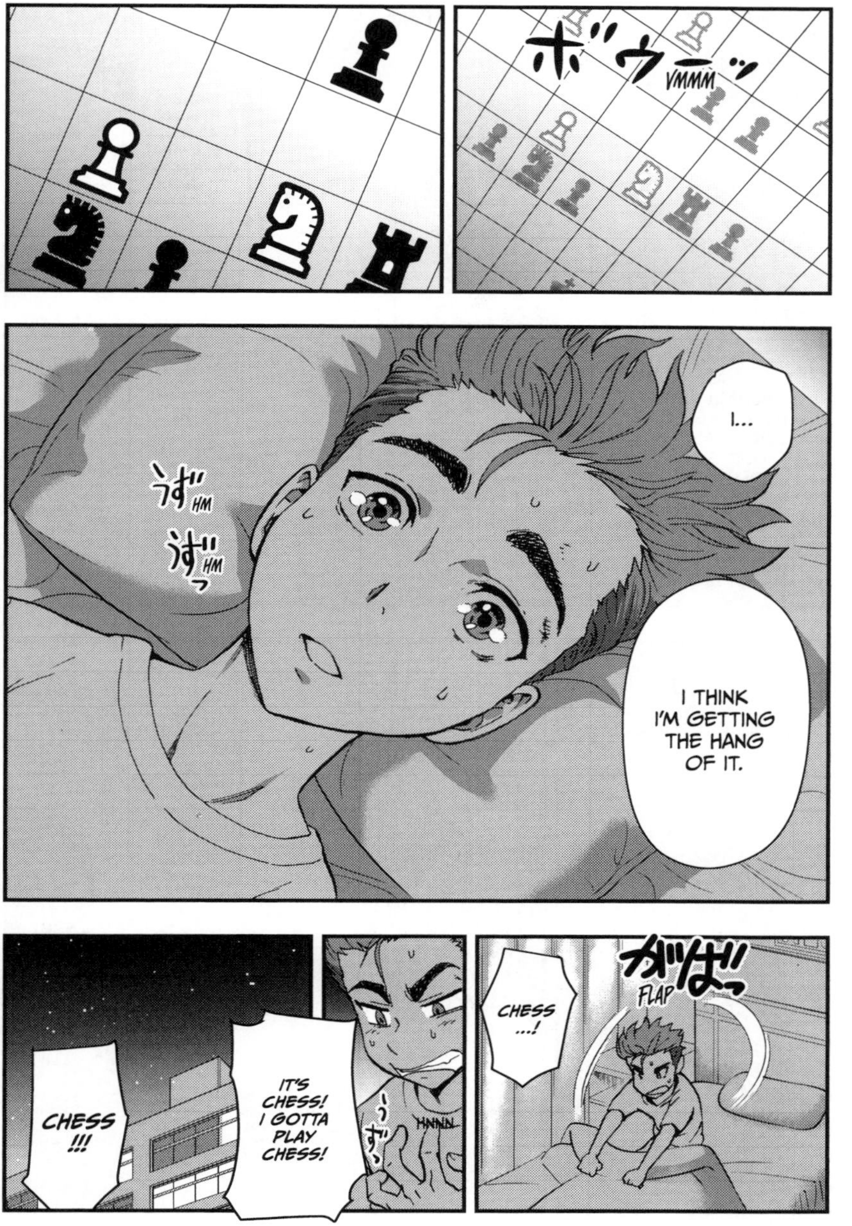
ボウーッ
VMMM
I...
うず HM
うずっ HM
I THINK I'M GETTING THE HANG OF IT.
ガばっ
FLAP
CHESS ...!
IT'S CHESS! I GOTTA PLAY CHESS!
うずっ
HNNN
CHESS !!!

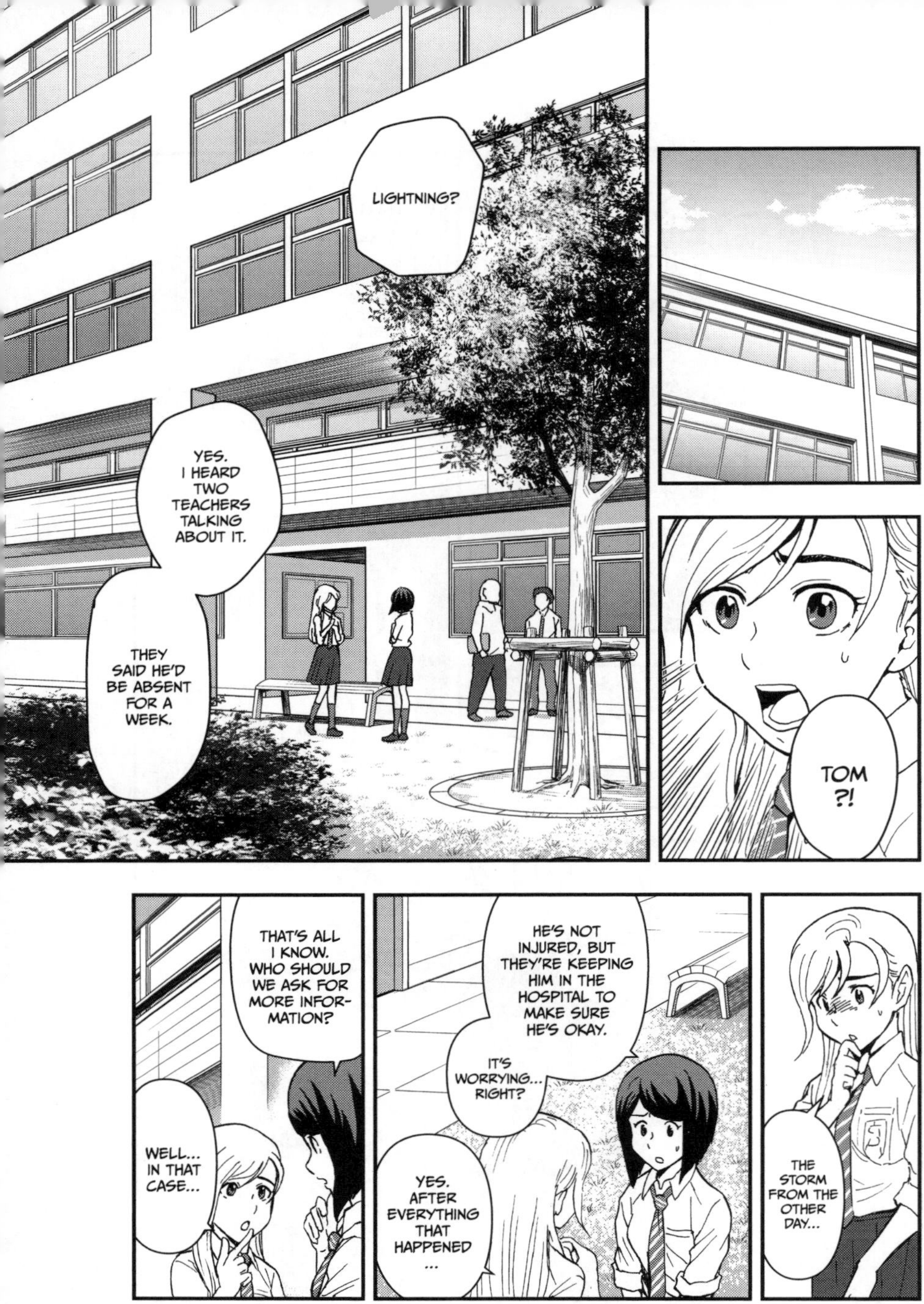
TOM ?!
LIGHTNING?
YES. I HEARD TWO TEACHERS TALKING ABOUT IT.
THEY SAID HE'D BE ABSENT FOR A WEEK.
THE STORM FROM THE OTHER DAY...
HE'S NOT INJURED, BUT THEY'RE KEEPING HIM IN THE HOSPITAL TO MAKE SURE HE'S OKAY.
IT'S WORRYING... RIGHT?
YES. AFTER EVERYTHING THAT HAPPENED ...
THAT'S ALL I KNOW. WHO SHOULD WE ASK FOR MORE INFOR-MATION?
WELL... IN THAT CASE...

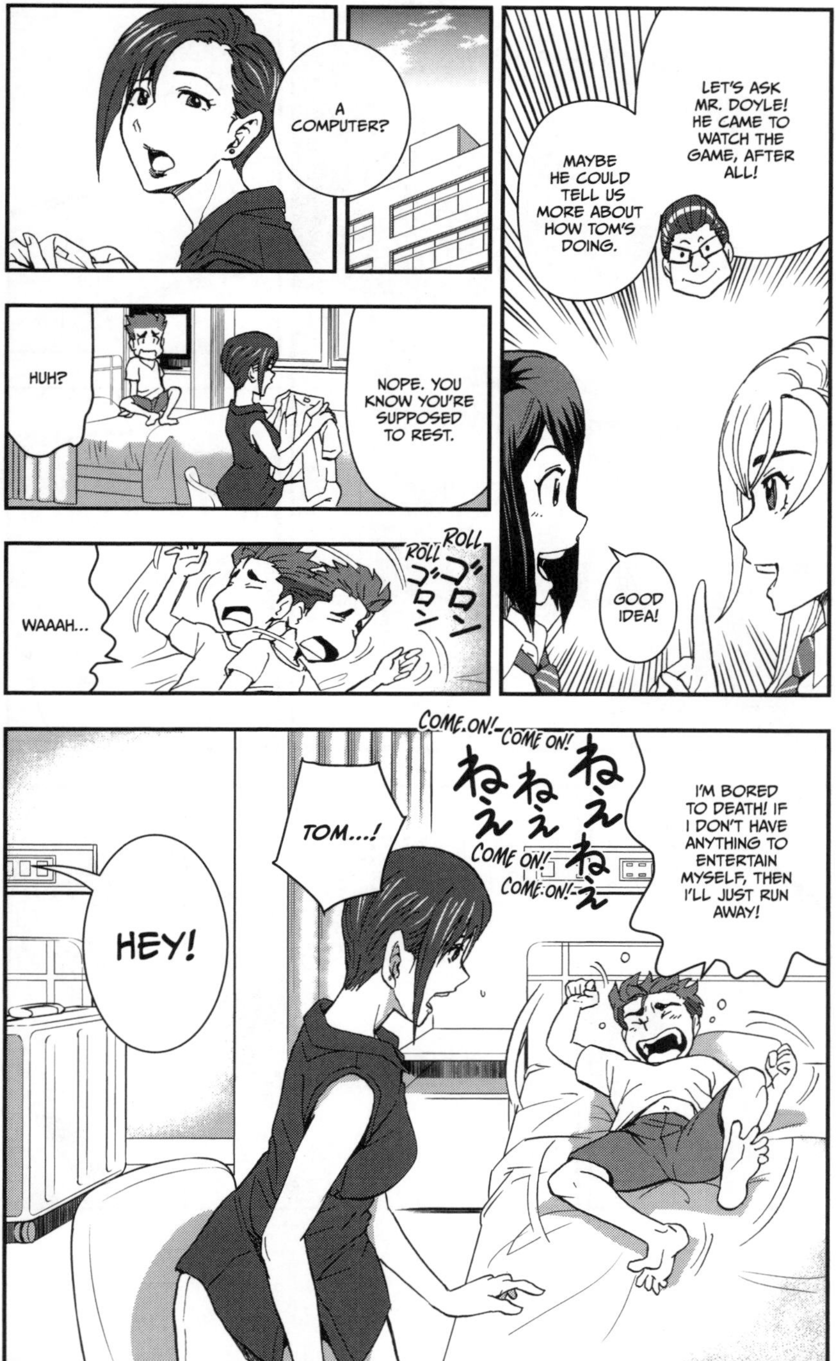
LET'S ASK MR. DOYLE! HE CAME TO WATCH THE GAME, AFTER ALL!
MAYBE HE COULD TELL US MORE ABOUT HOW TOM'S DOING.
GOOD IDEA!
A COMPUTER?
NOPE. YOU KNOW YOU'RE SUPPOSED TO REST.
HUH?
ROLL ROLL
ゴロンゴロン
WAAAH...
COME ON! COME ON! COME ON! COME ON!
ねえねえねえねえ
I'M BORED TO DEATH! IF I DON'T HAVE ANYTHING TO ENTERTAIN MYSELF, THEN I'LL JUST RUN AWAY!
TOM...!
HEY!

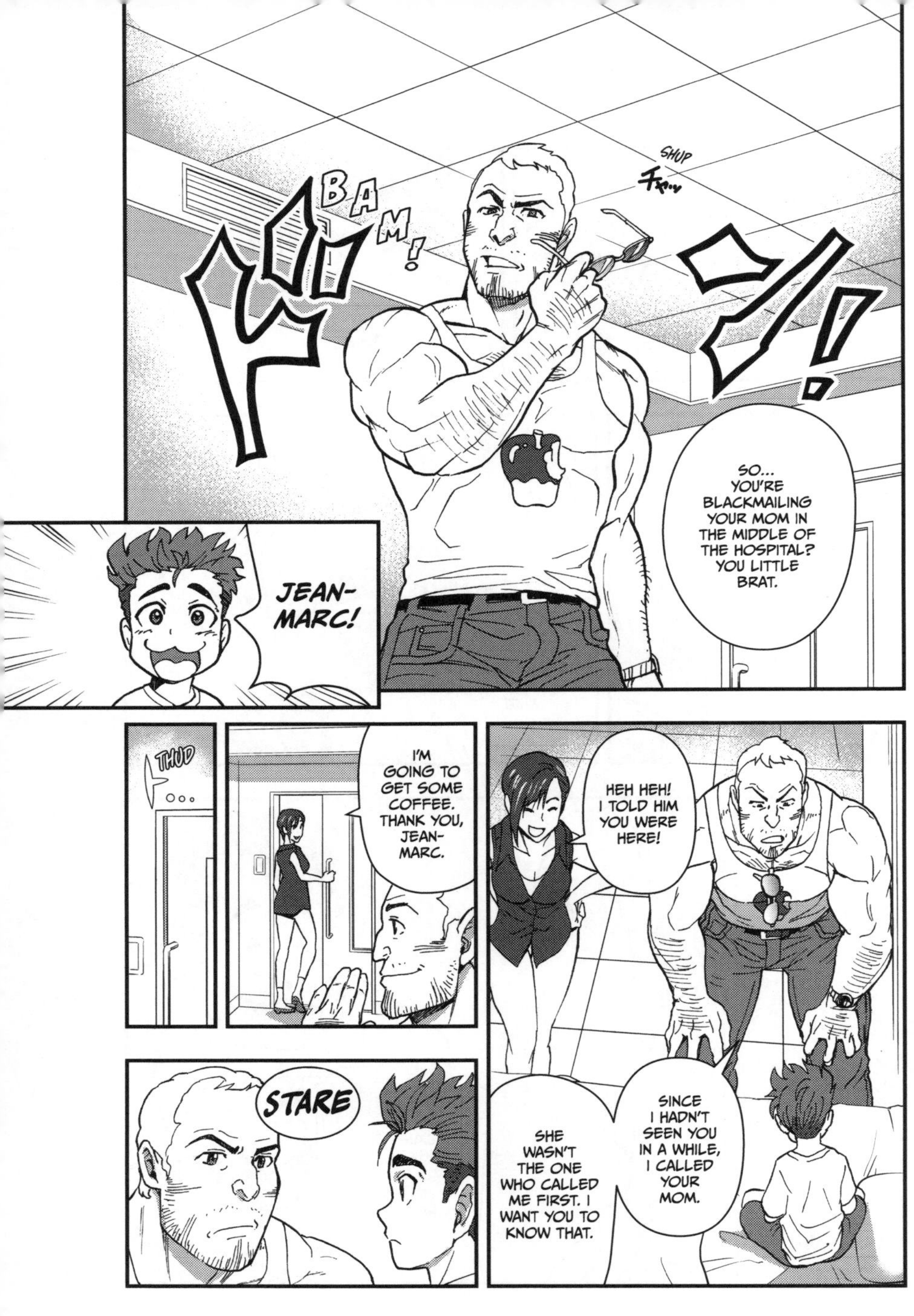
BAM!
SHUP
SO... YOU'RE BLACKMAILING YOUR MOM IN THE MIDDLE OF THE HOSPITAL? YOU LITTLE BRAT.
JEAN-MARC!
HEH HEH! I TOLD HIM YOU WERE HERE!
SINCE I HADN'T SEEN YOU IN A WHILE, I CALLED YOUR MOM.
SHE WASN'T THE ONE WHO CALLED ME FIRST. I WANT YOU TO KNOW THAT.
I'M GOING TO GET SOME COFFEE. THANK YOU, JEAN-MARC.
THUD
...
STARE

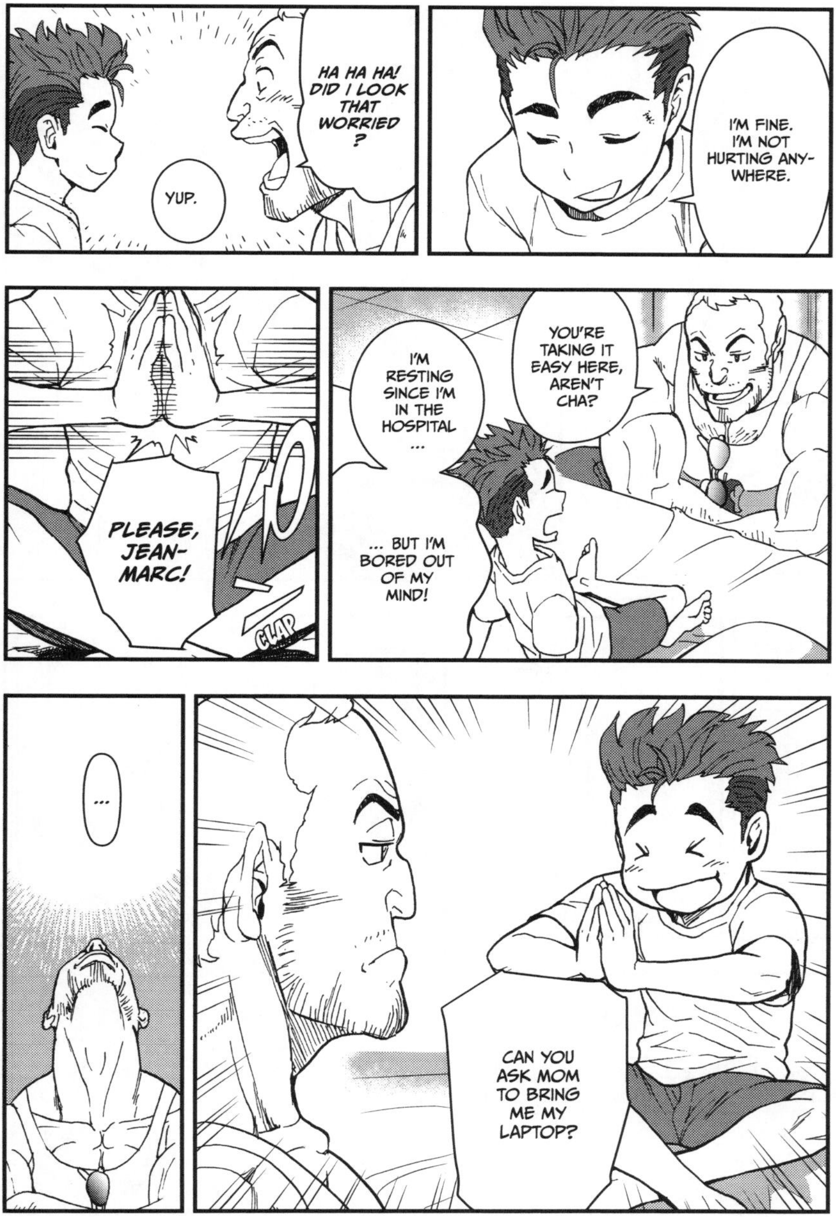
I'M FINE. I'M NOT HURTING ANY-WHERE.
HA HA HA! DID I LOOK THAT WORRIED?
YUP.
YOU'RE TAKING IT EASY HERE, AREN'T CHA?
I'M RESTING SINCE I'M IN THE HOSPITAL ...
... BUT I'M BORED OUT OF MY MIND!
CLAP
PLEASE, JEAN-MARC!
CAN YOU ASK MOM TO BRING ME MY LAPTOP?
...

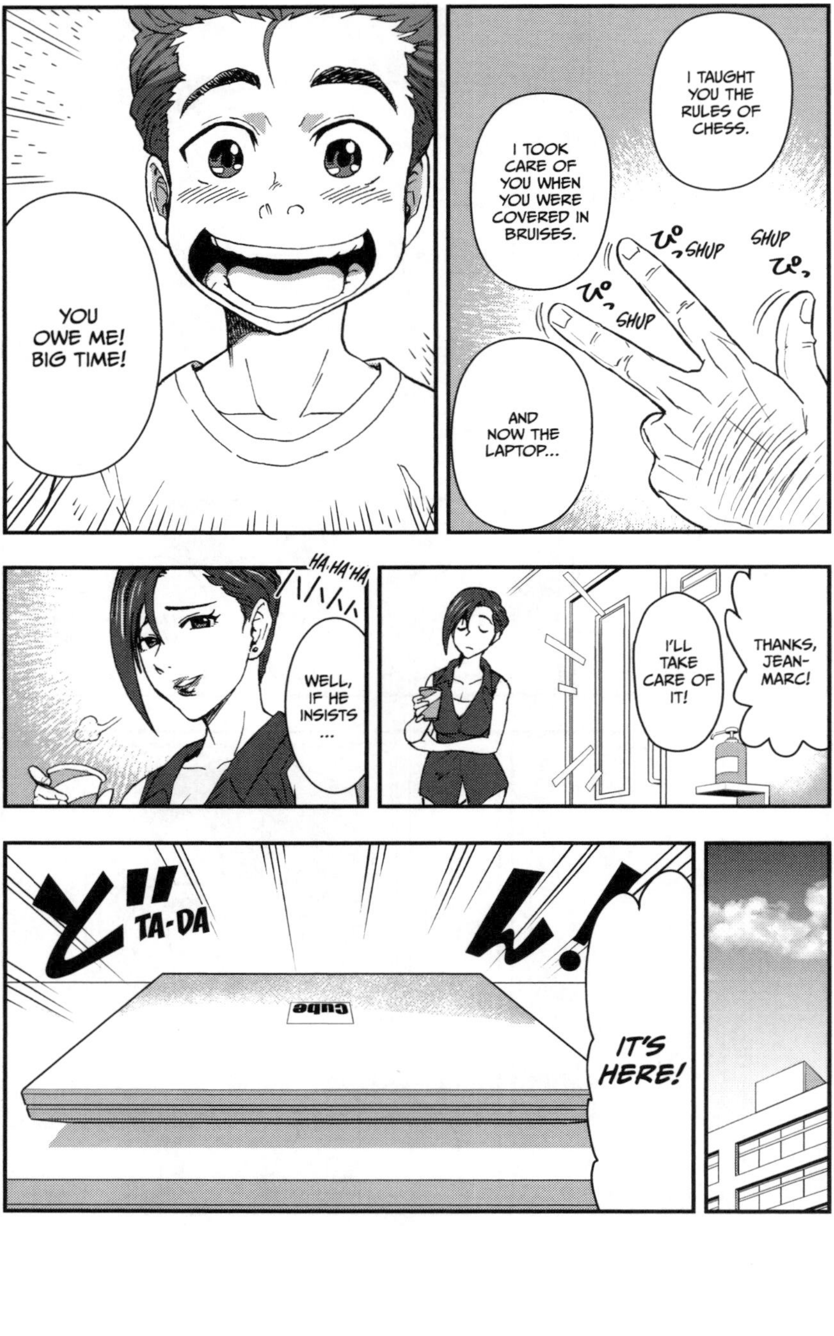
I TAUGHT YOU THE RULES OF CHESS.
I TOOK CARE OF YOU WHEN YOU WERE COVERED IN BRUISES.
ぴっ SHUP
ぴっ SHUP
ぴっ SHUP
AND NOW THE LAPTOP...
YOU OWE ME! BIG TIME!
THANKS, JEAN-MARC!
I'LL TAKE CARE OF IT!
ハハハ HA HA HA
WELL, IF HE INSISTS ...
TA-DA
Cube
IT'S HERE!

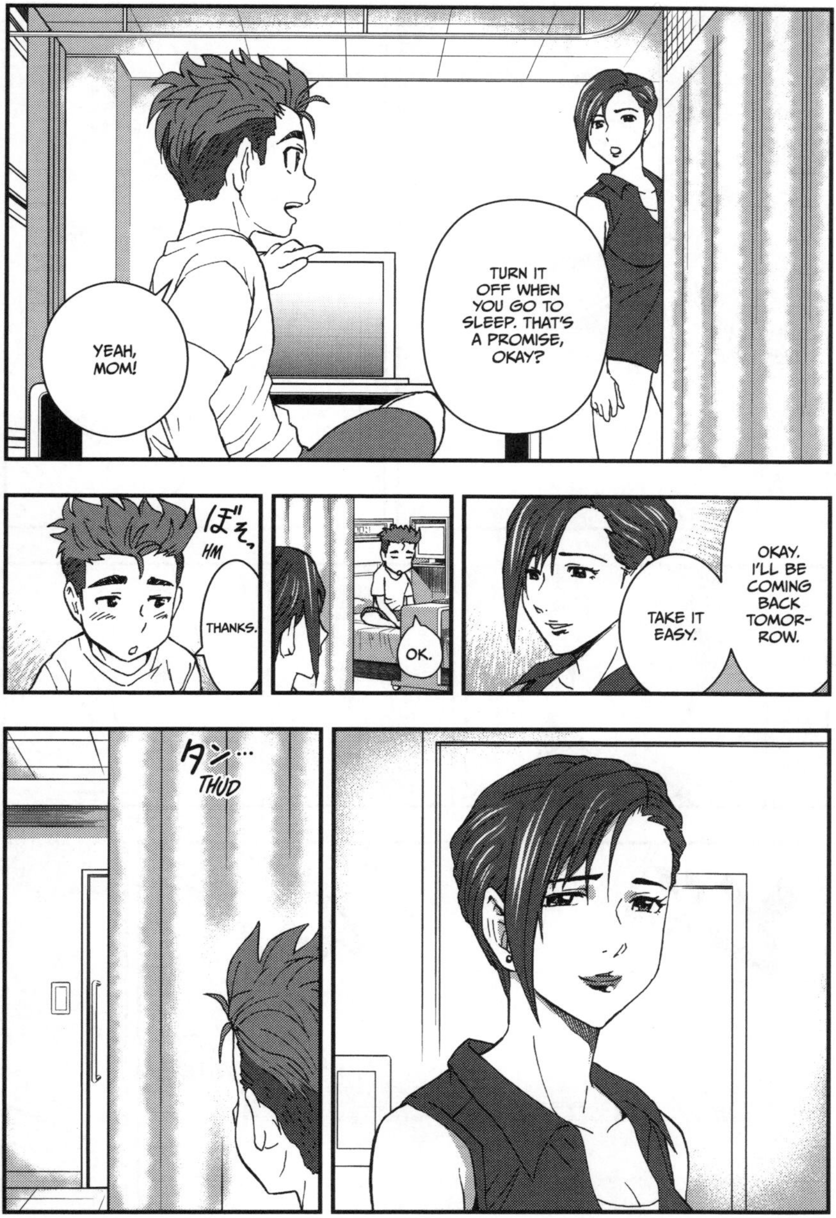
TURN IT OFF WHEN YOU GO TO SLEEP. THAT'S A PROMISE, OKAY?
YEAH, MOM!
OKAY. I'LL BE COMING BACK TOMOR-ROW.
TAKE IT EASY.
OK.
ぼそっ
HM
THANKS.
タン…
THUD

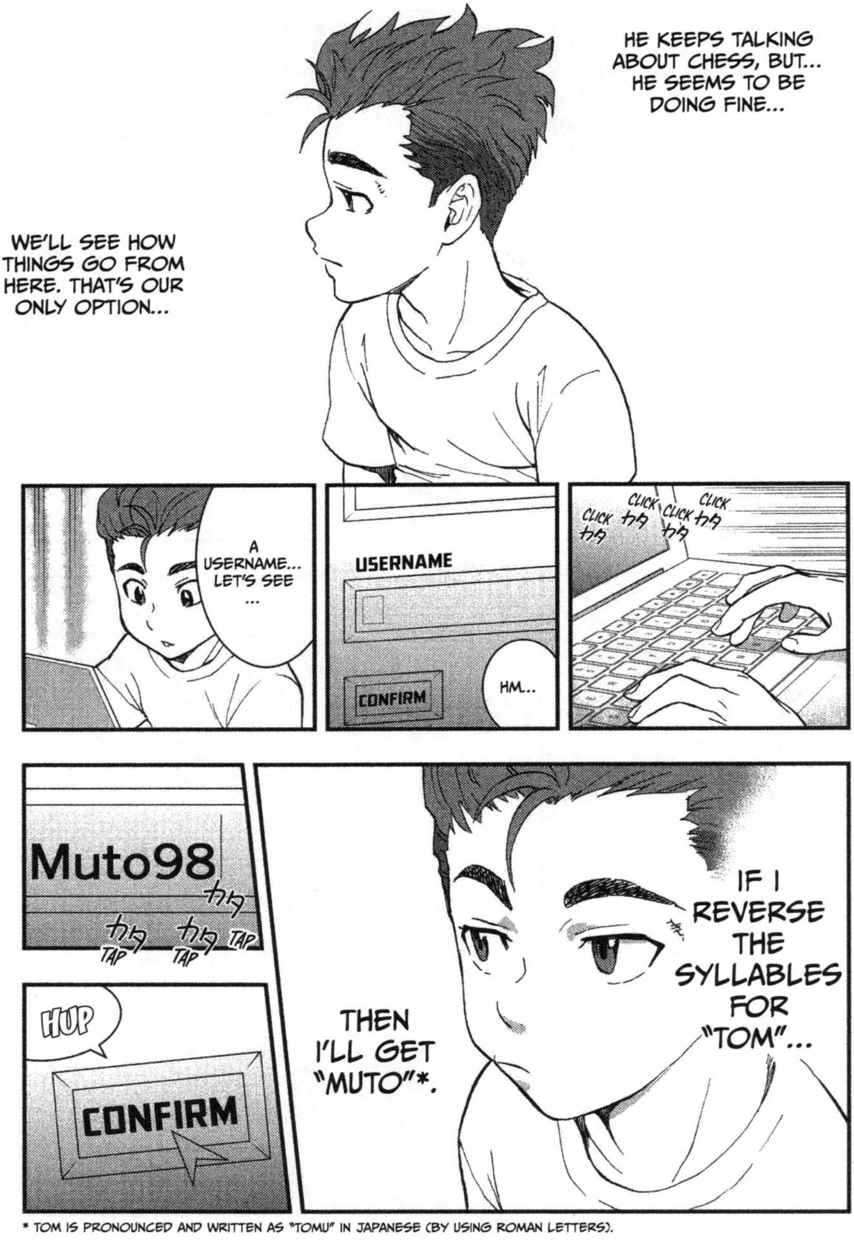
HE KEEPS TALKING ABOUT CHESS, BUT... HE SEEMS TO BE DOING FINE...
WE'LL SEE HOW THINGS GO FROM HERE. THAT'S OUR ONLY OPTION...
CLICK カタ
CLICK カタ
CLICK カタ
CLICK カタ
USERNAME
HM...
CONFIRM
A USERNAME... LET'S SEE ...
IF I REVERSE THE SYLLABLES FOR "TOM"...
THEN I'LL GET "MUTO"*.
Muto98
カタ TAP
カタ TAP
カタ TAP
HUP
CONFIRM

* TOM IS PRONOUNCED AND WRITTEN AS "TOMU" IN JAPANESE (BY USING ROMAN LETTERS).

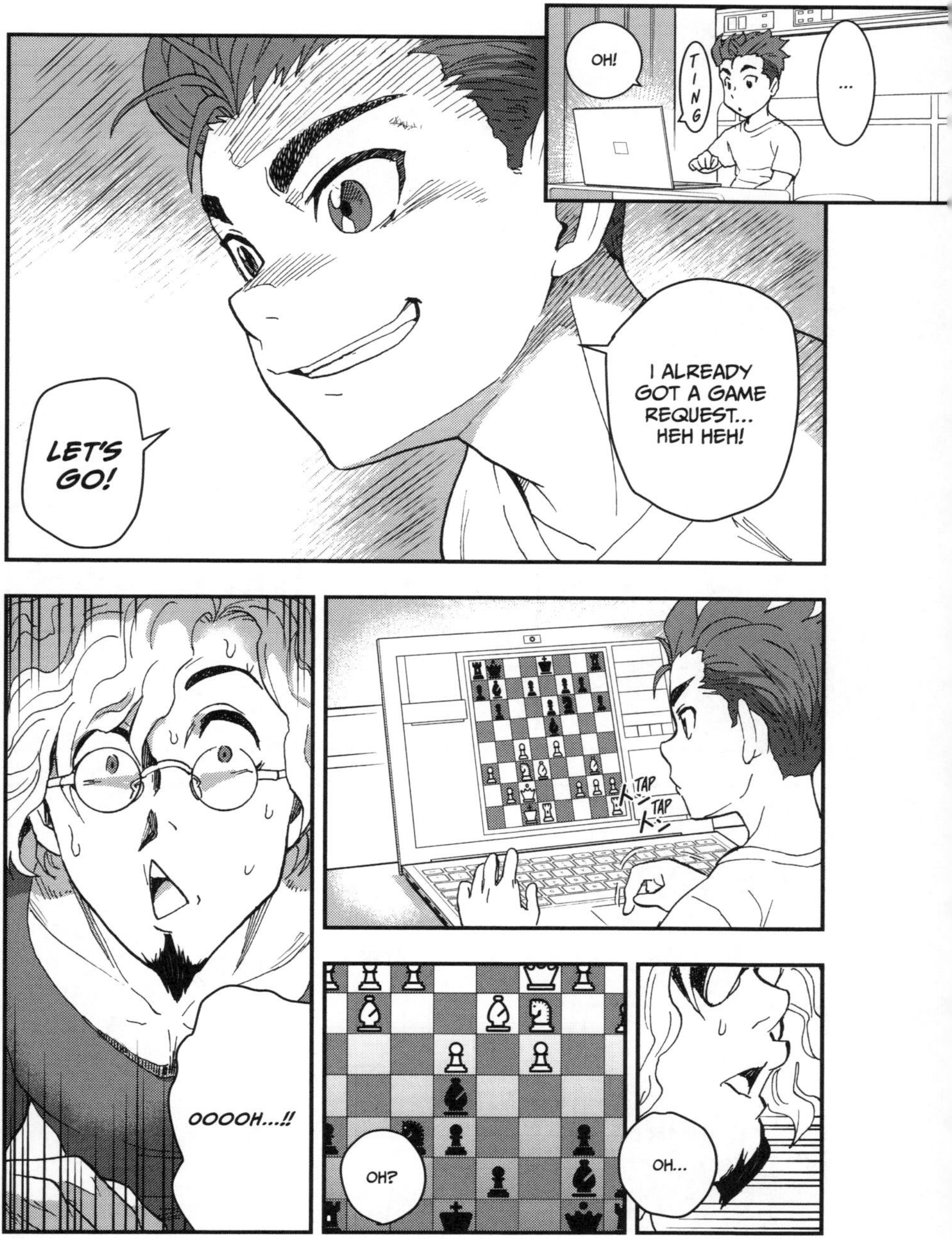
...
TING
OH!
I ALREADY GOT A GAME REQUEST... HEH HEH!
LET'S GO!
TAP
TAP
OH...
OH?
OOOOH...!!

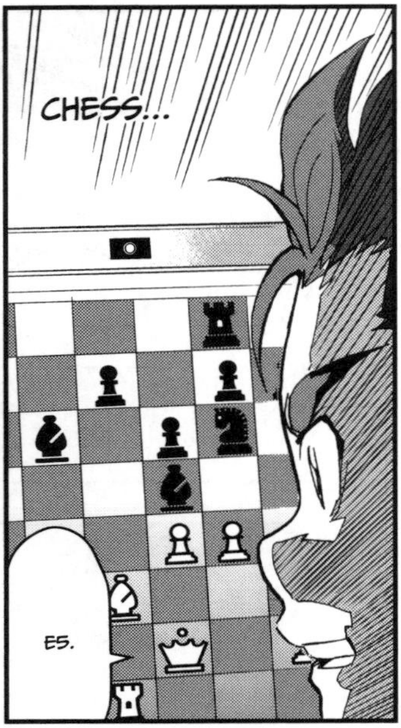
CHESS...
E5.

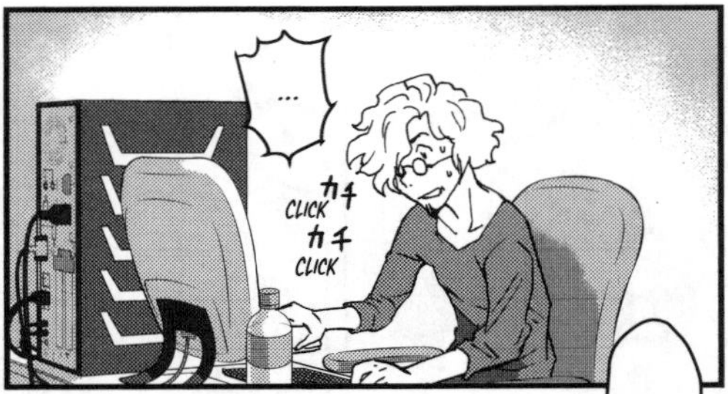
...
カチ
CLICK
カチ
CLICK

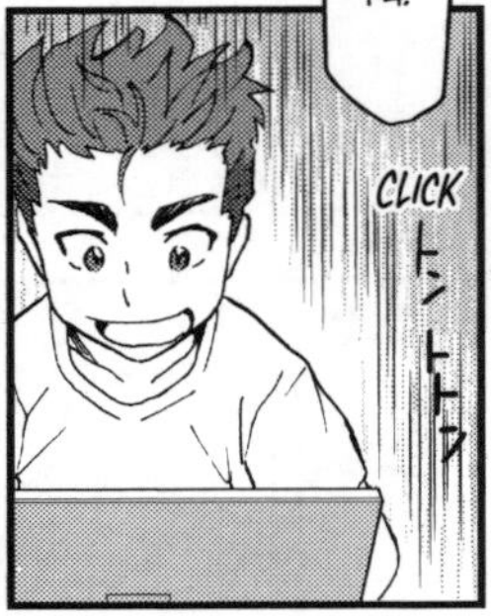
F4.
CLICK
トントン

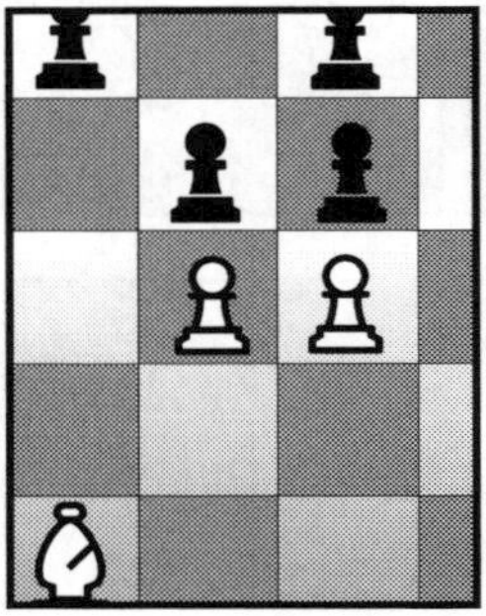

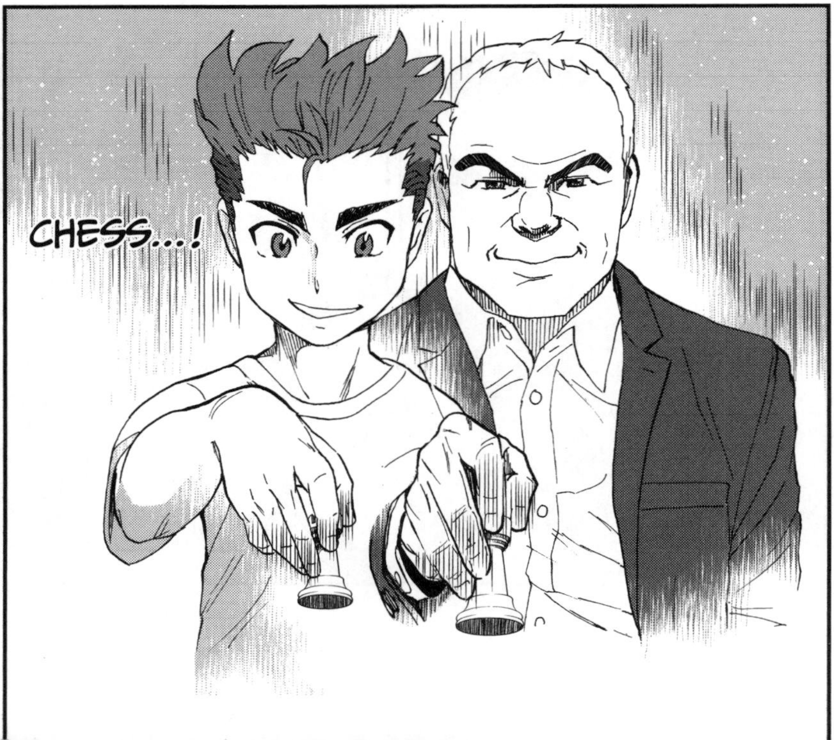
CHESS...!

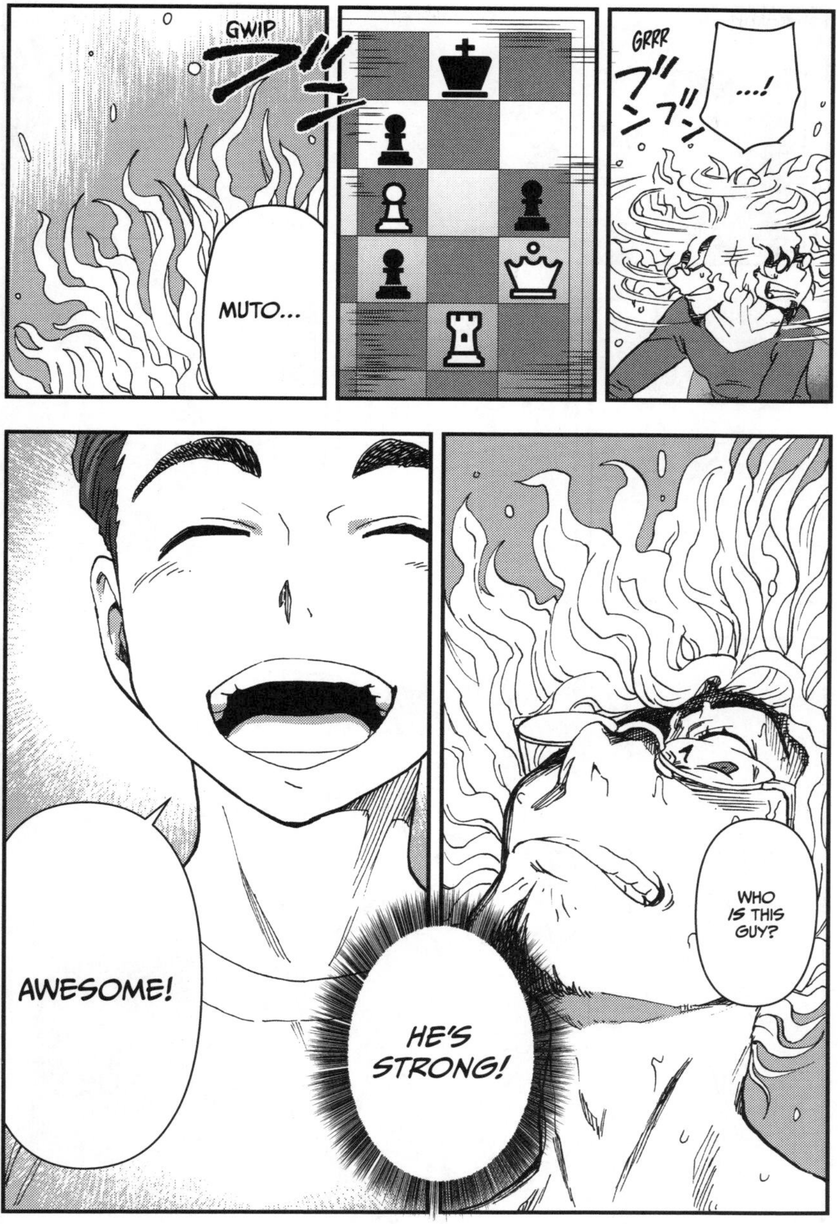
GRRR
...!
GWIP
MUTO...
WHO IS THIS GUY?
AWESOME!
HE'S STRONG!

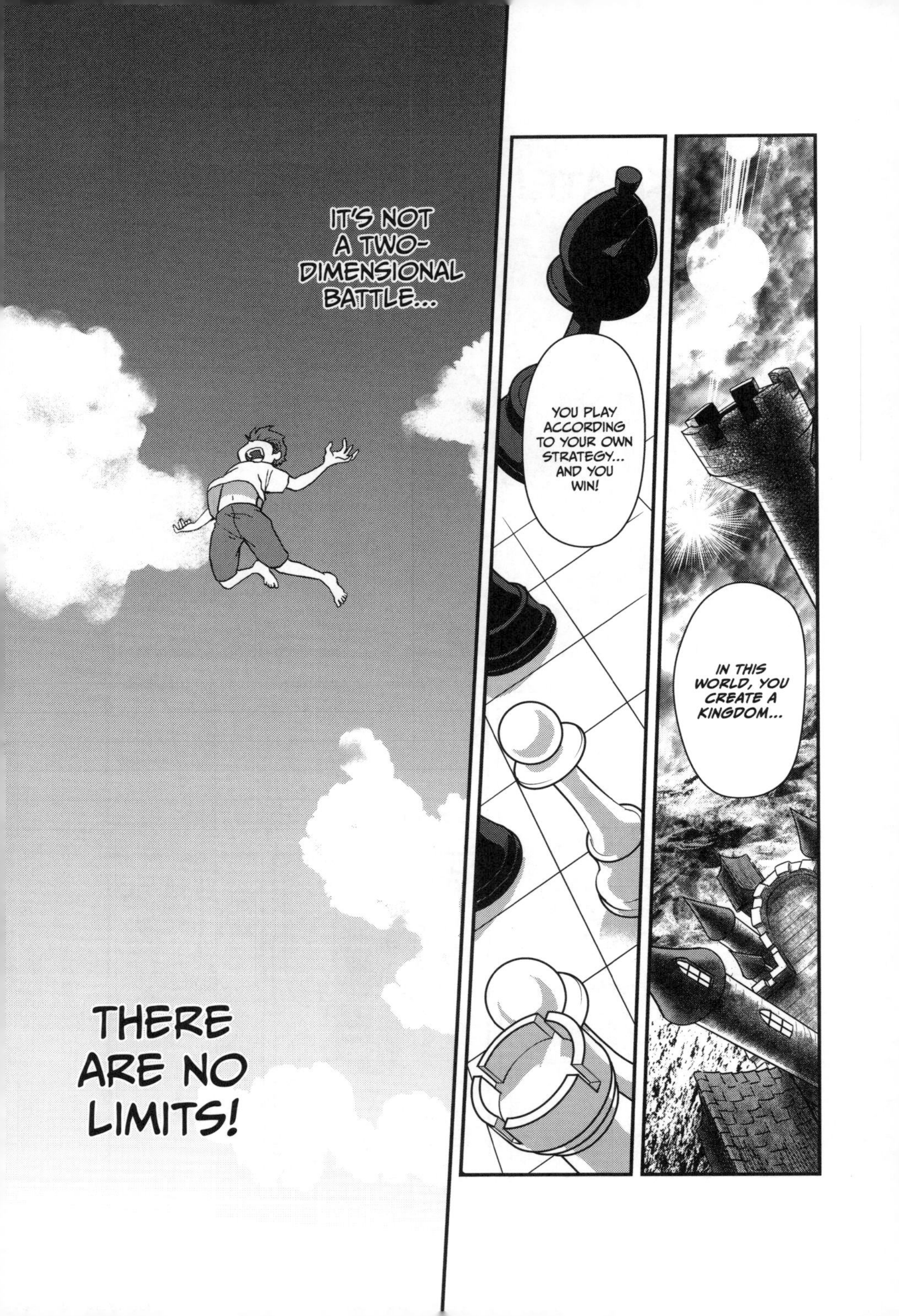
IN THIS WORLD, YOU CREATE A KINGDOM...
YOU PLAY ACCORDING TO YOUR OWN STRATEGY... AND YOU WIN!
IT'S NOT A TWO-DIMENSIONAL BATTLE...
THERE ARE NO LIMITS!

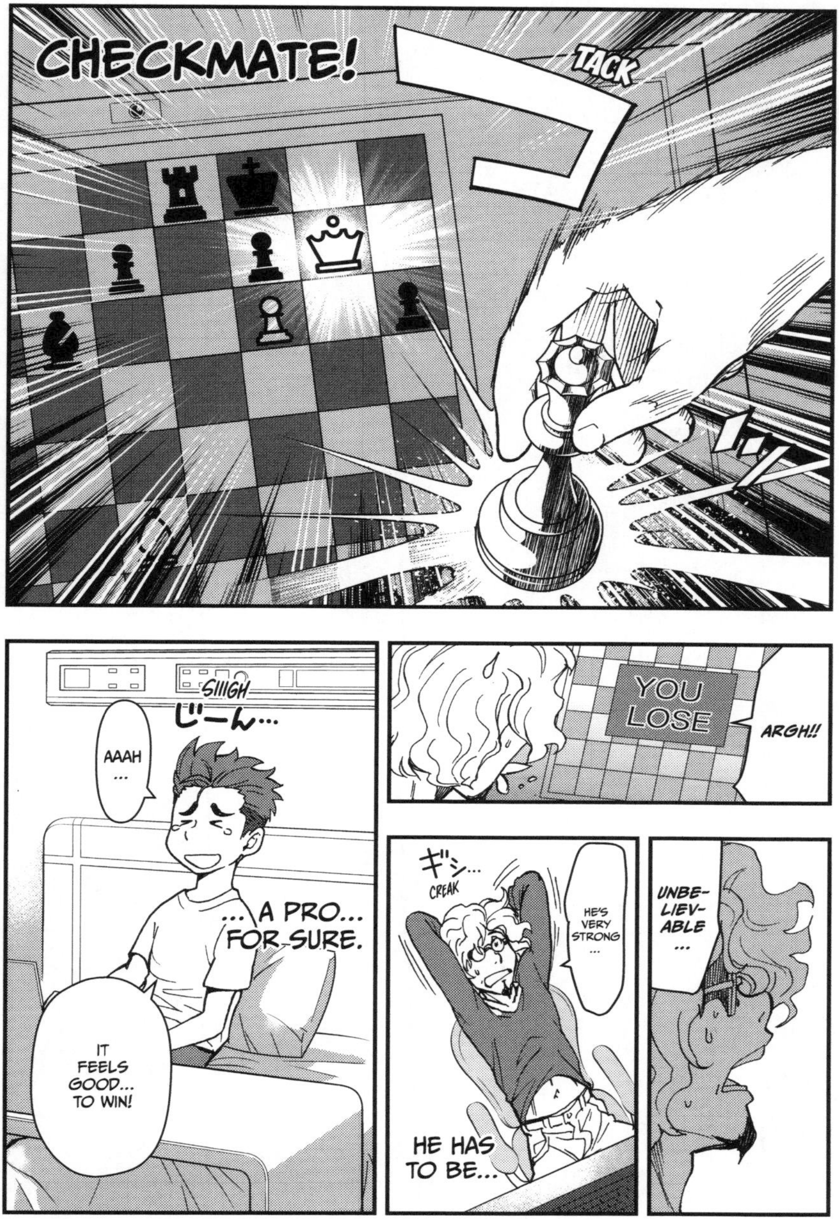

CHECKMATE!
TACK
YOU LOSE
ARGH!!
UNBE-LIEV-ABLE...
ギシ...
CREAK
HE'S VERY STRONG...
HE HAS TO BE...
SIIIGH
じーん...
AAAH...
... A PRO... FOR SURE.
IT FEELS GOOD... TO WIN!

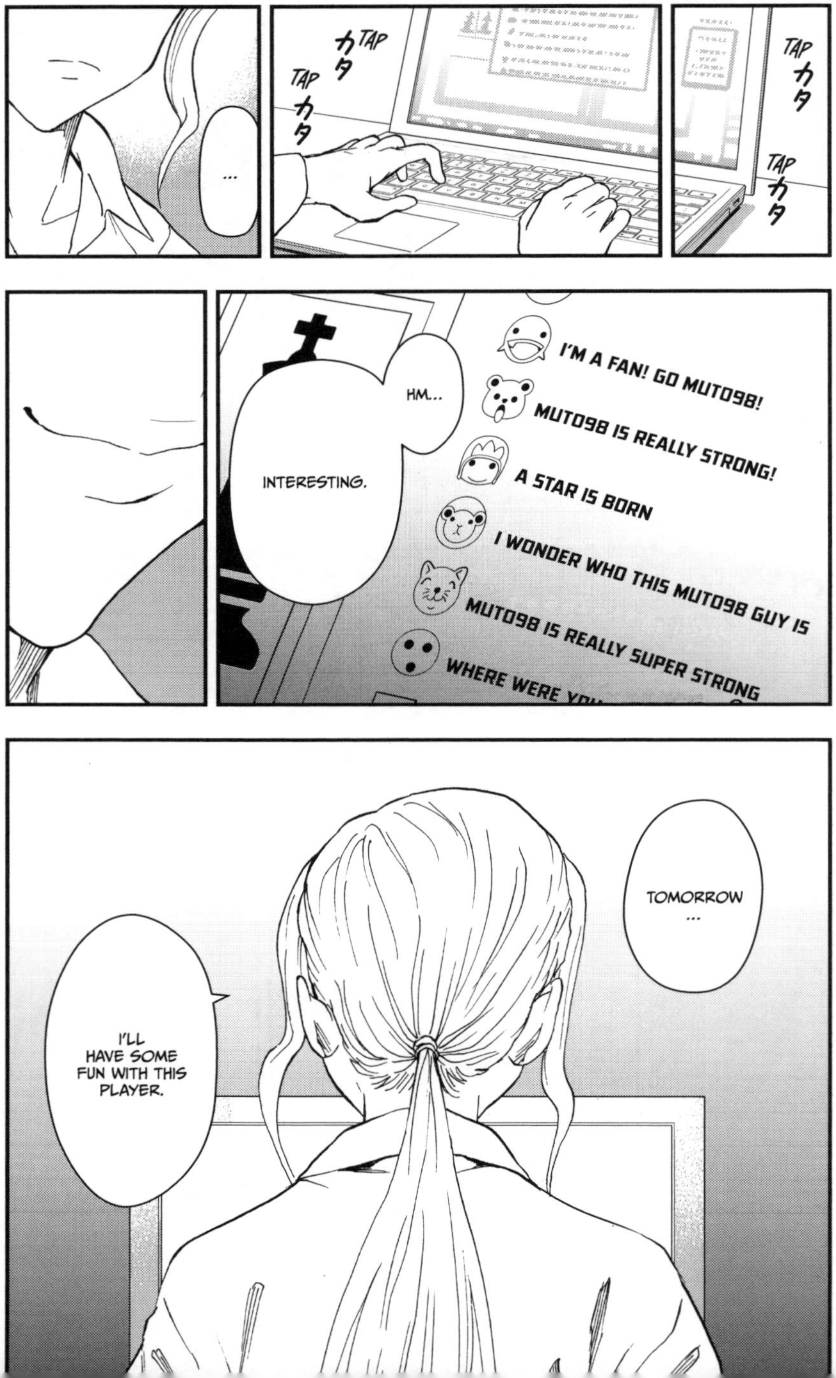
TAP カタ
TAP カタ
TAP カタ
TAP カタ
...
HM...
INTERESTING.
I'M A FAN! GO MUTO98!
MUTO98 IS REALLY STRONG!
A STAR IS BORN
I WONDER WHO THIS MUTO98 GUY IS
MUTO98 IS REALLY SUPER STRONG
TOMORROW...
I'LL HAVE SOME FUN WITH THIS PLAYER.

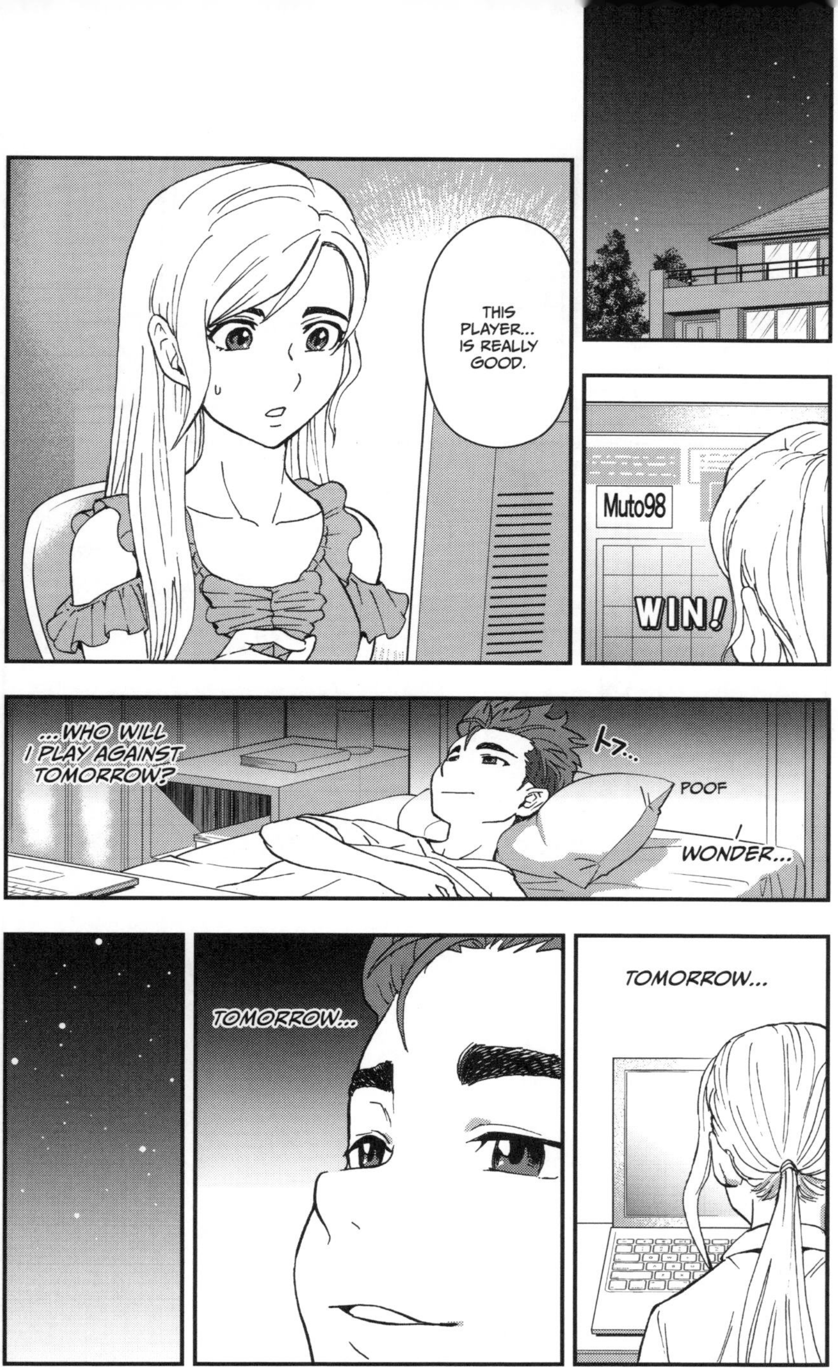
Muto98
WIN!
THIS PLAYER... IS REALLY GOOD.
トッ...
POOF
I WONDER...
...WHO WILL I PLAY AGAINST TOMORROW?
TOMORROW...
TOMORROW...

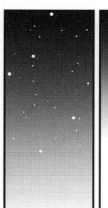

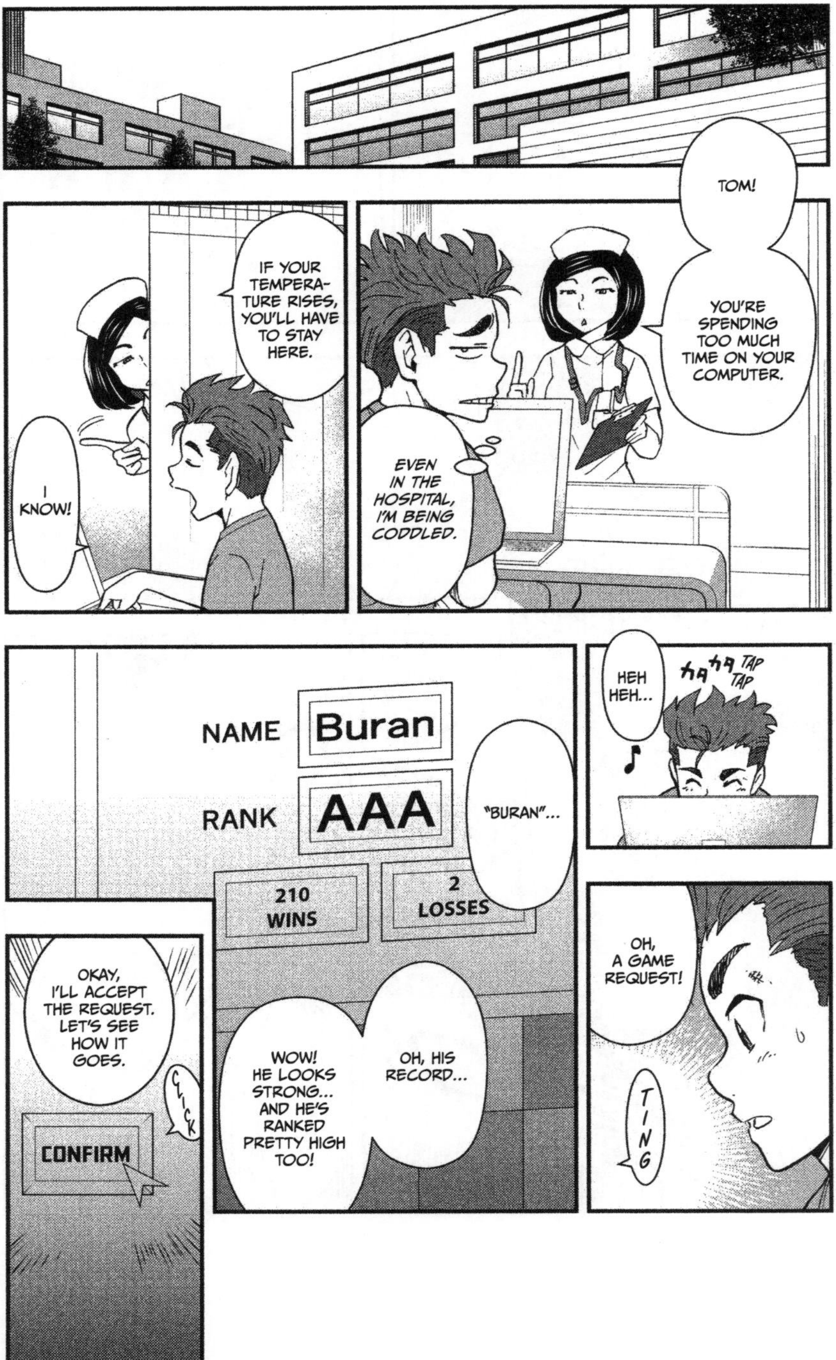
TOM!
YOU'RE SPENDING TOO MUCH TIME ON YOUR COMPUTER.
EVEN IN THE HOSPITAL, I'M BEING CODDLED.
IF YOUR TEMPERA-TURE RISES, YOU'LL HAVE TO STAY HERE.
I KNOW!
カタカタ TAP TAP
HEH HEH...
NAME Buran
RANK AAA
210 WINS
2 LOSSES
"BURAN"...
OH, A GAME REQUEST!
TING
OH, HIS RECORD...
WOW! HE LOOKS STRONG... AND HE'S RANKED PRETTY HIGH TOO!
OKAY, I'LL ACCEPT THE REQUEST. LET'S SEE HOW IT GOES.
CLICK
CONFIRM

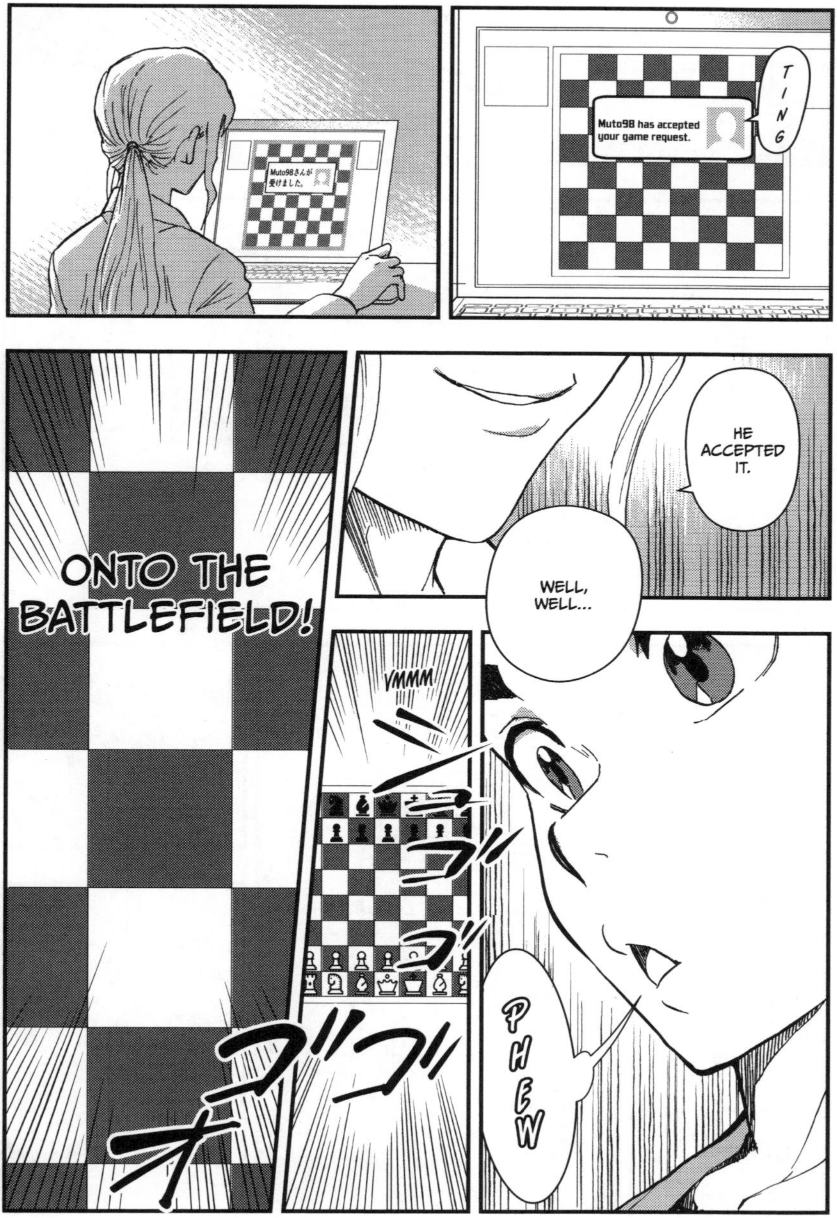
TING
Muto98 has accepted your game request.
Muto98さんが受けました。
HE ACCEPTED IT.
WELL, WELL...
PHEW
VMMM
ゴゴゴ
ONTO THE BATTLEFIELD!
ゴゴゴ
オ

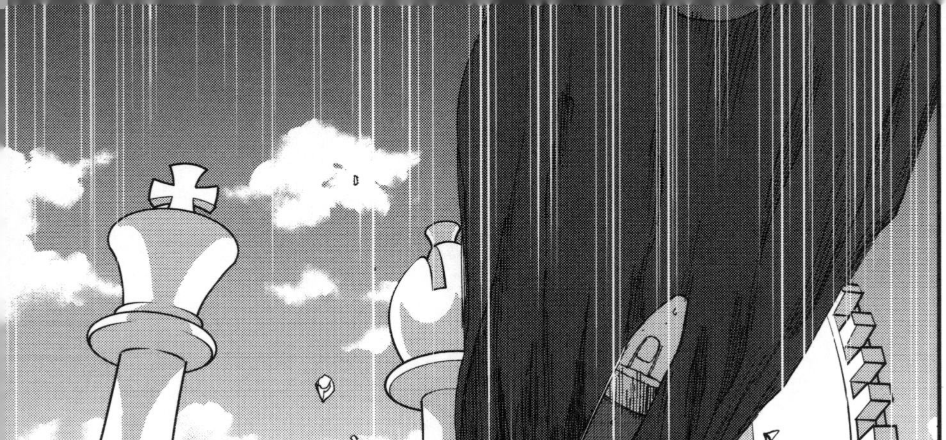
BAM

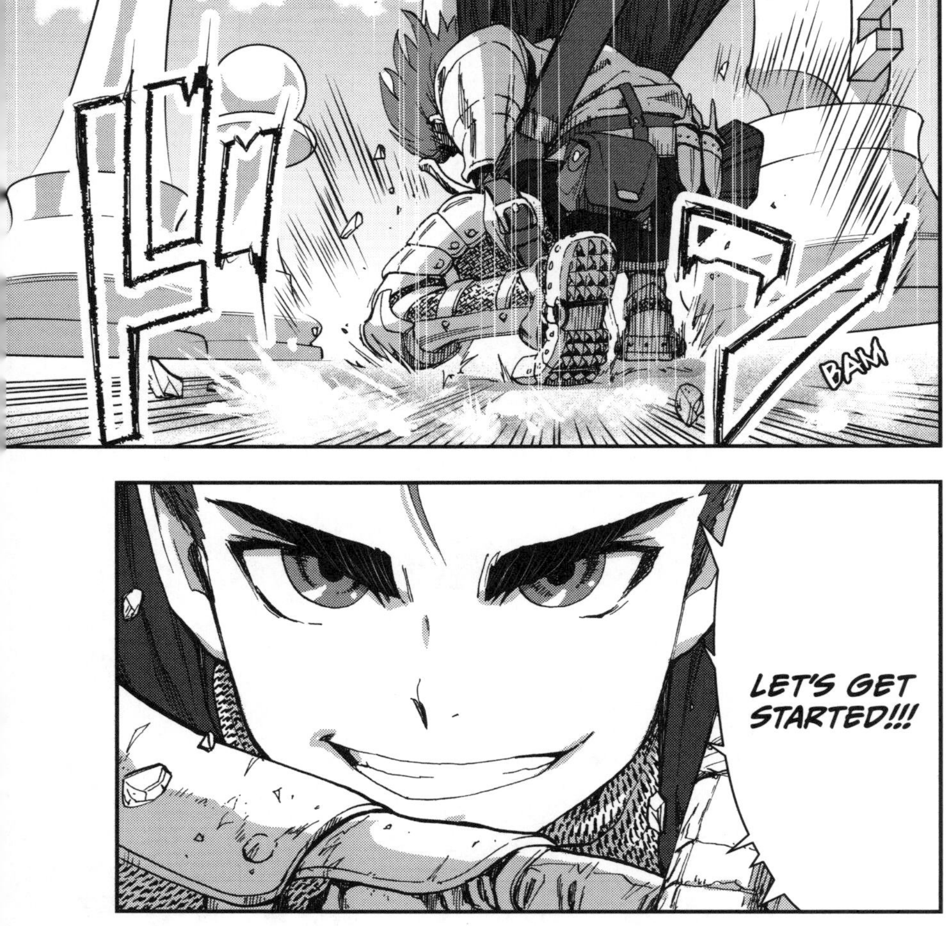
LET'S GET STARTED!!!

BLITZ

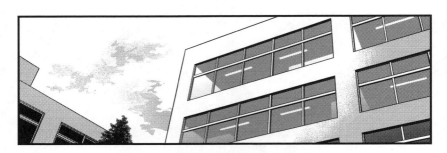

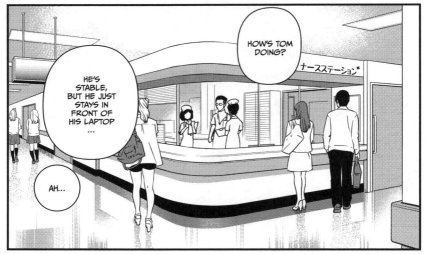

HOW'S TOM DOING?
ナースステーション*
HE'S STABLE, BUT HE JUST STAYS IN FRONT OF HIS LAPTOP ...
AH...

*NURSES' OFFICE

HE HAS TO TAKE IT EASY, THOUGH!
WHAT IS HE DOING ON HIS COMPUTER?
ACTUALLY ...
HE SEEMS TO BE PLAYING CHESS.
CHESS?
カタ TAP
TAP カタ

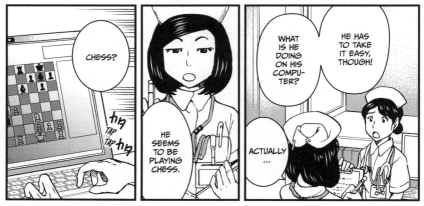

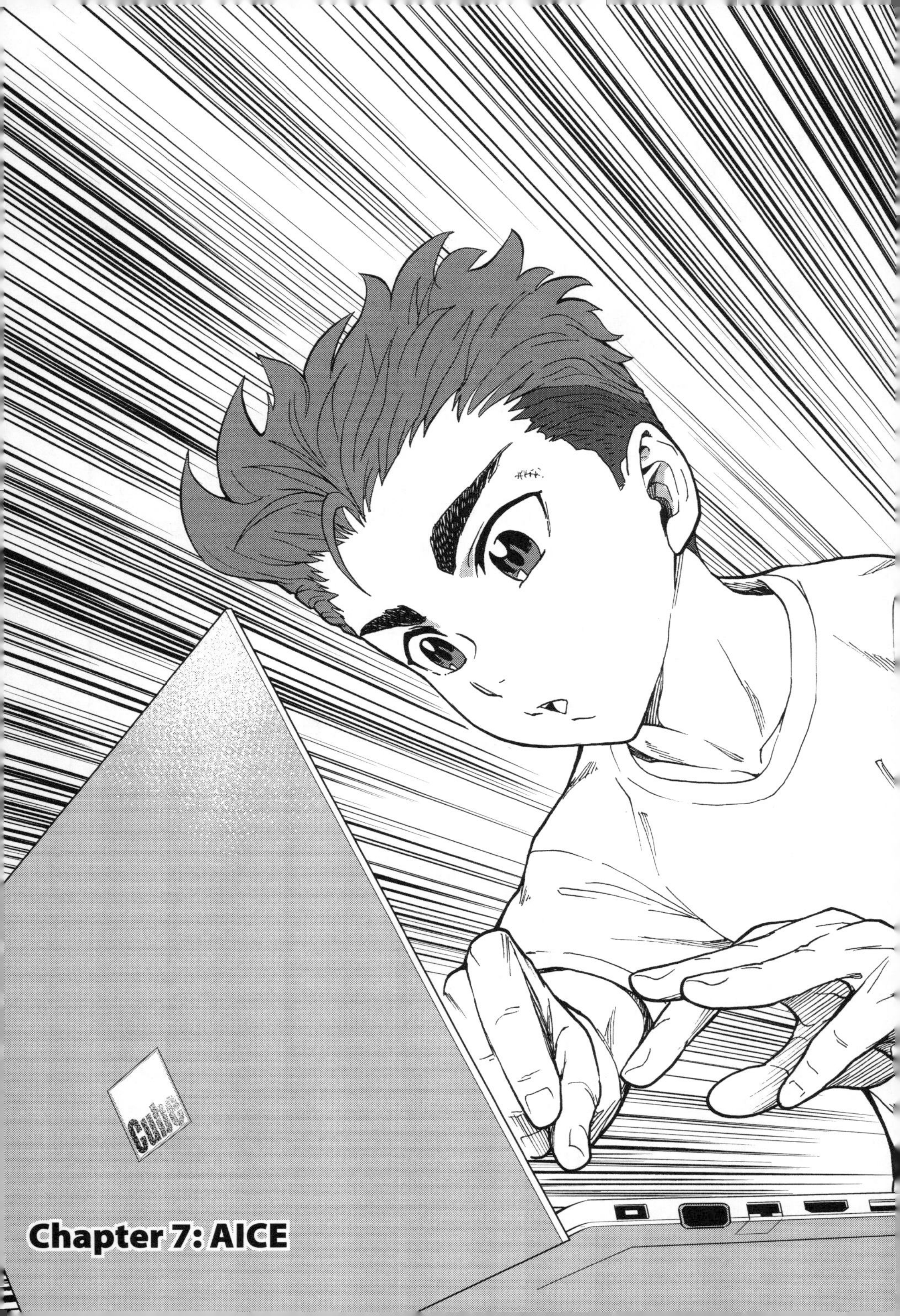
Cube

Chapter 7: AICE

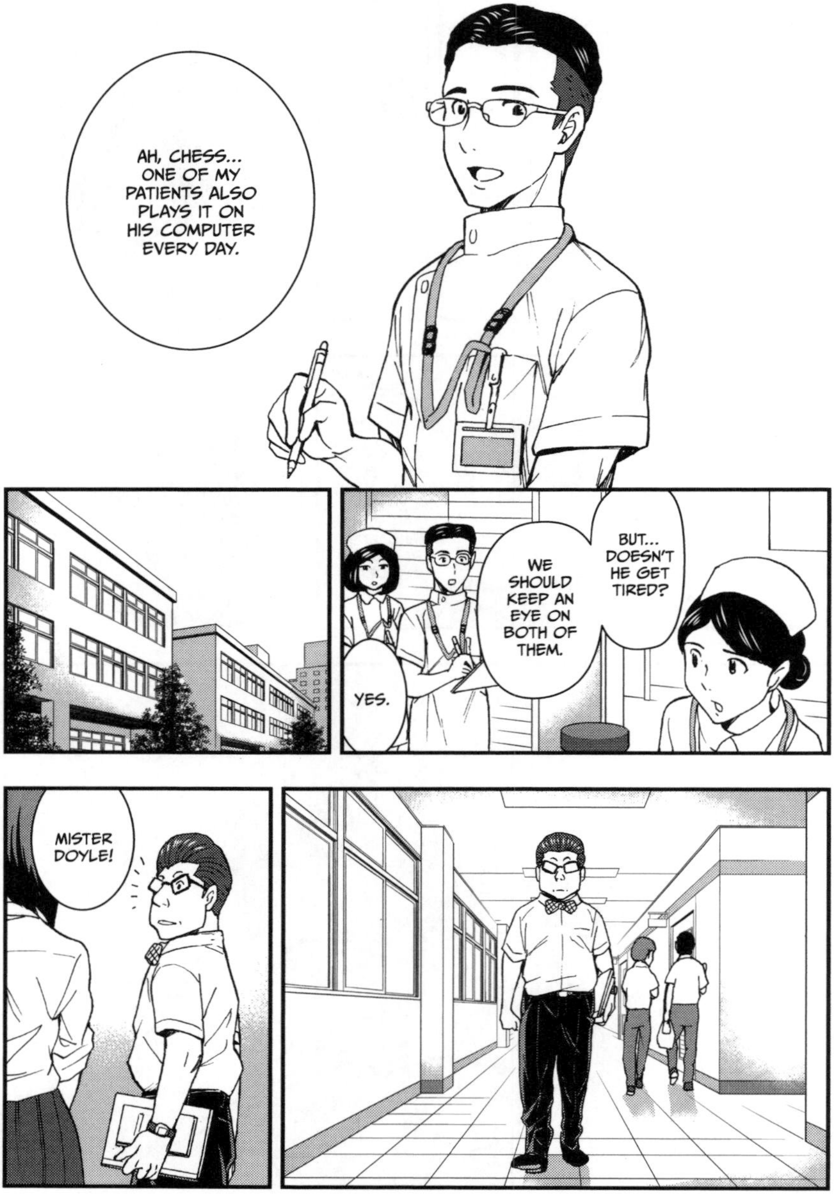
AH, CHESS... ONE OF MY PATIENTS ALSO PLAYS IT ON HIS COMPUTER EVERY DAY.
BUT... DOESN'T HE GET TIRED?
WE SHOULD KEEP AN EYE ON BOTH OF THEM.
YES.
MISTER DOYLE!

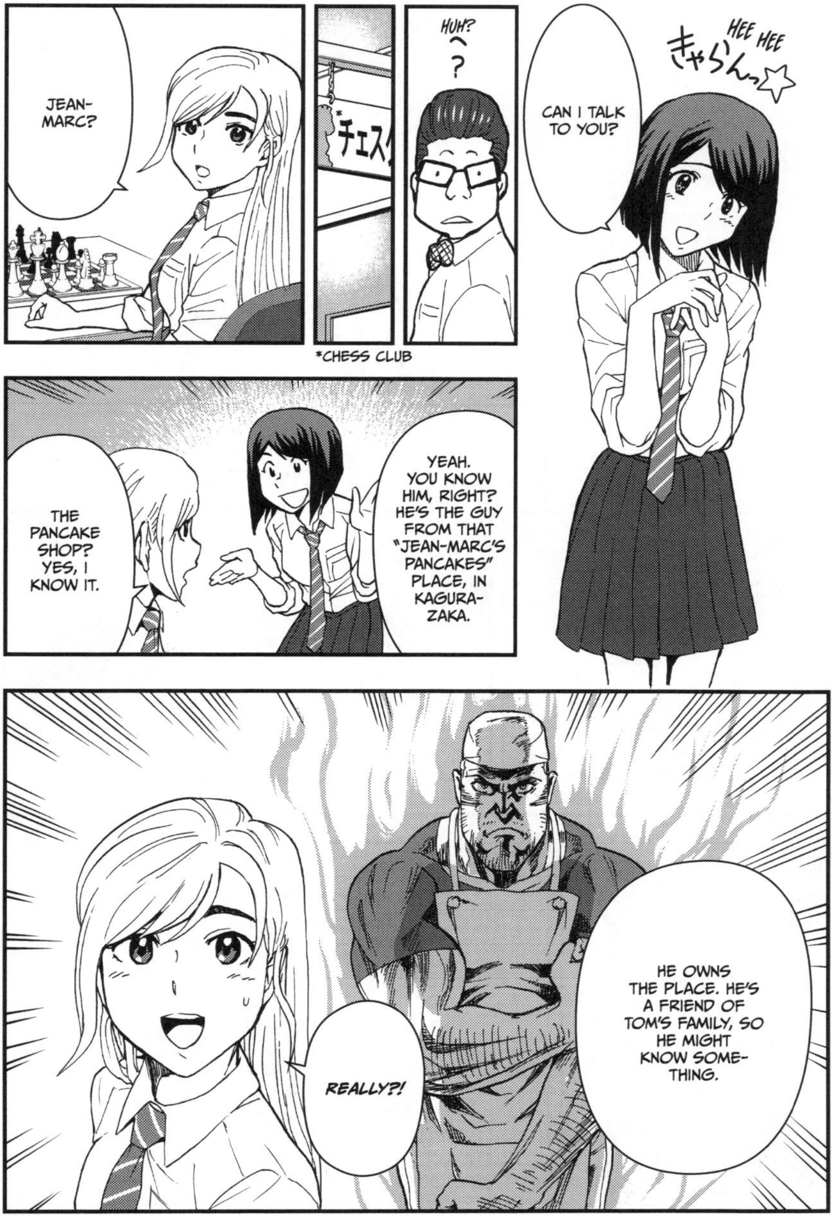
きゃらんっ☆
HEE HEE
CAN I TALK TO YOU?
へ？
HUH?
*チェス
JEAN-MARC?
*CHESS CLUB
YEAH. YOU KNOW HIM, RIGHT? HE'S THE GUY FROM THAT "JEAN-MARC'S PANCAKES" PLACE, IN KAGURA-ZAKA.
THE PANCAKE SHOP? YES, I KNOW IT.
HE OWNS THE PLACE. HE'S A FRIEND OF TOM'S FAMILY, SO HE MIGHT KNOW SOME-THING.
REALLY?!

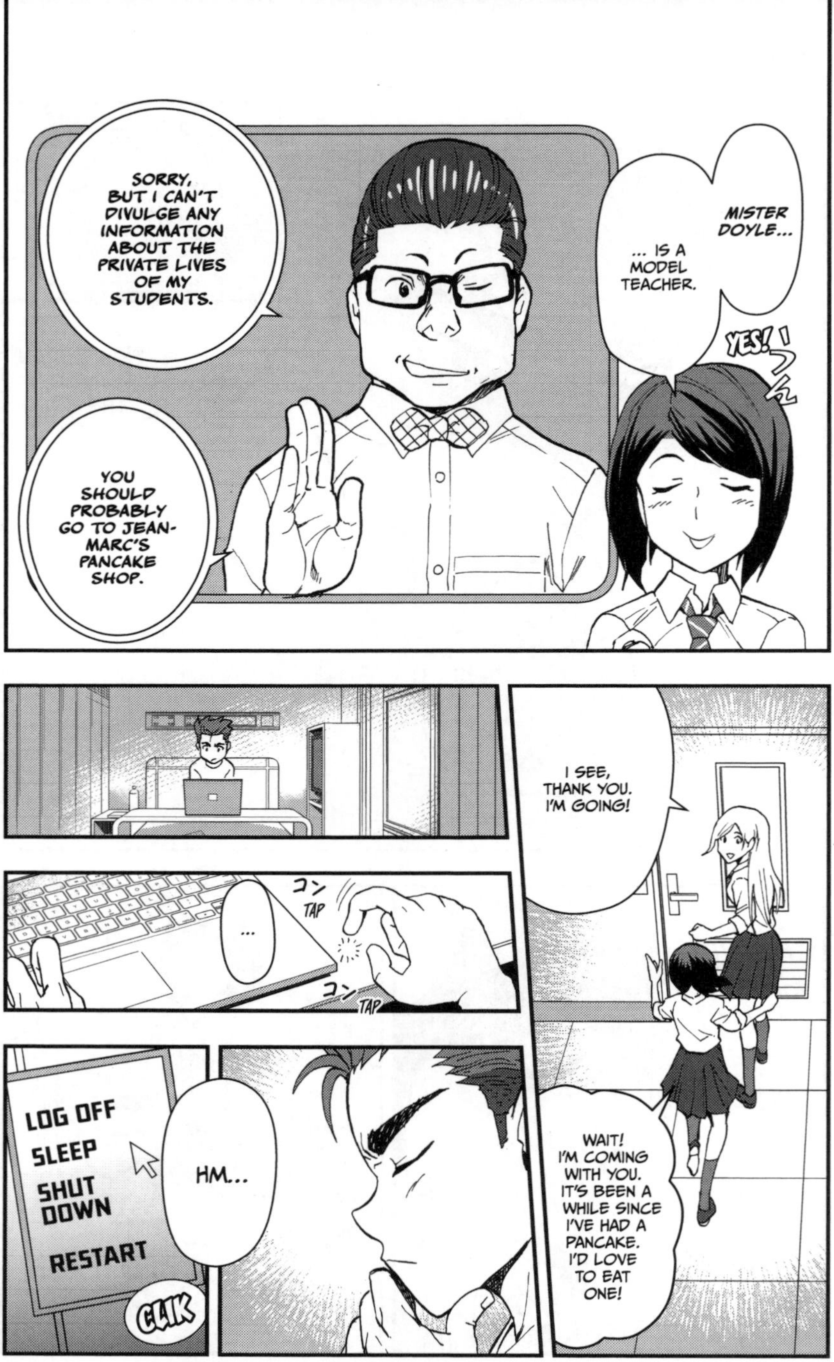
MISTER DOYLE...
... IS A MODEL TEACHER.
YES! うん
SORRY, BUT I CAN'T DIVULGE ANY INFORMATION ABOUT THE PRIVATE LIVES OF MY STUDENTS.
YOU SHOULD PROBABLY GO TO JEAN-MARC'S PANCAKE SHOP.
I SEE, THANK YOU. I'M GOING!
WAIT! I'M COMING WITH YOU. IT'S BEEN A WHILE SINCE I'VE HAD A PANCAKE. I'D LOVE TO EAT ONE!
コン TAP
...
コン TAP
HM...
LOG OFF
SLEEP
SHUT DOWN
RESTART
CLIK

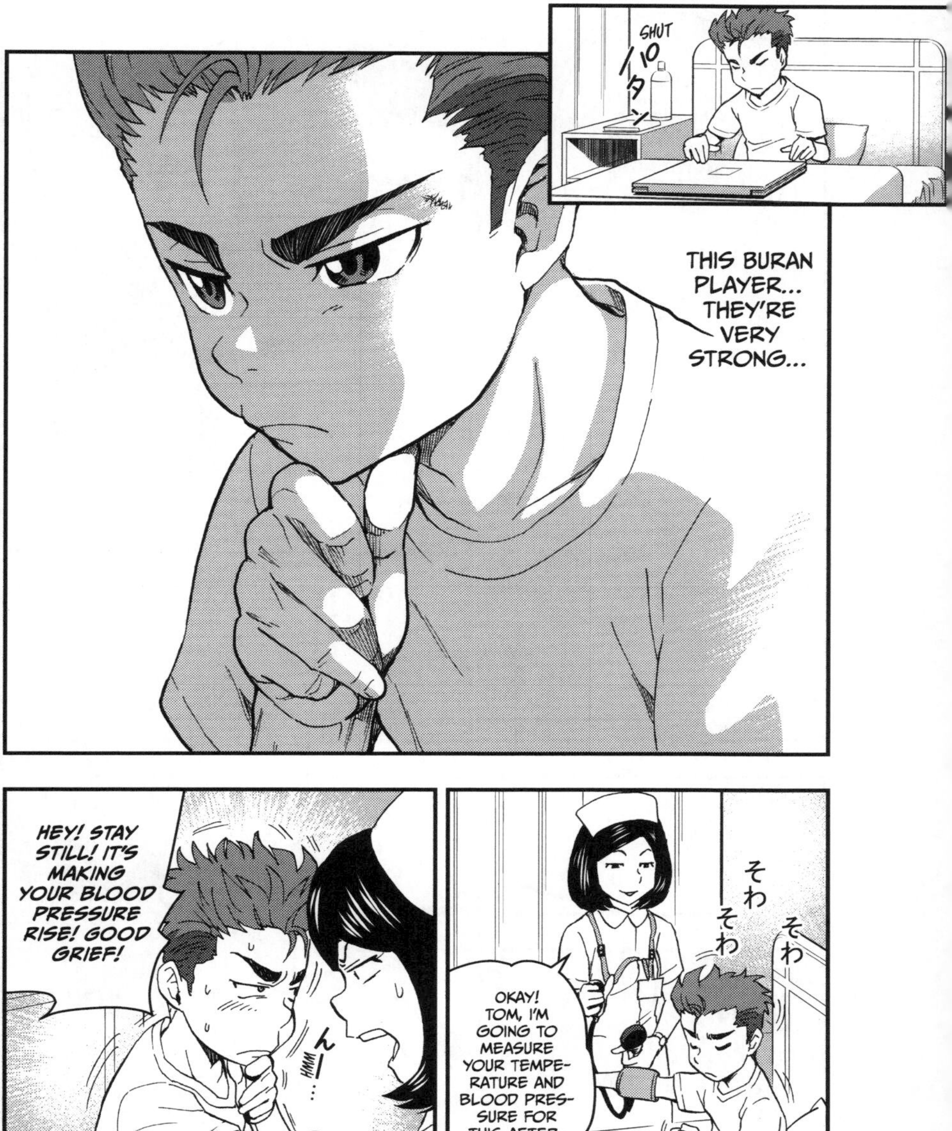
SHUT
パタン
THIS BURAN PLAYER... THEY'RE VERY STRONG...
そわ
そわ
そわ
そわ
OKAY! TOM, I'M GOING TO MEASURE YOUR TEMPERATURE AND BLOOD PRESSURE FOR THIS AFTERNOON.
HEY! STAY STILL! IT'S MAKING YOUR BLOOD PRESSURE RISE! GOOD GRIEF!
んー
HMM...

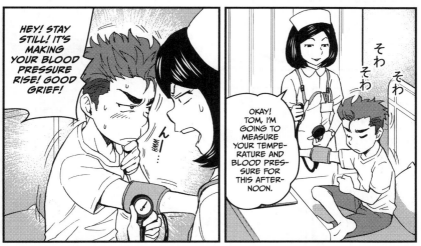

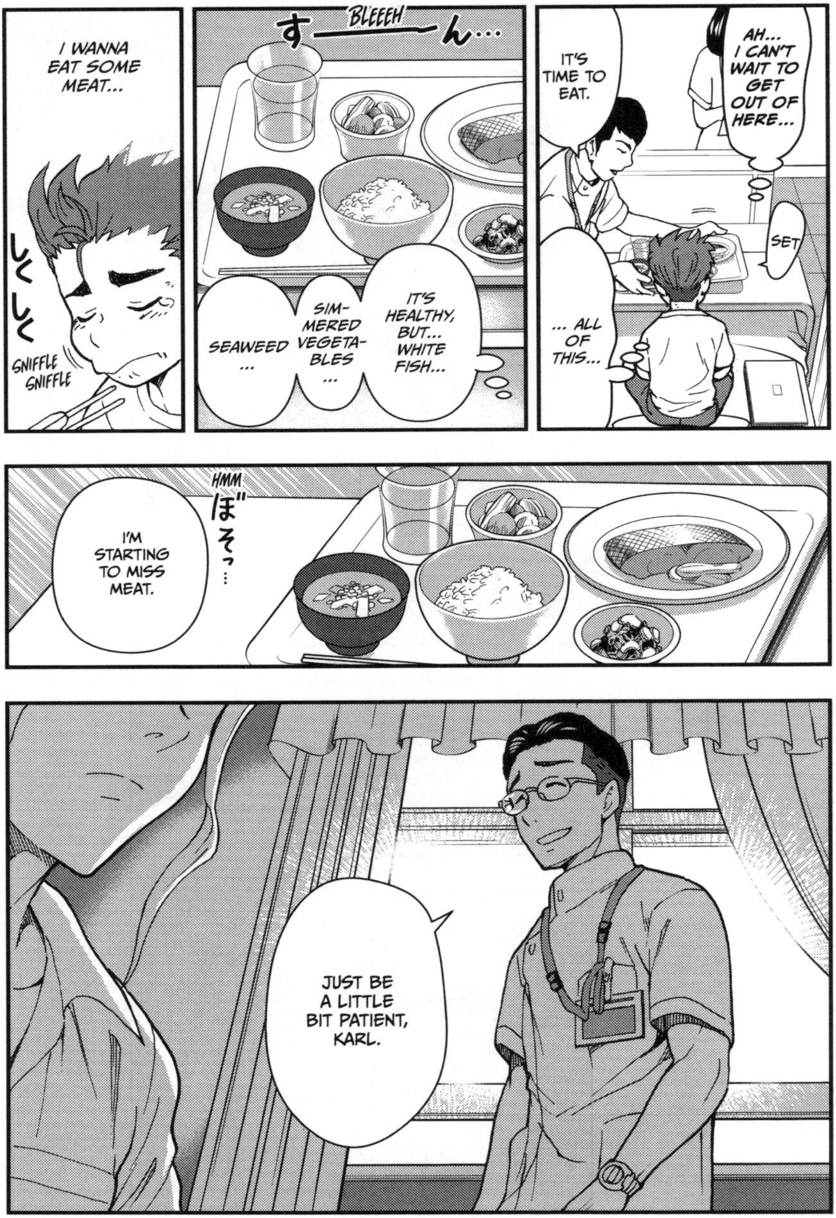
AH... I CAN'T WAIT TO GET OUT OF HERE...
IT'S TIME TO EAT.
SET
... ALL OF THIS...
すーーーん…
BLEEEH
IT'S HEALTHY, BUT... WHITE FISH...
SIM-MERED VEGETA-BLES ...
SEAWEED ...
I WANNA EAT SOME MEAT...
しくしく
SNIFFLE SNIFFLE
HMM
ぼそっ…
I'M STARTING TO MISS MEAT.
JUST BE A LITTLE BIT PATIENT, KARL.

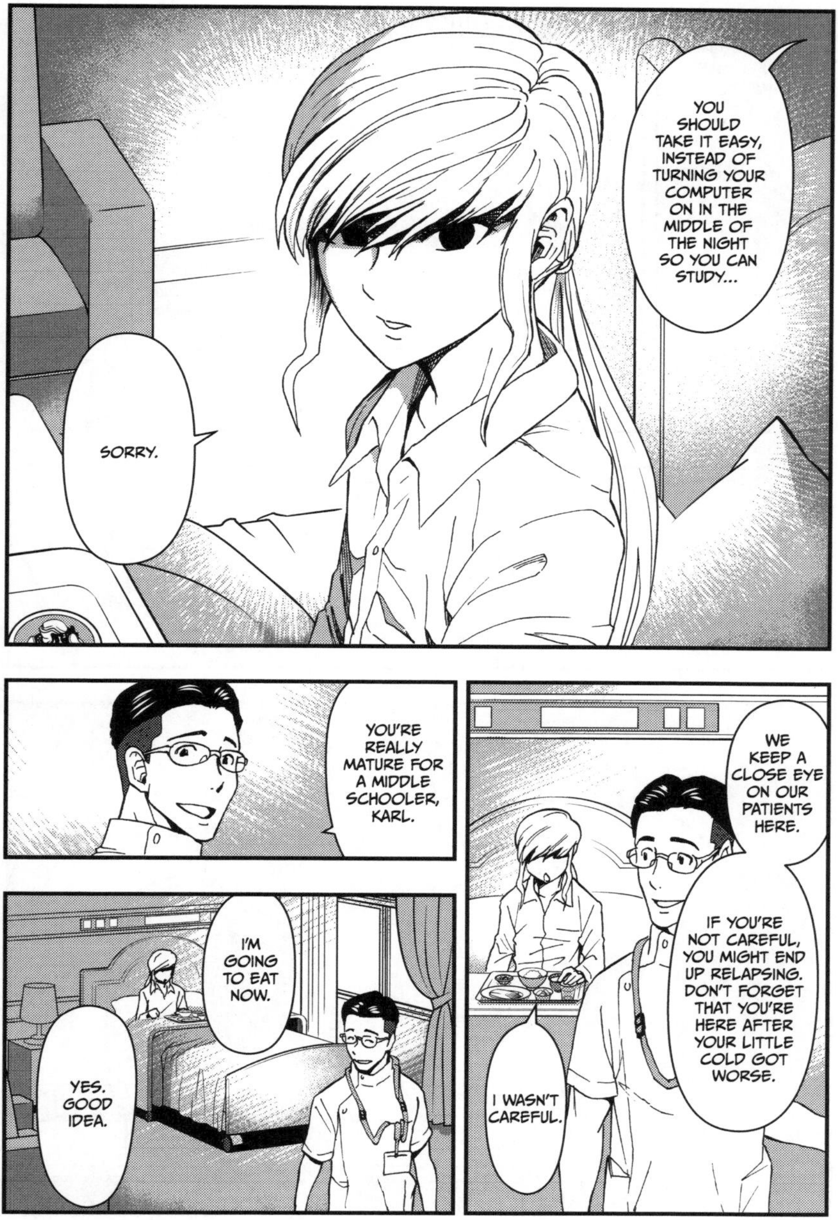
YOU SHOULD TAKE IT EASY, INSTEAD OF TURNING YOUR COMPUTER ON IN THE MIDDLE OF THE NIGHT SO YOU CAN STUDY...
SORRY.
WE KEEP A CLOSE EYE ON OUR PATIENTS HERE.
IF YOU'RE NOT CAREFUL, YOU MIGHT END UP RELAPSING. DON'T FORGET THAT YOU'RE HERE AFTER YOUR LITTLE COLD GOT WORSE.
I WASN'T CAREFUL.
YOU'RE REALLY MATURE FOR A MIDDLE SCHOOLER, KARL.
I'M GOING TO EAT NOW.
YES. GOOD IDEA.

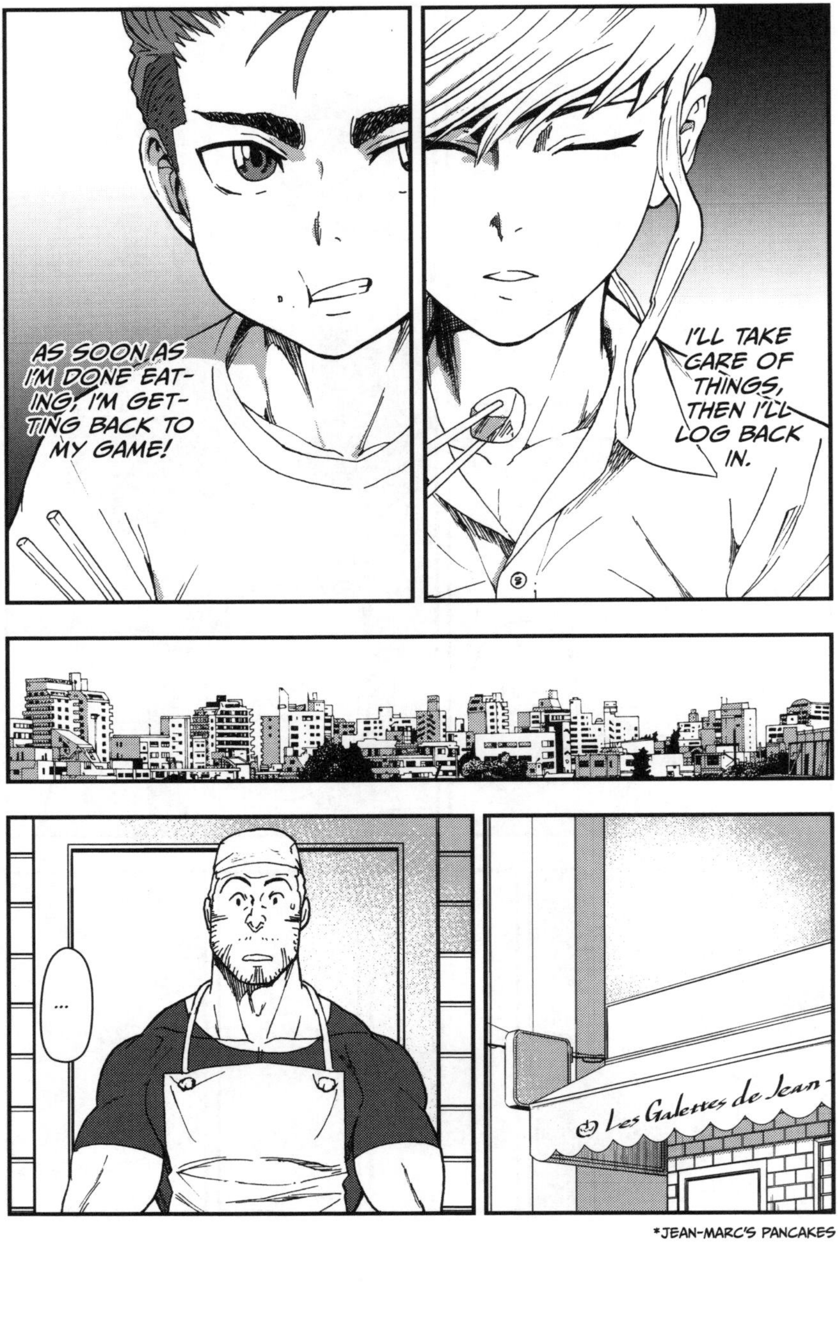
I'LL TAKE CARE OF THINGS, THEN I'LL LOG BACK IN.
AS SOON AS I'M DONE EATING, I'M GETTING BACK TO MY GAME!
Les Galettes de Jean-
...

*JEAN-MARC'S PANCAKES

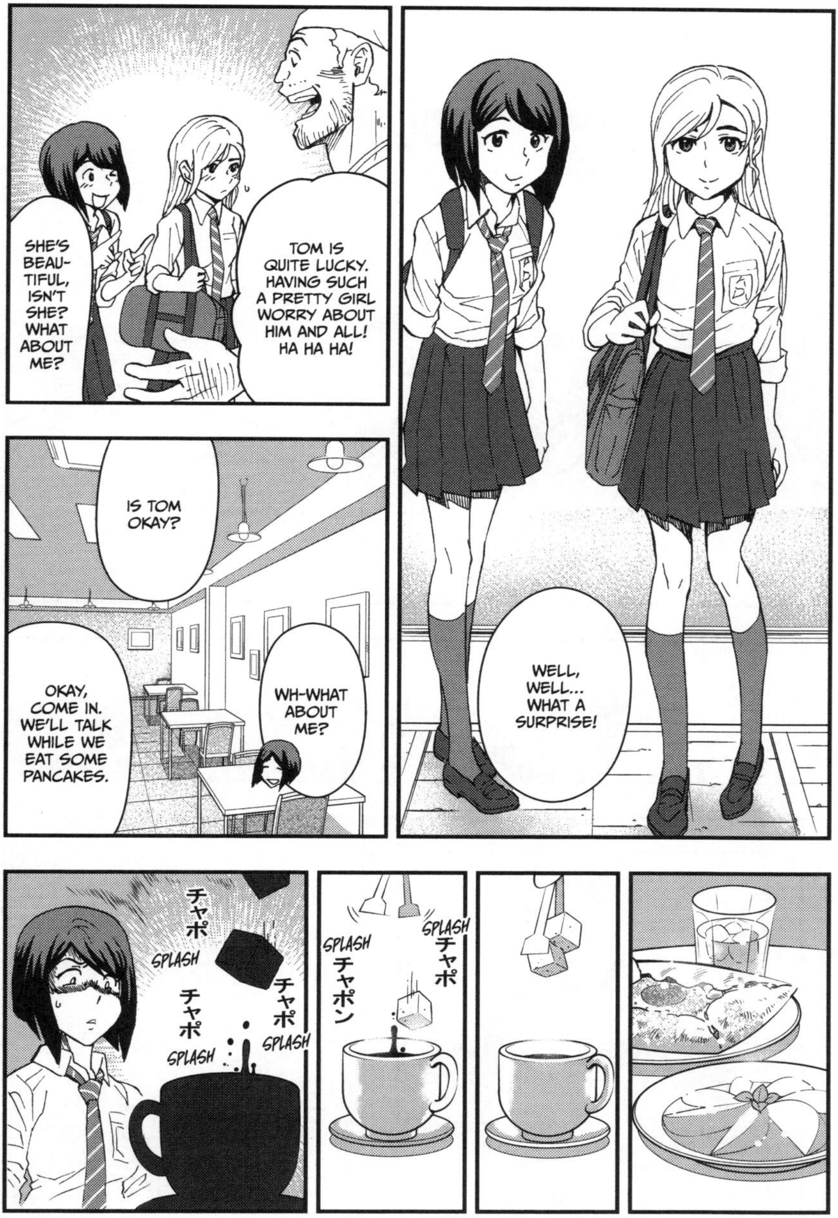
WELL, WELL... WHAT A SURPRISE!
TOM IS QUITE LUCKY. HAVING SUCH A PRETTY GIRL WORRY ABOUT HIM AND ALL! HA HA HA!
SHE'S BEAU-TIFUL, ISN'T SHE? WHAT ABOUT ME?
IS TOM OKAY?
WH-WHAT ABOUT ME?
OKAY, COME IN. WE'LL TALK WHILE WE EAT SOME PANCAKES.
SPLASH
チャポ
SPLASH
チャポン
チャポ
SPLASH
チャポ
SPLASH
チャポ
SPLASH

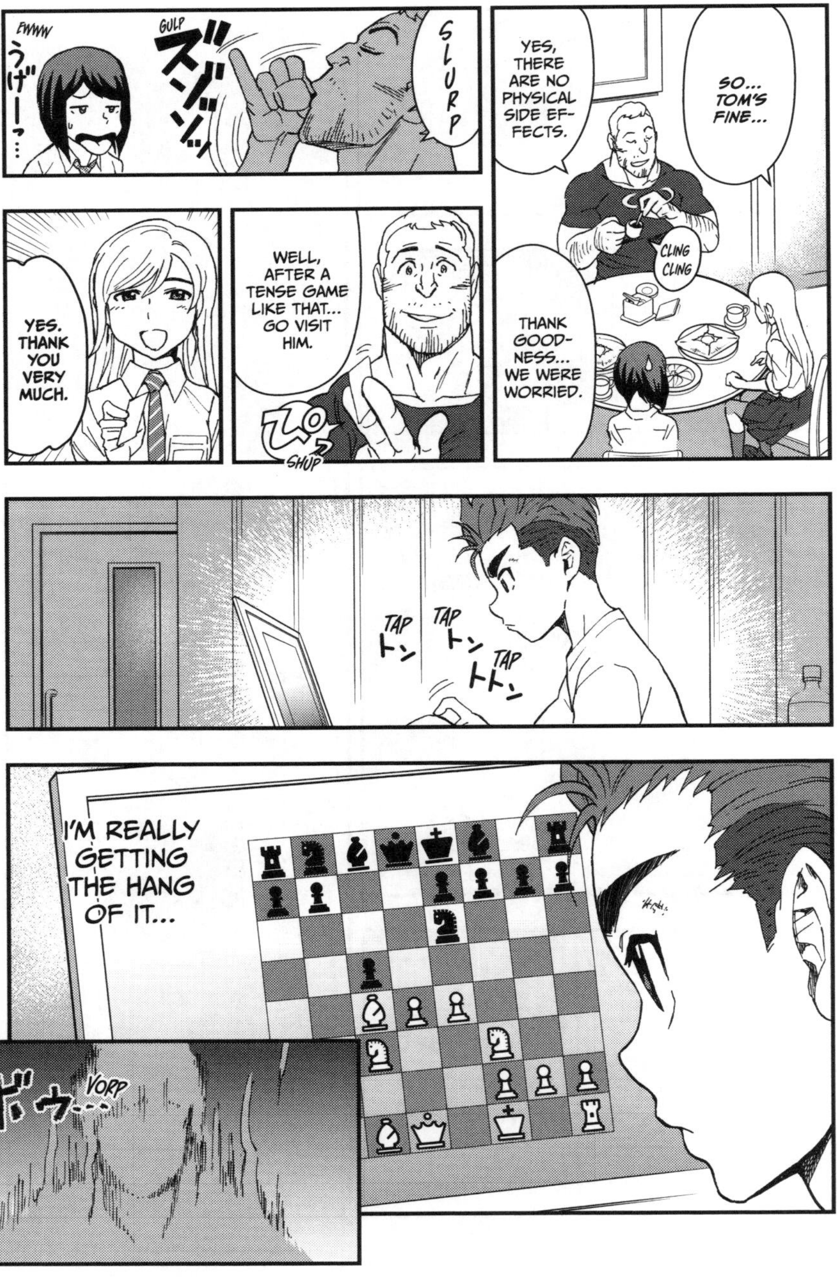
SO... TOM'S FINE...
YES, THERE ARE NO PHYSICAL SIDE EF- FECTS.
CLING CLING
THANK GOOD- NESS... WE WERE WORRIED.
SLURP
GULP
ズゾゾッ
EWWW
うげーっ...
WELL, AFTER A TENSE GAME LIKE THAT... GO VISIT HIM.
ぴっ
SHUP
YES. THANK YOU VERY MUCH.
TAP
トン
TAP
トン
TAP
トトン
I'M REALLY GETTING THE HANG OF IT...
ボウ...
VORP

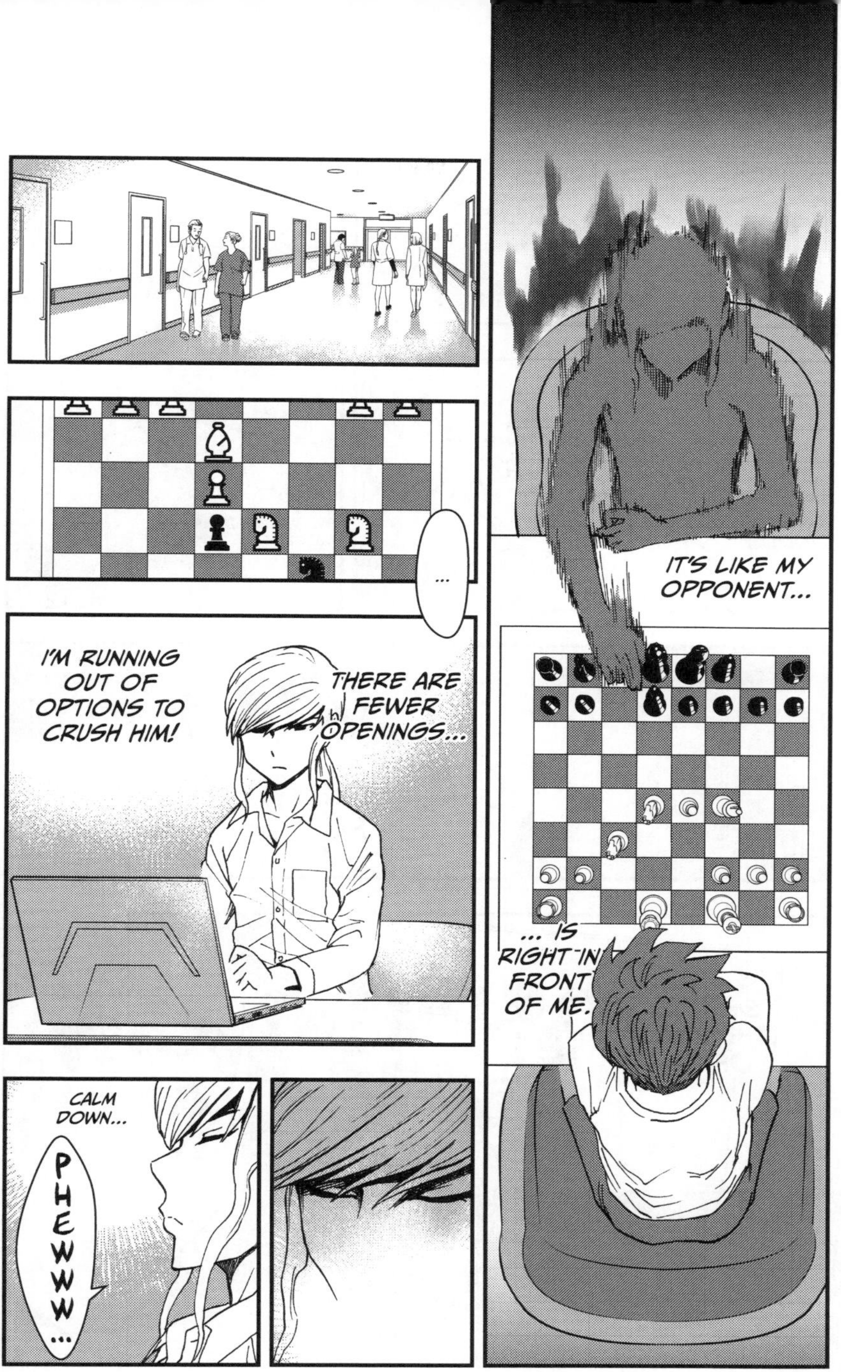
IT'S LIKE MY OPPONENT...
... IS RIGHT IN FRONT OF ME.
...
THERE ARE FEWER OPENINGS...
I'M RUNNING OUT OF OPTIONS TO CRUSH HIM!
CALM DOWN...
PHEWWW...

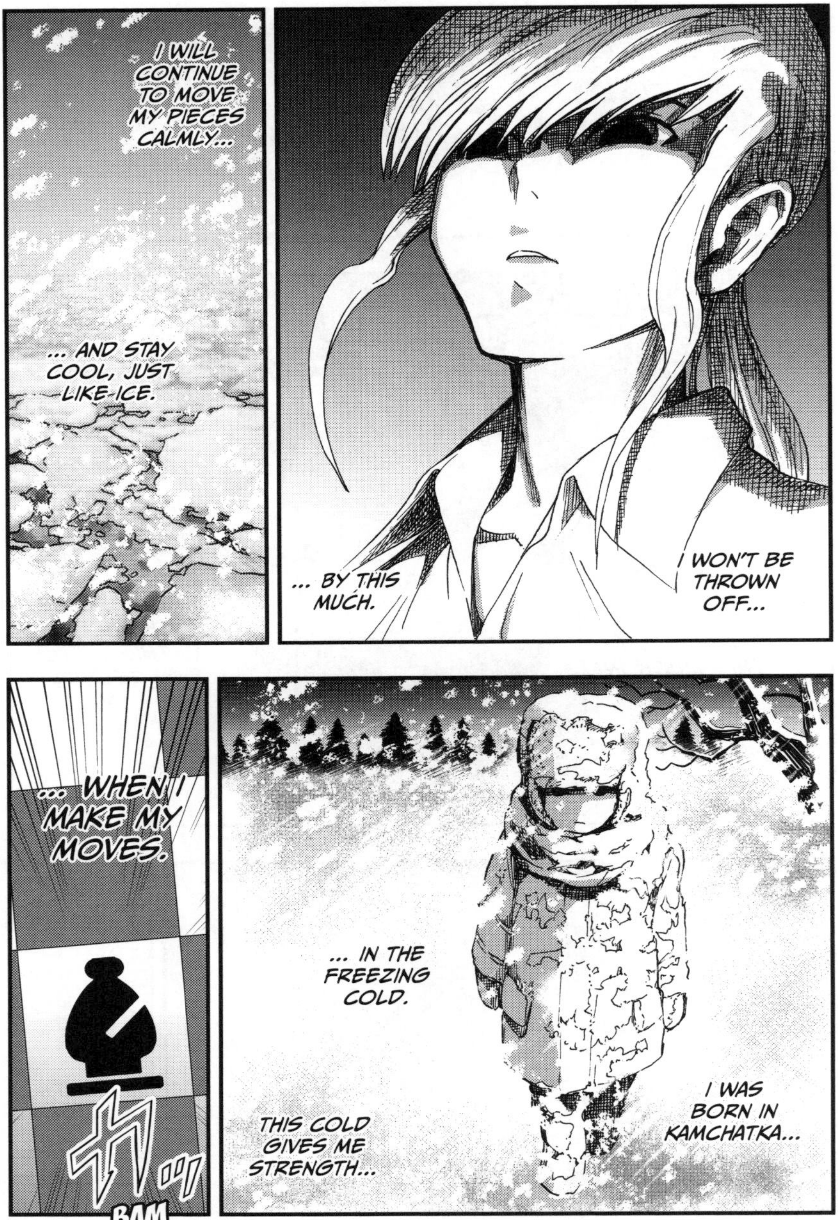

I WON'T BE THROWN OFF...
... BY THIS MUCH.
I WILL CONTINUE TO MOVE MY PIECES CALMLY...
... AND STAY COOL, JUST LIKE ICE.
I WAS BORN IN KAMCHATKA...
... IN THE FREEZING COLD.
THIS COLD GIVES ME STRENGTH...
... WHEN I MAKE MY MOVES.
BAM

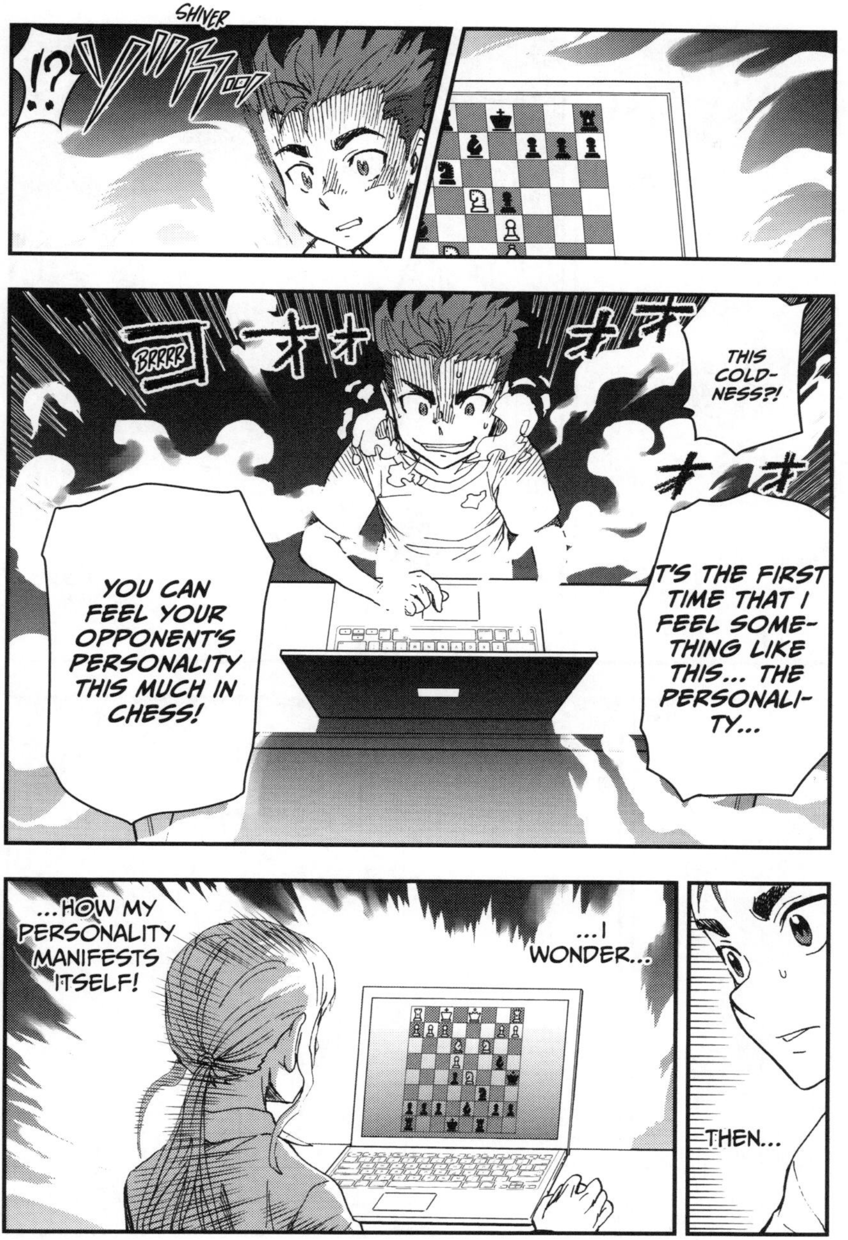
SHIVER
!?
BRRRR
THIS COLD-NESS?!
T'S THE FIRST TIME THAT I FEEL SOME-THING LIKE THIS... THE PERSONALI-TY...
YOU CAN FEEL YOUR OPPONENT'S PERSONALITY THIS MUCH IN CHESS!
THEN...
...I WONDER...
...HOW MY PERSONALITY MANIFESTS ITSELF!

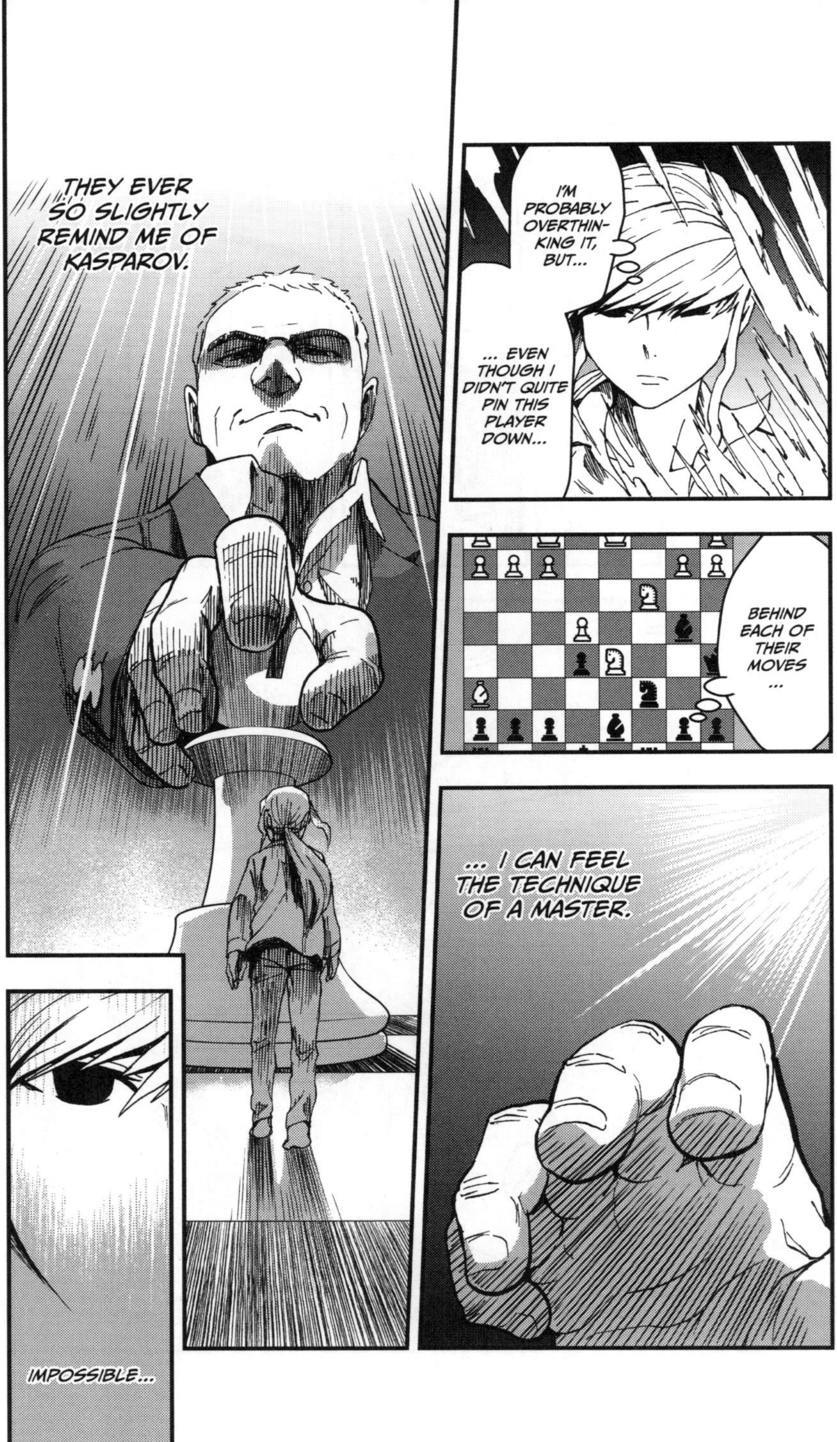
I'M PROBABLY OVERTHINKING IT, BUT...
... EVEN THOUGH I DIDN'T QUITE PIN THIS PLAYER DOWN...
BEHIND EACH OF THEIR MOVES ...
... I CAN FEEL THE TECHNIQUE OF A MASTER.
THEY EVER SO SLIGHTLY REMIND ME OF KASPAROV.
IMPOSSIBLE...

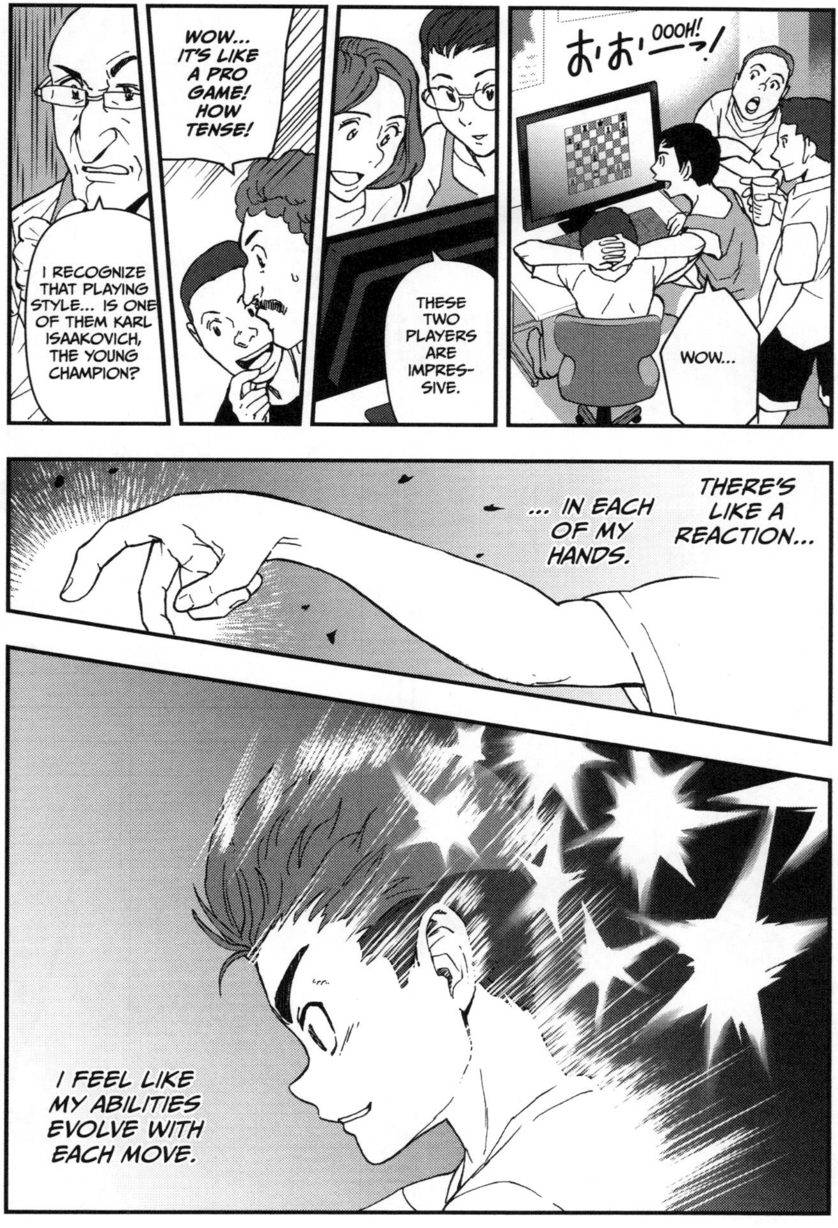
おおーっ!
OOOH!
WOW...
THESE TWO PLAYERS ARE IMPRES-SIVE.
WOW... IT'S LIKE A PRO GAME! HOW TENSE!
I RECOGNIZE THAT PLAYING STYLE... IS ONE OF THEM KARL ISAAKOVICH, THE YOUNG CHAMPION?
THERE'S LIKE A REACTION...
... IN EACH OF MY HANDS.
I FEEL LIKE MY ABILITIES EVOLVE WITH EACH MOVE.

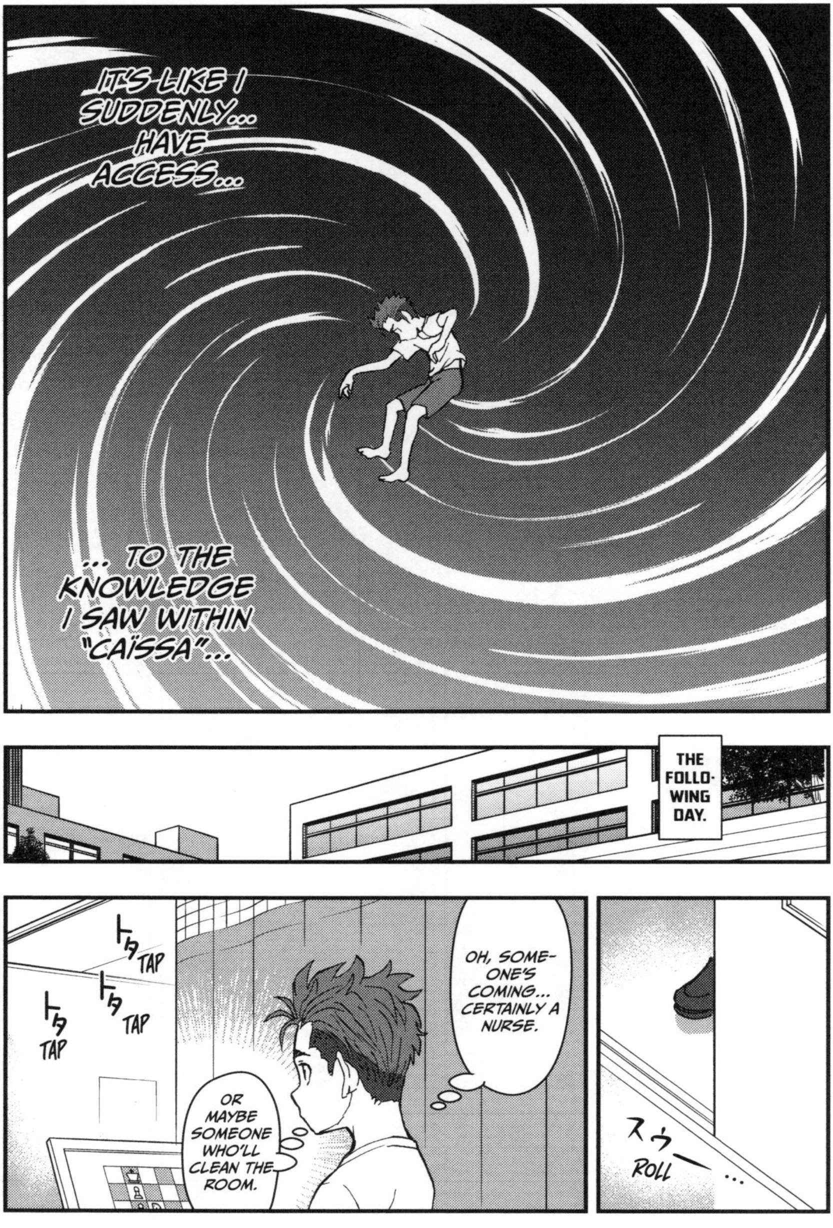
IT'S LIKE I SUDDENLY... HAVE ACCESS...
... TO THE KNOWLEDGE I SAW WITHIN "CAÏSSA"...
THE FOLLO-WING DAY.
スウー ROLL ...
トタ TAP
トタ TAP
トタ TAP
OH, SOME-ONE'S COMING... CERTAINLY A NURSE.
OR MAYBE SOMEONE WHO'LL CLEAN THE ROOM.

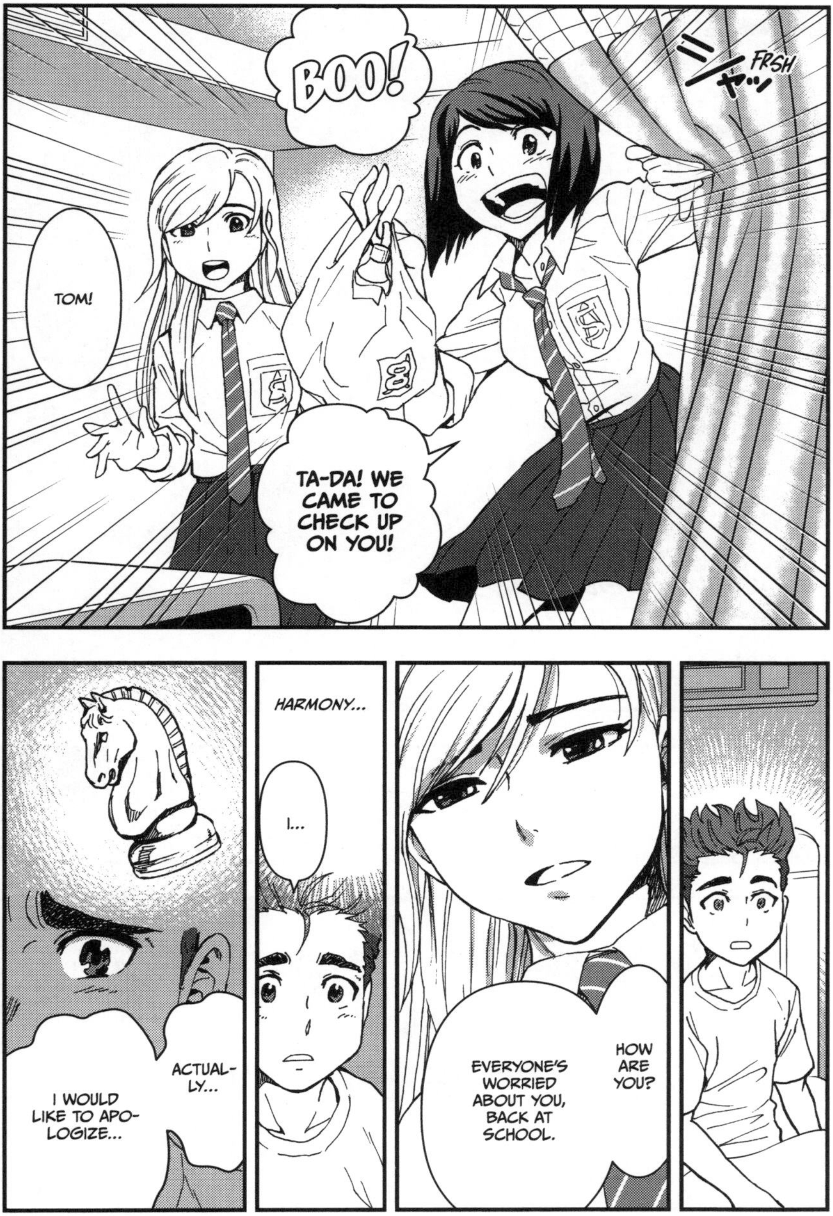
FRSH
BOO!
TOM!
TA-DA! WE CAME TO CHECK UP ON YOU!
HOW ARE YOU?
EVERYONE'S WORRIED ABOUT YOU, BACK AT SCHOOL.
HARMONY...
I...
ACTUAL-LY...
I WOULD LIKE TO APO-LOGIZE...

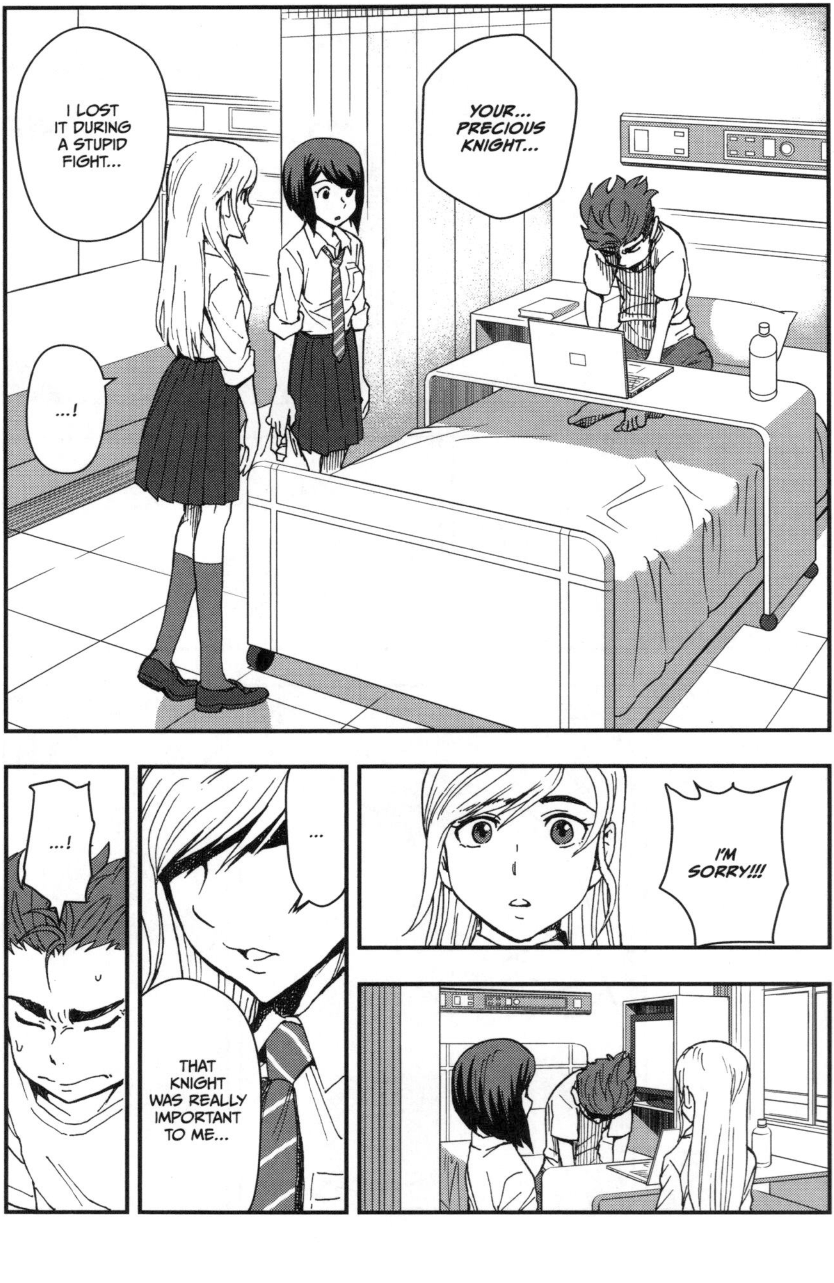
YOUR... PRECIOUS KNIGHT...
I LOST IT DURING A STUPID FIGHT...
...!
I'M SORRY!!!
...
THAT KNIGHT WAS REALLY IMPORTANT TO ME...
...!

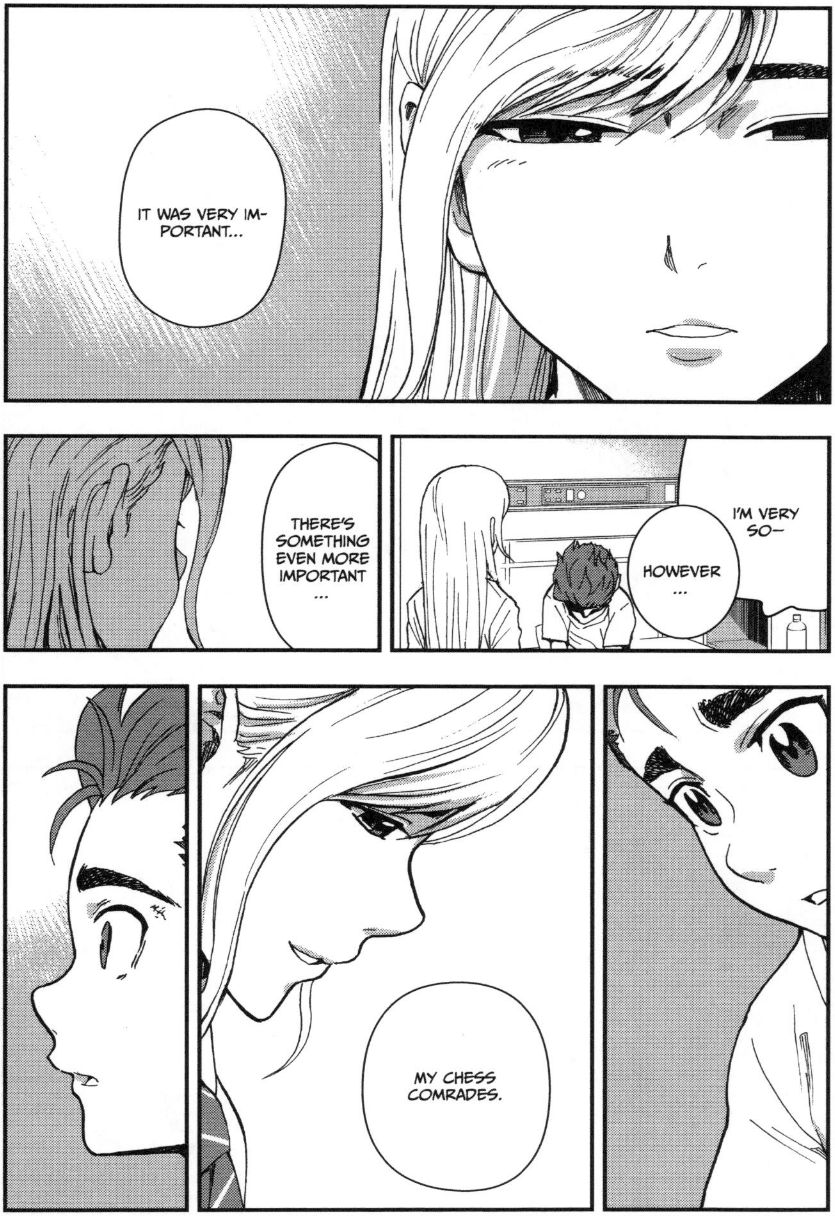
IT WAS VERY IMPORTANT...
I'M VERY SO—
HOWEVER ...
THERE'S SOMETHING EVEN MORE IMPORTANT ...
MY CHESS COMRADES.

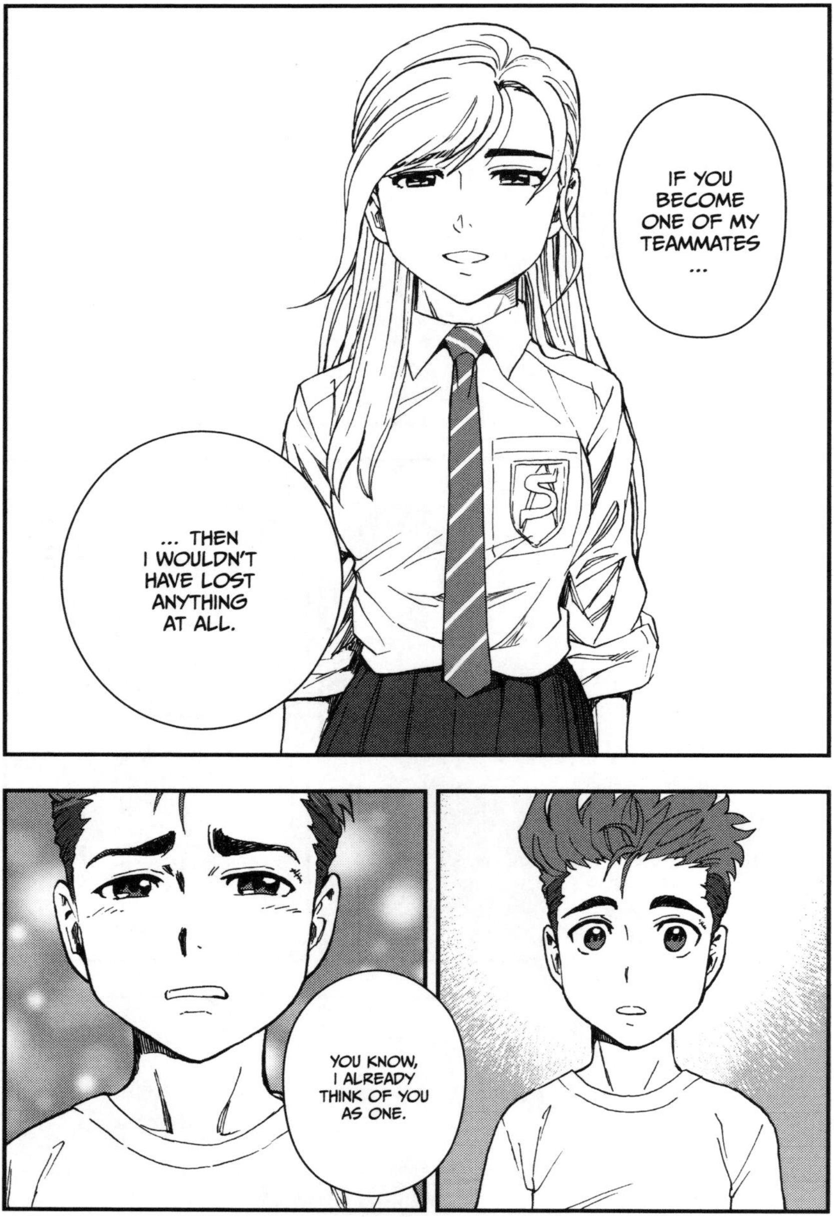
IF YOU BECOME ONE OF MY TEAMMATES ...
... THEN I WOULDN'T HAVE LOST ANYTHING AT ALL.
YOU KNOW, I ALREADY THINK OF YOU AS ONE.

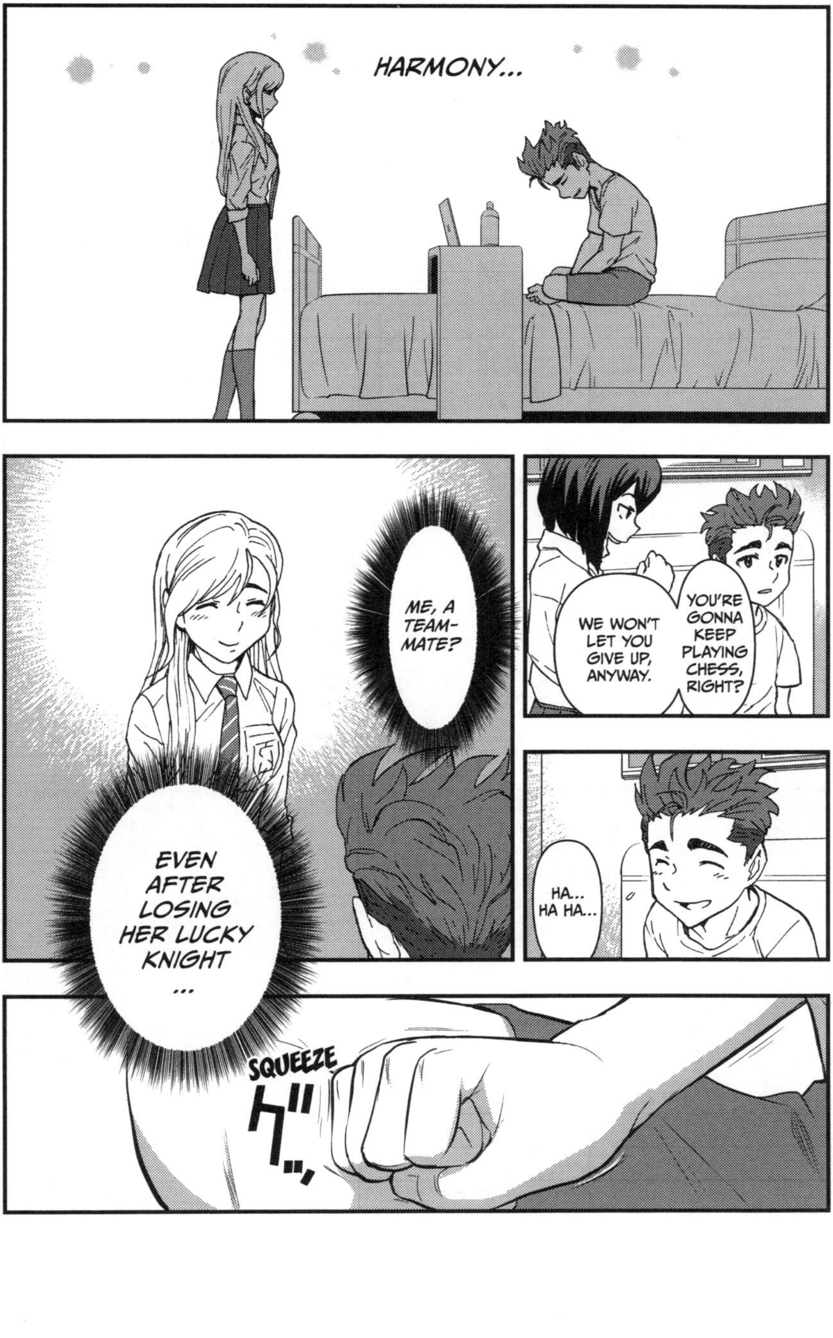
HARMONY...
YOU'RE GONNA KEEP PLAYING CHESS, RIGHT?
WE WON'T LET YOU GIVE UP, ANYWAY.
HA... HA HA...
ME, A TEAM-MATE?
EVEN AFTER LOSING HER LUCKY KNIGHT ...
SQUEEZE
グッ

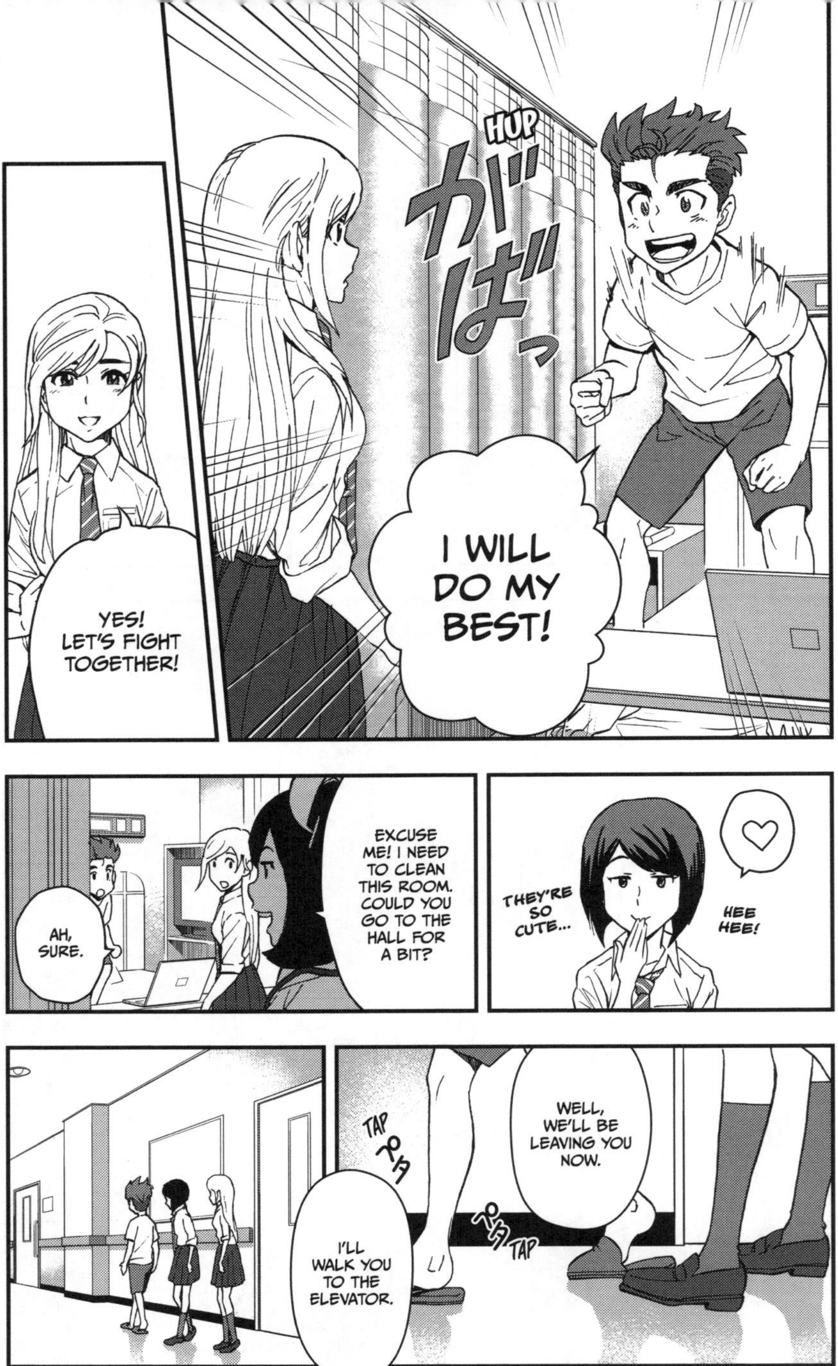
HUP
がばっ
I WILL DO MY BEST!
YES! LET'S FIGHT TOGETHER!
THEY'RE SO CUTE...
HEE HEE!
EXCUSE ME! I NEED TO CLEAN THIS ROOM. COULD YOU GO TO THE HALL FOR A BIT?
AH, SURE.
WELL, WE'LL BE LEAVING YOU NOW.
TAP
ぺた
ぺた
TAP
I'LL WALK YOU TO THE ELEVATOR.

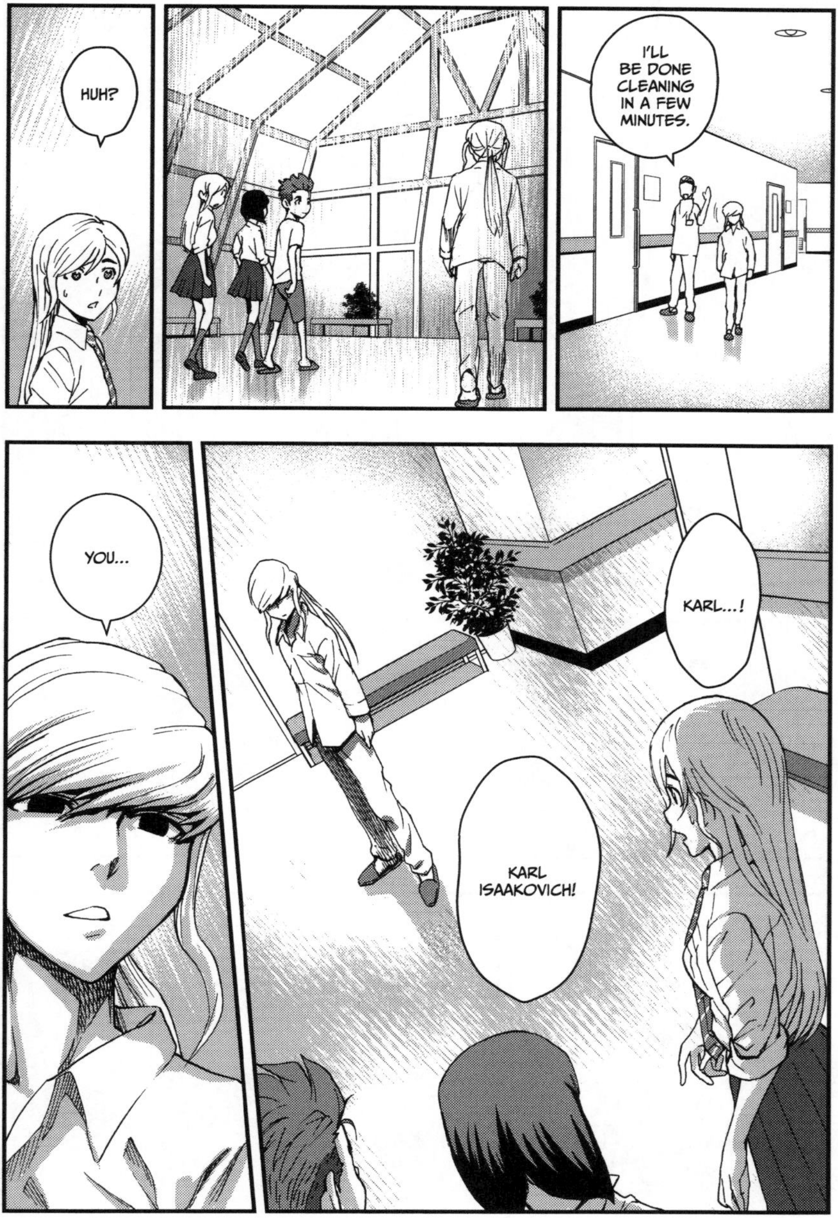
I'LL BE DONE CLEANING IN A FEW MINUTES.
HUH?
KARL...!
KARL ISAAKOVICH!
YOU...

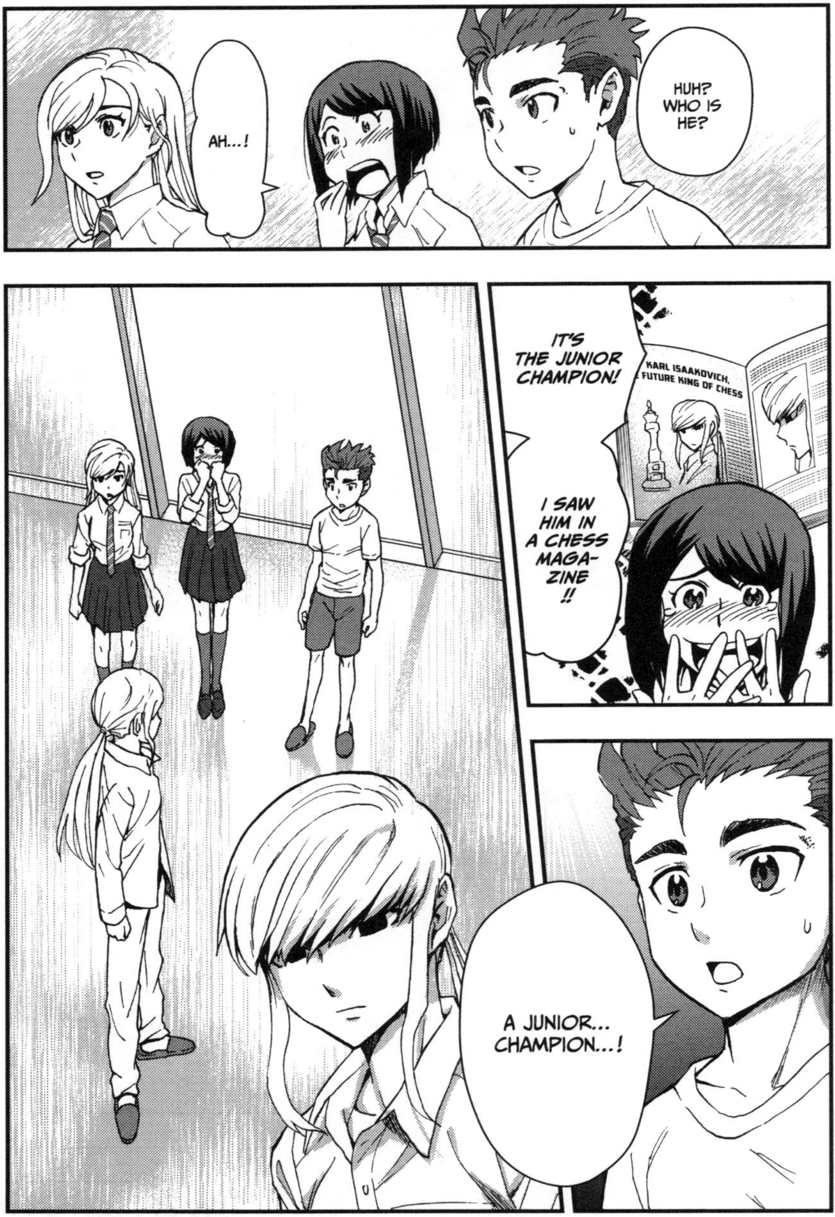
HUH? WHO IS HE?
AH...!
IT'S THE JUNIOR CHAMPION!
KARL ISAAKOVICH,
E FUTURE KING OF CHESS
I SAW HIM IN A CHESS MAGAZINE !!
A JUNIOR... CHAMPION...!

BLITZ

Chapter 8: Project T

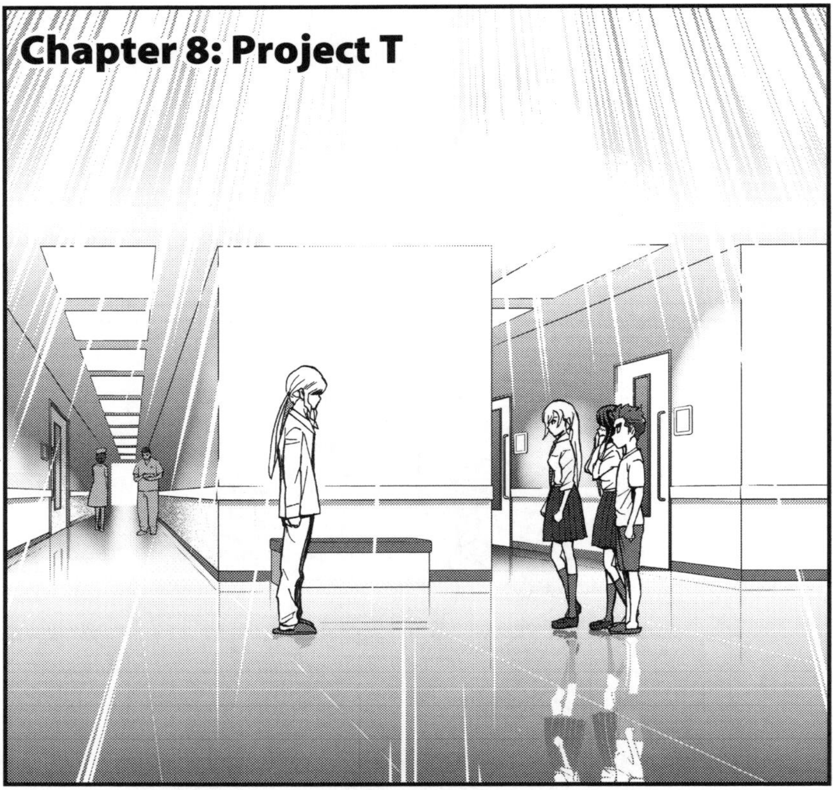

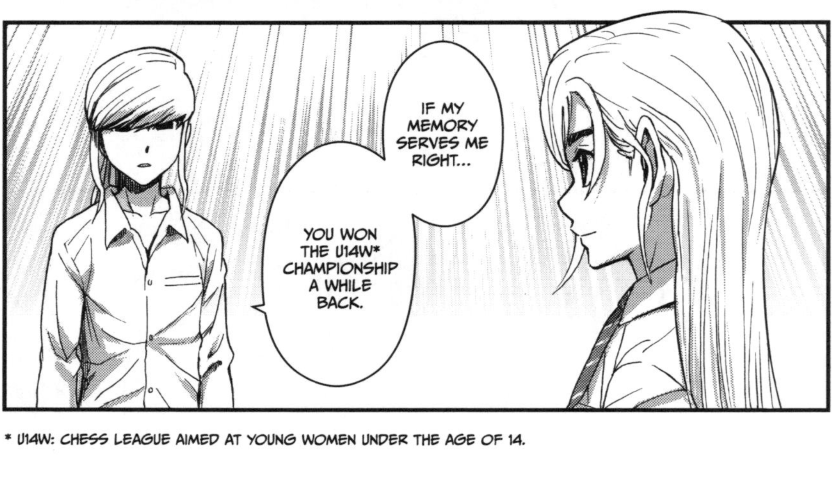
IF MY MEMORY SERVES ME RIGHT...
YOU WON THE U14W* CHAMPIONSHIP A WHILE BACK.

* U14W: CHESS LEAGUE AIMED AT YOUNG WOMEN UNDER THE AGE OF 14.

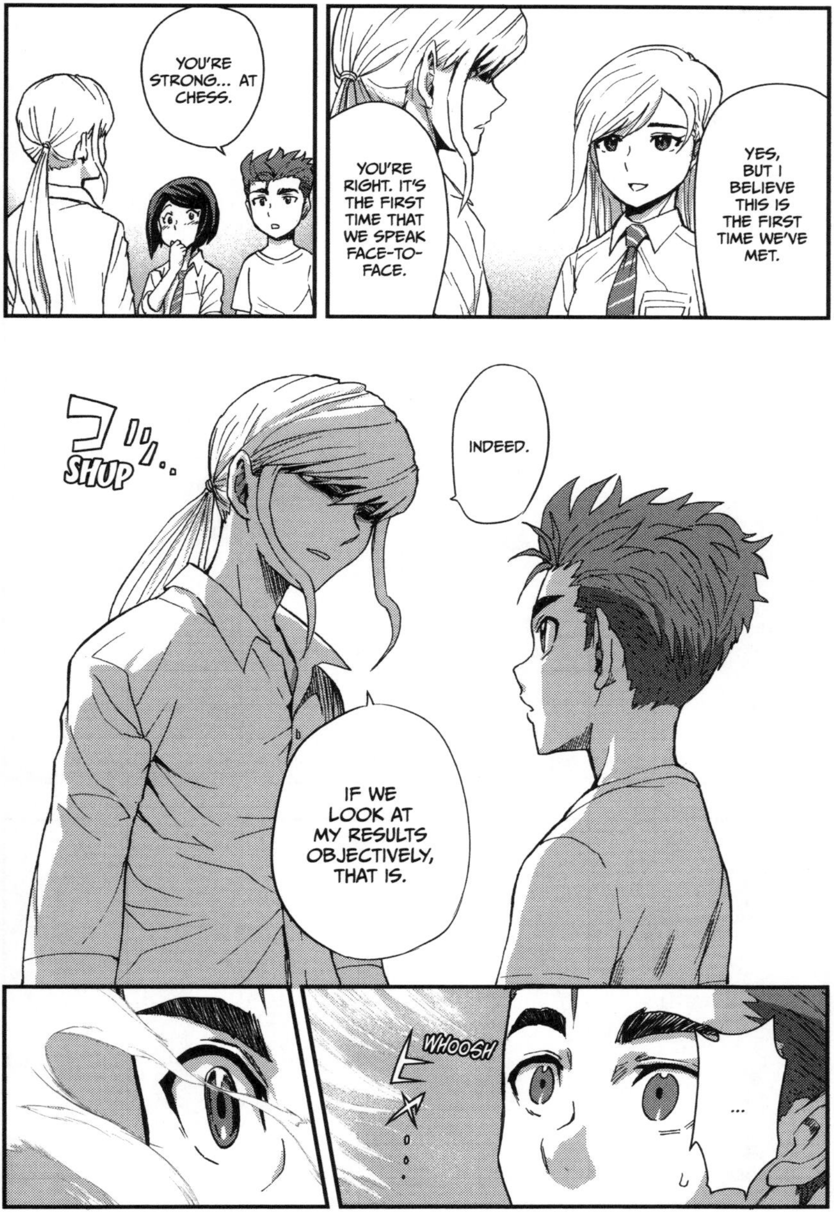
YES, BUT I BELIEVE THIS IS THE FIRST TIME WE'VE MET.
YOU'RE RIGHT. IT'S THE FIRST TIME THAT WE SPEAK FACE-TO-FACE.
YOU'RE STRONG... AT CHESS.
INDEED.
SHUP
IF WE LOOK AT MY RESULTS OBJECTIVELY, THAT IS.
WHOOSH
...

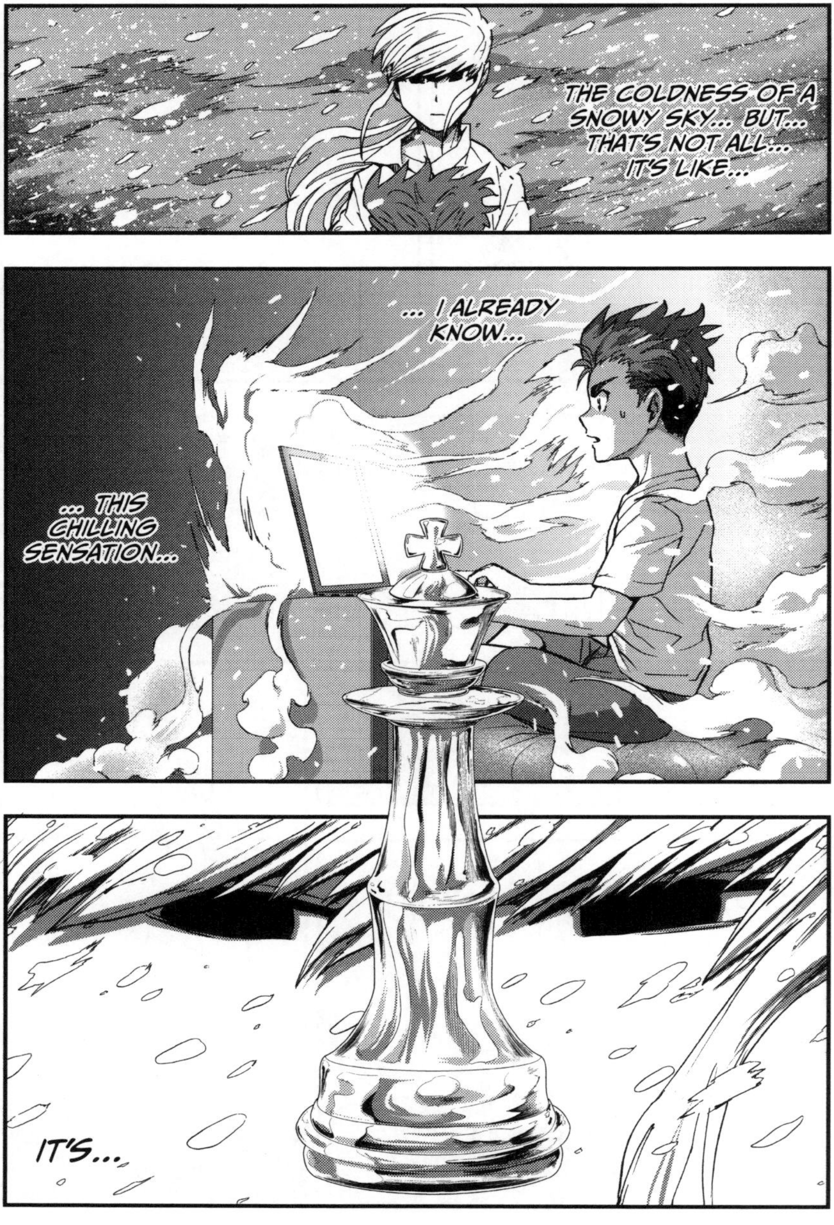
THE COLDNESS OF A SNOWY SKY... BUT... THAT'S NOT ALL... IT'S LIKE...
... I ALREADY KNOW...
... THIS CHILLING SENSATION...
IT'S...

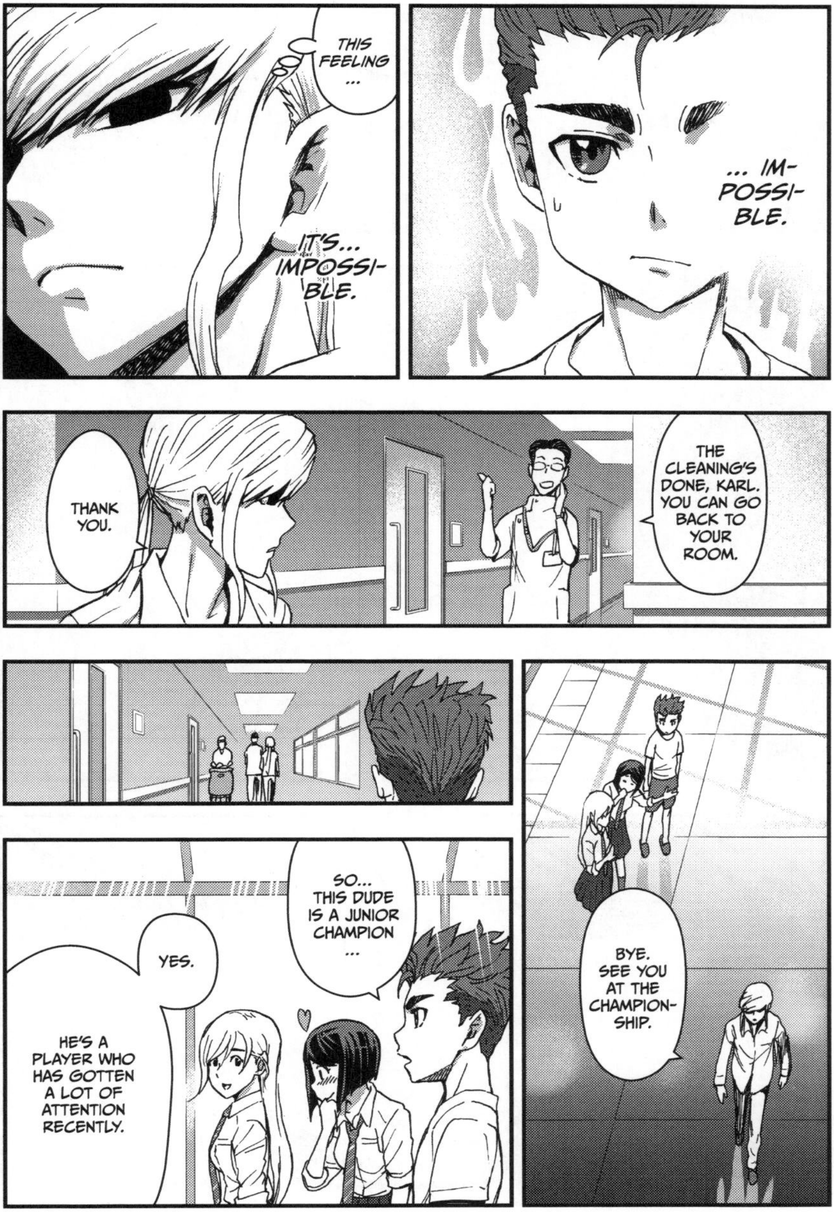
... IM-POSSI-BLE.
THIS FEELING ...
IT'S... IMPOSSI-BLE.
THE CLEANING'S DONE, KARL. YOU CAN GO BACK TO YOUR ROOM.
THANK YOU.
BYE. SEE YOU AT THE CHAMPION-SHIP.
SO... THIS DUDE IS A JUNIOR CHAMPION ...
YES.
HE'S A PLAYER WHO HAS GOTTEN A LOT OF ATTENTION RECENTLY.

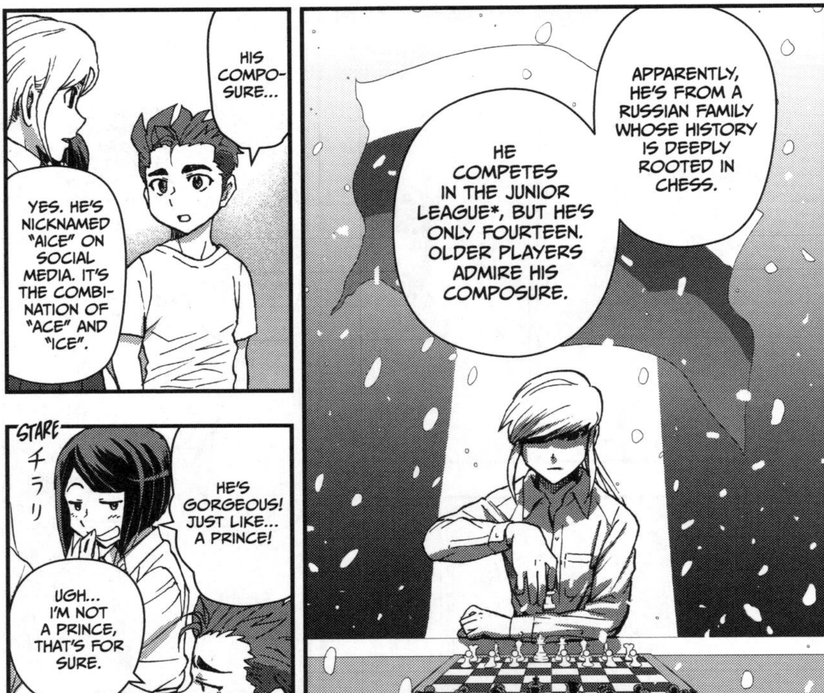
APPARENTLY, HE'S FROM A RUSSIAN FAMILY WHOSE HISTORY IS DEEPLY ROOTED IN CHESS.
HE COMPETES IN THE JUNIOR LEAGUE*, BUT HE'S ONLY FOURTEEN. OLDER PLAYERS ADMIRE HIS COMPOSURE.
HIS COMPO-SURE...
YES. HE'S NICKNAMED "AICE" ON SOCIAL MEDIA. IT'S THE COMBI-NATION OF "ACE" AND "ICE".
STARE
チラリ
HE'S GORGEOUS! JUST LIKE... A PRINCE!
UGH... I'M NOT A PRINCE, THAT'S FOR SURE.
I FEEL MORE LIKE A PAWN.

* JUNIOR LEAGUE: CHESS LEAGUE AIMED AT PLAYERS AGED BETWEEN 18 AND 20.

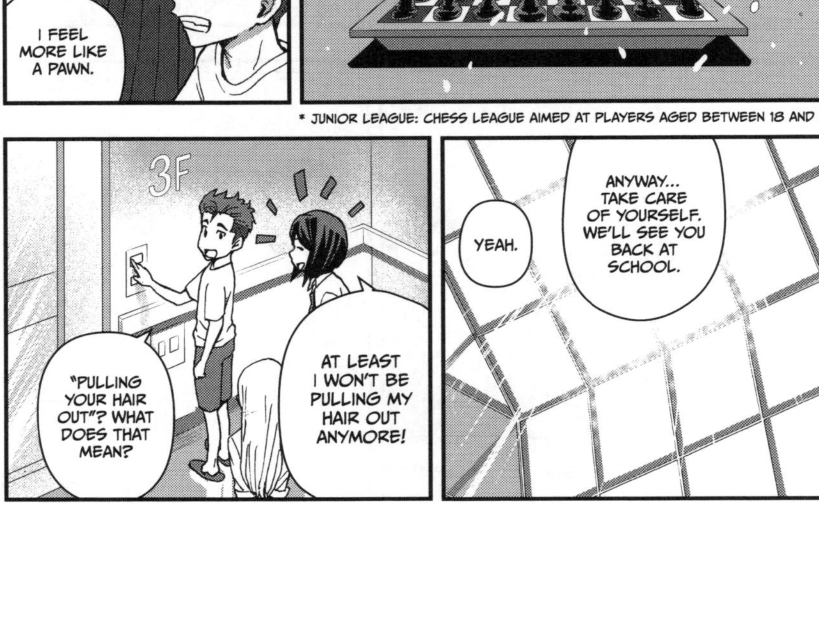
ANYWAY... TAKE CARE OF YOURSELF. WE'LL SEE YOU BACK AT SCHOOL.
YEAH.
3F
AT LEAST I WON'T BE PULLING MY HAIR OUT ANYMORE!
"PULLING YOUR HAIR OUT"? WHAT DOES THAT MEAN?

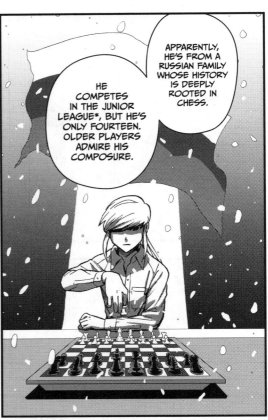

ALRIGHT, GET BETTER SOON!

BYE BYE! バイ♡
バイ♡

IT'S AN OLD EXPRESSION MY GRANDPA USED TO SAY, AND IT MEANS "TO WORRY".

HE WOULD SAY "NO MORE PULLING MY HAIR OUT!" WHEN THINGS GOT BETTER.

NO MORE PULLING MY HAIR OUT!

HA HA HA!

OH YEAH...

OLD-TIMER STUFF...

ケシ...
SHUT

YOU HAD A VISIT? THEY'RE VERY PRETTY.

YEAH...

HUP

は——...♡ AH...

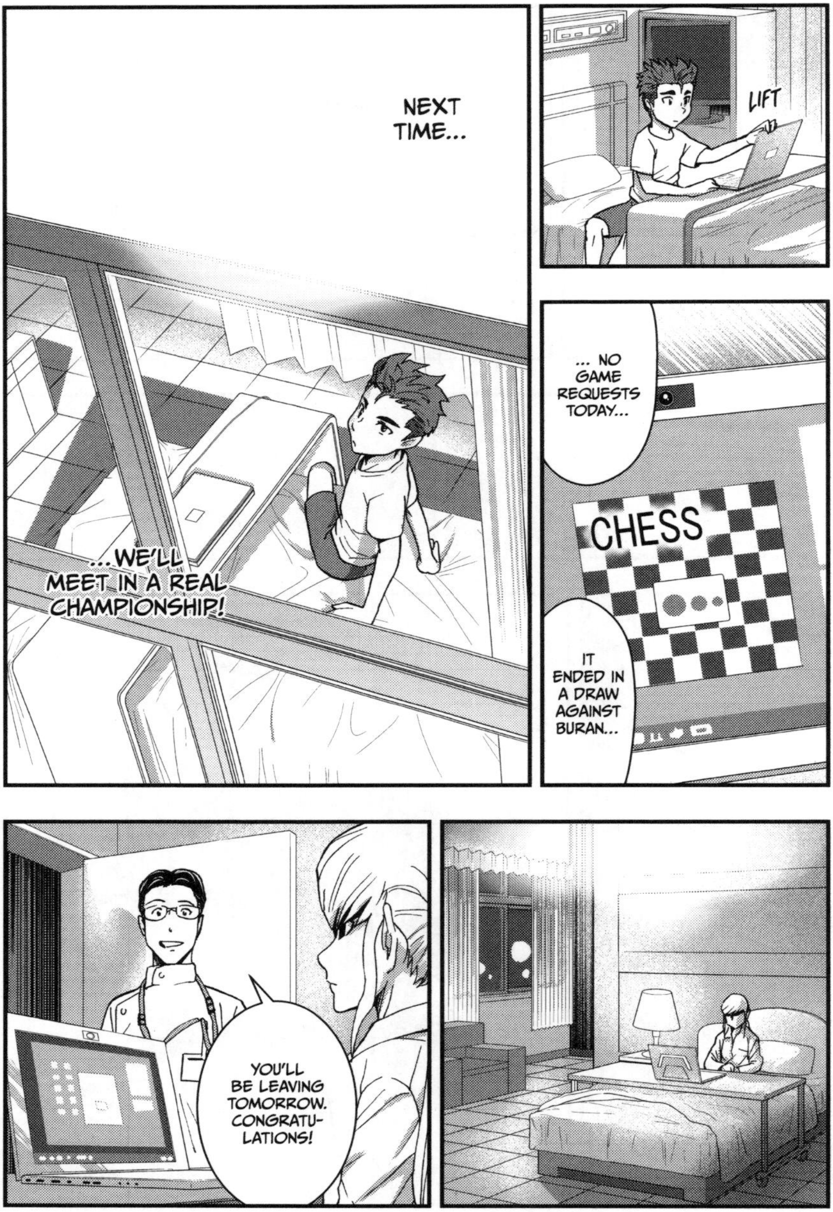
LIFT
... NO GAME REQUESTS TODAY...
CHESS
IT ENDED IN A DRAW AGAINST BURAN...
NEXT TIME...
...WE'LL MEET IN A REAL CHAMPIONSHIP!
YOU'LL BE LEAVING TOMORROW. CONGRATU-LATIONS!

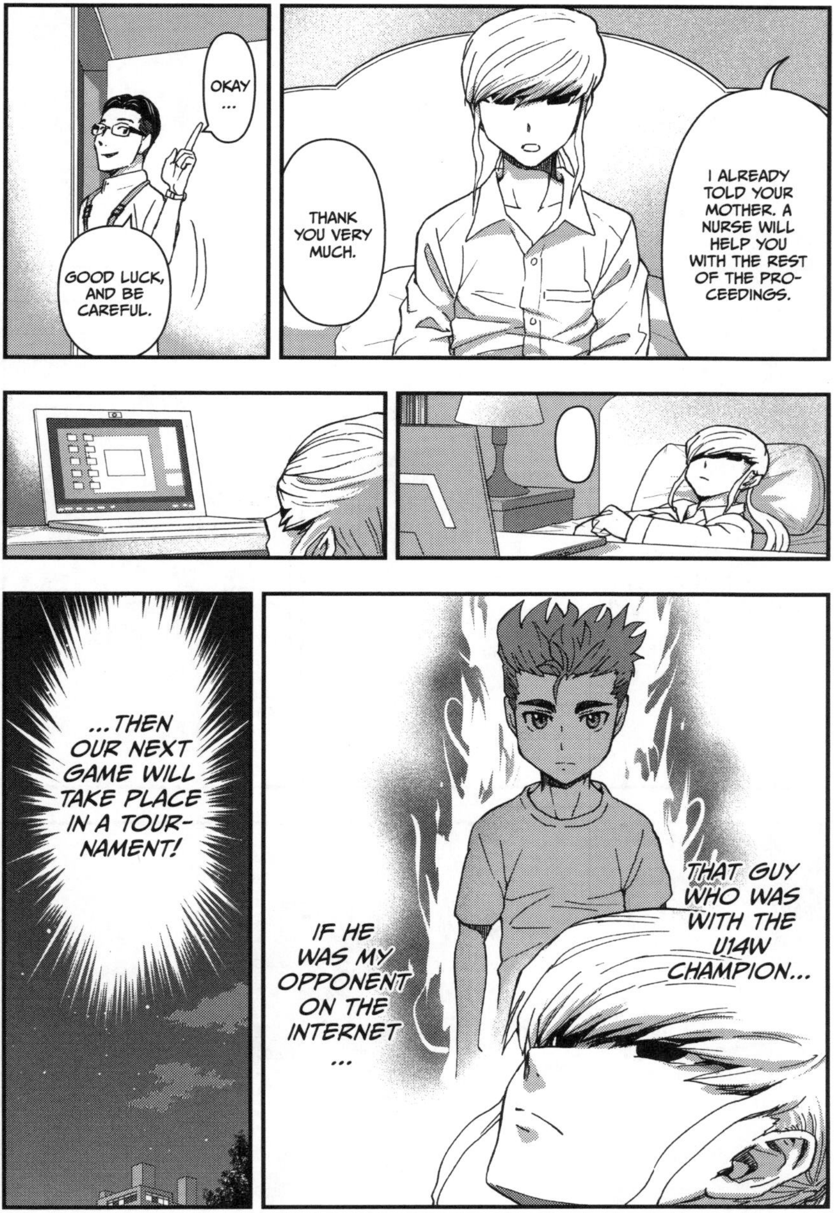
I ALREADY TOLD YOUR MOTHER. A NURSE WILL HELP YOU WITH THE REST OF THE PRO-CEEDINGS.
THANK YOU VERY MUCH.
OKAY ...
GOOD LUCK, AND BE CAREFUL.
THAT GUY WHO WAS WITH THE U14W CHAMPION...
IF HE WAS MY OPPONENT ON THE INTERNET ...
...THEN OUR NEXT GAME WILL TAKE PLACE IN A TOUR-NAMENT!

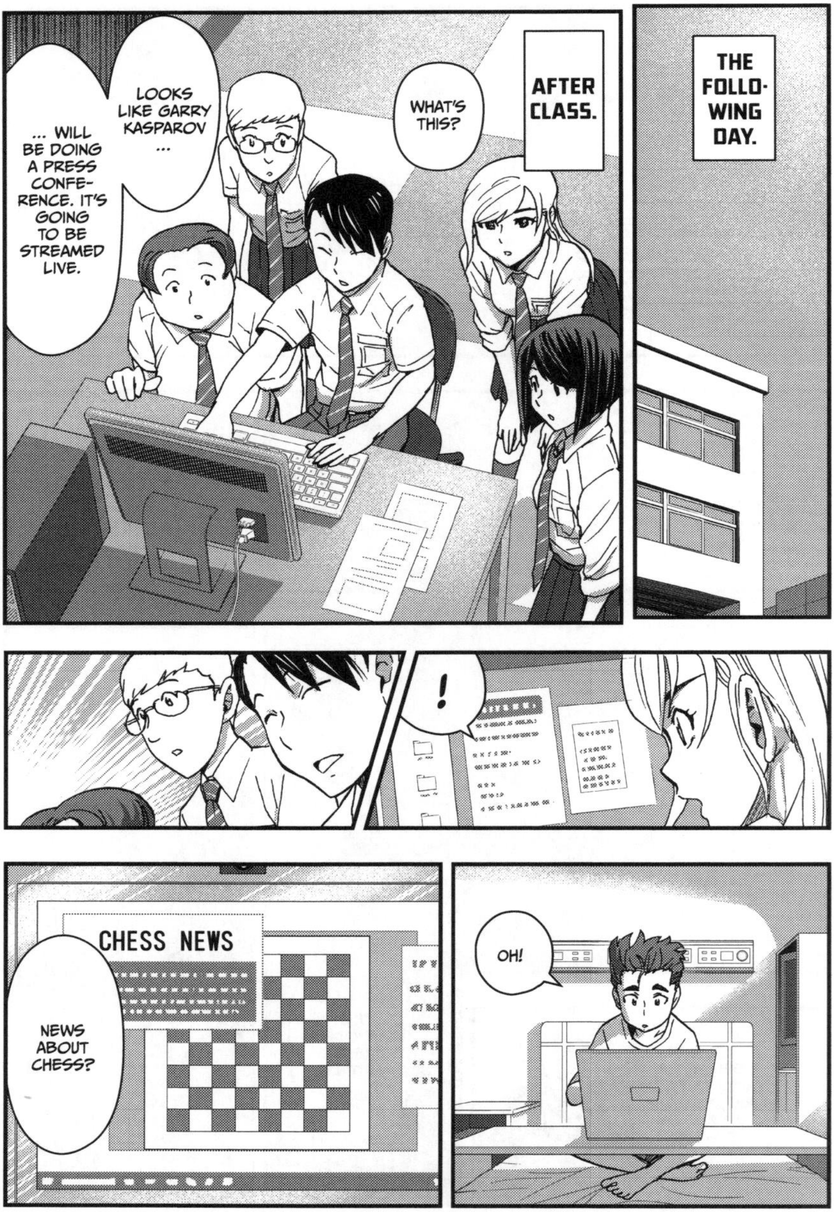
THE FOLLOWING DAY.
AFTER CLASS.
WHAT'S THIS?
LOOKS LIKE GARRY KASPAROV ...
... WILL BE DOING A PRESS CONFERENCE. IT'S GOING TO BE STREAMED LIVE.
!
OH!
CHESS NEWS
NEWS ABOUT CHESS?

MY GUT FEELING TELLS ME...

... IT'S GOING TO BE REALLY COOL!

PRINCIPALITY OF MONACO, MEDITERRANEAN COAST.

THE JOURNALISTS ARE ALL WAITING.

YOU CAN SEE MEDIA OUTLETS FROM ALL OVER THE WORLD ON THIS LIST.

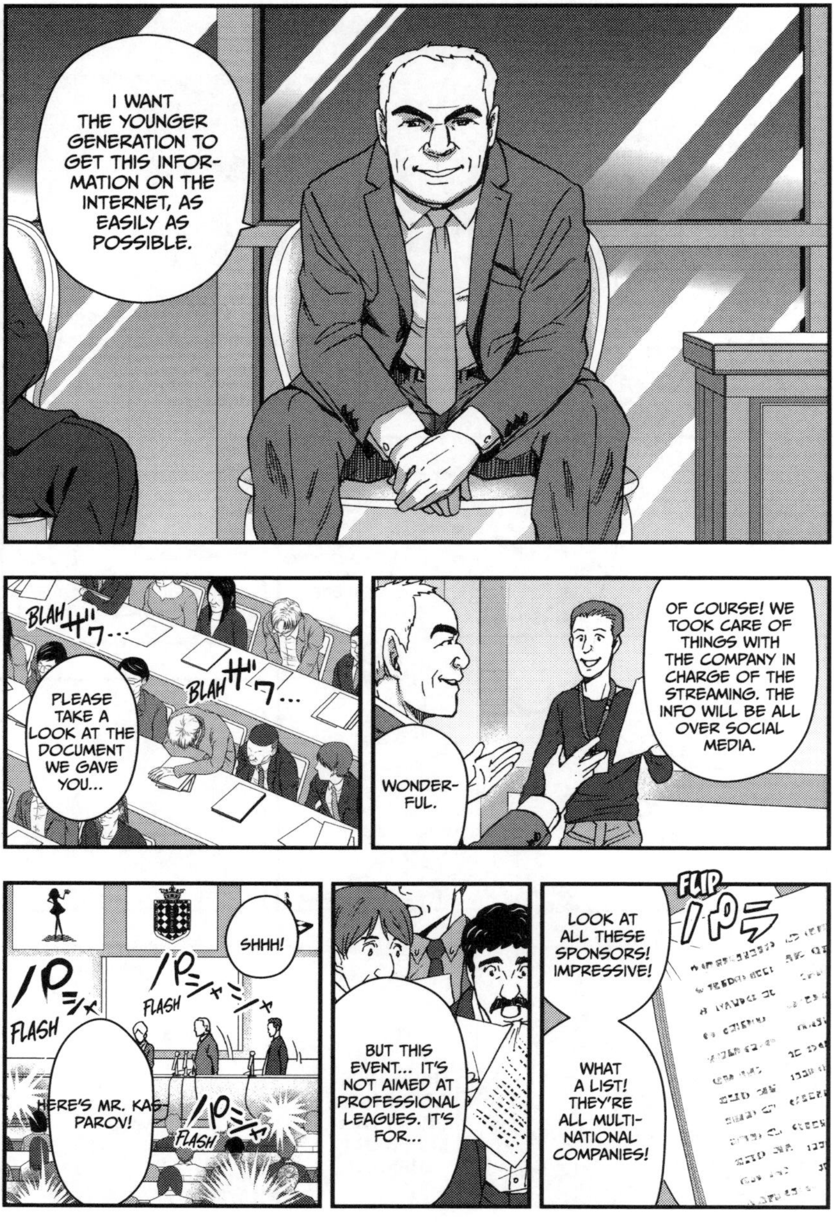
I WANT THE YOUNGER GENERATION TO GET THIS INFORMATION ON THE INTERNET, AS EASILY AS POSSIBLE.
OF COURSE! WE TOOK CARE OF THINGS WITH THE COMPANY IN CHARGE OF THE STREAMING. THE INFO WILL BE ALL OVER SOCIAL MEDIA.
WONDERFUL.
BLAH ザワ...
BLAH ザワ...
PLEASE TAKE A LOOK AT THE DOCUMENT WE GAVE YOU...
FLIP パラ
LOOK AT ALL THESE SPONSORS! IMPRESSIVE!
WHAT A LIST! THEY'RE ALL MULTINATIONAL COMPANIES!
BUT THIS EVENT... IT'S NOT AIMED AT PROFESSIONAL LEAGUES. IT'S FOR...
SHHH!
FLASH パシャシャ
FLASH パシャ
HERE'S MR. KASPAROV!
FLASH パシャ

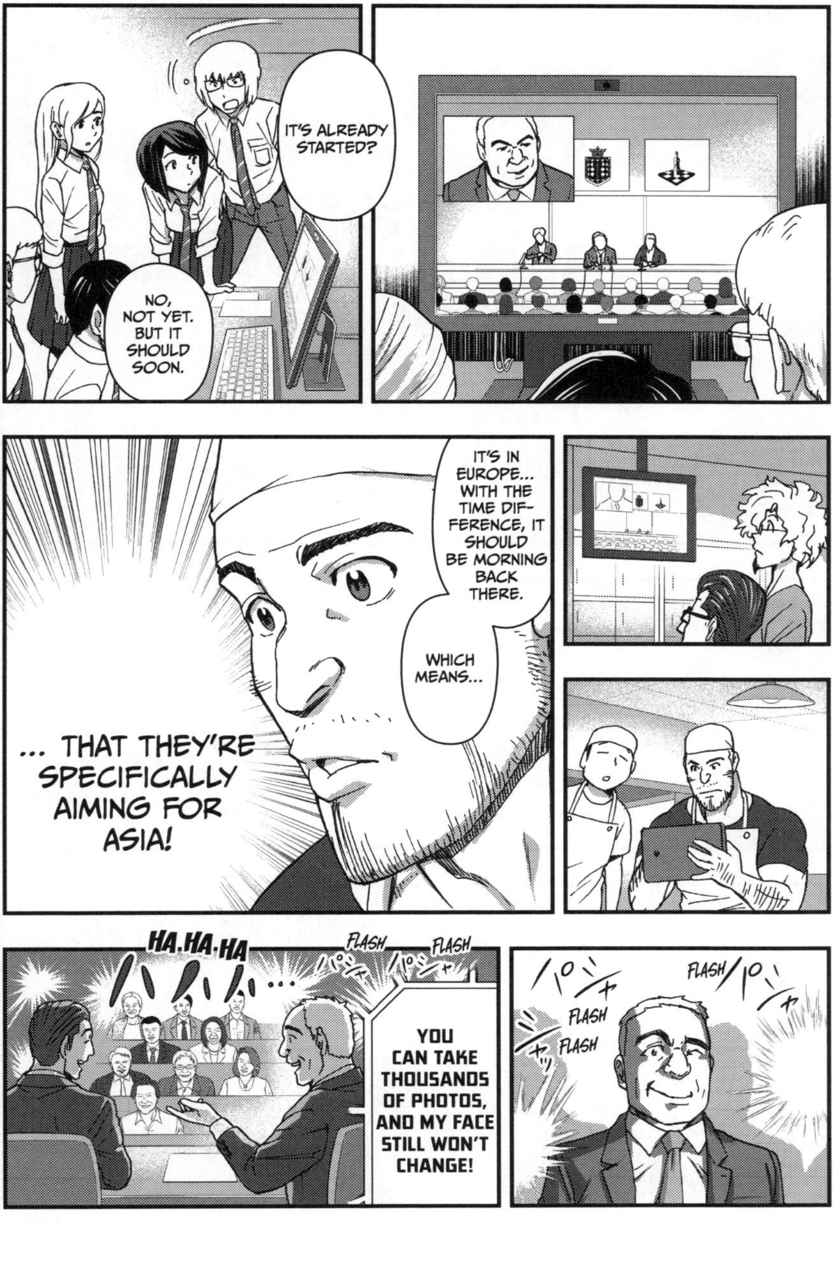
IT'S ALREADY STARTED?
NO, NOT YET. BUT IT SHOULD SOON.
IT'S IN EUROPE... WITH THE TIME DIFFERENCE, IT SHOULD BE MORNING BACK THERE.
WHICH MEANS...
... THAT THEY'RE SPECIFICALLY AIMING FOR ASIA!
FLASH
FLASH
FLASH
FLASH
HA-HA-HA
FLASH
FLASH
YOU CAN TAKE THOUSANDS OF PHOTOS, AND MY FACE STILL WON'T CHANGE!

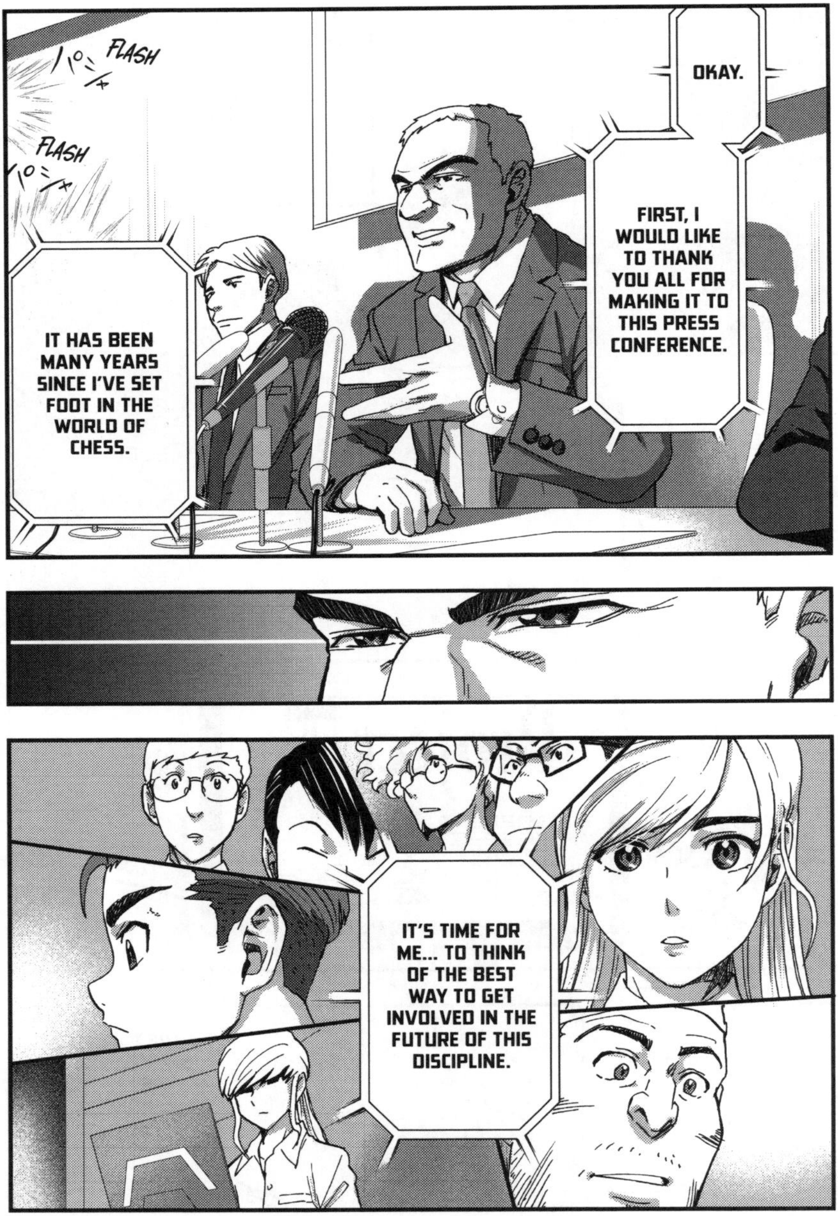
OKAY.
FIRST, I WOULD LIKE TO THANK YOU ALL FOR MAKING IT TO THIS PRESS CONFERENCE.
FLASH
FLASH
IT HAS BEEN MANY YEARS SINCE I'VE SET FOOT IN THE WORLD OF CHESS.
IT'S TIME FOR ME... TO THINK OF THE BEST WAY TO GET INVOLVED IN THE FUTURE OF THIS DISCIPLINE.

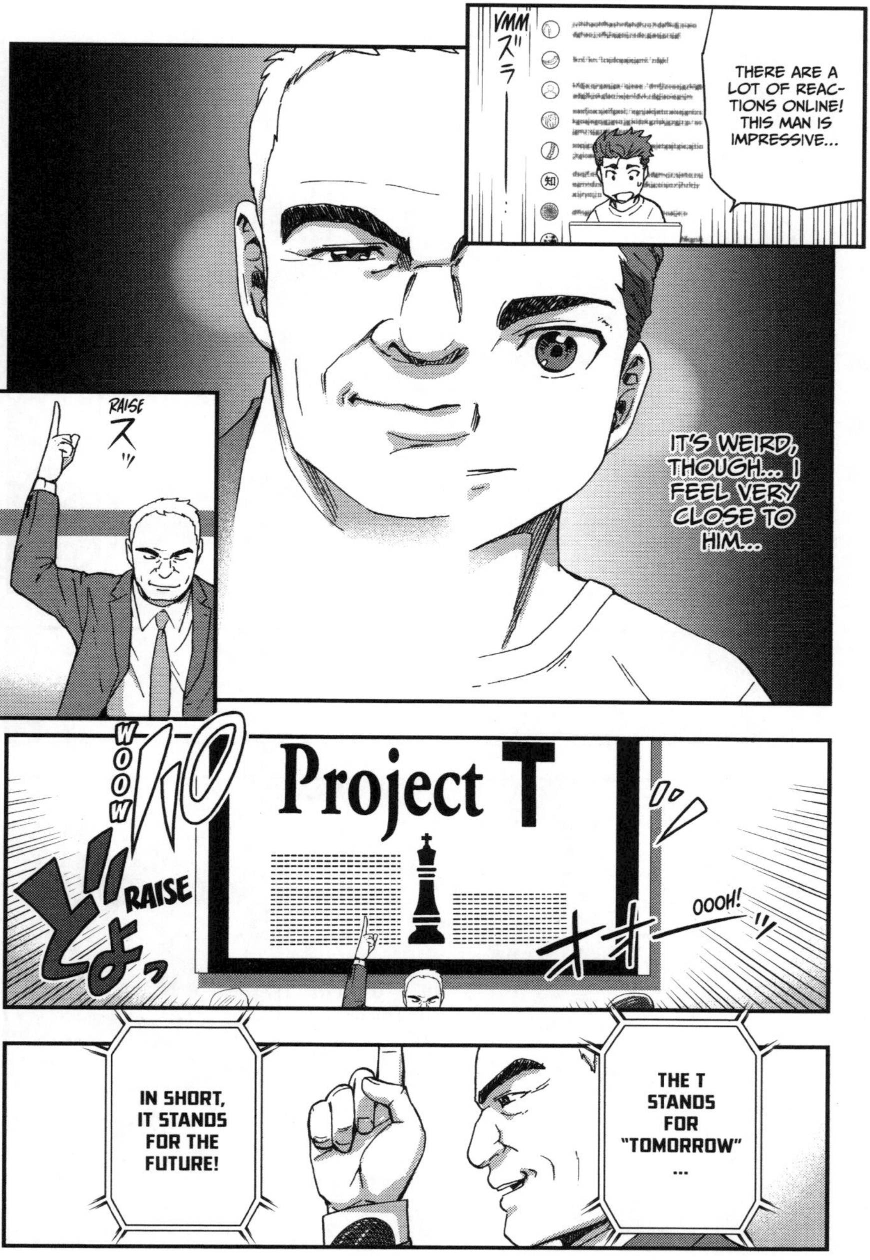
VMM
ズラー
THERE ARE A LOT OF REACTIONS ONLINE! THIS MAN IS IMPRESSIVE...
IT'S WEIRD, THOUGH... I FEEL VERY CLOSE TO HIM...
RAISE
スッ
Project T
OOOH!
オオー
WOOW
パ
RAISE
どよっ
THE T STANDS FOR "TOMORROW"...
IN SHORT, IT STANDS FOR THE FUTURE!

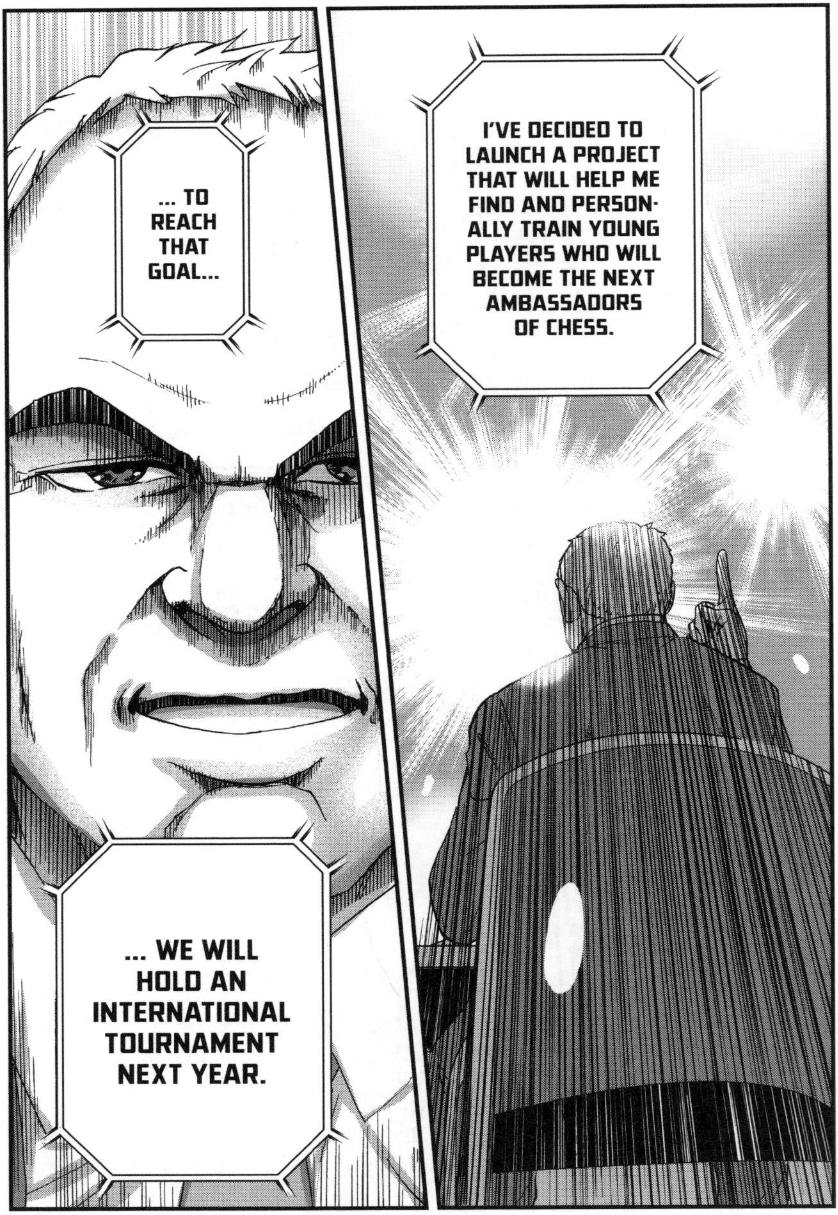
I'VE DECIDED TO LAUNCH A PROJECT THAT WILL HELP ME FIND AND PERSON-ALLY TRAIN YOUNG PLAYERS WHO WILL BECOME THE NEXT AMBASSADORS OF CHESS.
... TO REACH THAT GOAL...
... WE WILL HOLD AN INTERNATIONAL TOURNAMENT NEXT YEAR.

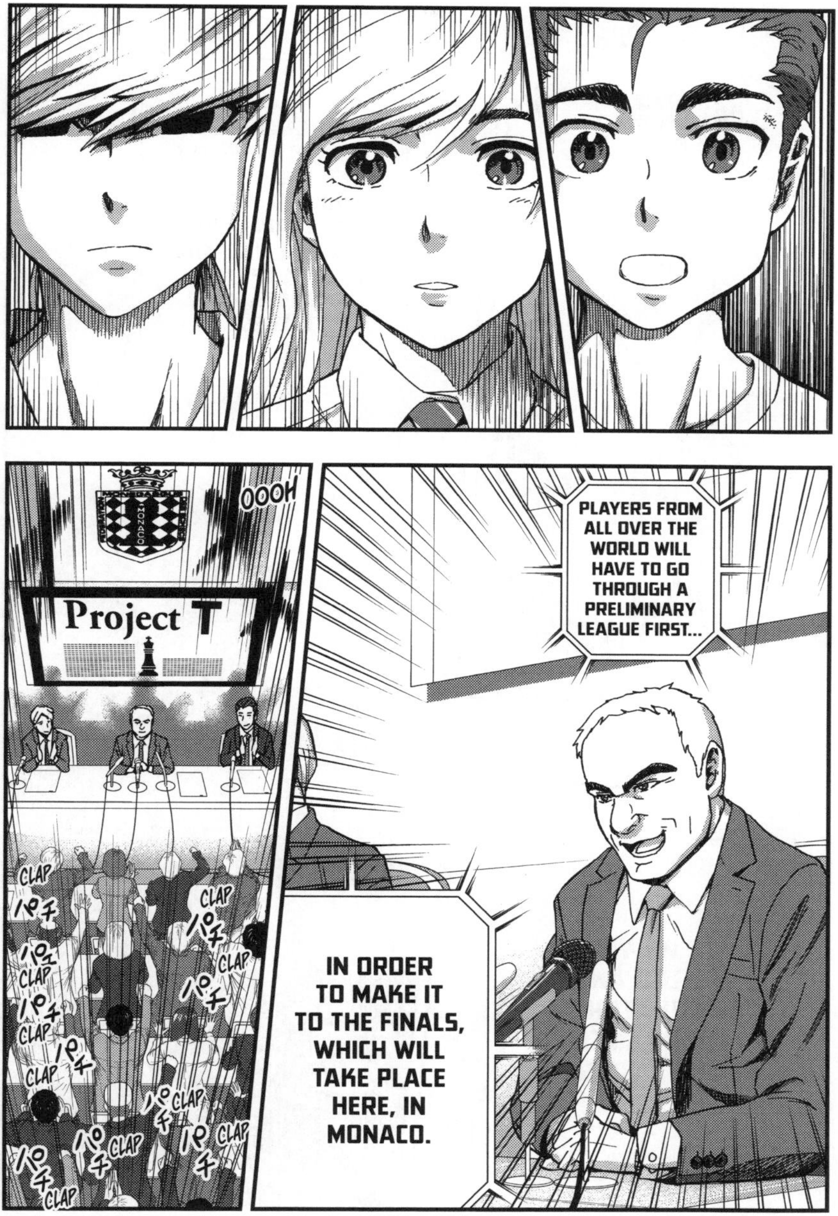
PLAYERS FROM ALL OVER THE WORLD WILL HAVE TO GO THROUGH A PRELIMINARY LEAGUE FIRST...
IN ORDER TO MAKE IT TO THE FINALS, WHICH WILL TAKE PLACE HERE, IN MONACO.
OOOH
MONACO
Project T
CLAP
パチ
CLAP
パチ
CLAP
パチ
CLAP

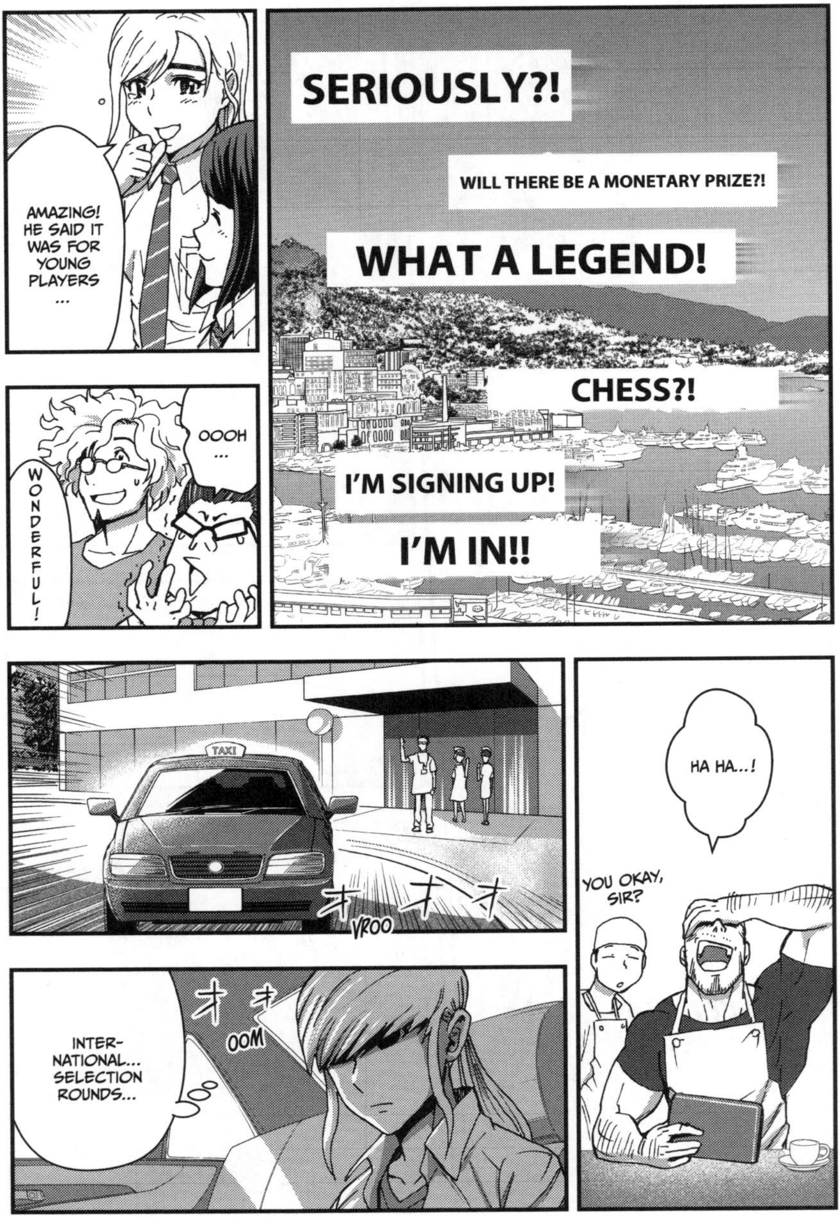
SERIOUSLY?!
WILL THERE BE A MONETARY PRIZE?!
WHAT A LEGEND!
CHESS?!
I'M SIGNING UP!
I'M IN!!
AMAZING! HE SAID IT WAS FOR YOUNG PLAYERS ...
OOOH ...
WONDERFUL!
HA HA...!
YOU OKAY, SIR?
オオオ
VROO
オオ
OOM
INTER-NATIONAL... SELECTION ROUNDS...

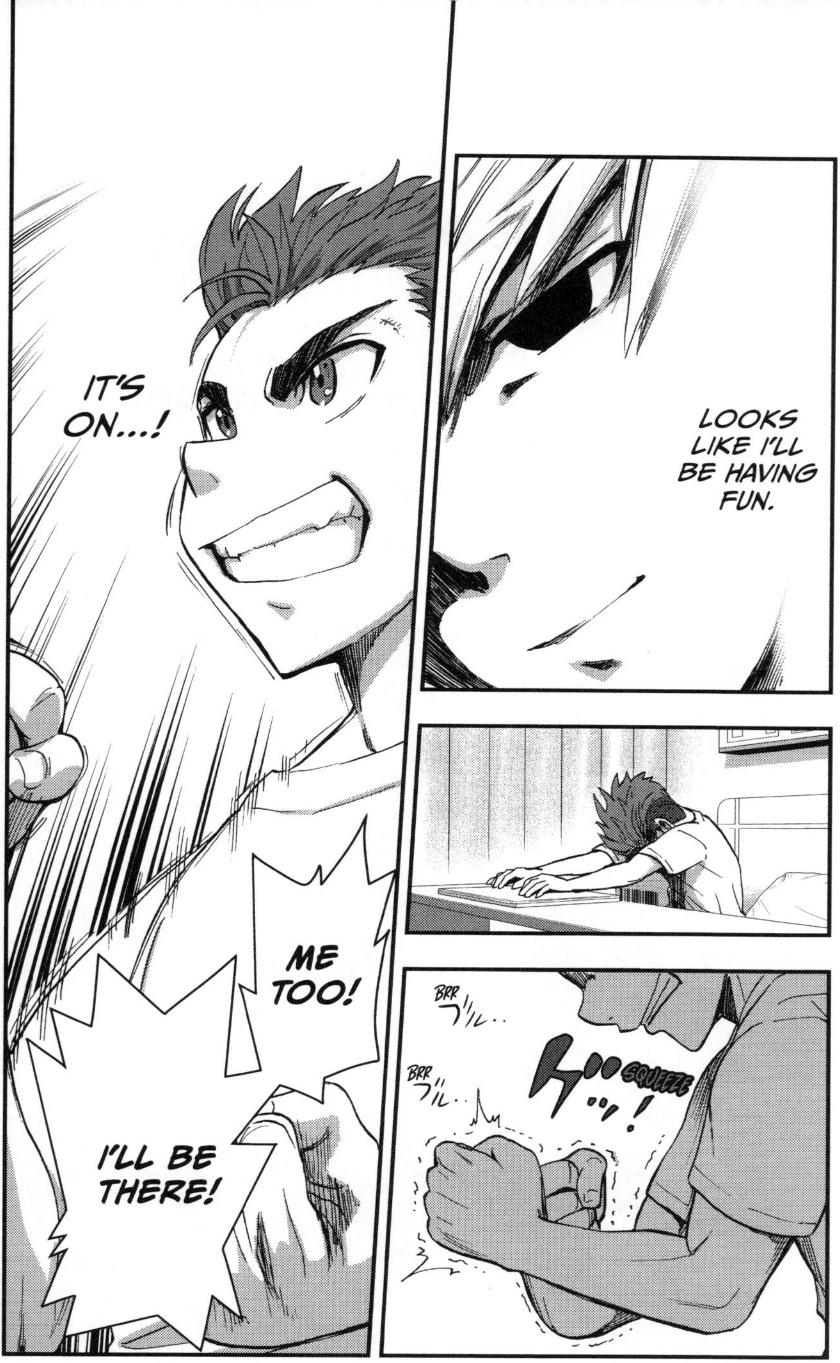
LOOKS LIKE I'LL BE HAVING FUN.
BRR
ブル‥
BRR
ブル‥
SQUEEZE
IT'S ON...!
ME TOO!
I'LL BE THERE!

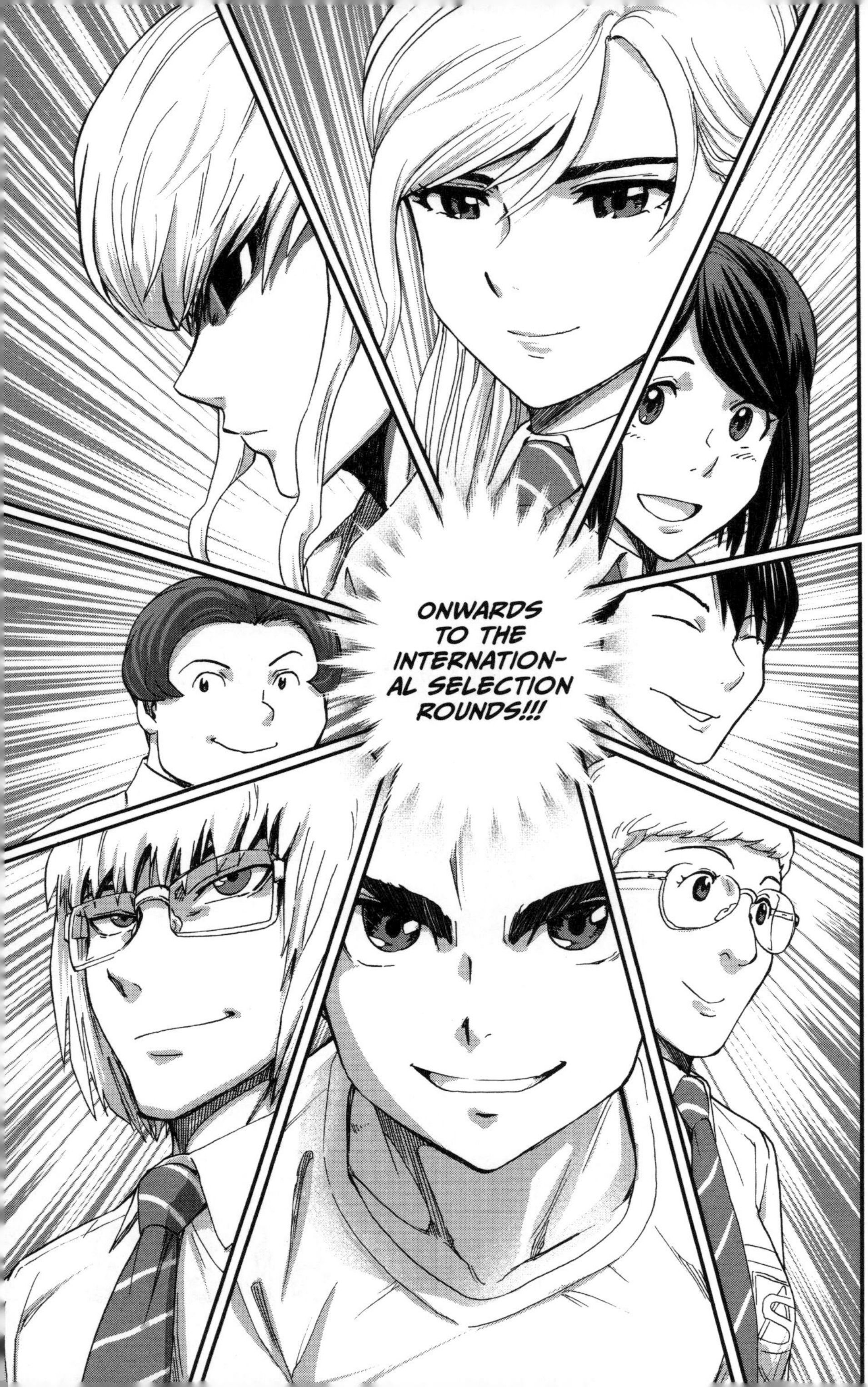
ONWARDS TO THE INTERNATION-AL SELECTION ROUNDS!!!

BLITZ

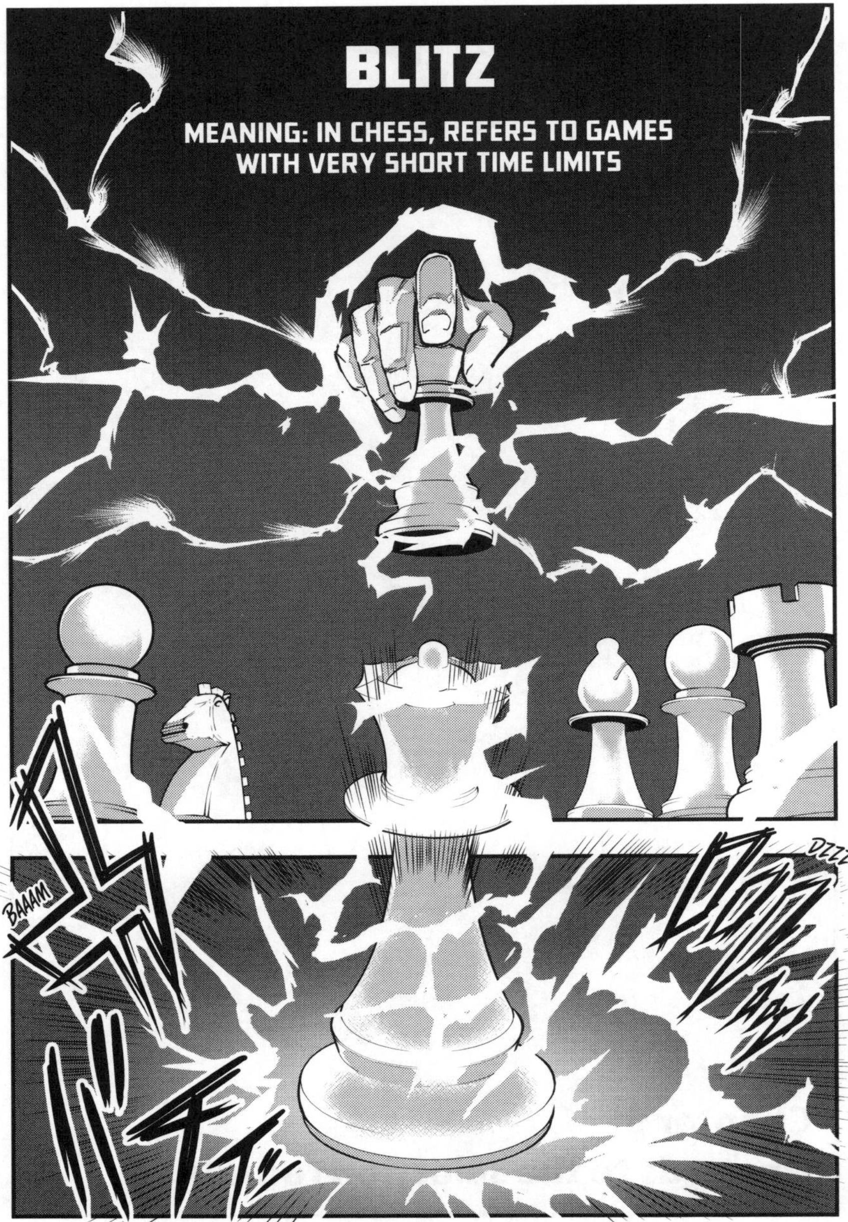
BLITZ
MEANING: IN CHESS, REFERS TO GAMES WITH VERY SHORT TIME LIMITS
DZZZT
BAAAM

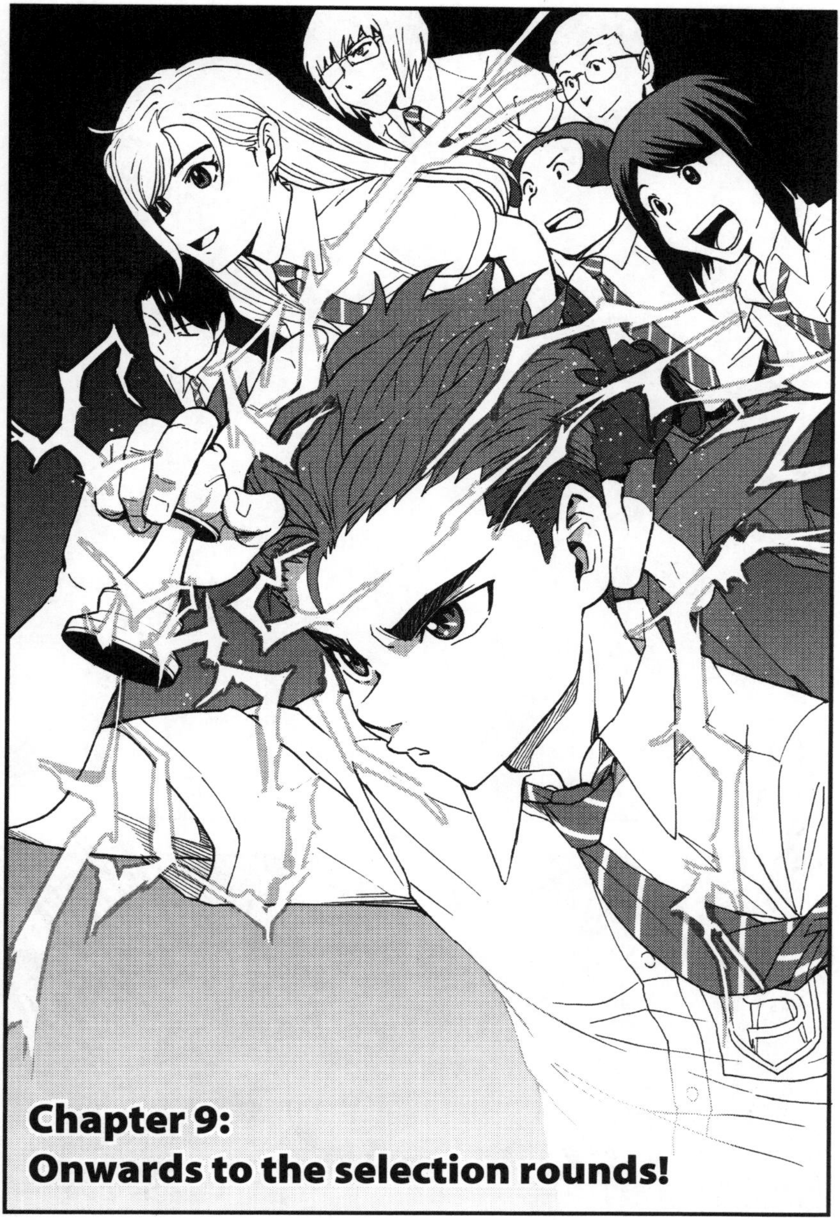

Chapter 9: Onwards to the selection rounds!

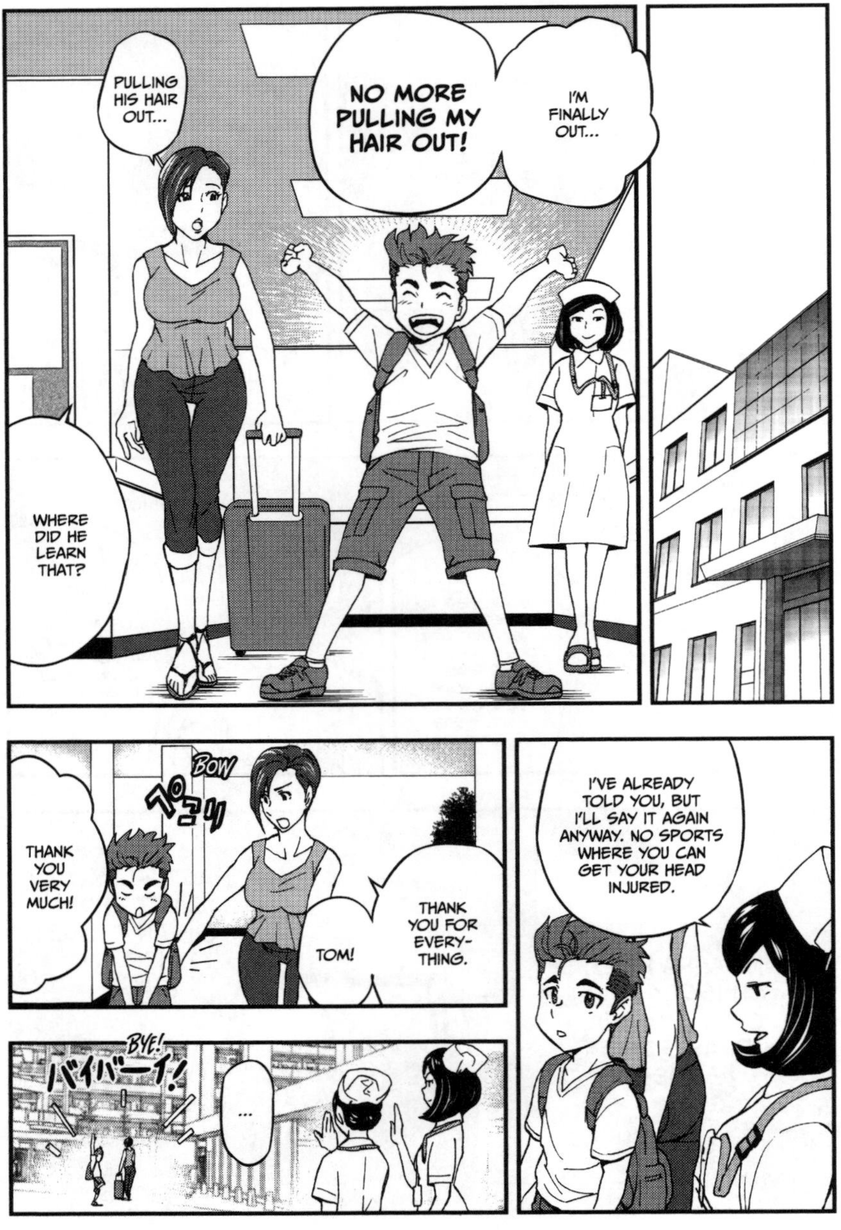
I'M FINALLY OUT...
NO MORE PULLING MY HAIR OUT!
PULLING HIS HAIR OUT...
WHERE DID HE LEARN THAT?
I'VE ALREADY TOLD YOU, BUT I'LL SAY IT AGAIN ANYWAY. NO SPORTS WHERE YOU CAN GET YOUR HEAD INJURED.
THANK YOU FOR EVERY-THING.
TOM!
BOW
ペコリ
THANK YOU VERY MUCH!
...
BYE!
バイバーイ!

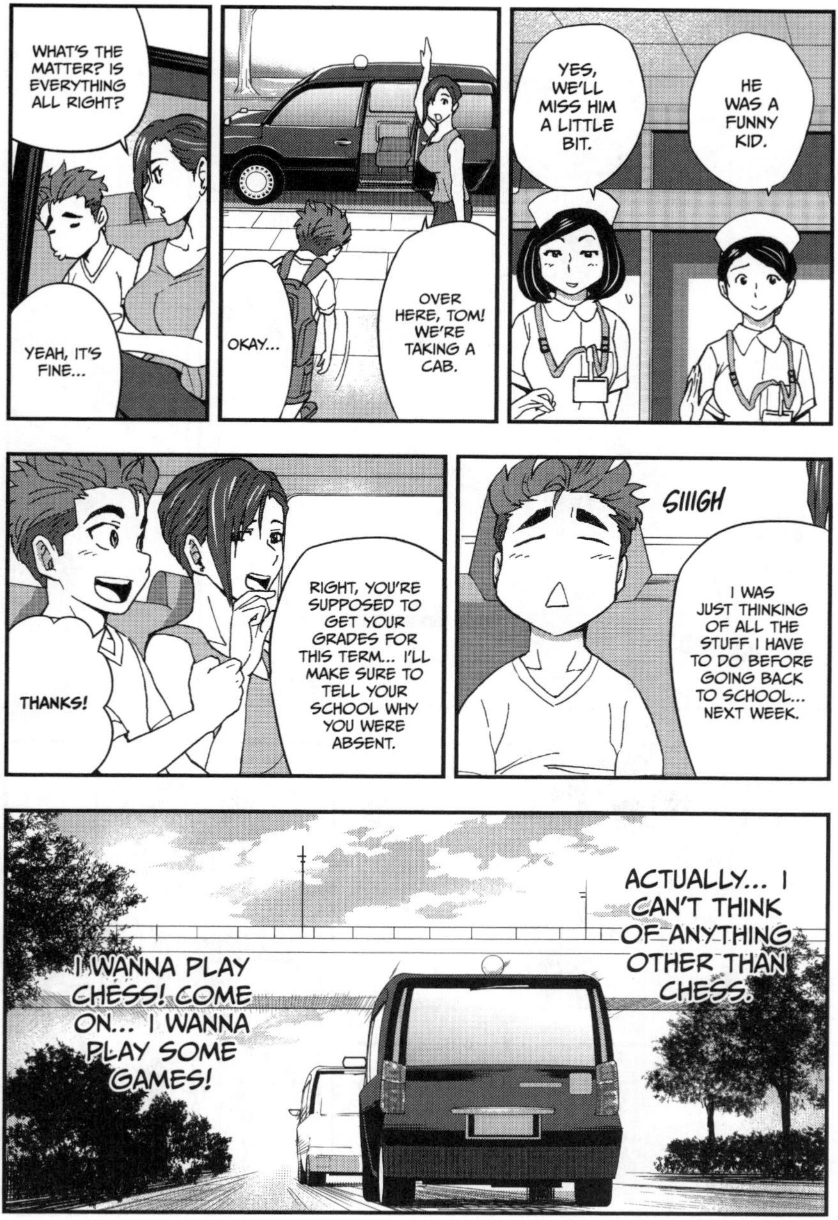
HE WAS A FUNNY KID.
YES, WE'LL MISS HIM A LITTLE BIT.
OVER HERE, TOM! WE'RE TAKING A CAB.
OKAY...
WHAT'S THE MATTER? IS EVERYTHING ALL RIGHT?
YEAH, IT'S FINE...
SIIIGH
I WAS JUST THINKING OF ALL THE STUFF I HAVE TO DO BEFORE GOING BACK TO SCHOOL... NEXT WEEK.
RIGHT, YOU'RE SUPPOSED TO GET YOUR GRADES FOR THIS TERM... I'LL MAKE SURE TO TELL YOUR SCHOOL WHY YOU WERE ABSENT.
THANKS!
ACTUALLY... I CAN'T THINK OF ANYTHING OTHER THAN CHESS.
I WANNA PLAY CHESS! COME ON... I WANNA PLAY SOME GAMES!

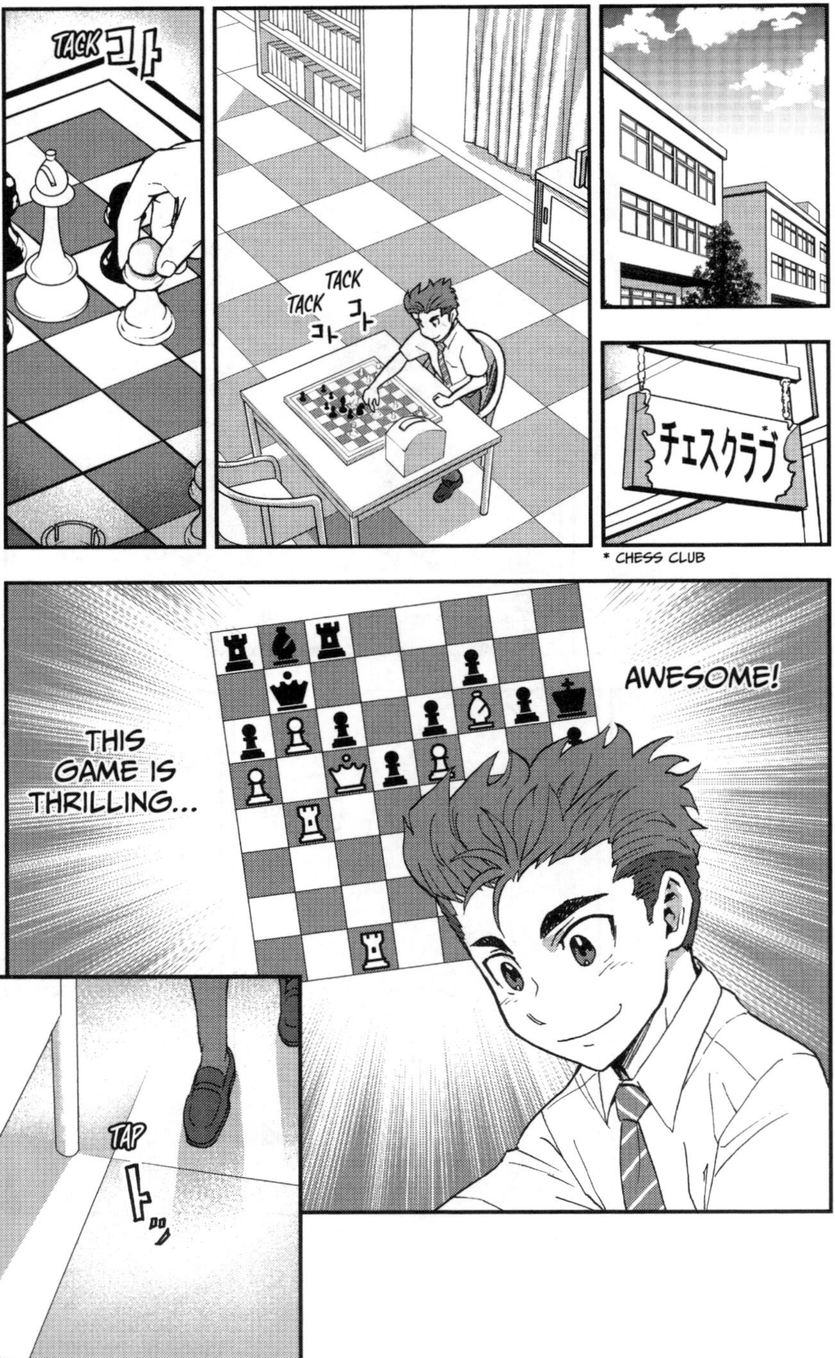
チェスクラブ*
* CHESS CLUB
TACK
コト
TACK
コト
TACK
コト
AWESOME!
THIS GAME IS THRILLING...
TAP
トッ

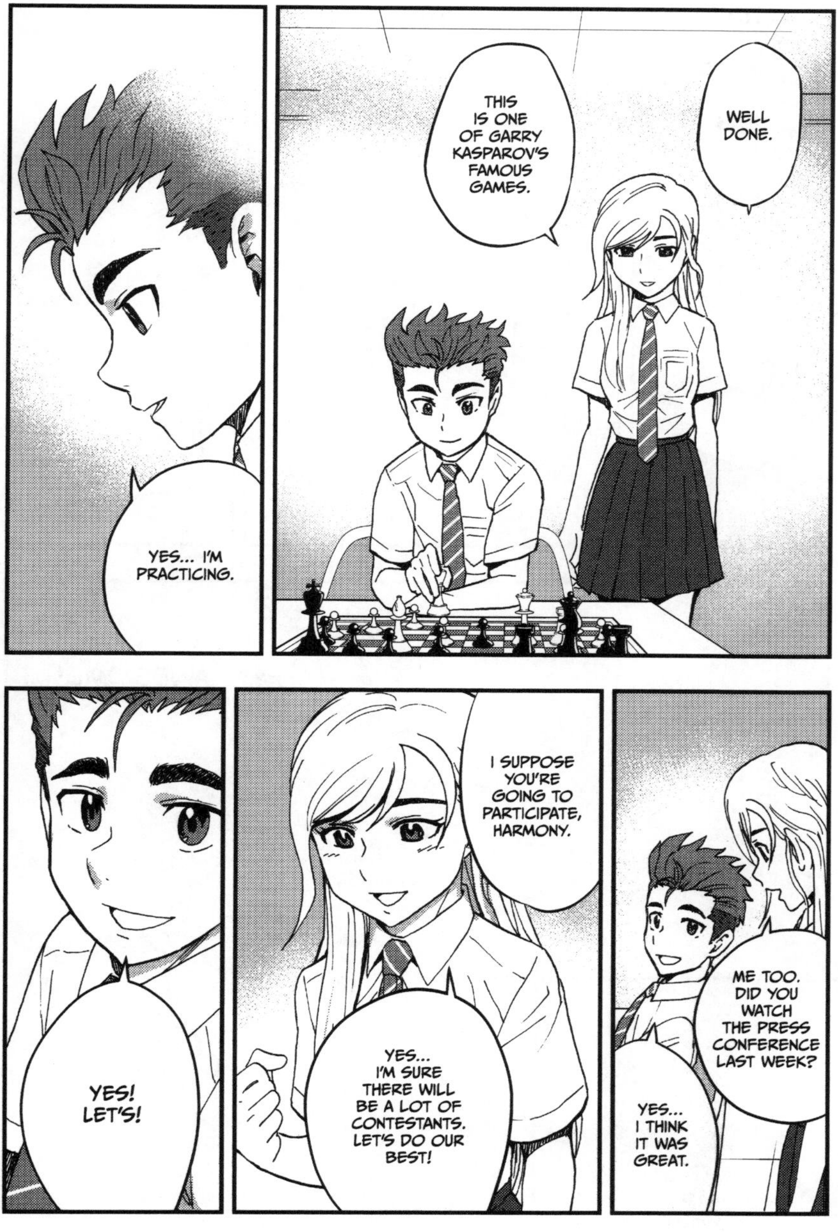
WELL DONE.
THIS IS ONE OF GARRY KASPAROV'S FAMOUS GAMES.
YES... I'M PRACTICING.
ME TOO. DID YOU WATCH THE PRESS CONFERENCE LAST WEEK?
YES... I THINK IT WAS GREAT.
I SUPPOSE YOU'RE GOING TO PARTICIPATE, HARMONY.
YES... I'M SURE THERE WILL BE A LOT OF CONTESTANTS. LET'S DO OUR BEST!
YES! LET'S!

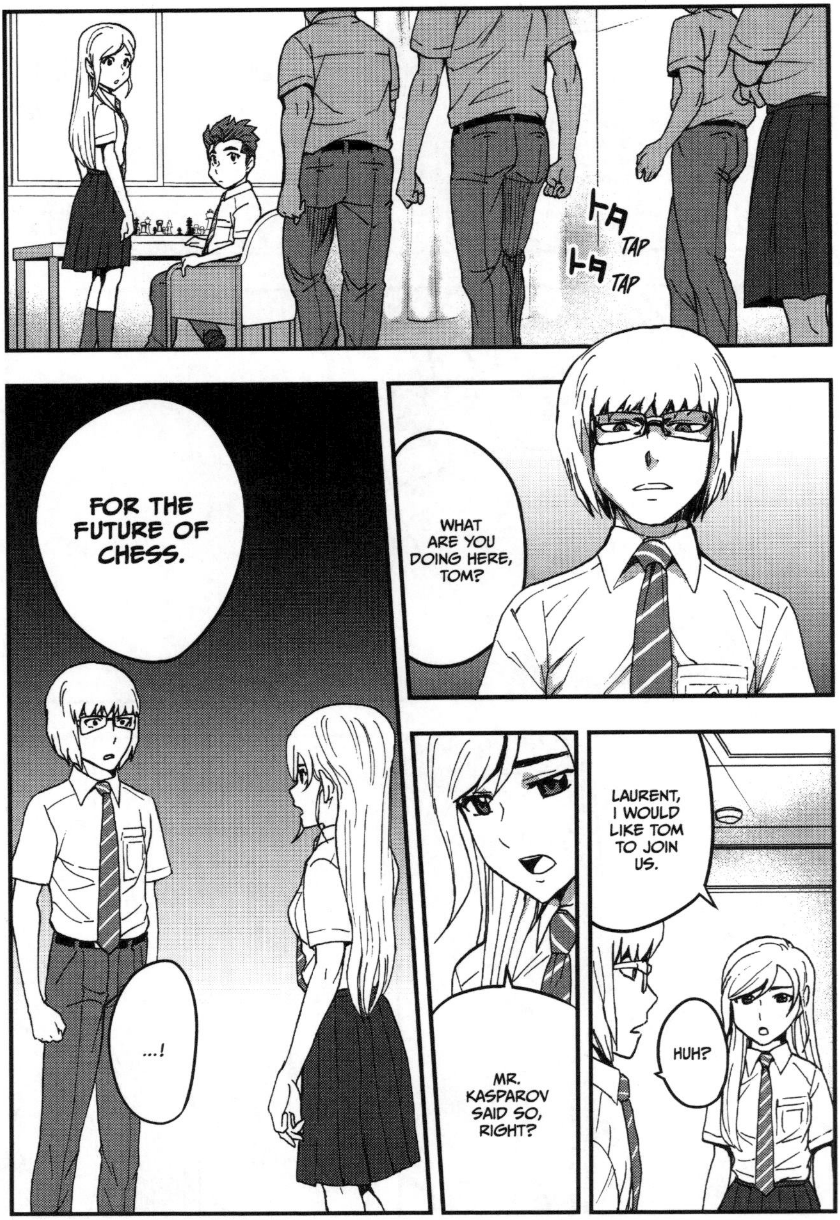
トタ TAP
トタ TAP
WHAT ARE YOU DOING HERE, TOM?
LAURENT, I WOULD LIKE TOM TO JOIN US.
HUH?
MR. KASPAROV SAID SO, RIGHT?
FOR THE FUTURE OF CHESS.
...!

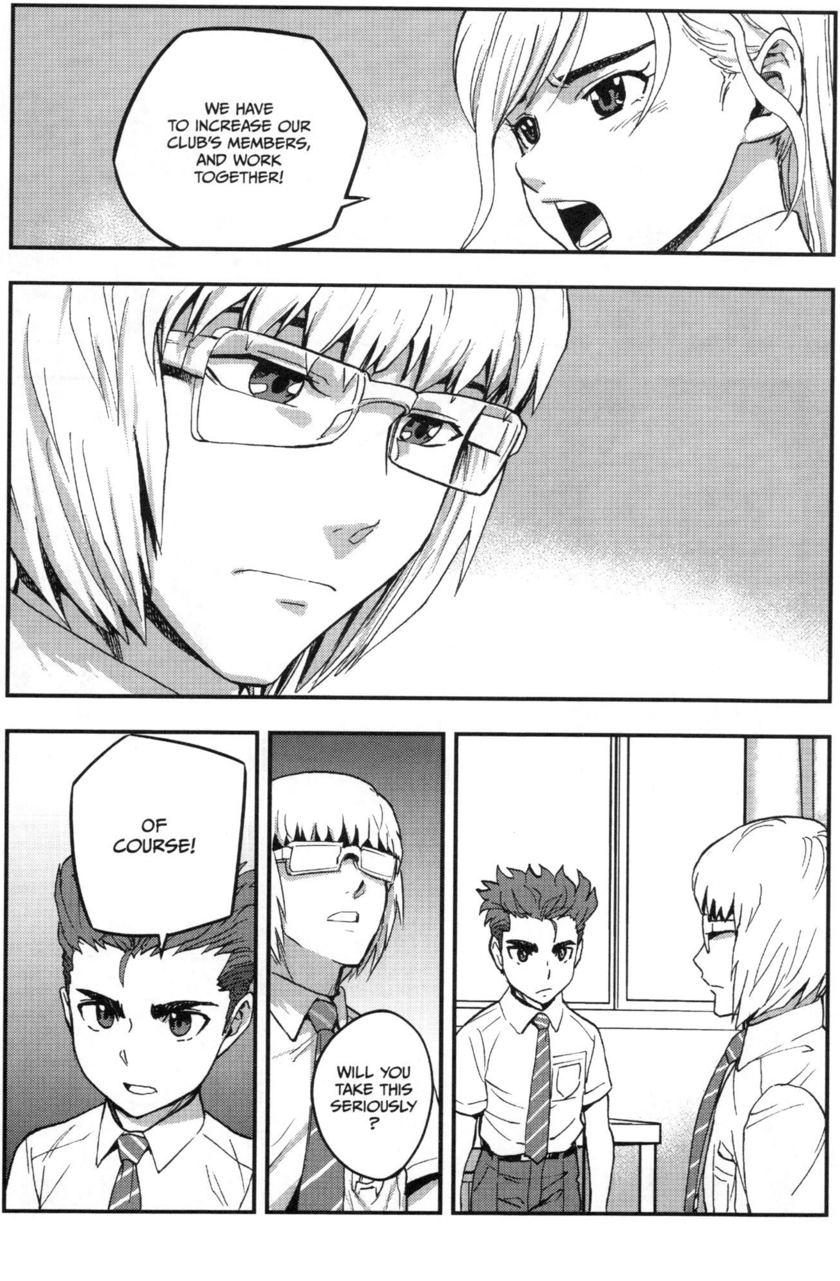
WE HAVE TO INCREASE OUR CLUB'S MEMBERS, AND WORK TOGETHER!
WILL YOU TAKE THIS SERIOUSLY?
OF COURSE!

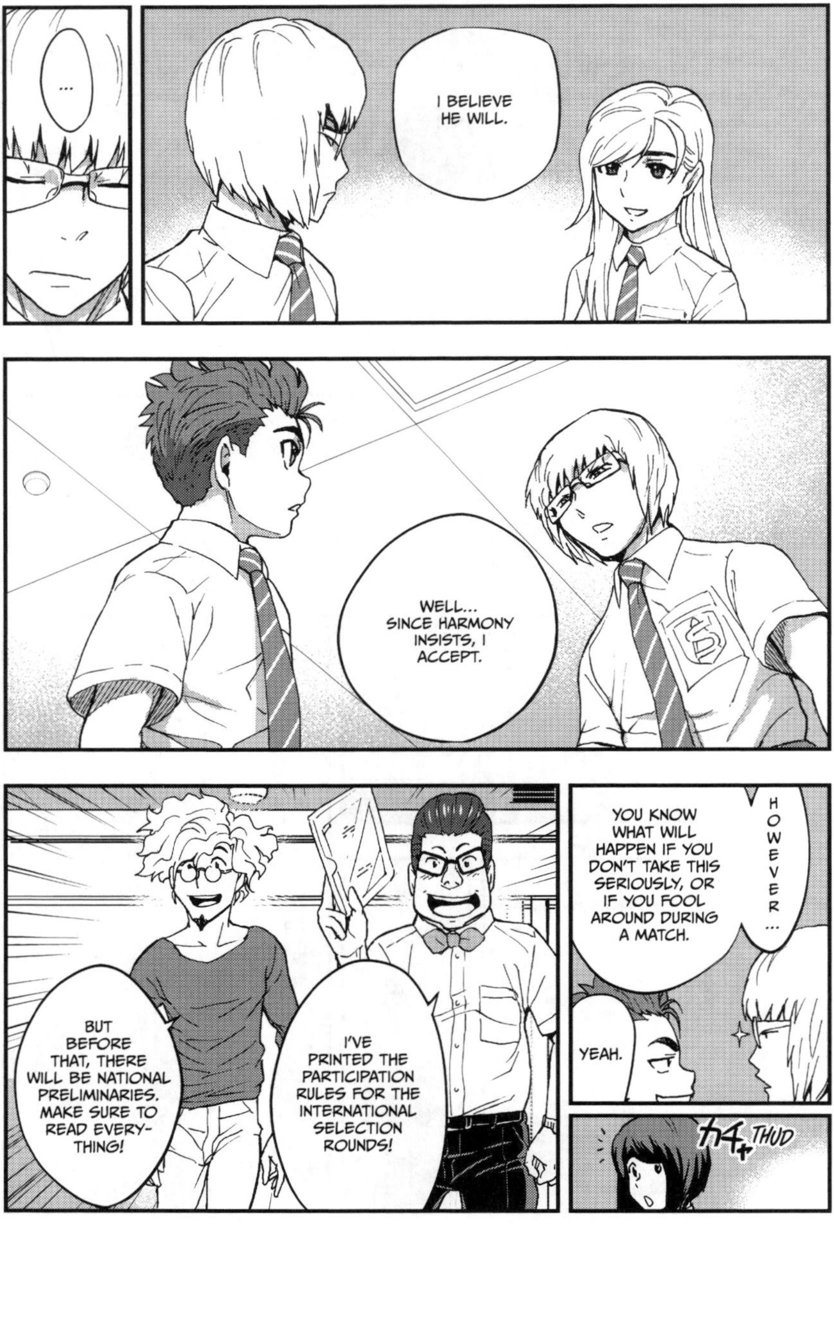
I BELIEVE HE WILL.
...
WELL... SINCE HARMONY INSISTS, I ACCEPT.
HOWEVER...
YOU KNOW WHAT WILL HAPPEN IF YOU DON'T TAKE THIS SERIOUSLY, OR IF YOU FOOL AROUND DURING A MATCH.
YEAH.
THUD
I'VE PRINTED THE PARTICIPATION RULES FOR THE INTERNATIONAL SELECTION ROUNDS!
BUT BEFORE THAT, THERE WILL BE NATIONAL PRELIMINARIES. MAKE SURE TO READ EVERY-THING!

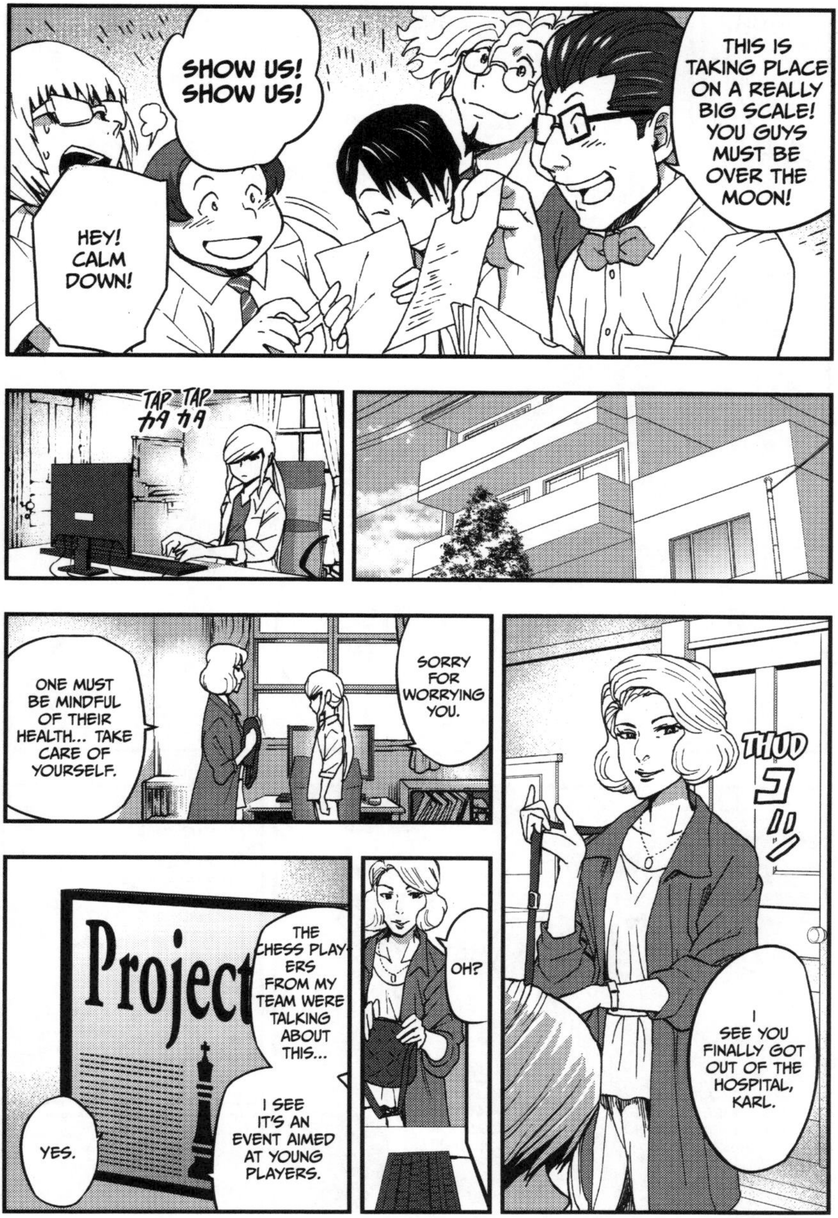
THIS IS TAKING PLACE ON A REALLY BIG SCALE! YOU GUYS MUST BE OVER THE MOON!
SHOW US! SHOW US!
HEY! CALM DOWN!
TAP TAP
カタカタ
THUD
コッ
I SEE YOU FINALLY GOT OUT OF THE HOSPITAL, KARL.
SORRY FOR WORRYING YOU.
ONE MUST BE MINDFUL OF THEIR HEALTH... TAKE CARE OF YOURSELF.
OH?
THE CHESS PLAYERS FROM MY TEAM WERE TALKING ABOUT THIS...
I SEE IT'S AN EVENT AIMED AT YOUNG PLAYERS.
Project
YES.

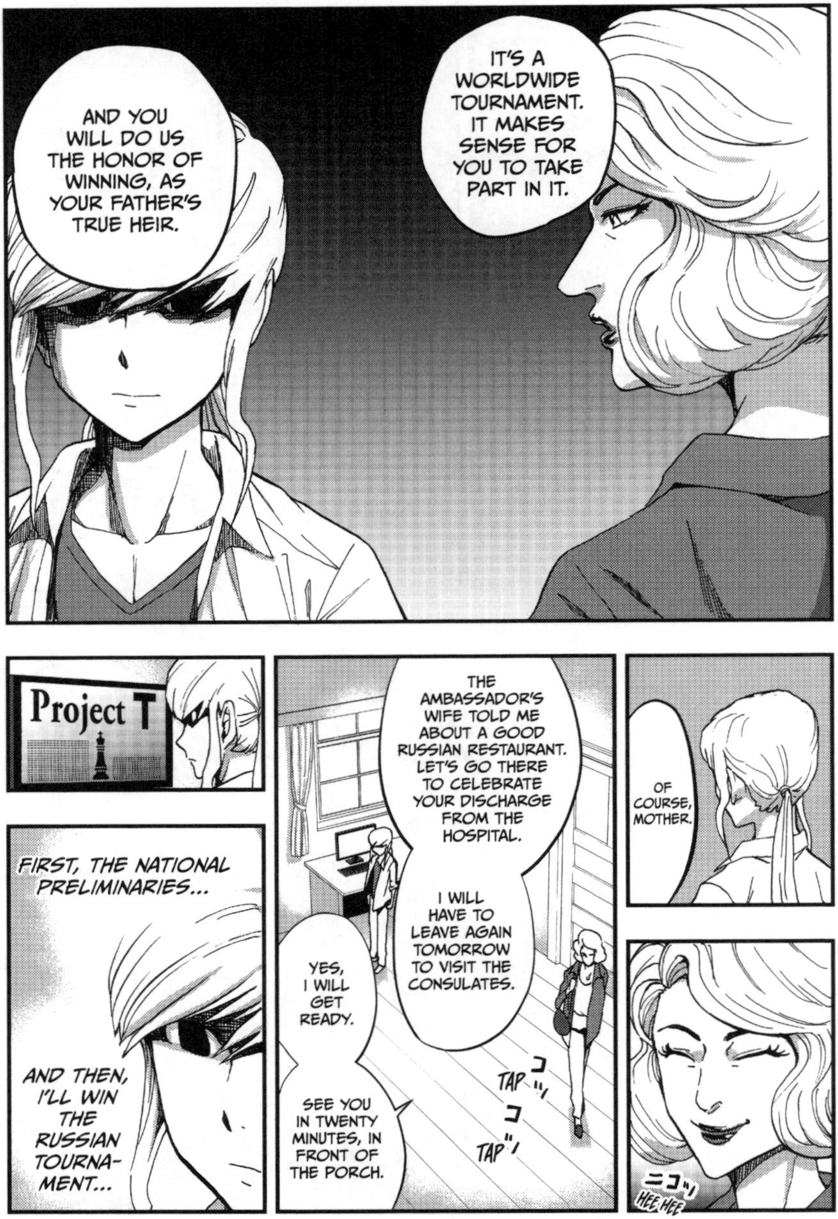
IT'S A WORLDWIDE TOURNAMENT. IT MAKES SENSE FOR YOU TO TAKE PART IN IT.
AND YOU WILL DO US THE HONOR OF WINNING, AS YOUR FATHER'S TRUE HEIR.
OF COURSE, MOTHER.
HEE HEE
THE AMBASSADOR'S WIFE TOLD ME ABOUT A GOOD RUSSIAN RESTAURANT. LET'S GO THERE TO CELEBRATE YOUR DISCHARGE FROM THE HOSPITAL.
I WILL HAVE TO LEAVE AGAIN TOMORROW TO VISIT THE CONSULATES.
TAP
TAP
YES, I WILL GET READY.
SEE YOU IN TWENTY MINUTES, IN FRONT OF THE PORCH.
Project T
FIRST, THE NATIONAL PRELIMINARIES...
AND THEN, I'LL WIN THE RUSSIAN TOURNAMENT...

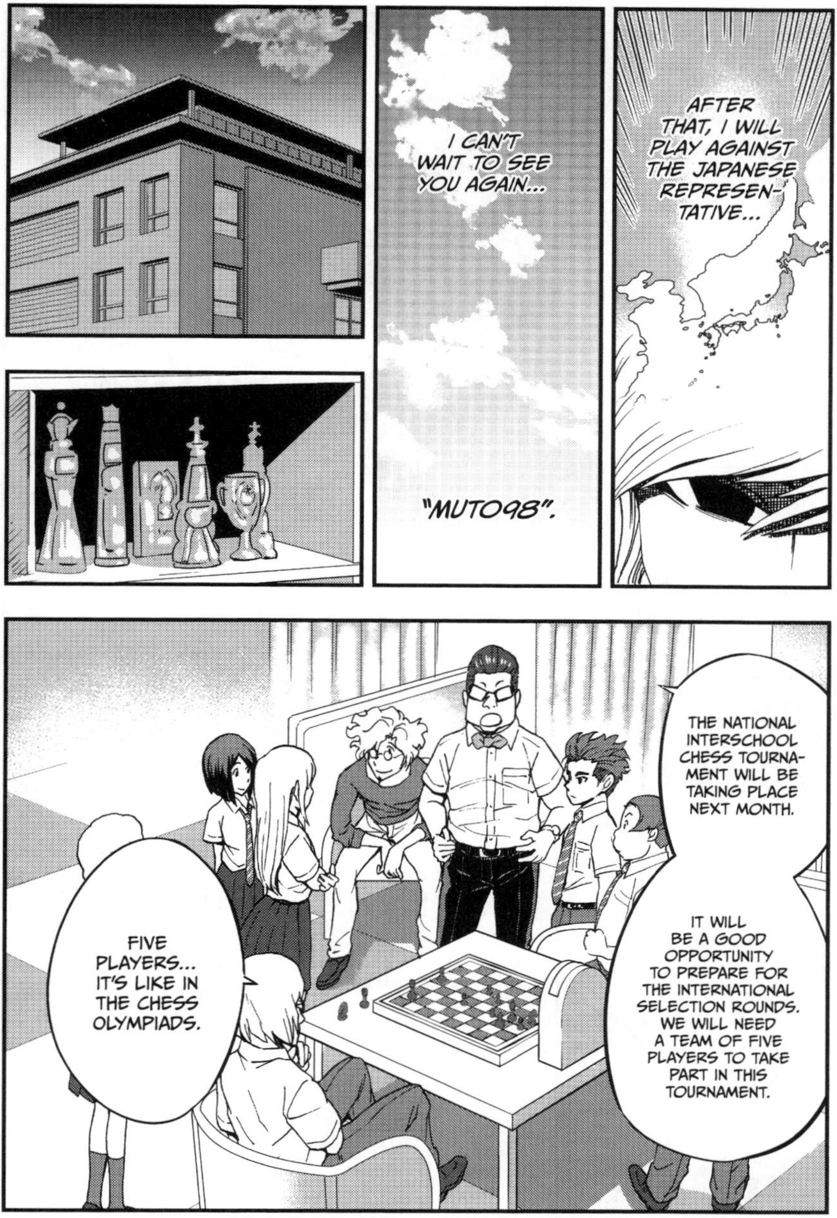
AFTER THAT, I WILL PLAY AGAINST THE JAPANESE REPRESEN-TATIVE...
I CAN'T WAIT TO SEE YOU AGAIN...
"MUTO98".
THE NATIONAL INTERSCHOOL CHESS TOURNA-MENT WILL BE TAKING PLACE NEXT MONTH.
IT WILL BE A GOOD OPPORTUNITY TO PREPARE FOR THE INTERNATIONAL SELECTION ROUNDS. WE WILL NEED A TEAM OF FIVE PLAYERS TO TAKE PART IN THIS TOURNAMENT.
FIVE PLAYERS... IT'S LIKE IN THE CHESS OLYMPIADS.

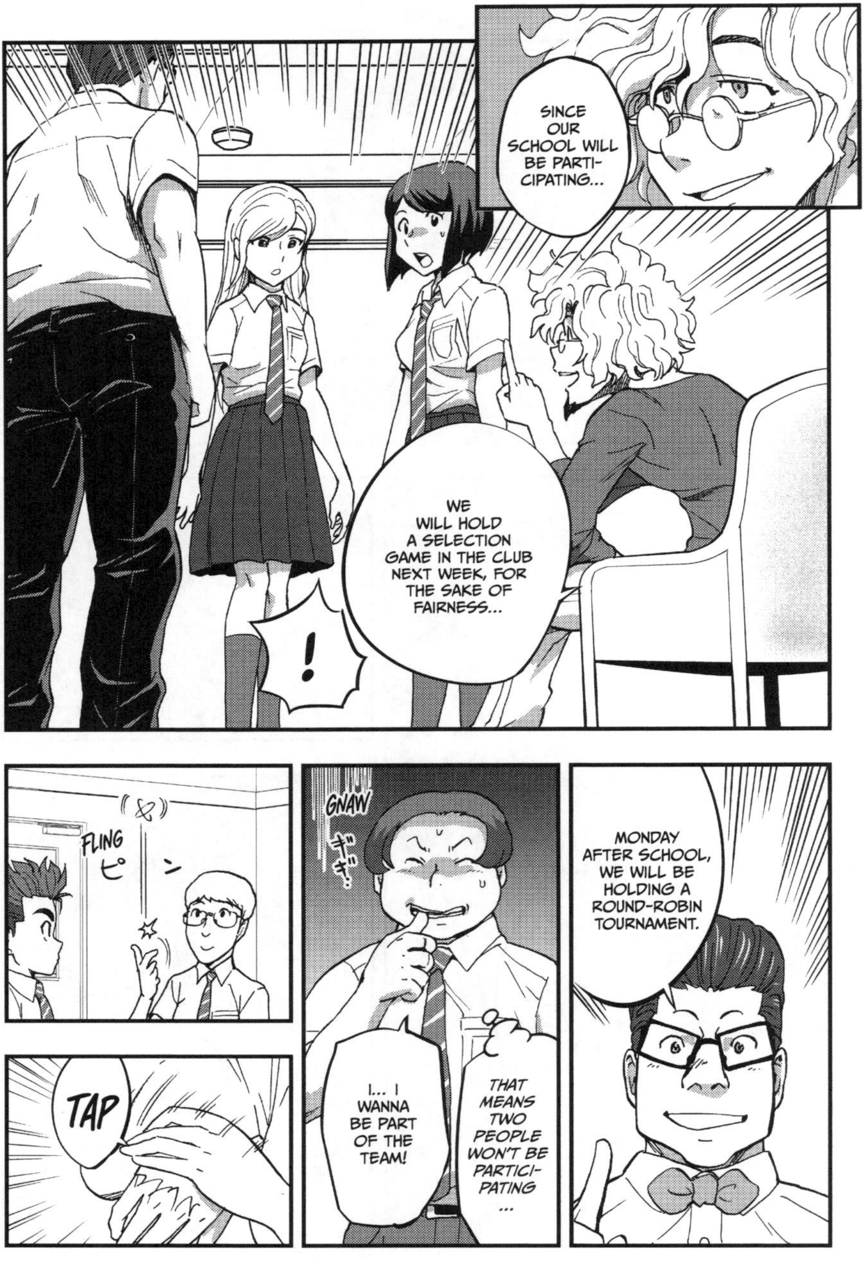
SINCE OUR SCHOOL WILL BE PARTI-CIPATING...
WE WILL HOLD A SELECTION GAME IN THE CLUB NEXT WEEK, FOR THE SAKE OF FAIRNESS...
!
MONDAY AFTER SCHOOL, WE WILL BE HOLDING A ROUND-ROBIN TOURNAMENT.
GNAW
ギギ…
THAT MEANS TWO PEOPLE WON'T BE PARTICI-PATING ...
I... I WANNA BE PART OF THE TEAM!
FLING
ピン
TAP

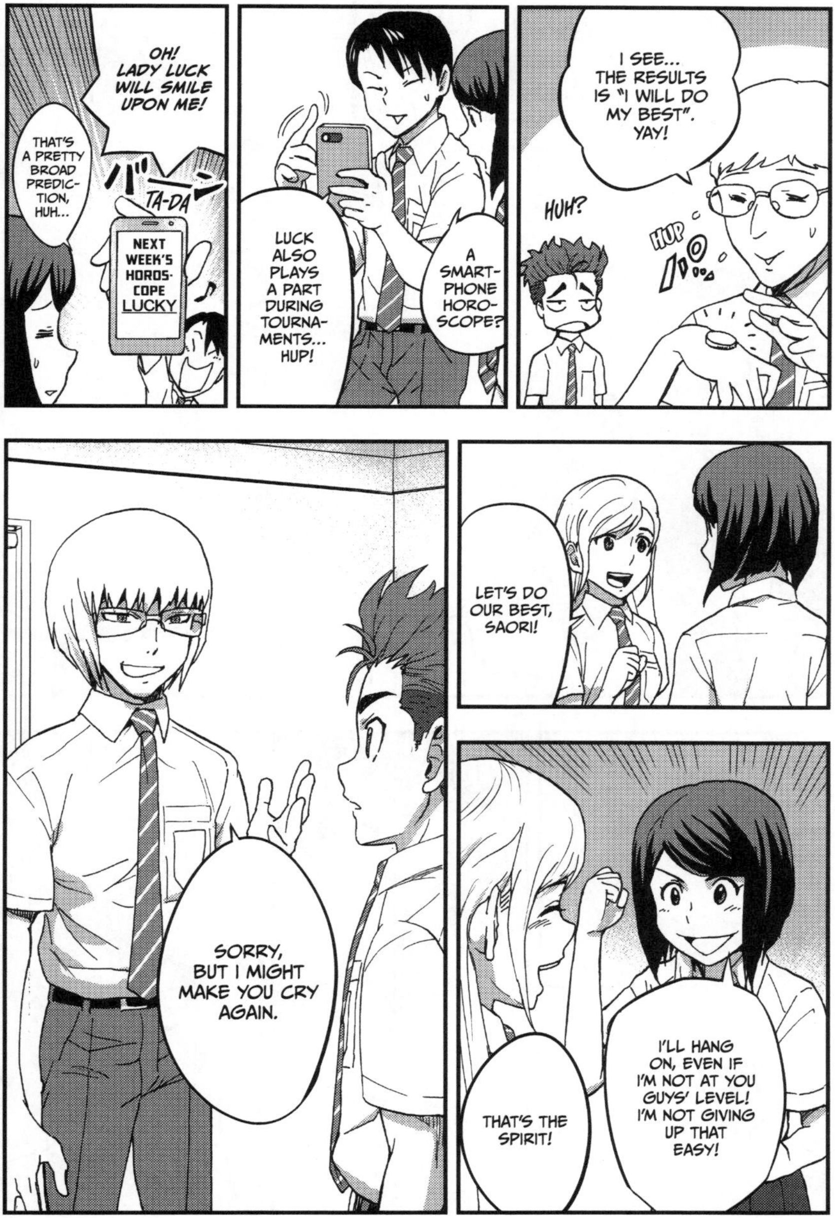
I SEE... THE RESULTS IS "I WILL DO MY BEST". YAY!
HUH?
HUP
A SMART-PHONE HORO-SCOPE?
LUCK ALSO PLAYS A PART DURING TOURNA-MENTS... HUP!
OH! LADY LUCK WILL SMILE UPON ME!
TA-DA
NEXT WEEK'S HOROS-COPE LUCKY
THAT'S A PRETTY BROAD PREDIC-TION, HUH...
LET'S DO OUR BEST, SAORI!
I'LL HANG ON, EVEN IF I'M NOT AT YOU GUYS' LEVEL! I'M NOT GIVING UP THAT EASY!
THAT'S THE SPIRIT!
SORRY, BUT I MIGHT MAKE YOU CRY AGAIN.

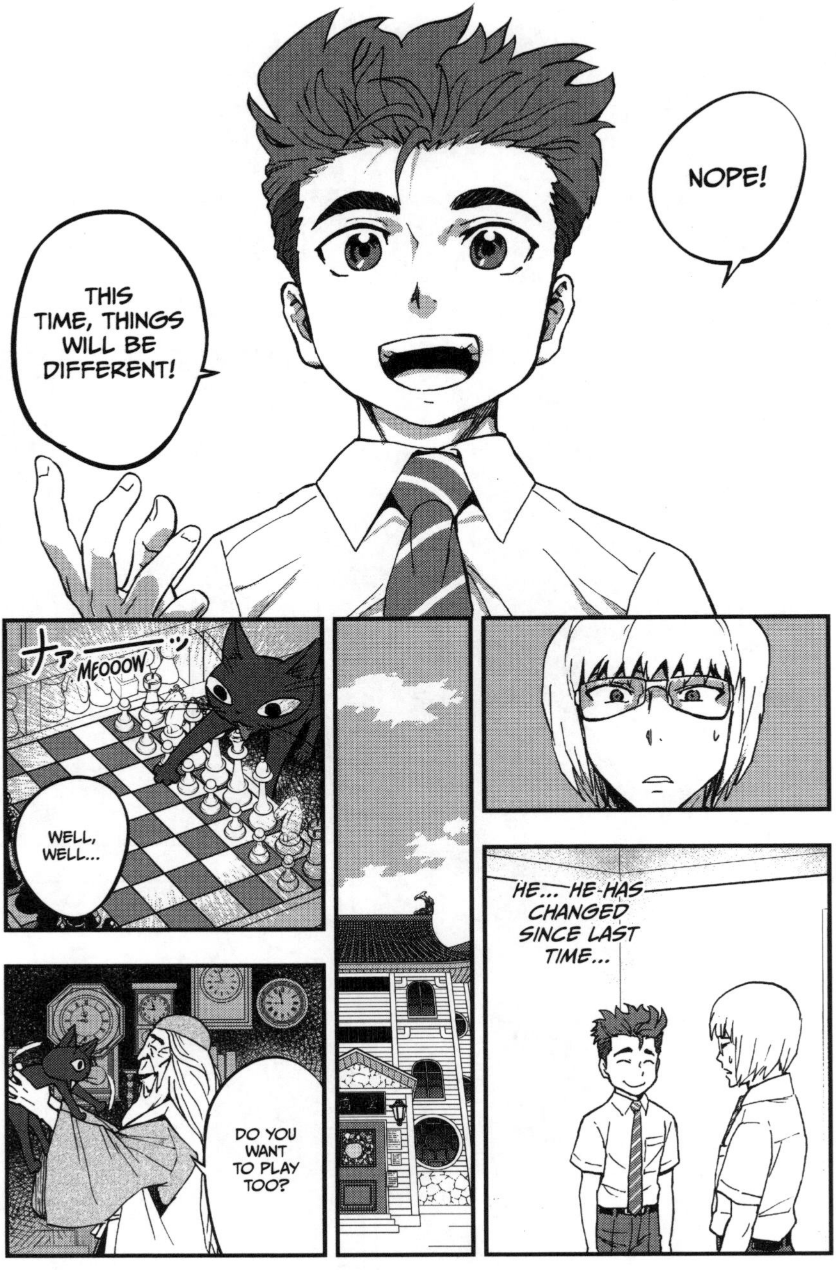
NOPE!
THIS TIME, THINGS WILL BE DIFFERENT!
HE... HE HAS CHANGED SINCE LAST TIME...
ナァーーッ
MEOOOW
WELL, WELL...
DO YOU WANT TO PLAY TOO?

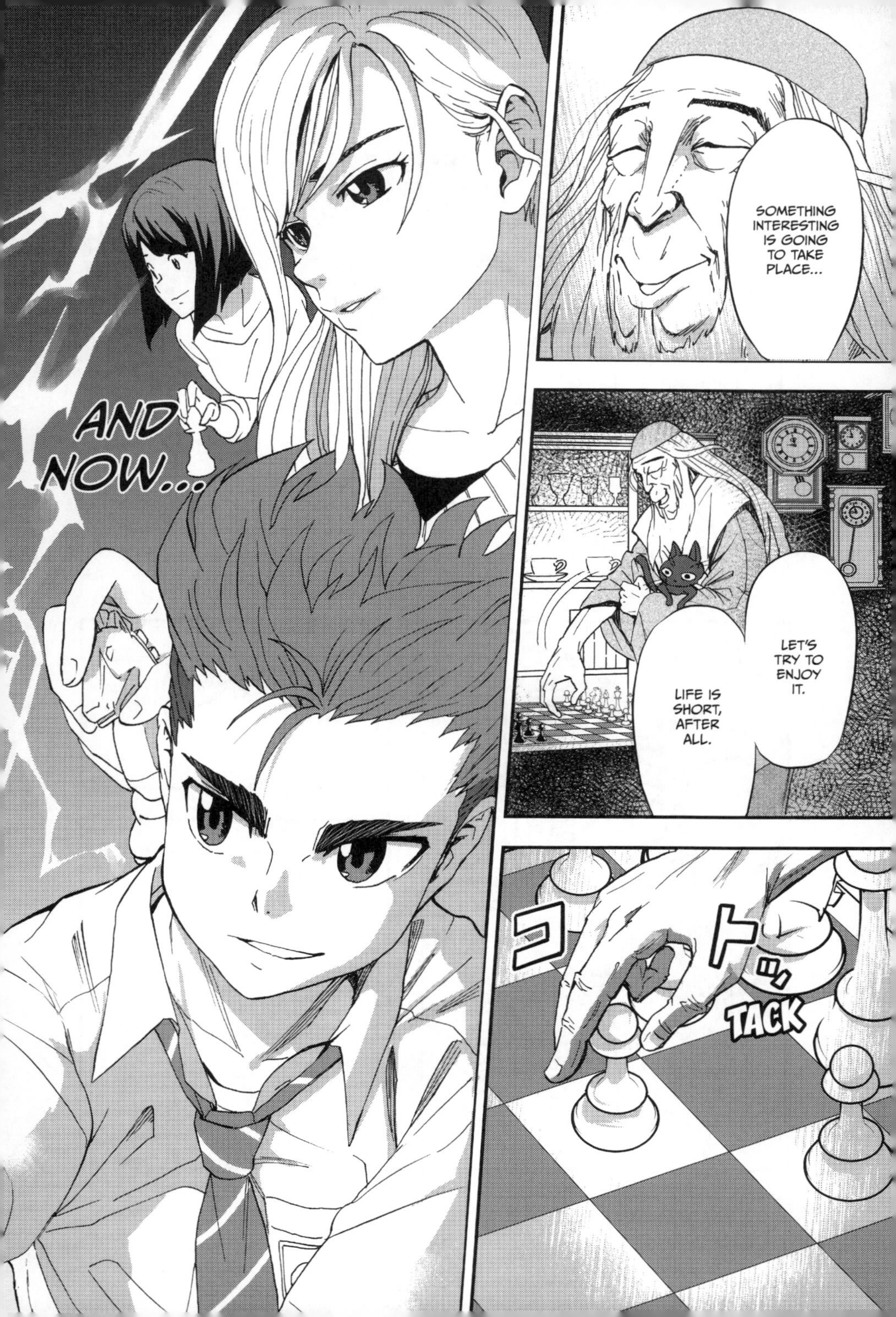
SOMETHING INTERESTING IS GOING TO TAKE PLACE...
LIFE IS SHORT, AFTER ALL.
LET'S TRY TO ENJOY IT.
コトッ
TACK
AND NOW...

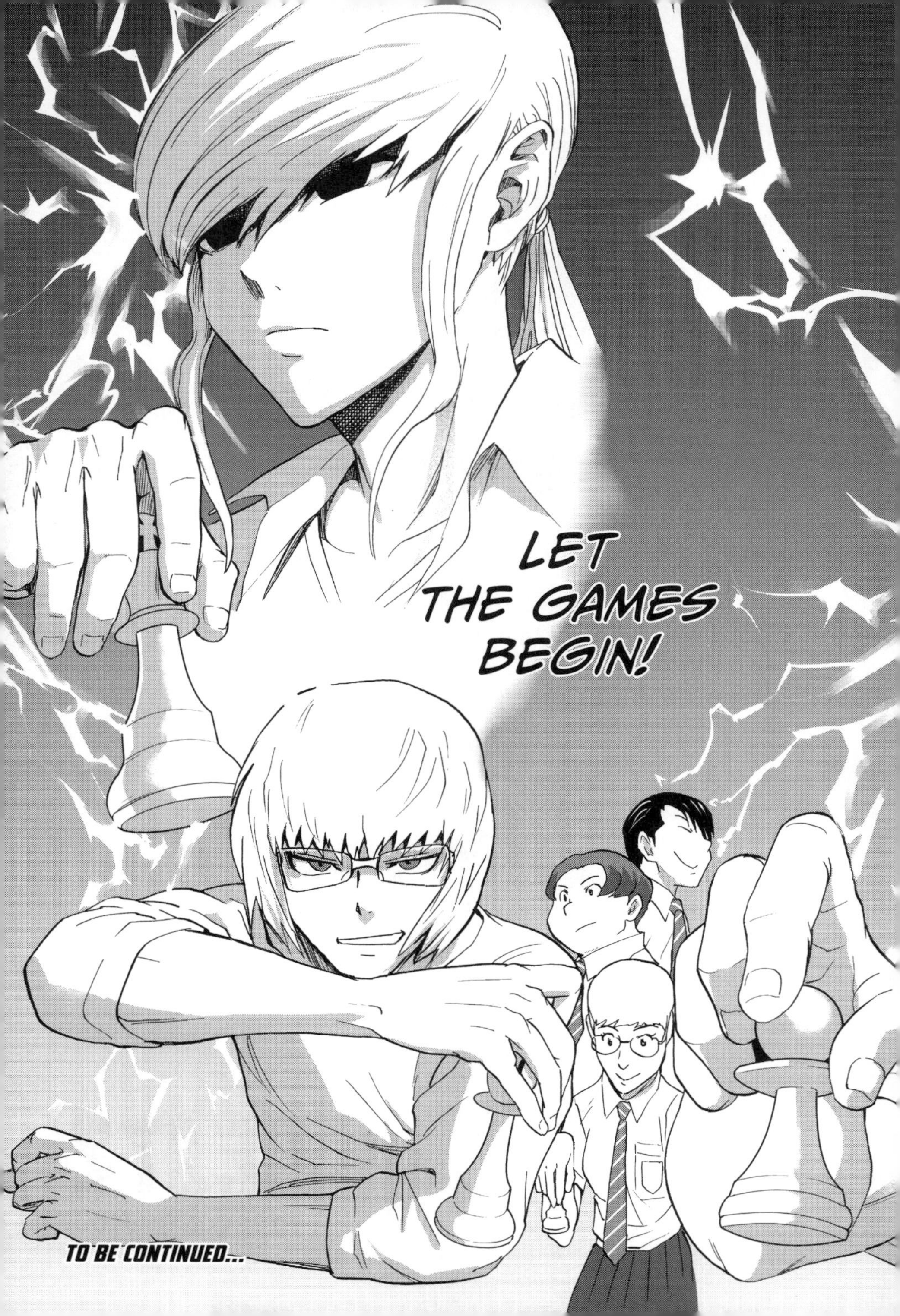
LET THE GAMES BEGIN!
TO BE CONTINUED...

BLITZ

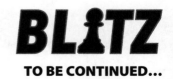

TO BE CONTINUED...

Written by Cédric Biscay and drawn by manga artist Daitaro Nishihara, Blitz is overseen and sponsored by none other than Garry Kasparov!

"I have always devoted myself to democratize chess by any means possible. This is a unique opportunity to do so, especially in Japan, where the game is not as popular as Shogi. If you wish to communicate efficiently, you have to use the target audience's language. In a way, manga is the mother tongue of many young people. That is why Cédric's invitation seemed to be the perfect opportunity to promote chess towards a new public, by using a media that is both visual and dynamic."

Garry Kasparov

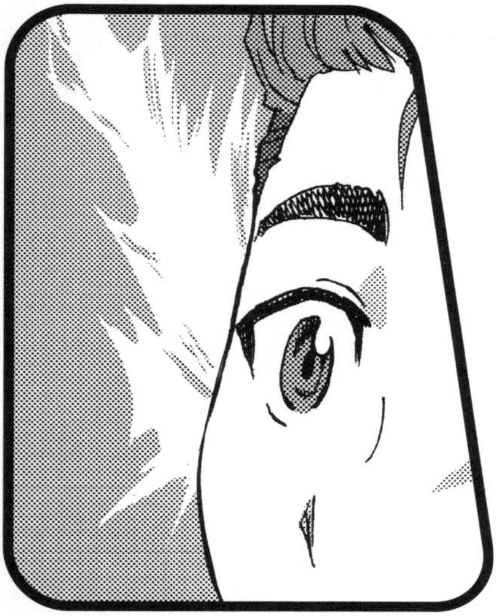

AFTERWORD

INTUITION

We would all love to have superpowers. Extraordinary abilities that are reminiscent of some of the most amazing superheroes. For example, we could see things faster and from farther away. Knowing things, in a way. We could make better decisions, and be creative enough to find the best solutions. We could instantly make the right moves, feel the best way to go and follow the right path. We could even anticipate the thoughts and actions of our friends and other people.

It would be wonderful if we could be more intelligent, more aware of our surroundings, and if we could meet the challenges that we impose on ourselves head-on, even if they seem impossible at the beginning.
What if we could?

What if we really could have those abilities?

After his little incident, Tom awakens to new sensations. He manages to have bouts of stupendous intuition, albeit more or less consciously. He can feel which piece to move, and he moves it automatically. He starts to sense his opponent's personality.

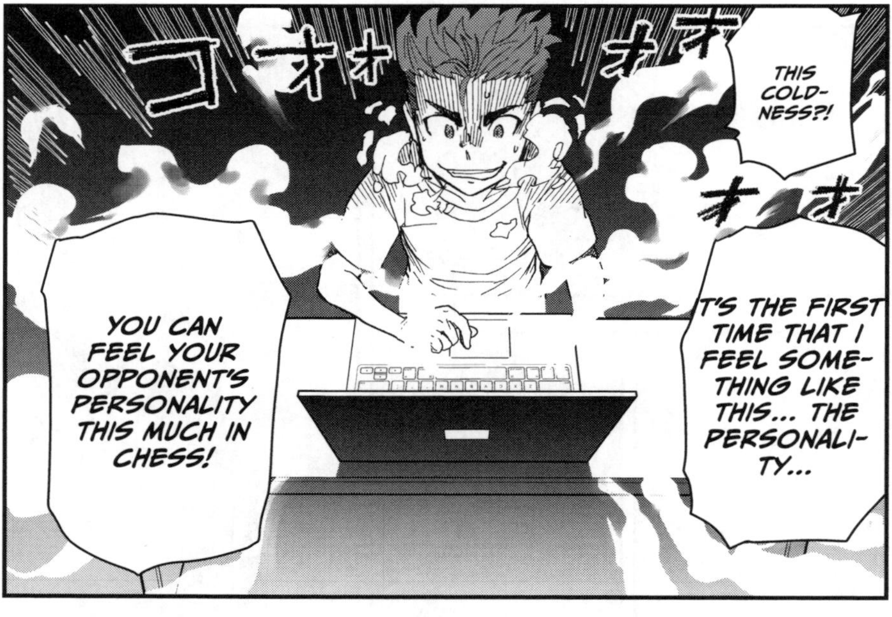
THIS COLD-NESS?!
T'S THE FIRST TIME THAT I FEEL SOME-THING LIKE THIS... THE PERSONALI-TY...
YOU CAN FEEL YOUR OPPONENT'S PERSONALITY THIS MUCH IN CHESS!

He is so receptive to the emotions of his mother and friends that he can spontaneously anticipate their thoughts and actions.

And you? You probably already had the feeling that something would or was about to happen. Or the feeling of seeing or knowing something, without being able to tell where that knowledge came from. At that moment, you know something, but you have no idea how you know it!

That's the magic of intuition.

Intuition can be perceived as a certainty, a conviction or something obvious. It can take the form of a sensation, or a feeling. It can also take the form of a little voice in your head. A sort of internal wisdom. Creative people call it inspiration. For scientists, it is more akin to that "Eureka!" moment. A sort of revelation or a stroke of genius. When it comes to policemen and journalists, intuition is more like a gut feeling, or relying on their instinct or sixth sense...

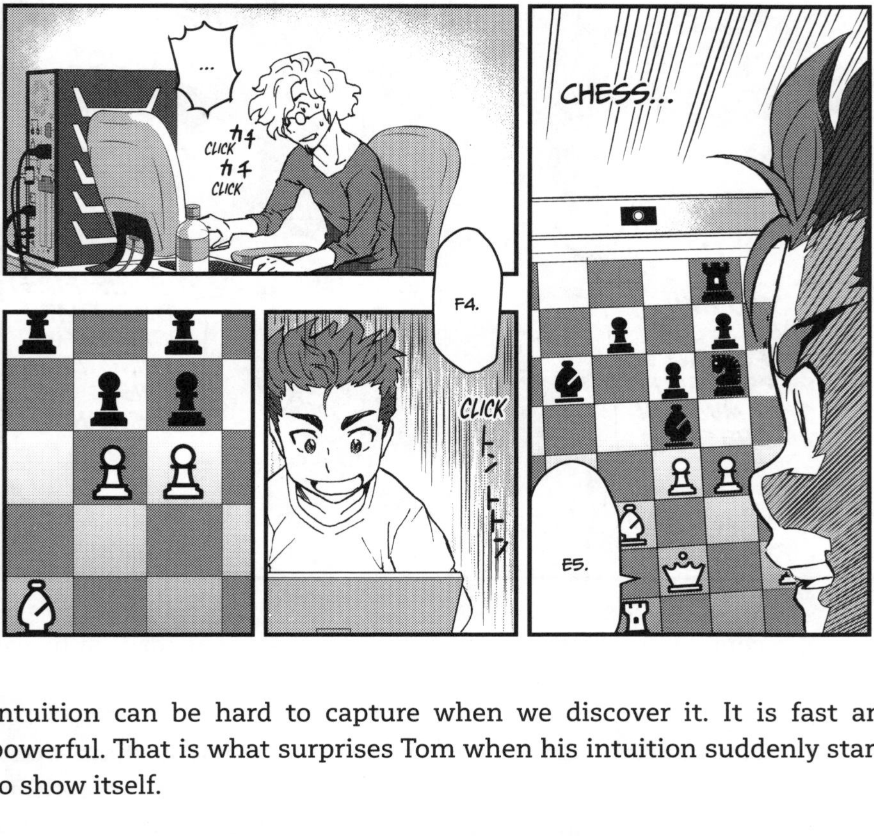
CHESS...
E5.
...
CLICK カチ
カチ CLICK
F4.
CLICK

Intuition can be hard to capture when we discover it. It is fast and powerful. That is what surprises Tom when his intuition suddenly starts to show itself.

Intuition is a type of knowledge that is independent from reason. It is difficult to understand by design. Intuition gives you the information without having to think, or calculate, or analyze things. You do not need any information to start with! It comes to you spontaneously. It is the result of a peculiar way of seeing the world. It is a direct and spontaneous

form of understanding: getting access to the knowledge within us.
By the way, did Tom get his powers after the storm made his VR set explode? Or did he have them beforehand, and the accident just helped make them spring to life? We will uncover the mystery as Tom's adventures go on.

You could easily get access to your intuition, just like Tom.

Intuition is a reality that has been studied by scientists for decades, and there have been a lot of discoveries made over the years. Researchers have uncovered many keys that allow us to reach our intuition in order to use it and make it evolve. That means that every one of us has that ability, like learning the piano, tennis or chess.

Intuitive thinking is a process that takes place from within, even if we are not aware of it. It is a perceptive process that manifests itself in the body. It takes the form of reflexes or automatic actions, and that gives way to a feeling. That is the phenomenon of foreboding. In turn, these feelings can make images or ideas pop into our minds.
Think of a question that you are asking yourself. A question that requires you to make a choice, right here, right now. For example: "Would it be better to do this (choice 1) or that (choice 2)?"

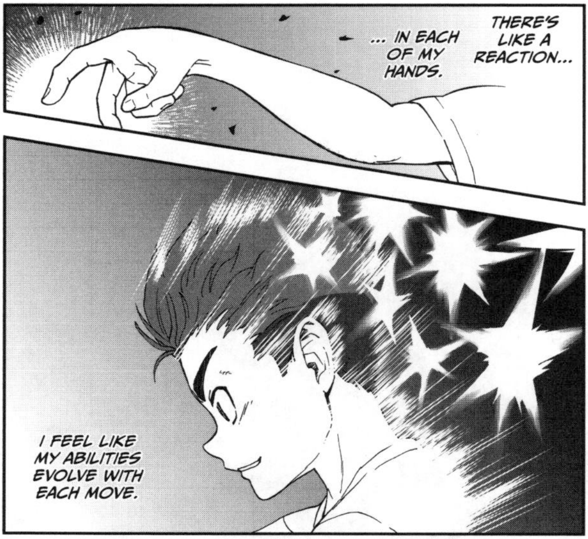
THERE'S LIKE A REACTION...
... IN EACH OF MY HANDS.
I FEEL LIKE MY ABILITIES EVOLVE WITH EACH MOVE.

Pick two possibilities of your choosing. Two possibilities that match one of your current interrogations. Then, imagine yourself walking in the direction of choice 1. Imagine that choice 1 is right in front of you and that you are walking towards it.

How does it feel inside you?
How do you feel?
Do you feel light? Do you have a spring in your step? Or do you feel blocked, and your feet heavy?
Now do the same thing for choice 2.
How do you feel when you picture yourself walking in that direction?
In which direction does your body take you to more easily?

Which direction does your heat seem to sway?

Like the old merchant told Tom, **there is a complete harmony between the past, the present and the future.** It is up to us to reach for that harmony, and to go on an adventure. Just like Tom and the merchant. Let us go on an adventure to uncover the extraordinary abilities that are hiding deep within, and that are only looking to come out in the open so we can be our best.

Alexis Champion

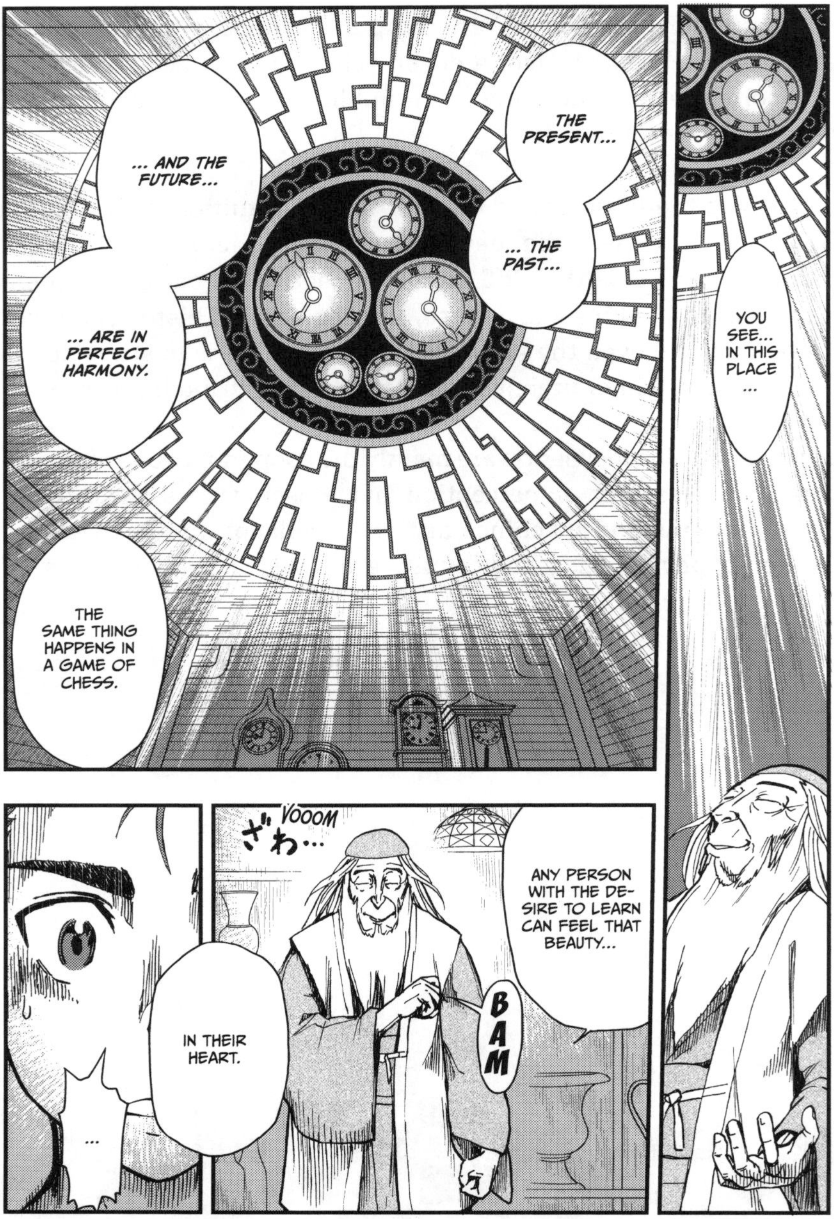
YOU SEE... IN THIS PLACE ...
THE PRESENT...
... THE PAST...
... AND THE FUTURE...
... ARE IN PERFECT HARMONY.
THE SAME THING HAPPENS IN A GAME OF CHESS.
VOOOM
ざわ…
ANY PERSON WITH THE DE-SIRE TO LEARN CAN FEEL THAT BEAUTY...
BAM
IN THEIR HEART.
...

Alexis Champion

Alexis Champion has a doctorate in computer science, with a specialization in artificial intelligence. Over a dozen years, he has been a researcher, then a computer projects director in public and private laboratories, as well as in service companies.

Alexis is also the founder and director or iRiS Intuition. It is a company dedicated to the use, the development and the scientific research of intuition. Since 2008, iRiS has been active in various fields, like manufacturing, banking and finance, archaeology and history, energy, law, management and even the arts. The purpose of iRiS is to study decision-making in uncertain or urgent situations, creativity and innovation.

The areas that Alex focuses on are mainly the cooperative use of reasoning and intuition, research on perception and consciousness, the differences between humans and machines and their collaboration, as well as the perfection of physiological and cognitive abilities of human beings.

Garry Kasparov

Born in 1963 in Baku, in Azerbaijan, Garry Kasparov first became champion of the U18 chess tournament of the USSR at the age of twelve. At 17 years old, he won the title of the U20 world championship. In 1985, at 22 years old, he became known worldwide as the youngest chess champion in history.

He defended titles five times, in a legendary game series against his greatest rival, Anatoly Karpov.

Kasparov broke Bobby Fischer's record in 1990, and his record was unbeaten until 2013.

His famous games against IBM's Deep Blue supercomputer in 1996-97 have played a major role in the introduction of artificial intelligence in the world of chess.

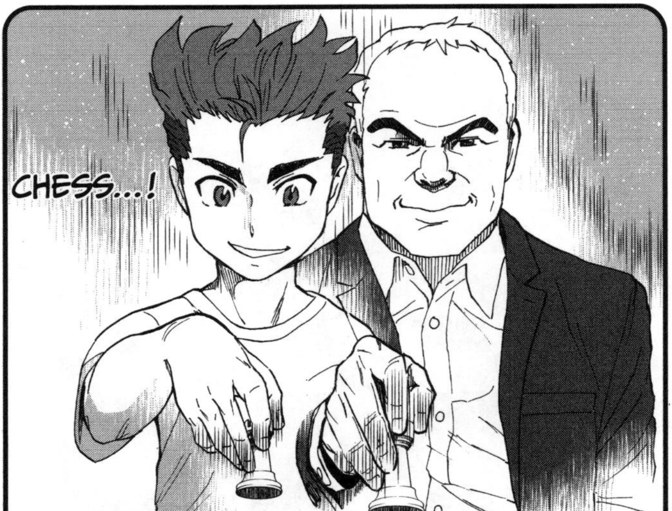
CHESS...!

SPECIAL THANKS TO

Garry Kasparov
Kosta Yanev
Dasha
Mariana
Alexandra Kovcic
Yuma Shinano
Toru Nakayama
Alexis Champion
Tsukasa Mori

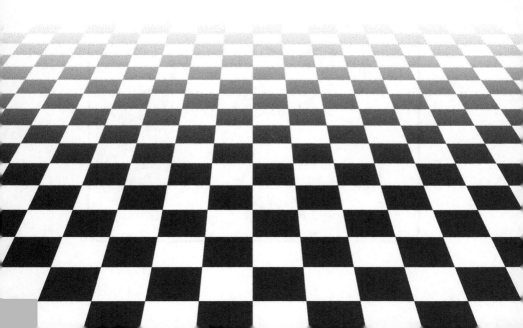

I am writing these few lines alone,
but this manga is an incredible
collaboration between Monaco, Japan,
France and the United States.
A dream that comes true thanks
to a great team. Enjoy!

Cédric Biscay
 @CEDRICBISCAY

original idea: CÉDRIC BISCAY
illustrator: DAITARO NISHIHARA
written by: CÉDRIC BISCAY & HARUMO SANAZAKI
editorial direction: YASUHARU SADAIE & SAHÉ CIBOT

coordination: DOMINIQUE LANGEVIN
translation and lettering: STUDIO MAKMA

cover illustration: DAITARO NISHIHARA
colorization: HERVÉ TROUILLET
counsel: JEAN MICHEL RAPAIRE, SÉBASTIEN JOIE

FOR ABLAZE
managing editor RICH YOUNG
editor KEVIN KETNER
designers RODOLFO MURAGUCHI
& CINTHIA TAKEDA CAETANO

BLITZ VOL 1. Published by Ablaze Publishing, 11222 SE Main St. #22906 Portland, OR 97269. BLITZ © IWA / Shibuya Productions. All rights reserved. Ablaze and its logo TM & © 2022 Ablaze, LLC. All Rights Reserved. All names, characters, events, and locales in this publication are entirely fictional. Any resemblance to actual persons (living or dead), events or places, without satiric intent is coincidental. No portion of this book may be reproduced by any means (digital or print) without the written permission of Ablaze Publishing except for review purposes. Printed in Mexico. This book may be purchased for educational, business, or promotional use in bulk.
For sales information, advertising opportunities and licensing email: info@ablazepublishing.com

10 9 8 7 6 5 4 3 2 1

Publisher's Cataloging-in-Publication data

Names: Biscay, Cédric, author. |Sanazaki, Harumo, author. | Nishihara, Daitaro, artist. |
Kasparov, G. K. (Garri Kimovich), contributor.
Title: Blitz , vol. 1 / writers: Cedric Biscay & Harumo Sanazaki; artist: Daitaro Nishihara; featuring Garry Kasparov.
Description: Portland, OR: Ablaze, LLC., 2022.
Identifiers: ISBN: 978-1-68497-076-6
Subjects: LCSH Chess—Comic books, strips, etc. | Kasparov, G. K. (Garri Kimovich)—
Comic books, strips, etc. | Graphic novels. | BISAC COMICS & GRAPHIC NOVELS / Manga / General
Classification: LCC PN6790.B43 .B57 v. 1 2022 | DDC 741.5—dc23

 /ablazepub  @AblazePub @AblazePub

www.ablaze.net

To find a comics shop in your area go to:
www.comicshoplocator.com

**DOWNLOAD THE GAME
FOR FREE!**

TOP!

THIS IS THE BACK OF THE BOOK!

This manga collection is translated into English, but arranged in right-to-left reading format to maintain the artwork's visual orientation as originally drawn and published in Japan. Start in the upper right-hand corner and read each word balloon and panel right-to-left.